RENEWAL IN CHRIST

RENEWAL IN CHRIST

AS THE CELTIC CHURCH LED "THE WAY"

by
Edward W. Stimson

Edward W. Stimson

VANTAGE PRESS
New York   Washington   Atlanta   Hollywood

Grateful acknowledgement is given for permission to quote:

1. The poem "The Ways" by John Oxenham, chosen for the Frontispiece because it so aptly identifies "The Way in Christ" with the strongly willing, responsible, moral decisiveness so emphasized in historic Celtic Christianity, as expressed by a modern Christian influenced by that heritage. (See page ix.)

2. The poem "The Scholar and His Cat," written by a lonely Irishman serving in faraway Austria long ago, translated by Robin Flower, as reported in Diana Leatham's *Celtic Sunrise,* published by Hodder and Stoughton. (See page 266.)

3. The Table of United Presbyterian Church Trends from *The Presbyterian Layman* of February 1976. (See page 294.)

4. The poem "I'd Never Need a Shrink, I Think" by Dorie Volk. (See page 297.)

AN HONEST BLURB

Dr. E. W. Stimson's volume entitled *RENEWAL IN CHRIST: As the Celtic Church Led "The Way"* is written in the prophetic vein. For the prophets recovered older truths and insights in their religious tradition and brought them to bear upon their contemporary problems. This is what Dr. Stimson has done with the Celtic version of the Christian tradition. Equally appreciated is his gospel emphasis upon Christian mysticism or the charismatic experience in personal religion and its social expression. This volume proposes a recovery of a neglected segment of our Christian heritage as a corrective to imbalance and as a guide for the future. Here is a fresh and, we believe, creative perspective for the Christian church in our time.

R. W. Frank

(Robert Worth Frank, Ph.D., is former president and professor of philosophy and ethics at McCormick Theological Seminary, Chicago.)

To: EMILY CAMPBELL McLEAN STIMSON,

My Life-Partner in Christ's Ministry, whose an-
cestral heritage helped this Germanic Anglo-
Saxon to appreciate the Celts, and whose encouragement, patience, constructive criticism, and loving help have graced these more than two-score
years in Christ in family and Church.

Jesus, knowing that the Father had given all things into His hands, and that He had come from God and was going to God, rose from supper . . . and girded himself with a towel . . . (saying) "I have given you an example . . . a servant is not greater than his master."   —John 13:3, 4, 15, 16.

PAINTING BY E. W. STIMSON

The Celtic Invocation of Christ

Christ with me, Christ before me,
Christ behind me, Christ in me,
Christ beneath me, Christ above me,
Christ to right of me, Christ to left of me,
Christ where I lie, Christ where I sit, Christ where I arise,
Christ in the heart of every person who thinks of me!
Christ in the mouth of every person who speaks to me!
Christ in every eye that sees me!
Christ in every ear that hears me!

—(From the sixth-century *Lorica* or "Breastplate"
Prayer of Spiritual Armor ascribed to Patrick)

You shall receive power when the Holy Spirit has come upon you; and you shall be my witnesses in Jerusalem and in all Judea and Samaria and to the end of the earth,　　　　　—*Acts* 1:8

And now I am no more in the world, but they are in the world, and I am coming to Thee. Holy Father, keep them in thy name which thou hast given me, that they may be one, even as we are one. . . . I have given them thy word; and the world has hated them because they are not of the world, even as I am not of the world. . . . I do not pray for these only, but also for those who are to believe in me through their word, that they may all be one; even as thou, Father, art in me, and I in thee, that they also may be in us, so that the world may believe that thou hast sent me.　　　　—*John* 17:11, 14, 20, 21

You know that those who are supposed to rule over the Gentiles lord it over them, and their great men exercise authority over them. But it shall not be so among you; but whoever would be great among you must be your servant, and whoever would be first among you must be slave of all. For the Son of Man also came not to be served but to serve, and to give his life as a ransom for many.—*Mark* 10:42-45

The Ways

To every man there openeth
A Way, and Ways, and a Way;
And the High Soul climbs the High Way,
And the Low Soul gropes the Low,
And in between, on the misty flats,
The rest drift to and fro.
But to every man there openeth
A High Way, and a Low.
And every man decideth
The Way his soul shall go.

—*John Oxenham* (Used by Permission)

CONTENTS

10. Broadly tolerant spiritual ecumenicity after Jesus' prayer. Liberty in Christ allows for rich diversity.

Irish pilgrim missionary exiles / life and ministry of Columban in Gaul, Switzerland, and Italy / instructing the pope / Willibrord, Boniface, and other Irish and English missionaries to the Lowlands, German lands, and as far East as Kiev / Irish scholars educate Europe.

VIII. Resurgence of "the Way's" Independence: 1637-1776 269

Why American Colonies shut out Anglican bishops / Erastianism and the Protestant Reformation / *Sing A Song Of Sixpence* for Henry VIII / Scottish Covenanters / the Long Parliament and Westminster Assembly of Divines / Cavaliers and Roundheads / Cromwell's "Protectorate" / restoration of Erastian persecution / Greyfriars Cemetery / emigration to America / The Great Awakening: William Tennant, Sr's Log College / Jonathan Edwards, George Whitefield, Gilbert Tennant; controversy and missionary success / spiritual undergirding of American independence / John Witherspoon / Separation of Church and State.

IX. "The Way" in Christ Largely Forsaken 293

Shrinking memberships, Church Schools, and benevolences / analyses by Dean Kelley and John Fry / the social idealist coalition of Neo-orthodox and liberals embarks upon "rule or ruin" tactics, with universal reconciliationism, alienating the laity / recent American oldline churches' policy appraised in light of Ten Essentials found in New Testament and Celtic Churches, and in The Great Awakening: Evangelical faith; Biblical enlightenment; humble piety; charismatic inspiration; realistic theology vs. Tillich, Barth, et al.; missionary withdrawal; steadfast personal morals vs. *situation ethics*; realistic social ethic for Church and society vs. the acculturated Christ of socialist idealism; humble Church leadership vs. heirarchical polity; ecumenical unity of Spirit with rich variety—Lambeth or Geneva.

X. "The Way": Uniting and Renewing All Churches 345

God's diversity / COCU's dilemma / Real Apostolic Succession / conciliarism or monarchy? / Federal Union / spiritual unity / the call to renewal.

Maps

FOREWORD

The Church's ideas, programs, and activities need frequent testing. If not tested, they can get out of balance. An idea or a program may become an end in itself, not subservient to the higher ends for which the Church exists. When it does, it becomes idolatrous, a matter of proximate significance accorded ultimate significance.

Fortunately, idolatries do not go unchallenged very long. There are prophets who sound warnings against them. "I hate, I despise your feasts, and I take no delight in your solemn assemblies" (Amos 5:21). Prophets are disaffected and disaffecting, disturbed and disturbing people. They are not inclined to give the full, well-argued case. Rather, they want to sound one side, that to which balance needs to be restored.

In this book, Ed Stimson, a Presbyterian minister and leader, has sounded a prophetic note. He has used history to do so, and he has used it well. A reader need not agree with his conclusions at every turn to appreciate the care with which he has studied the history of early Celtic Christianity. Moreover, he makes some points about the character of apostolic Christianity as reflected in Celtic Christianity which we today need to ponder. Although he sometimes comes down too hard on one side, he has, for the most part, told the story the way it was.

The reader will recognize readily the motive for Ed Stimson's book. He has written as a deeply concerned churchman who feels that his own denomination, the United Presbyterian Church, leaned too far toward social ministries and activities and too far away from evangelism and missions. He would not, I judge, deny the propriety of the former, but he pleads for balance, in line with Celtic Christian interests to which he ties his own heritage.

I share his concern for balance. My own experience with

church social ministries has led me to conclude that a congregation needs the physique of a Charles Atlas to do the work of a ninety-five pound weakling. Often, the proportions get turned around. A ninety-five pound weakling tries the work of a Charles Atlas. The result is sometimes embarrassing, always disappointing. Any extension of the Church's ministries should be built upon a firm base, such as the author describes.

This book can be recommended, therefore, to Christians who are seriously interested in the life and work of the Church. Ed Stimson writes with verve and clarity. Even when you cannot agree with his opinions, you can appreciate his insights, his humor, and his concern for the Church.

E. Glenn Hinson
Louisville, Kentucky
November 1974

RENEWAL IN CHRIST

PREFACE

"Little Boy Blue, come blow your horn,
    The sheep's in the meadow, the cow's in the corn!
Where's the little boy who looks after the sheep?"
    "He's under the haycock, fast asleep!"
"Go wake him, go wake him!" "Oh no, not I,
    For if I do he'll be sure to cry!"

Those who know the writer may chuckle at any self-identification with "Little Boy Blue," either in size or disposition. Yet, for many years, as one of the lesser boys called to tend the sheep, I have been haunted with fear of deserving such a judgment. Did not our Lord himself warn us to watch, lest he come suddenly and find us asleep? Are not his sheep straying? Especially after the New Life Movement of Evangelism in the late '40s and '50s faltered, proving more ephemeral than we had hoped, and when secular relevance through worldly means, and an ecumenism of unified ecclesiastical power and efficiency became the most avid goals of the leaders of the denominations, the signs of the times became disturbing. The church was more eager to throw open the gates of the lush meadow of technological material prosperity to sheep and goats indiscriminately, the world over, than to lead the sheep to high pastures. Twice, quixotically, I attempted to blow my horn as Little Boy Blue, sending letters of warning to all United Presbyterian ministers and sessions. Most of my colleagues resented my attempt to wake them up, or would not believe there was any danger.

Still, the churches were beginning to shrink. More and more, people were bypassing The Way In Christ for a lush, pleasure-driven materialism. The churches became polarized. Mission-giving languished. Society paid less and less attention to what the churches said. The moral standards of the Gospel were more and more openly flaunted as a superficial Christendom died.

Wherein is real hope for the renewal of Christ's Church in our time? With what light must she shine to illumine the darkness of the late twentieth century? Such questions were wracking my mind in 1964 as we planned to plumb the plight of Christ's Way in lands formerly important to Christendom. Over a generation earlier, graduate study had been fruitful in Scotland and Germany. What was God doing there now, and in Scandinavia, and behind the iron curtain, through His Church? Interviews with knowledgeable churchmen were arranged through the helpful offices of the World Council of Churches, seeking trends hopeful of renewal.

The prospect was largely discouraging. One rare evidence of spiritual vitality was in the Soviet Union. Though there, the Russian Orthodox Church appeared mostly to be an empty shell, tolerated and largely controlled for state propaganda purposes, the Protestant Union Church of Baptists, Mennonites, and Pentecostals evidenced unmistakably real Christian vitality. The Thursday-night service we attended, one of five each week, was jammed with movingly sincere worshipers, many of them young adults. We had no contact with the free church underground.

Everywhere in the free West, worship in state churches was pitifully attended by only 1 to 5 percent of their nominal members. The Church had lost its influence as the major moral and spiritual factor in society. Taxes for state churches were widely resented, and pastors were considered mere public functionaries. Socialism and economic well-being contributed to religious indifference. The Danes have a proverb, "It is necessary to have a broad back to carry good days." Why depend upon God when all seems to be going well, and you can depend upon the state, which guarantees welfare from birth to death?

In the Scandinavian countries, Free churches still were generally more alive, but in Sweden even they had been losing 3 percent to 4 percent a year of late. Marxist natural philosophy and scientific materialism had generally so permeated popular thinking that most people had adopted a wholly this-world outlook as adequate to life. Where, as in Scotland, the churches had tried to have a progressive social outlook, it made little difference. With cars and boats, there was a general weekend exodus to the seaside, so that in Hawick, in the Scottish Borders, where I had preached to good congregations in one of three parish churches, all flourishing in 1931, the one church into which they had combined was struggling in 1964. Even the Iona Fellowship hadn't brought renewal to Scotland. Why had Dr. George MacLeod's promising movement, bringing the church's ministers closer to the laboring man, made no greater dent in the widespread indifference?

Even so, we finished our tour with a long delayed pilgrimage to the Holy Isle of Iona off the west coast of Scotland, and there our trip came to an unexpected climax, and this book was born. There, in the sixth century, Columba made his headquarters for the mission that first converted most of Scotland. As I stood by the rough stone site of Columba's little prayer cell, and knelt in the barren simplicity of the tiny Relig Oran Chapel nearby, a haunting question formed in my mind, changing the nature of my quest, and promising a strangely different answer to the problem of Church renewal. Why, I wondered, had this remote island, only three miles long and two wide, far out on the fringe of ancient civilization, become the Westminster Abbey of the sixth and seventh centuries? Here lie buried at least forty-eight kings, Scottish, Irish, Norwegian, and one from France. One, Kenneth, son of Erc, first united the thrones of the Picts and Scots. Duncan and Macbeth, immortalized by Shakespeare, both lie here. Why had kings come here for confession, advice, and consecration? How did this small isle, in the distant semibarbarian wilderness, become in a real sense the rival of Rome as the center of affairs for this world and the world to come?

From this island, the Picts of northern Scotland were won to Christ, and the Saxons of Northumbria, in fact most of the Anglo-Saxon invaders of what was to become England, as far south as the Thames. From here and from the North of Ireland nearby, and from England after they evangelized her, went forth the missionaries who won the barbarians then controlling the ravaged continent of Europe, in the Lowlands, among the Franks, in Switzerland, Northern Italy, among the Gothic peoples of Germany, and as far east as Kiev. What was it in the life of that ancient Celtic Church that gave to them alone the spiritual power and light to illumine Europe after the fall of the Roman Empire and the night of the Dark Ages? Wherein did they differ from the much larger but moribund and largely sterile churches surviving around the Mediterranean and in the continuing Eastern Empire? In that difference must be the essence of Christ's Way!

One arresting coincidence impressed me. The date of Columba's death on Iona, A.D. 597, was the same year that Augustine, under orders from the first real Pope, Gregory the Great of Rome, landed at Canterbury to begin the first Roman Catholic mission to the pagan Anglo-Saxons. In my dim memories of early Church history, English Christianity had begun with Augustine. Then where had Columba come from? From the North of Ireland, with its flourishing church among the Scots, planted by Patrick when he came in 432. Then where did Patrick come from? From somewhere in Britain. And what sort of church was there in Britain in Roman or even pre-Roman times? I came back to the polarized, floundering church of my homeland with this question uppermost.

The reading of a recent biography of *St. Patrick* by R.P.C. Hanson, the Bishop of Clougher in Northern Ireland, convinced me that this early British Celtic Church was far more important than I had known. Pastoral duties in Omaha prevented the sustained study demanded by my quest. Still the subject haunted my early morning prayer-meditations, and on October 8, 1970, under strong guidance of a seeming Revelation, I arose in the wee sma' hours and hurriedly scribbled down the whole outline of a book on "The Way of the Spirit of Christ" through the centuries of Church history. "The Way," "in Christ," as taught and exemplified by Jesus and lived in the New Testament Church, spread abroad by faithful apostles and intrepid missionaries, was spiritually alive and contagious in the teeth of persecution for over 200 years. It was "in the world yet not of the world." Its faith was pure, its organization simple, its spirit humble. Strong circumstances tempted the leaders of the Church to depart from that "Way" with its freedom in Christ experienced as Holy Spirit. Yet far out on the western fringe, whence faith on the continent must be reborn, and whence the morning-star of Reformation and the resistance to establishment and the rebirth of missionary zeal would spring forth in later times, the true Way was kept unspoiled. So I was given a new, fresh perspective of the whole of Christian history. Here was hope for renewal in any dark age.

To test the validity of this thesis would require more study and research. It called for another trip to the British Isles in the summer of 1971, to search out some of the historic sites and traditions of the ancient Celtic churches and their brave but humble stands for freedom in Christ until suppressed by the alliance of the Rome-Canterbury way with the Crown.

In Northern Ireland, we visited Moville Abbey, Bangor, Downpatrick, Saul, and Armagh, the haunts of Columba and his teacher Finnian, of Columbanus, and especially of Patrick. In the Library of Trinity College, Dublin, we saw the Book of Kells with its gloriously illuminated pages, and the Book of Armagh containing the *Confession* of Patrick and his *Letter to Coroticus*—the best literary evidence of the spiritual nature of the Celtic Church. We visited the Vale of Glendalough, and Kells, where the Columban monks from Iona fled from the Vikings around A.D. 800, and Tara, seat of the ancient High Kings of Ireland, and Slane, where tradition claimed Patrick built his Easter fire, confronting the order of the pagan High King.

In Wales, our attempts to find traditional sites of significance for Pelagius and Merlin were rather fruitless, but at Llandaff Cathedral near Cardiff, the dean introduced us to Father Harold Rue, retired librarian of the cathedral, an Anglican monk of the Merfield Fathers of Yorkshire, and a great enthusiast of early Celtic Church history. He gave us a helpful summary of Welsh traditions, including a meaningful account of the meeting of the Welsh bishops with Augustine at the River Severn in A. D. 603, quite in contrast to the lame explanation of this meeting given in A.D. 731 by the Venerable Bede in his *Ecclesiastical History of the English People*.

We attended the annual Anglican Pilgrimage to Glastonbury on the last Saturday in June. Its celebration contained no reference to ancient traditions. There was no mention of the claimed coming of Joseph of Arimathea, of the early Wattle Church, or of the legends about King Arthur and Guinevere, whose graves are marked in the grounds of the ruined abbey. At Redruth in Cornwall, we visited tin mines in operation for 3,000 years, where Phoenician and Jewish traders had settlements in the trade that furnished tin to make bronze for the Bronze Age in the Mediterranean area. At Tintagel on the rocky Cornish coast, beyond the castle ruins associated in legend with the conception of King Arthur, we found the archaeologically identified ruins of Celtic monastic settlements of the fifth century.

In London, near the Tower, we saw the replica of the stone plaque to Classicianus, latter-first-century governor of Britain; the Church of Saint Peter upon Cornhill with its tradition of being the first Christian church in London, its fourteenth-century brass plaque claiming the first building on the site was built by King Lucius in A.D. 179; and Roman ruins in the crypt of Saint Bride's Church unearthed by World War II bombing. In the record office in Chancery Lane, we sought out the Domesday Book, researching the reference to the Church of Saint Mary in Glastonbury, Somerset, having "twelve hides of land on which taxes were never paid." Tradition claims King Arviragus of the Silures gave this land to Joseph of Arimathea when their party arrived from Gaul in the first century! In the British Museum, we visited the archeological finds of religion in fourth century Britain; Christian mosaic floors and wall paintings from Roman villas, together with one dedicated to the Celtic god Nodens.

York was celebrating the 1900th Anniversary of the founding of the city by the Romans in A.D. 71. An impressive outdoor pageant portrayed episodes of the Betrayal of King Caractacus, by his cousin Queen Aricia of the Brigantes after the Silurian leader had resisted the Romans for nine years (first century); the Crowning of Constantine as emperor by his soldiers at York, (fourth century); and the Conversion of the Saxon King and his Priest of Wotan by Paulinus of Canterbury (seventh century).

At Lindisfarne, the Holy Island near Berwick, we saw where Aidan from Iona led in the second and permanent conversion of Northumbria, and where Saint Cuthbert was later abbot. At Whitby, we visited the abbey where in 663 (revised date) King Oswy called the Synod and made the fateful decision for Rome and against Iona, sending home the Columban monks. In Scotland, we visited the Isle of Skye, finding two traditional sites of foundations by Columba: a chapel ruin on a tiny island in Portree Harbor, and the Columbcille Monastery ruin south of Kilmuir. Finally, Mr. Eric Crosbee of the Planning Commission of Scotland, long our Edinburgh friend, found for us the Ordinance Survey of Britain in the Dark Ages. Its archeologically identified sites, the Celtic in blue, pagan Anglo-Saxon in black, and Christian Anglo-Saxon in red depict the issue clearly. Blue symbols scattered broadly everywhere north of Hadrian's Wall, west of Offa's Dike in Wales, and beyond blue Glastonbury in the Cornwall Peninsula, prove the importance and tragic fate of the Celtic Church.

Full exploration of recent scholarly developments in this field of history to test my thesis, free it of legendary bias, and discover whether it was already redundant had to await retirement. In 1972, we moved to Louisville with its two helpful seminaries. A fine survey of "The History of the Early Church" under Dr. Catherine Gunsaulis at the Louisville Presbyterian Seminary, and an excellent and most helpful course on "Early Christian Institutions And The Concept of the Church" under Dr. Glenn Hinson at the Louisville Southern Baptist Theological Seminary, together with use of a carrel for extensive reading in the Presbyterian Seminary Library, confirmed and reinforced my earlier intuitive surmise. Much scholarship had already advanced, proving the importance of Christ's Way during the Celtic-Roman period in Gaul and Britain. Dom Louis Gougaud, the French Benedictine Monk of Saint Michael's Abbey, Farnborough had begun it with his *Gaelic Pioneers of Christianity* in 1923, and his *Christianity in Celtic Lands* in 1932. Diana Leatham, in 1951, in her superb little outline of Celtic Christianity, *Celtic Sunrise,* was extremely helpful. In its introduction, Dr. George F. MacLeod, founder of the Iona Community asks, "Were the Celtic Saints instinctive moderns before their time? A whole book awaits the writing on some such theme." What a challenge! James A. M. Hanna, a Louisville Seminary alumnus, published *A History of the Celtic Church* in 1962. James Bulloch's Iona Lectures of 1961 were published in 1963, *The Life of the Celtic Church.* Then, there was the intensive scholarship of Nora Chadwick, including even a popular Pelican Original paperback, *The Celts,* and finally, in 1974, the famous Church historian, John T. McNeill, long at Union Seminary, New York, proved my attraction to the importance of a long-undervalued epoch was sound by publishing his definitive history, *The Celtic Churches.* The history is amply written, but the obvious message for Christians today in this Christian experience has not been drawn from it. The Celtic Church had the original and living Way in Christ unalloyed. This the twentieth-century Church must recover if its life in all the dimensions of real Christianity is to be renewed—and so I must try to tell the story.

Yet, how to bridge the gap to the thought-world of that ancient time? Years ago, the renowned preacher of Edinburgh, James Black, wrote a delightful book of children's story sermons entitled *The Unlocked Door.* One of them, "The Tragedy of Humpty Dumpty," unlocked a door for me. He said Humpty Dumpty is

not only a Nursery Rhyme. It is a "potted drama" or a piece of great epic poetry, with all the concerns of pity and terror and fate at its heart . . . one of the world's earliest sagas of adventurous folly and luckless mischance.

Then he proceeded to explore its deeper meanings for life with such wisdom that I was alerted to the profound insights into life and history often hidden in the folklore of Mother Goose. I have used some of the best to unlock some doors in these chapters.

I am grateful to Dr. Glenn Hinson for his critical appraisal and encouragement after reading an early draft of these pages with his specialized knowledge of this field. I am also indebted to my daughter Marjorie for stenographic help.

Chapter I

HOW THE WAY CAME TO BRITAIN

The ancient cross on the Holy Isle of Iona was a Celtic Cross, with a circle, the symbol of Jesus' resurrection. It was the Cross of Saint John, whose teaching stressed eternal life by way of the Cross.[1] The market crosses of ancient Ireland and Scotland were of this form. The crude cross cut into the great stone slab over Patrick's grave by the Cathedral of the Holy Trinity at Downpatrick, near Belfast, is the same symbol. John was exiled on the Isle of Patmos for refusing to submit to the secular power of the Roman Empire.

Much later Saint Andrew was made the Patron Saint of Scotland. The Cross of Saint Andrew, a white "X" on a blue ground, and a later Cross of Saint Patrick, a similar red "X" on a white ground, were combined with a dominant red cross on white of Saint George of England to form the Union Jack, the flag of the British Isles. Well they might, for these were the symbols of the medieval churches of Scotland, Ireland, and England united under the Crown, established under and subordinate to the state. Saint Andrew's Cross succeeded the Celtic Cross of Saint John in Scotland when Queen Margaret won the Kirk in Scotland to the Rome-Canterbury power in the eleventh century. Ireland had succumbed earlier, when Patrick's earlier faith was subjugated and eclipsed by the beginning of the eighth century. The martial religion of the English Kings who patronized Saint George, the dragon-slayer, won its victory over the humble Celtic Church in Northumbria in 663.

The ancient Celtic Cross was treasured by a Church which

Map: Roman Britain—Celtic Tribes

shunned worldly pomp and allegiance, and maintained its precious freedom to share eternal life witnessing to Christ's truth and love. John had written of Jesus' promise that his faithful disciples would know the truth that makes men free.[2] Through direct succession of John's disciple in Asia Minor, Polycarp, the martyred Bishop of Smyrna, and his young disciple Irenaeus Bishop of Lyons in Gaul, this early tradition of the Way in Christ had been brought to Celtic Britain. It was an independent, humble church, in the world yet not of it, rich in the Spirit and therefore fruitful, able to preserve The Way unspoiled through Roman times and the Dark Ages when the barbarians overran the empire.

We must first trace the strength and fruitful characteristics of this church in Britain before the Anglo-Saxons destroyed it in the mid-sixth century. This may seem a strange and futile anachronism to members of the recent "now generation." or to existentialists who insist upon "the immediacy of faith." We do not resent their needed corrective. New life in Christ is always an immediate, living experience of the eternal, risen, living Lord. Yet, encounter with the living Christ is not a complete faith, nor is it self-explanatory. Christianity is a historical religion. Promising the Holy Spirit, Jesus said, "He will take of mine and declare it to you."[3] The Apostle Paul's vivid encounter on the Damascus Road was an overwhelming mystery until it was related to his previous experience. He asked, "Who are you, Lord?" The enlightening reply was "I am Jesus whom you are persecuting," and he was guided to await instruction from the church in Damascus. Patrick, with vivid awareness of Christ in his call to serve in Ireland, had to be trained for many years in the church of which his father had been a deacon and his grandfather a Presbyter. True, Christianity must be caught, not just taught, but it must be caught from its demonstration in a living fellowship of disciples. Christ is in the midst of us when two or three are gathered in His name.[4] Jesus sent his disciples out two by two, Paul took companions on all his missionary journeys, and Patrick went with several companions to Ireland. Christian love must be shared between those already in Christ to be demonstrated contagiously. The Way in Christ must be maintained and propagated through a living Church in social communion. Therefore, we must attempt to recover the all-but-missing link between the old Catholic Church of the first two centuries on the Continent of Europe and the Church Patrick founded in Ireland in the fifth century, the Celtic Church in Britain which was important in the growth of our heritage.

WHO WERE THE CELTS?

Until recently, many Americans have thought of the Celtics as a Boston Irish basketball team. They are Celts by long descent. Called *Keltoi* by the ancient Greeks and *Galli* by the Romans, the Celts' earliest known homeland was in Central Europe north of the Alps. Having early mastered iron-working, and superb as horsemen, they spread over Europe in successive waves, mounting a massive expansion in the sixth century B.C., sweeping into Gaul, Iberia, Northern Italy, Greece, and Asia Minor. Successive invasions populated Britain and Ireland. So their Iron-Age culture dominated most of Europe in a rather unorganized manner, prior to the period of the Greek and Roman Empires. Some areas they invaded only to plunder. Wherever they established their upland farming, aristocratic culture, they fortified hilltops, *oppida,* to protect the ruling nobles. About 390 B.C., they sacked Rome, and in 279 B.C., Delphi in Greece. One tribe, the Galatae, settled in the vicinity of modern Ankara in Asia Minor, appearing as the Galatians in the New Testament, retaining their Gallic tongue as a second language as late as the fourth century A.D.[5] This link with Asia Minor may have had some influence upon the growth of the legend of the coming of a Trojan chieftain, Brut, to Britain following the siege of Troy.

Recent discoveries indicate they even colonized in what was to become North America. A New Zealander, Barry Fell, a marine biologist turned ancient linguist, in tracing the languages of the Maori, studied Egyptian hieroglyphics, the Punic writings of the Phoenicians and Carthaginians, and the Ogam writings of the Celts. At Harvard University, he has translated hitherto undecipherable North American inscriptions found widely from New England to Minnesota and Iowa from his knowledge of Egyptian, Punic, and Ogam. Thomas Fleming, in a *Reader's Digest* article of February 1977 reviews Fell's book, *America B.C.,* under the title of "Who Really Discovered America?" Iberian Celts of Tarshish and the Carthaginians seem to have collaborated in a highly developed trade route between America and the Mediterranean with colonies of miners, hunters, and trappers in America sending copper, furs, and hides over the Atlantic for hundreds of years before the destruction of Carthage by the Romans.

Ancient and modern fads in scholarship have depicted the Celts as barbaric primitives, little better than savages. The Romans, as prejudiced enemies, called them bloodthirsty headhunters and cannibals. Modern writers, following Darwin's discovery of biological evolution, assumed primitive beginnings wherever real knowledge was lacking. Archaeological research has discovered otherwise. Aristocratic burial mounds, in which the deceased were interred upon well-wrought wagons with ornate gear and utensils, unearthed in the upper Danube and Rhine valleys have identified the Hallstatt and La Tene Cultures of the seventh and sixth centuries b.c. in the Celtic homeland. Nora Chadwick tells of their superb art styles, especially in metal-work, and of the skill of their wheelwrights, carpenters, and blacksmiths, producing technically advanced four-wheel wagons and lighter war chariots, great two-edged longswords, and decorated fire-dogs for chieftains' hearths, and concludes, "In general the technological level of the La Tene Celts, with very few exceptions, was equal to, and in some matters surpassed that of the Romans.[6]

Little wonder Julius Caesar's two probes into Britain after his conquest of the Celts in Gaul, in 55 and 54 b.c., met strong military resistance and convinced him an occupation would be too costly. Around a.d. 40, Cunobelinus, Shakespeare's Cymbelline, chieftain of the Belgic Tribe in South Britain, forged a kingdom of surrounding tribes and issued his own coinage for a wealthy trade with Rome. When the invasion finally came a century later than Julius Caesar's vain hope, the Celtic Britains were not, as the Venerable Bede erroneously reports from poor Roman sources, an easy prey.[7] It took the Emperor Claudius' leading generals nine years, after the first disastrous battle in a.d. 43, to subjugate the Silures, who would not accept defeat. Even then, the Silurian King Caradoc (Caractacus) escaped to the Brigantes in Northumbria, hoping to raise further resistance, and was not captured, but betrayed by his cousin Aricia, queen of the Brigantes and sent to Rome in chains. There he was able to make his own defense before Claudius in faultless Latin. Soon Roman nobles were freely intermarrying as equals with the Celtic British aristocracy.

Philosophical men of wisdom, called Druids, were the religious leaders of the Celts, advising kings and training the younger nobles in the memorized sacred, legal, and cultural heritage. In A.D. 61, the Roman General Suetonius Paulinus took a legion to destroy the continuing center of Druid spiritual power on the Isle of Anglesey off the northwest coast of Wales. Druid spiritual resistance had to be crushed. During his absence, the Iceni Tribe, early collaborators with the Romans, revolted in moral protest and disgust. Seneca, chief counselor to Nero, had loaned their king a huge sum to build a Roman-style capital city. The king had died, leaving a will making Seneca an heir to guarantee the debt, but Seneca graspingly demanded immediate repayment. Roman soldiers sent to force this oppression violated Queen Boudicca (Boadicea) and raped her daughters. Boudicca roused the neighboring southeastern tribes, overran Colchester and Verulam, and burned London, slaughtering the Roman citizenry. Paulinus' legion, rushing back from the destruction of the Druidic groves on Anglesey, defeated Boudicca's untrained and disorganized hordes at battle in Flintshire, the queen committing suicide on the field.

From 71 to 83, the Roman legions, then under General Agricola, fought to subjugate the Brigantes, Silures, and Caledonians, the culminating battle being fought in the Perthshire Highlands at Mons Graupius. In 119, the Emperor Hadrian came and planned a wall, built in 120-123, from the Solway to the Tyne, to keep out the undefeated Picts. It was no easy conquest!

Thereafter, with Roman legions stationed in forts at Caerleon in southeastern Wales, at Chester and at York, protecting all of Britain east and south of these outposts, and with Roman roads radiating to the forts from London, peace was kept for over 300 years. Towns grew as centers of Roman civilization. Bath and Verulamium vied with Italian cities in elegance. Aristocratic British farmers, their lands cultivated by serfs, lived in villas with plumbing and central heating, adorned with frescos and mosaics, with a luxury not equaled again until the nineteenth century.[8] Those who accepted Roman rule and collaborated enjoyed an unprecedented peace and prosperity similar to the American Southern plantation culture during slave days. The older Druidic religious philosophy and remnants of Celtic aristocracy were kept underground. The older popular Celtic polytheism was allowed to flourish along with, and to be identified with the worship of the gods of the old Roman pantheon. Commerce with the Continent flourished. It was into this cultural situation that another repressed, persecuted, philosophically superior faith infiltrated into Britain.

THE MYSTERY OF THE CELTIC CHURCH IN BRITAIN

Exactly when the Church began in Celtic Britain, no one knows. Generally, in church history courses, it is practically ignored. If mentioned, it has been treated as of little importance. A number of causes have deprived posterity of the evidence of the real nature and merit of this Church. The ancient Celts had practically no written literature, using their Ogam alphabet very seldom, as their culture stressed a strong preference for oral literature and memorizing. What was finally written down, centuries later, of the traditions of the bards of Wales and Brittany, was so legendary and palpably wide of historical facts as to be of little historical use. Secondly, Celtic culture in Britain was subjugated by the Romans for 350 years, who for the first 250 of those years officially persecuted Christianity, stifling open literary activity. Thirdly, the area where the British Celtic Church grew most was ruthlessly overrun by the conquering pagan Anglo-Saxons, who utterly destroyed all Christian religion and Roman culture in the area they seized, forcing all to flee who would not be enslaved. Gildas the Wise, writing of "The Overthrow of Britain" almost contemporaneously in 560 from Wales says "I shall not follow the writings and records of my own country, which, if there were any of them, have been consumed by the fires of the enemy or have accompanied my exiled countrymen to distant lands."[9] Fourthly, the later contest for supremacy between the state-oriented Rome-Canterbury hierarchy patronized by the kings, and the stubborn, independent Celtic churchmen of Wales, Ireland, Scotland, and Northumbria, enduring over 200 years, left the victors to write the history. The first English church historian, the Venerable Bede, writing *A History of the English Church and People* at Jarrow in Northumbria in 731 sets the tradition of denigrating the earlier Celtic Church, often showing his bias. He is careful to tell how in 431 " . . . the Roman pontiff Celestine sent Palladius to the Scots (Irish) who believed in Christ to be their first bishop"[10] when Palladius lasted only a year, left Ireland and died, but totally omits any mention of Patrick, of whom Aidan from Iona who had converted Northumbria was a successor! Fifthly, prejudice of the conquering English against their Welsh, Irish, and Scottish subjects has tended to suppress appreciation of Celtic Britain and her earlier faith.

> Taffy was a Welshman, Taffy was a thief,
> Taffy came to my house and stole a piece of beef.

Later, he came and stole a marrow bone and a silver pin. The rhyme has drilled prejudice and distrust of the Welsh in English children's minds for centuries. Anglo-Saxons had to justify their cruel aggression by despising the descendants of their victims as lying thieves and scoundrels. They also held their heroes up to ridicule:

> When good King Arthur ruled his land
>   He was a goodly King,
> He stole three pecks of barley meal
>   To make a bag-pudding;
> A bag-pudding the King did make,
>   And stuffed it well with plums,
> And in it put great lumps of fat
>   As big as my two thumbs.
> The King and Queen did eat thereof,
>   And noblemen beside;
> And what they could not eat that night
>   The Queen next morning fried!

By stealing three pecks of barley meal, King Arthur betrays his Welsh kinship to Taffy. This rhyme was in the John Newbury's *Original Mother Goose Melody,* issued in London in 1760. Scholars have shared the prejudice. Matthew Arnold declared that because of their extreme unreliability, no English writer would seriously consider information contained in Welsh literature. Granted that the fertile imaginations of poetic Celts have given wings to this judgment, yet it has not worked to produce a fair atmosphere for recovering Celtic Church history.

Sixthly, modern seekers for believable Church history have been turned away by the lush, weedy growth of legendry that has grown to fill the void:

> Old King Cole was a merry old soul,
>   And a merry old soul was he:
> He called for his pipe and he called for his bowl,
>   And he called for his fiddlers three.

This glimpse of ancient Celtic tradition in our earliest English nursery rhyme may be a symbol of the frustrating difficulties that confront our search.[11] His pipe dates the ditty after Sir Francis Drake and Sir Walter Raleigh introduced tobacco into England in 1586, whereas King Cole, or Coel in the Welsh-Breton tradition accepted by Geoffrey of Monmouth, was a legendary third century King. The Welsh tradition of King Coel has his daughter Helena marry the Roman Caesar Constantius Chlorus and become the mother of Constantine the Great. Recalling how Helena, the mother of Constantine, helped him make Christianity the state religion of the Roman Empire, this would be great news about Christians in Britain in the Roman period. Sadly, the best Roman evidence reveals the real Helena as an Illyrian innkeeper's daughter who was never in Britain, since Constantius 'Chlorus divorced her for state reasons and remarried when he accepted the emperorship of the West. Constantine joined his father in York only a year before Constantius Chlorus's death and Constantine's crowning there in 306, and was no son of British soil. Was King Coel a real personage? We are tempted to improvise:

> Fiddle-diddle-diddle-diddle-diddle went the fiddlers,
>   A merrie companie,
> Where the bards in song through the winters long
>   Made fantastic historie!

For this was the setting of the Welsh-Breton traditions that survived the night of the Dark Ages, the oral traditions of the Bards of Wales and of Brittany in the Celtic area of Northern France, composed and recited to amuse and please the nobles and their "merrie companie" passing the bowl around the fire in the great hall through long winter evenings. So we have in a number of Welsh manuscripts, like *The Brut Tysilio,* the account of the reigns of successive Celtic kings in Britain, from the legendary Brut, grandson of Aeneas, a Trojan prince who led his ships from Southern Italy a generation after the siege of Troy, out through the Gates of Hercules and after stopping in Gaul, to Britain. These traditions are also the source of part of the development of the King Arthur legend, expanded in the French romances compiled by Thomas Malory in *Le Morte d' Arthur.*

Geoffrey of Monmouth's twelfth century *Histories of the*

Kings of Britain in Latin caused this legendary to be believed as history until modern times. Geoffrey said he based his Historia on an ancient manuscript in the Breton tongue brought from Brittany. Many modern scholars have claimed he spun the stories out of his own fertile imagination, as he did an earlier tale about Merlin which he included. Three considerations indicate Geoffrey was truthful in claiming an Armorican source. Too much of the action takes place in Gaul, including a sojourn conquering part of Gaul by the ancient legendary Brut on the way to Britain, and a tremendous campaign and sojourn of King Arthur in Gaul before his ceremonial crowning in Britain. The Welsh Geoffrey would have little motive to fabricate this. Secondly, the theory that the Welsh manuscripts are only summary translations from Geoffrey's Latin doesn't stand scrutiny. Comparison of English translations of Geoffrey's *Historia* and of one Welsh tradition clearly shows Geoffrey expanding and improving upon some text like the latter, but depending upon it for details.[12] Thirdly, Dom Gougaud, the French Benedictine scholar, has researched a part of the history of Brittany which explains part of the development. For three hundred years, kings of Celtic Brittany tried to persuade the popes that they had a right to have their own archbishop at Dol, to resist the dominance of the Frankish archbishop of Tours, and wanted to prove that King Arthur had had archbishops who crowned him in Britain while he ruled that part of Gaul.[13] The Celts in Brittany had fled there from Britain, driven by the conquering Anglo-Saxons and the horrible plague of the sixth century, hardly a glorious memory. Their later heroic aspirations sorely needed a glorified heritage in song and story, more satisfying than the real history of abject defeat and terrified escape, and the bards earned their pay, shaping their best traditions to suit these purposes. So the glories of King Arthur! History does not deny that there was an Arthur. His real great victory at the Siege of Badon Hill around 490 stayed off the Anglo-Saxons for a generation.

Yet the whole Arthurian legend furnishes us no real information about the Christian Church in fifth-century Britain. There is little religion in the tales. The bards were secular minstrels, and when they wanted to glorify Arthur, would read customs of much later origin, such as the ritual crowning of kings by archbishops, back into a time when no archbishop had ever been known in Britain.

Another fiddler with Celtic Church history was a researcher for the Venerable Bede. Bede in 732 tells a tale about the coming of Christianity to Britain which Gildas the Wise in 560, and the Papal archives, and all Continental writers prior to Bede should have known about, but never mentioned. He says that King Lucius of Britain in A.D. 167 sent to Pope Eleutherius a request that he be made a Christian, and the Pope immediately sent two missionaries who quickly converted the whole British people![14] No one questioned how this could be when there was no king of all Britain under the Romans, and Roman persecution would hardly have permitted such a wholesale conversion. Nor did the Celtic Church in Britain look to Rome for leadership. Yet Nennius, a Welsh historian of the ninth century, Geoffrey of Monmouth in the twelfth, and most other historians until modern times, were misled by Bede's assertion, and often embroidered it. Geoffrey inserted it in his *Historia,* and expanded it into an immediate organization of three archbishoprics and twenty-eight diocesan bishoprics, to take over the offices of as many archflamens and flamens of the Roman cultus of Caesar Augustus—this under Roman rule when Christians were being persecuted and the bishop of Lyons was soon martyred in Gaul. Dom Gougaud makes it plain that there were never any diocesan bishops in the Celtic Churches. Britain saw no archbishop until the coming of Augustine in 597. The transition to new Christian titles of such Roman territorial offices took place on the Continent after Constantine, but never in Britain. One might deduce that archbishops are not in the Apostolic Succession, but in Flamenic Succession!

A late nineteenth-century German scholar, Adolph Harnack, researching in the Vatican Library in Rome solved the riddle.[15] Bede had told how he had received information from the Vatican Library from Nothelm, a priest from London. Harnack found the note in the sixth-century *Liber Pontificalis* about King Lucius Aelius Septimas Megas Abgarus XI of Birtha in Edessa making such a request. Nothelm pounced too eagerly upon this notation, thinking it referred to Britain.[16] The Church he served, Saint Peters upon Cornhill in London, still advertises King Lucius as its original founder, in A.D. 179, with a brass plate above a mantel in its vestry, cast in the Middle Ages, shown to substantiate the claim.

A more attractive legend of earliest Christianity in Celtic Britain is associated with the ancient wattle Church long revered as the earliest built in all Christendom at Glastonbury, south of Wales near the Bristol Channel. There the monks cherished a story of the coming of Joseph of Arimathea and a company of twelve early disciples of Jesus in A.D. 37. Arviragus, king of Cornwall, whom he had known earlier while visiting as a Jewish tin merchant at the Cornwall mines, is said to have given Joseph twelve hides of land of Ynniswitrin (Glastonbury). These are noted in the Domesday Book as never having been taxed. So Joseph's party built the wattle church, and converted part of the family of Caradoc, king of the Silures. Welsh tradition recounts that Joseph was sent to Britain from Gaul by Philip the Apostle. Caradoc allowed the freedom of Rome after his famous defense before the Emperor Claudius, built a palace there for his family with his rents from Wales, and his daughter Gladys, called Claudia as a protege of the emperor, was married to Rufus Pudens, a young Roman nobleman. He had seen service with the army in Britain, where a pagan altar dedicated by him has been found. The nuptials were celebrated in a poem by a contemporary Roman poet, Martial. Friendship between this family and the Apostle Paul is claimed, during and after his first Roman imprisonment, Paul ordaining Claudia's brother Linus the first Bishop of Rome, and baptizing the children of Pudens and Claudia, who were later famous martyrs. All three, Linus, Pudens and Claudia, are identified with the Christians sending greetings through Paul in the closing salutation of the Second Epistle to Timothy. Simon the Zealot, Aristobulus, and Paul are said to have visited Britian. There is a "Pauline Way" up from the sea near Llandaff. There is no tradition in Spain of Paul's having fulfilled his former purpose to go there, and if he was once released from Roman detention, could have undertaken the farther journey to the farther end of the known world before writing his last pastoral Epistles.

The best support of the Joseph of Arimathea tradition is in the late sixteenth-century *Church Annals From Christ's Birth to 1198* by the Vatican Librarian, Cardinal Caesar Baronius. He guardedly tells of a tradition under the year A.D. 35 in Gaul, of Joseph of Arimathea, Lazarus, Mary Magdalene, Martha, and others being set adrift on the Mediterranean without sails or oars, making their way to Philip in Gaul who sent them on to Britain.[17] William of Malmesbury, a competent historian of the twelfth century visited Glastonbury, was convinced by the monks, and wrote *On The Antiquity of the Church at Glastonbury,* telling much about the ancient wattle church there and the legend of its building.[18] The claim that "Joseph was a tin merchant," heard for centuries in the Cornish tin mines is not totally unbelievable, as these mines have been used for 3,000 years, furnishing tin for the Mediterranean in the Bronze Age and attracting Phoenician and Jewish tin merchants to Cornwall.

Yet, in tracking down the "twelve hides of land," which we found mentioned as never having paid taxes in the *Domesday Book,* we discovered in Scott-Stokes' translation of William of Malmesbury's *On The Antiquity of the Church at Glastonbury,* Appendix D, a listing of other royal sources of just twelve hides of early Church of Glastonbury land accredited to seventh-century kings recounted from the Abbey records by Malmesbury.

The claim that Britain was first evangelized under the Emperor Tiberius in A.D. 37 may be traced to a curious general claim in Tertullian's *Apology* of the early third century, stating that Tiberius sought to persuade the Roman Senate to investigate the doctrine of Christ, and fostered Christian missions throughout the world. Eusebius, the fourth-century Church historian repeated this, wanting to feel favorable about Roman Emperors from his association with Constantine, and his widely circulated history was the evident source of a queer statement by Gildas that the islands of Britain,

stiff and cold with frost in a distant region of the world remote from the visible sun . . . received the holy precepts of Christ . . . at the latter part, as we know, of the reign of Tiberius Caesar, by whom his religion was propagated without impediment.[19]

Gildas' claim supplies the early date, as Tiberius died in A.D. 37.

While Archbishop Ussher and later historians relied heavily upon the evidence of William of Malmesbury for the Joseph of Arimathea tradition, his writing is ambiguous. There are two editions of his most famous history, *Acts of the Kings of the English,* one repeating the King Lucius tale, the other the Joseph story. The two are not compatible, for if Joseph started the active Church in Britain, the Lucius request could hardly have been necessary. Scholars question which was William's later judgment.

The Roman Catholic Church and the British Crown have officially acknowledged the Joseph of Arimathea claim since the fifteenth century. The Councils of Pisa, Constance, and Siena affirmed the prior antiquity of the British Church when this was challenged by France and Spain. The right of British delegates to Christian Councils to stand first in the serial recognition of historic Christian realms was granted, accepting the British claim that Joseph of Arimathea brought the faith of Christ to Great Britain immediately after Christ's passion. Yet even if Joseph, Paul, or any other early Christians visited Britain, there is no evidence of any significant growth or impact of Christianity in Britain in the first century. Most scholars today avoid all of these intriguing traditions like the plague!

ACCEPTABLE EVIDENCE OF THE WAY IN CELTIC BRITAIN

As late as 1937, Kenneth Scott Latourette of Yale could say in his *A History of the Expansion of Christianity* that the archaeological remains of Christianity in Great Britain in the pre-Anglo-Saxon times were very slight, and the literary records tantalizingly fragmentary, with the inference that British Christianity came from Gaul, centering first among the Latin-speaking townsmen, with few members among the wealthy, and coming to prominence slightly later than on the adjacent continent.[20] His inference remains true, but the evidence has been increased, affording glimpses of a quite influential church, growing slowly.

Gildas the Wise's few words about the period are descriptive:

These rays of light were received with lukewarm minds by the inhabitants, but they nevertheless took root among them in a greater or less degree until the nine years of persecution of the tyrant Diocletian.[21]

This earliest historian of the sixth century could recount no traditions from British sources, no tales of missionary heroes or church leaders until the first martyrs, who, from his Continental sources, he supposed, suffered under the Diocletian persecution.

The earliest written sources are the Ante-Nicene Church Fathers, who boast of beginnings of the faith in Britain toward the end of the second century. Irenaeus, who became bishop of Lyons in central Gaul in 177, says that the Church was dispersed throughout the whole world. He mentions Germany, Spain, Gaul, Libya, and Egypt, pointedly omitting Britain so nearby. Could he have made the general boast if he knew of no church there? This was Gaul's mission territory. Recent Roman persecution in Gaul had martyred his predecessor, Bishop Pothinus of Lyons. Most probably escapees from that persecution had sought refuge in neighboring Britain, and were beginning the first real evangelizing there, and Irenaeus would be careful not to expose them, trusting Christian readers to sense his obvious meaning.

In A.D. 190, Tertullian of North Africa wrote in his *Answer To The Jews* a listing of the peoples then known to believe in Christ, including:

(in) the haunts of the Britons—inaccessible to the Romans but subjugated to Christ—the name of Christ who is already come reigns.

He had heard that Christianity had penetrated the part of Britain beyond the rule of the Roman Legions. Origen of Alexandria (185-284), in his homilies, made similar claims of the goodness of Christ being "diffused among the Britons." There was much travel for trade in Roman times, and we may assume that the first Christians in Britain were among the Roman- and Greek-speaking traders and artisans in the Rome-built cities of the latter part of the second century. Churches would be small groups meeting in homes quietly to escape persecution.

The renowned early martyrs in Britain should be assigned to the Decian (250), Gallian (251-53), or Valerian (257-59) persecution, when thousands of the faithful were lost throughout the Empire. The Anglo-Saxon Chronicle does not follow Gildas, as Bede and others did, in assigning the deaths of Alban of Verulam, and Aaron and Julius of Caerleon to the Diocletian persecution after 301, giving an earlier date, 283. Gildas, quoting his general Continental sources says the martyrs:

erected trophies to their glorious martyrdom even in the gates of the City of Jerusalem. For those who survived hid themselves in woods and deserts and secret caves.

There are no deserts in Britain, nor were trophies of British marytydom erected in faraway Jerusalem! The clinching reason for dating these British martyrs long before the Diocletian persecution is that the Roman emperor of the West, Constantius Chlorus, refused to implement the Diocletian persecution in his portion of the empire.[22]

All we know of the martyrs Aaron and Julius is that Bede says they were citizens of the City of Legions, i.e., Caerleon. Bede gives three whole pages to the story of the martyrdom of Saint Alban of Verulamium. A priest, Fortunatus, described as mentioning "all the blessed martyrs who came to God from every part of the world" is quoted:

> In fertile Britain's land
> Was noble Alban born.

Alban, when still a pagan, gave shelter to a Christian priest who was fleeing from agents of persecution. Observing the fugitive's steadfast prayer and vigil, Alban was suddenly touched by the grace of God, and began to follow the priest's example of faith and devotion. Receiving Christian instruction in his home from the hiding priest, Alban renounced his idolatrous paganism and sincerely accepted Christ. When word reached the Roman authorities about the hidden fugitive, soldiers were sent to search the house. Seeing them coming, Alban donned the priest's long cloak, surrendered himself in the place of his guest and teacher, and was led bound before the judge.

The judge was furious with the attempted deception, threatened Alban with torture and death, but gave him the option of reduced sentence if he would sacrifice to the Roman gods. Alban fearlessly confessed his faith in Christ, said these sacrifices were to devils, and those who sacrificed to idols doomed to the pains of hell. He was mercilessly flogged, but bore the torments gladly and would not renounce Christ. He was ordered to be decapitated, and went to the place of his execution with prayer. The first appointed executioner threw down his sword, fell at Alban's feet, and was martyred with him. We may omit several miracles with which mistaken earlier piety surrounded Alban's death before it reached Bede over 470 years later, as they detract from rather than add to the witness.

Having sown the seed of martyrdom, the Celtic Church in Britain must have grown stronger during the final years of the third century. Two significant events, one barely mentioned in Bede's history and the other totally omitted, give us our greatest clues to the strength of the Church in Britain before Christianity became the state religion of the empire.

The first was the crowning of Constantine as emperor by his troops in York in 306, after which they supported him in conquering the world, to share the toleration of Christianity his father had practiced in the West throughout the empire, resulting in the eventual conversion of Constantine and the establishment of official Christianity as the empire religion. Curious that Bede should merely say this, in the midst of a section decrying the Arian heresy, which he erroneously assumes to have infected the British Isles:

> At this time, Constantius, a man of exceptional kindness and courtesy, who had governed Gaul and Spain during the lifetime of Diocletian, died in Britain. His son Constantine, the child of Helena his concubine, succeeded him as ruler of Gaul. Eutropius writes that Constantine, proclaimed Emperor in Britain, succeeded to his father's domains. In his time the Arian heresy sprang up. . . . [23]

We shall have to explore Briton Christians' part in this later.

The second event was the participation of British bishops in the Council of Arles in Southern Gaul in 314. Constantine called for a council of bishops from Gaul and Britain to settle the Donatist Controversy, and three British bishops attended, one from York, one from London, and one from Caerleon. So, prior to any rapid growth of the Church in Britain under official Roman aegis, there was a strong enough Church in Britain to send three bishops to a church council in Arles! Two were from places that were primarily military installations, indicating close contacts between the Church and the Roman military in Britain! The British bishops at Arles participated in the condemnation of the North African Donatist schismatics who had refused to forgive former church members who had lapsed in their witness to save their skins in the recent Diocletian persecution; in a decision that moral fault in the character of a cleric does not invalidate his sacraments; and in the recognition of the then current Roman system of calculating the date of Easter, the system long kept in the Celtic churches stubbornly resisting later changes dictated by Rome. This latter could account for Bede's not mentioning participation at Arles—or his Roman sources not telling him about it.

There is no evidence of participation by British bishops in the Council of Nicea in 325 called to define the Person of Christ. Athanasius, its champion, later said that the British Church accepted its findings, though there was little interest in hair-splitting Greek philosophical definitions in the later Eastern councils by the distant, practical-minded Britons. In 360, a council at Rimini on Italy's Adriatic Coast with 400 bishops in attendance drew more than three British bishops, for it was remarked that three of them took advantage of the offer of the Emperor Constantius to draw their travel expenses from Imperial funds, rather than be a burden to their church brethren. Bishops who were only missionary pastors without dioceses might well not have constituencies prepared to support such a journey!

Archaeological evidence of the flourishing Church in Britain in the fourth century is growing. The town of Calleva Atrebatum at Silchester was completely excavated, beginning in 1890. Built by Agricola in the late first century, the Roman City had four pagan temples, but near the forum, obviously built later, was a small edifice forty-two by twenty-seven feet, fitting specifications of early basilican type Christian churches of the fourth century on the Continent and in North Africa, with nave, aisles, transepts, apse, and a narthex. So small a building could have served only a minority of the town's two thousand inhabitants. Others used the round temple of Mars, also apparently active to the end of the Roman period. Tolerance ruled in Britain after the empire became officially Christian, with active Christians a real minority still.

At Lullingstone in Kent, part of a country villa was adapted to church use. When fire destroyed it in the late fourth or early fifth century, its walls collapsed into the basement, preserving colored frescos in restorable condition for 1500 years. One room had a repeated design of the Greek Chi Rho within a wreath of leaves and buds. A larger room for assembly had painted on the west wall six full-length human figures about four feet tall, side by side, and separated by decorative pillars. Each figure was clothed in a long rich robe, adorned with a cross from chin to ankles, posed with hands outstretched palms upward in the ancient attitude of prayer. The south wall was decorated as over an altar with a large Chi Rho emblem with Alpha and Omega symbols in a large wreath. The same motifs have been found in the vicinity of Rome and at Dura Europos in Upper Syria.

In the large room of the British Museum where these reconstructed frescos are exhibited, there is a Christian mosaic pavement from Thraxton, Hampshire, and another, larger, with Christian symbols in splendid condition from Hinton, Saint Mary's, Dorset. Christian tombstones from the Roman period have been found in Cumberland, Westmoreland, and Cornwall. A villa in Chedworth in Gloucestershire has the Chi-Rho monogram worked into its mosaics: a similar one from Frampton, Dorset, includes both the Chi Rho and a representation of Neptune in its pavement pattern, the pagan motif persisting in the decorative art, but the villa builder including the symbol of his new faith.

Christian artifacts have survived: a Chi-Rho adorned pewter plate found in Appleshaw, Hants; fish symbols on finger rings; bowls suspended by chains with the cross and fish in the decorative motif found at Faversham, Lullingstone, Salisbury, and elsewhere; a fine repousse silver flagon found on Taprian Law in East Lothian, with a frieze depicting the Temptation of Eve, Moses striking the Rock, and the Adoration of the Magi, accompanied by a colatorium or wine-strainer for the Eucharist.

Yet, along with these, there are reminders that paganism survived. The heathen revival under the Emperor Julian the Apostate in 360-61 was short-lived and more philosophical than realistic, yet a stone pedestal found in 1891 at Cirencester seems to date from this time. Shortly thereafter, in 364-67, in the Severn Valley near Lydney on the edge of the Forest of Dean, a large group of Roman-style buildings were erected, with baths, shops, a temple, and a guest house for visitors, all to honor Nodens, the ancient hunter-god of the Forest of Dean. His hilltop above Lydney had been sacred as long as men could remember, and he was reputed to heal. Eight thousand Roman coins, most dating from the fourth century, uncovered in the area prove the new shrine was popular, and that after the reestablishment of Christianity following the downfall of Julian, there was no intolerance in Britain. Christian faith need fear no competition as truth, unshackled, will prevail.

The latter-fourth-century British Church produced a missionary, a famous heretic scholar, and a military champion of Christian orthodoxy.

The missionary was Ninian, called Ringan among the Lowland Scots, born around 360, the son of a British chieftain in Cumberland or North Wales. Bede is responsible for the tradition that he studied and was consecreated a bishop in Rome,

27

and studied in Gaul with Saint Martin of Tours on the return journey, bringing Martin's form of monasticism to Britain. He is said to have secured masons from Tours to build his stone church at Whithorn on the Galloway Coast, north of Wales, called Ad Candidam Casam (At the White House). Martin of Tours died in 397 while it was a-building, so it was dedicated in his name. From there, Ninian conducted his mission to convert the Southern Picts. Discovery of an eighth-century poem on Saint Ninian containing no mention of Rome or Tours has raised scholarly question whether Bede and/or Picthelm, Bishop of Whithorn in Bede's day, both of whom were avid Roman partisans, may have invented these details. Archaeological evidence does attest Ninian's early history at Whithorn. His was probably a mission from the British Churches in Wales, prior and similar to Patrick's to Ireland.

The scholar and famous heretic was Pelagius, whose Latin name, meaning "of the sea," is a translation of the Welsh name Morgan. A lay brother, perhaps forty years of age, he crossed to the Continent at the turn of the century, was enthused by the spiritual rigor of the monastery of Saint Martin at Tours, but later appalled by the low morality he found in Rome, supposedly one of the great centers of Empire Christianity. Fluent in Latin and Greek, he was intellectually of the caliber to tilt with both Jerome and Augustine of Hippo, combating the excesses of asceticism and the denial of the importance of the human free will.

The Christian military leader was Magnus Clemens Maximus. A Roman official of Spanish origin, he was converted to Christ in Britain. Arian heresy had swept the Continent, distressing the British Church. Orosius calls Maximus "a man of vigor and integrity, worthy to be an Augustus, who was made Emperor by the Army against his will." At the time the troops acclaimed him "Augustus," he was a newly baptized Christian in the orthodox British persuasion. His troops remembered what their predecessors had accomplished with Constantine less than a hundred years earlier, and made him their leader to champion Orthodoxy in the empire. Crossing, they defeated Gratian in Gaul, where Maximus reigned in Trier for three years, recognized as Augustus there by Theodosius and Valentinian II. He and his family were favorably impressed with Saint Martin of Tours and his monastery at Marmourtier. In 387, he invaded Italy, driving out Valentinian, but was defeated and killed in battle with Theodosius at Aquileia in 388. This brave adventure, failing to repeat the pattern of the glorius Constantine, denuded Britain of troops, leaving her western coasts vulnerable to raids from the Scots of North Ireland. While remnants of his army settled in Brittany, his son Plebig returned to North Wales, there to found a family monastic settlement, Llanbeblig, like Saint Martin's in Gaul. Not many years later, Scots from North Ireland raiding Britain's unprotected west coast took Patrick into slavery.

In 406, the barbarian Franks, Burgundians, Vandals, Alans, and Suevi overran Gaul and the Western Empire expired. Again the British army assayed the role of world savior. The first two men they crowned, Marcus and Gratian were speedily murdered, but the third, named Constantine but no relation to the former emperor, led another army from Britain into Gaul. There he was hoodwinked, defeated, and killed and his army was scattered. Again Britain was denuded of troops, and left open to the raids from the Northern Scots of Dalriada, the Picts, and the Saxons. When Rome fell to the Visigoths in 410, the British provincials declared their independence of Roman rule, but were soon imploring remnants of Roman power for help.

Another type of invasion threatened the Church. One Agricola, a Pelagian son of an Italian Bishop, brought the Pelagian heresy in exaggerated form to Britain, and received an enthusiastic popular response. To stem the tide, the British bishops asked for help from the church in Gaul. Obviously, they looked to Gaul rather than Rome as their Mother Church. Calling a Synod, the bishops of Gaul sent Germanus, bishop of Auxerre, and Lupus, bishop of Troyes. Great crowds greeted them in churches, in the streets, and in the fields, exhibiting a widespread popular interest in Christian theology. Having corrected the heretics, Germanus made a pilgrimage to the tomb of the martyr Alban at Verulam. He concluded his visit by directing British troops in a bloodless "Alleluia Victory" over some invading Saxons. Stationing the troops above a narrow defile through which the unsuspecting Saxons were approaching, he gave the signal for a mighty shout of "Alleluia!" three times, panicking the enemy column so that they threw away their weapons in headlong flight.

During the visit, Germanus and another of his party, a deacon named Palladius, observed that the British Church was doing nothing to evangelize the Scots in Northern Ireland, where many Christians had been taken into slavery. Rather than presume upon the British prerogative on their own, they reported to Rome, and shortly thereafter Palladius was commissioned in 431 "to the Scots (Irish) who believe in Christ to be their first Bishop."[24] He stayed in Ireland only one year, then died among the Scots in Northern Britain. Hearing of this, in 432, the chastened British Synod stirred itself to send Patrick, who had long wanted this service, as their missionary to Ireland.

After the departure of the Roman government and army from Britain, what was left of the former tribal nobility, spoiled and weakened by eleven generations of Roman coddling, formed a coalition of petty chieftains under Vortigern of Central Wales. So, poorly led, they foolishly invited Saxons to settle the British coastal lowlands as mercenary defenders against the Picts and Scots. They learned to rue the day. Saxons swarmed in, ever increasing their territorial holdings and demands, and craftily, by a ruse, slew most of the British leaders unarmed in a banquet hall. Around 490, Ambrosius Aurelianus, a Cornish king brought up in Brittany, returned to unite and lead the British in resistance. The famous Arthur was either Aurelianus' Welsh name, or was his chief general and successor. After many battles, the great victory at the siege of Badon Hill (Bath) in about the year 493 won respite from the Saxon scourge for a generation.

During this respite, monasticism gained great popularity in Wales. Dubricius, bishop of Hereford, and Illtyd, who founded Llaniltyd, or Llantwit Major in Glamorganshire, were the leaders. Dubricius inspired and ordained Saint Samson of Caldey Island, and Saint Teilo who founded Llandaff. Illtyd taught Maelgwyn, abbot of Bangor on Dee, Gildas the Wise, the historian, and both Saint Samson and Saint Paul Aurelian, the two greatest missionaries to Brittany. Saint David of Menevia, patron saint of Wales, founded his strict monastic settlement on the bleak, barren southwest tip of Wales at this time, and in 560 was the clerk of the Welsh Synod of Menevia which, at that time of dread and penitence, confirmed the Penitential Discipline of the Welsh Church. That same year, Gildas wrote his lament, *Of The Conquest of Britain,* blaming the sins of the British kings and clergy for the Saxon scourge, as it was the dire judgment of God.

The yellow plague of 547 had weakened the Britons, many of them escaping to Brittany from the disease. Just before 560, the Anglo-Saxons rose up in force, and drove all the Celts who would not be their slaves out of the major part of Britain with relentless fury. All Celts who would not die or be enslaved emigrated to Wales, Cornwall, or over the Channel into Brittany, where many escapees from the plague and remnants of former British armies awaited them. Thereafter, stark paganism ruled supreme in Britain everywhere East of Wales and Cornwall for half a century.

If more proof is needed of the importance of the Celtic Church in Britain prior to the Saxon invasion, we may offer three unquestioned literary citations. Of the coming of Augustine to Canterbury in 597, Bede writes,

> On the east side of the city stood an old church, built in honor of St. Martin during the Roman occupation of Britain, where the Christian Queen of whom I have spoken went to pray. Here they first assembled to sing the psalms, to pray, to say Mass, to preach, and to baptize, until the King's own conversion to the faith gave them greater freedom to preach and to build and *restore* churches everywhere.[25]

Later, Bede tells how Augustine threatened the Welsh bishops he summoned to meet him at the bank of the Severn with Divine judgment if they would not join him in evangelizing the Anglo-Saxons, and recounts the sequel when Ethelfrid slaughtered 1,200 of the 2,100 monks of the Monastery of Bangor Iscoed when they prayed against the king of Northumbria's victory in battle.[26] It was some church, with 2,100 monks in one monastery! Bede didn't mind telling this when it put that church in a bad light.

The third evidence is in Eddius Stephanus' contemporary *Life of Wilfrid,* the biography of the great eighth-century Northumbrian abbot. For the dedication of his splendid new church at Ripon Abbey, Wilfrid had assembled the Christian Kings and other dignitaries. While he had this audience before the altar, Wilfrid first thanked them for the lands they had already given him, then:

> He went on to enumerate holy places in various parts of the country which the British clergy, fleeing from our own hostile sword, had deserted. God would indeed be pleased with the good Kings for the gift of so much land to our bishop. They gave Wilfrid land

around Ribble, Yeadon, Dent, and Catlow, and in other places too.[27]

These were lands they admitted their ancestors had stolen from the Church in one area of Britain. The Church had become wealthy in the more than two hundred years between the Edict of Toleration and the Saxon scourge.

Yet all this tells us little of the faith and spiritual life of this Church. What qualities in his British heritage gave Patrick his foundation for the sound Church he planted in Ireland? What made this Way flower into mission while the Church on the Continent remained so sterile?

Chapter II

CHRIST'S WAY IN CELTIC BRITAIN ASSESSED

We now need to plumb the all but lost heritage of Patrick in the Celtic Church of Britain in greater depth. Our only extant written sources, a little homily *On The Christian Life,* written around 425 by a Briton bishop named Fastidius, and Gildas the Wise's queer lament over *The Conquest of Britain* around 560 give us limited evidence. Jesus' words, "By their fruits ye shall know them," suggest that we may judge the church in Britain by Patrick and his writings. We also know about the roots of the British Church. It was a Bible-educated church, and was nurtured by traditions from the Continent, particularly from the second- and third-century church in Gaul. Yet, to think of this church in Britain as merely a missing link, or a bridge between better known churches in Ireland and Gaul is too mechanical a metaphor. A biological metaphor would come closer to reality. A species of plant evolving new qualities, yet keeping its basic characteristics as it spreads from land to land, adapting to changing climate guided by the immanent creative mind of God would be a better figure,[1] for the church in Britain with a history of over 350 years had its own developments. Yet the Church is a Divine-human social organism, subject to leading of the Holy Spirit who guides into new truth, and to the vagaries of human freedom, and to the influences of its cultural environment. So, knowing Patrick's rich writings, and much about the life of the early Church on the Continent, and the constant

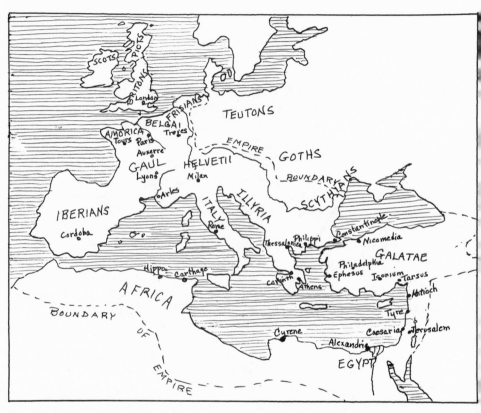

Map: Some Sites of Church History in the Roman Empire

content of the Scriptures, and somewhat about the Celtic cultural heritage, we have clues to use for interpreting with more meaning the bare events cited in Chapter I.

Since Patrick grew up and was educated in Britain, most of what he wrote and planted in Ireland can confidently be assumed to have come from the British Church's life. Further, distinctive characteristics of Patrick's Irish version of The Way, when they match identical peculiarities in the Welsh, Cornish, and Breton versions, and may be traced back to the time when they flourished in the earlier Continental Mother Church, may indicate just when the British Church was firmly planted. If Continental Church developments forsook these characteristics, the planting of the British Church with its stable eugenic strains must have antedated the Continental mutations. Four such widespread Celtic Church practices indicate a British Church beginning in the late second century: the absence of any metropolitan bishops, or any diocesan organization for bishops; the practice of marriage among the clergy with no celibate rule; worship confined to the Triune God, with no adoration of the Virgin nor prayers to Mary and the Saints; and most important, close fellowship with the immanent and ever-present Christ as loving Savior and Friend, with none of the transcendent distance of the fourth-century Eastern and Roman Continental development of Christ feared and worshiped as "Christus Pantocrator," "Christ Almighty." So He was painted high in the apses of the new empire churches looking like the former pagan Olympic Jupiter.

From Patrick's Irish Church, we discern ten essential characteristics or areas of Church life integrated in the whole and living Way of the true Church, which he may have brought from the church in Britain and which that church might earlier have derived from the Scriptures and her Mother Church in Gaul:

1. An evangelistic faith and practice.
2. Biblical education.
3. Devoted piety, in public worship, private prayer, and charity.
4. Charismatic inspiration in gifts and works of the Holy Spirit.
5. Clear, realistic Trinitarian doctrine.
6. Faithful missionary outreach.
7. Strict and steadfast personal ethics.
8. Constructive but relativistic and independent social ethics.

9. Humbly ordered Church government.
10. Broadly tolerant spiritual ecumenicity.

As best we may with the evidence at hand, we shall attempt to explore these characteristics in the life of the British Celtic Church, in varying degrees of its faithfulness, straying, or neglect from time to time, as her example, both positive and negative, affected the Church in Ireland.

1. Evangelistic Faith and Practice: The Druids and Toleration

Even without written evidence, it could be assumed that the faith and practice of the early Celtic Church in Britain was evangelical and evangelistic. No other faith could take root and grow in a pagan Celtic culture or in towns planted and controlled by Roman overlords and military rulers serving an empire officially persecuting The Way. The Gospel had to be experienced in its reality under those conditions to be contagious. Only when Christianity becomes socially accepted or established under the state, and it becomes profitable or politically advantageous to profess to believe in Christ, can church members who lack a saving faith and a passion for souls become common. When the threat of martyrdom was the price of faith, only those who knew vital redemption in Christ dared to profess Him, and knew they must! Who were the first believers, the first presbyters, the first bishops, we do not know, for they sought and received no open acclaim, but they knew and loved and served Christ personally, or no Church would have grown.

They had the New Testament with its emphasis upon new life in Christ to feed their faith. Jesus had promised that where two or three would gather in His Name, he would be in their midst.[2] In his priestly prayer of intercession in the Temple Court that night after they left the upper room, Jesus had prayed for his disciples down through the ages, "that they all may be one; even as Thou, Father art in me, and I in Thee, that they also may be in us."[3] Paul, who wrote, "if anyone is in Christ he is a new creation; the old has passed away, behold the new has come,"[4] uses the term "in Christ" dozens of times in his letters, so that William Barclay in *The Mind of Paul* calls it Paul's favorite phrase, "not so much the essence of Paul's theology as it is the summary of his whole religion." That Patrick took this faith from Britain to Ireland is evident from the heart of the sixth-century Breastplate Prayer, "The Lorica" ascribed to Patrick as representing his faith, these lines being most likely from his pen:

> Christ with me, Christ before me,
> Christ behind me, Christ in me,
> Christ beneath me, Christ above me,
> Christ to right of me, Christ to left of me,
> Christ where I lie, Christ where I sit, Christ where I arise,
> Christ in the heart of every person who thinks of me!
> Christ in the mouth of every person who speaks to me!
> Christ in every eye that sees me!
> Christ in every ear that hears me!

The greatest Church Father of the Mother Church in Gaul, Irenaeus of Lyons, wrote a compendium of the evangelistic preaching of the original apostles sometime around A.D. 200 entitled "Proof of the Apostolic Preaching." Useful for catechetical instruction and widely circulated as mentioned in Eusebius, it has survived in an Armenian translation from the original Greek made in the sixth century. If used by the faraway Armenians, it was surely helpful in the Gallic Churches' mission in Britain. Pertinently, Irenaeus wrote:

> Thus then does the Word of God in all things hold the primacy, for He is true man and Wonderful Counsellor and God the Mighty, calling man back again into communion with God, that by communion with Him we may have part in incorruptibility. . . .
>
> Taught by Him, and witnesses of all His good works and of His teaching, and of His passion and death and resurrection, and ascent into heaven after the bodily resurrection were the Apostles, who, after the descent of the power of the Holy Spirit were sent by Him into the whole world and carried out the calling of the Gentiles, showing mankind the way of life, turning them back from idols and from fornication and from selfish pride, purifying their souls and their bodies through the baptism of water and of the Holy Spirit, dispensing and administering to the faithful the Holy Spirit they had received from the Lord.[5]

Prominent in the Apostolic message as summarized by Irenaeus is the use of the argument for Jesus' Messiahship from the detailed fulfillment of Old Testament prophecies. Scores of texts from the Law, Prophets, and Psalms are quoted with the early Apostles' and Irenaeus' interpretation of them as applying to the Trinity and the Conception, Birth, Ministry, Passion, Resurrection, Ascension, and Entry into Heaven of Jesus.

Since the Jews of the Dispersion carried on much of the commercial trading of the Roman Empire, as they continued to do in the Europe of the Middle Ages, and they were protected in their practice of monotheism and excused by special imperial privilege from having to participate in the public cult of emperor worship, their Sabbath synagogue worship everywhere attracted thoughtful natives to belief in one God. These God-fearers were seldom converted to full Judaism with its circumcision and rigid dietary rules, yet they furnished the most likely prospects for becoming Christian converts, in the practice of Paul and the other early Apostles. The language of trade was Greek. The Septuagint translation of the Old Testament in common use in the synagogues throughout the empire was in Greek. The New Testament of the first three centuries was in Greek and the ritual of the early Christian Church was in that language. We may readily assume that there was fellowship in the cities Rome built for trade and military government in Britain between intelligent Jewish traders and aristocratic Celtic families with their philosophical Druidic faith in God the Creator and ruler of the universe. Irenaeus' "Proof of the Apostles' Preaching" with its argument from Old Testament prophecy would be useful in the evangelizing of such God-fearers in Britain.

To appreciate the evangelistic opportunity, approach, and success of the second- and third-century Christian disciples in Celtic Britain, we should learn all we can of the Druidic religion. It has been both over-maligned and denigrated by some, and romanticized by others. The romancing stems largely from the modern Order of Druids, a friendly society founded as an imitation of the ancient Druids, in London in 1781, spreading to America (1833), Australia, and Germany. Ancient Roman historians, in their accounts of the Druids, were more or less biased, to rationalize the Roman oppression of these spiritual leaders of their enemies in war. A rescript of Augustus Caesar forbade Roman citizens to practice druidical rites. Under Tiberius, the Druids were suppressed by a decree of the Senate, which had to be renewed in A.D. 54 by Claudius to meet the emergency in Britain. They were so outlawed and driven underground because their wisdom, high morale, and spiritual influence were a threat to Roman authority. The punitive expedition led by General Paulinus against the Holy Isle, Mona (Anglesey), in 61 proved their importance. Tacitus' account of this invasion, which sounds like an eyewitness report, probably stems from his father-in-law Agricola, the general who later conquered most of Britain and who was present as a young officer attending Gen. Suetonius Paulinus.

Suetonius Paulinus ... prepared to attack the Island of Mona, which had a powerful population and was a refuge for fugitives. He built flat-bottomed vessels to cope with the shallows and uncertain depths of the sea. Thus the infantry crossed, while the cavalry followed by fording, or, where the water was deep, swam by the side of the horses.

On the shore stood the opposing army with its dense array of armed warriors, while between the ranks dashed the women, in black attire like the Furies, with hair dishevelled, waving brands. All around the Druids, lifting their hands to heaven, and pouring forth dreadful imprecations, scared our soldiers by the unfamiliar sight, so that, as if their limbs were paralysed they stood motionless and exposed to wounds. Then, urged by their General's appeals and mutual encouragement not to quail before a troop of frenzied women, they bore the standards onwards, smote down all resistance, and wrapped the foe in the flames of his own brands.

A force was next set over the conquered, and their groves, devoted to inhuman superstitions, were destroyed. They deemed it indeed a duty to cover their altars with the blood of captives and to consult their deities through human entrails.[6]

This is obviously a biased account to justify the sacrilege of destroying the sacred groves, priests, and priestesses of a religion the Romans did not dare to tolerate. The armed defense of the sanctuary island is exaggerated. The futile attempt, lacking sufficient military defense, to frighten the Roman legions, should not fool us into thinking this was the level of the Druids' own intelligence and sophistication. To be sure, they practiced magic, and tried it on the legionnaires.

Pliny A.D. 23-79 says the Druids were magicians, working with water, globes of balls, air, stairs, fire-lights, basins, and axes, mixing this with medicine, astrology, and mathematical arts, with a tradition from the Persian Zoroaster, and arts loved by Orpheus, Pythagoras, Empedocles, and Plato, still highly honored in Britain. As they deemed mistletoe, and the oak tree on which it grows, to be sacred, Pliny derived their name from the Greek word for "oak," "Drus" meaning "Oak-Priests." He describes the ceremonial gathering of the mistletoe. Two white bullocks are brought beneath a tree, which the priest in white vesture climbs to shear the mistletoe with a golden hook, then slaughters the beasts with many orisons, offers a sacrifice, and makes a broth of the mistletoe, which is supposed to promise fertility in man or beast.

Dio Chrysostom, a contemporary of Pliny, says of the Druids,

It is they who command, and kings and thrones of gold, dwelling in splendid palaces, are but their ministers, and the servants of their thought.

The most objective description of the Druids is by Julius Caesar who observed them first-hand during his *Gallic Wars*:

Throughout Gaul there are two classes of persons of definite account and dignity. As for the common folk, they are treated almost as slaves ... One consists of the Druids, the other of Knights. The former are concerned with divine worship, the due performance of sacrifices, public and private, and the interpretation of ritual questions: a great number of young men gather about them for the sake of instruction, and hold them in great honor ... It is they who decide in almost all disputes ... and if any crime has been committed or murder done, if there is any dispute about succession, or boundaries, they also decide. ... Of all the Druids one is chief ... It is believed that their rule of life was discovered in Britain and transferred thence to Gaul. ...

Report says that in the schools of the Druids they learn by heart a great number of verses, and therefore some persons remain twenty years under their training. ... They make use of Greek letters ... the cardinal doctrine which they seek to teach is that souls do not die, but after death pass from one to another. ... besides this they have many discussions as touching the stars and their movement, the size of the universe, and of the earth. ...

The Gauls affirm that they are descended from a common father, Dis, and say that this is the tradition of the Druids. For that reason they determine all periods of time by the number not of days, but of nights, and in their observance of birthdays, and the beginnings of months and years, day follows night.

Dis was the god of the dark underworld. When we speak of "fortnights," we still honor the custom of measuring time by nights rather than by days. Caesar's reference to the rule of life coming to Gaul from Britain locates the center of Druid power and instruction for the Celts in his day, but the use of Greek letters indicates an earlier source of their philosophy. Caesar's account contains a lengthy description of the ritual sacrifice of criminals to the gods by fire in large woven wicker baskets, which may be taken as a bit self-serving. Accusation of human sacrifices justified his wars of conquest, as the Romans, who had abolished ritual human sacrifices only a short time previously, were wont to exaggerate this practice in describing their enemies. Caesar's account generally is of a highly law-abiding, quite civilized, aristocratic culture.

Our best insight into the thinking and teaching of the Druids comes from a source not mentioned in histories we researched, *The Refutation of All Heresies* by Hippolytus, Bishop of the Port of Rome, (155-235).

The Druids, Progenitors of Their System

And the Celtic Druids investigate to the very highest point the Pythagorean philosophy after Zamolxis (Zametris), by birth a Thracian, a servant of Pythagoras became to them the originator of this philosophy. The Celts esteem these as prophets and seers, on account of their foretelling to them certain events from calculations and numbers by the Pythagorean art; on the methods of which very art we shall not keep silence, since also from these some have presumed to introduce heresies; but the Druids resort to magical rites likewise.[7]

Pythagoras combined together astronomy, geometry and music, and so he proclaimed that the Deity is a Monad . . . His theory of numbers was learned from the Egyptians . . . says the soul is immortal and subsists in successive bodies. . . . The world is a musical harmony and the sun performs a circuit in accordance with harmony. He also touched on magic . . . ordered his disciples not to eat beans . . . enjoined silence . . . He was burned along with his disciples in Croton, Italy . . . . leading them down into cells he made them to live a solitary life.[8]

If Hippolytus is as correct about the Druids as he is about Pythagoras, we have our most important clue. We know much about Pythagoras beyond his mathematical discovery regarding the square of the hypotenuse of right triangles. The history of philosophy tells of his greatness as a philosopher, religious leader, and political reformer. Born in Samos on the Aegean around 575 B.C., he traveled in Greece, Egypt, and Asia in quest of wisdom, and settled around 530 B.C. in Crotona, Italy. A group of 300 ascetic scholars gathered under his strict rule of "ipse dixit"—"He himself has said it." It was a mystical community with elaborate ritual, requiring of probationers five years of silence, practicing temperance and moral self-control. Along with mathematics, astronomy, medicine, and music they cultivated arts, crafts, and gymnastics in a social, philosophical, and religious brotherhood, monotheistic and highly moral. Pythagoras never committed his philosophy to writing, preferring the disciplined understanding of memorization.

An aristocratic reformist, Pythagoras' political reform movement elevated Crotona to top position among the Greek cities of Southern Italy. Democratic opposition caused him to migrate to Metapontus in 495 B.C., but organized branches of his movement in other cities formed a loose political and economic alliance by placing his pupils in prominent magistracies. The rising tide of democracy destroyed his brotherhood a generation after his death. Some of his followers were killed, others like Zamolxis exiled. Meanwhile, the spiritual philosophy of Pythagoras was influential upon Socrates, Plato, and Aristotle over against the materialists.

For Pythagoras, number was the key to reality. He discovered that basic musical harmonies depend upon simple numerical ratios between the dimensions of instruments (strings, pipes, bars, disks), so the whole world may be interpreted through mathematics as also in astronomy and physics. Dominant notes of the universe are proportion, order, and harmony. In his tables of opposites were straight and crooked, good and evil, light and darkness. In his ascetic ethics, happiness is the perfection of the soul's virtue in the harmony of love, wisdom, and friendship. Thus, the soul at death may enter upon a state superior rather than equal to its present life, according as the soul has lived for God, for the world, and for itself.

Of the elementary bodies, earth, fire, air, water, and ether, fire is the supreme element, the symbol of the divine principle in nature. It is concentrated into a central sun, the hearth of the universe and the abode of the Supreme God. Around it revolve three spheres: the Ouranos, embracing the earth and the counter-earth which we never see on the opposite side of the sun; the Cosmos, embracing the moon and the planets; and the Olympus, with the fixed stars. Pythagoras' disciples developed this into the heliocentric theory of the cosmos.[9]

There is considerable historical evidence to confirm Hippolytus' claim. In Ireland, where the Druidic schools were not suppressed, but incorporated into Christian universities, producing the great centers of learning in the sixth-century monasteries, the four Pythagorean subjects; mathematics, astronomy, music, and medicine were taught along with the Bible and Theology. Diana Leatham, commenting upon the Celtic flair for mathematics, says, "Even in pre-Christian times the works of Pythagoras were known to them." She tells of the turmoil caused in the eighth century by an Irishman, Firgil, Bishop of Salzburg in Germany, when he taught the Pythagorean doctrine then current in the Irish schools that the earth was not flat but round. Rival Roman missionaries reported this heresy to the pope, one of them being Boniface, the bishop of Mainz. Pope Zachery's answer survives, the thought garbled by having passed through two uncomprehending minds. Firgil is said to believe "that there are under the earth another earth and other men or sun and moon." This Pope Zachery denounced as a "perverse and unrighteous doctrine, an offense alike to God and to his own soul." Yet Firgil remained unconverted at Salzburg for forty years, and his belief in the antipodes continued to be taught in the ninth century by a more famous Celtic scholar, John the Scot.[10]

Fire had religious significance among the Druids. The legend of Patrick's Easter Fire contest with King Leary of Ireland at Slane is witness. In 1971 we found the Midsummer Night Solstice Fire still observed at Castle an Dinas in Cornwall, an ancient Briton Celtic oppidum site. There is no clear evidence of how much of the Pythagorean philosophy was preserved in the oral traditions of the Druids, who kept the custom of writing nothing down. They were also an aristocratic culture, with only the sons of the nobility receiving philosophical and scientific training. Therefore, as among the ancient Romans, the continued worship of many traditional gods was both tolerated and maintained. There were nature spirits, local tribal deities, and gods similar to those of the Roman pantheon, with which similar deities were identified and became merged. Yet Welsh tradition also tells of a symbol which every Druid bore on the front of his miter, of three rays or glories of light, representing the triple aspect of the ineffable God: the Creator of the Past, the Conserver of the Present, and the Renovator (i.e.,

Destroyer and Recreator) of the Future:—Beli, Taran, and Yesu. Procopius, the Byzantine historian of the sixth century, who was private secretary to Belisarius, accompanying him on his Persian, African, and Gothic campaigns in the time of Justinian wrote:

Hesus, Taranis, Belinus, unus tantumodo Deus unum Deus Dominum universi Druides solum agnoscunt.

If this was so, the Celts were wide open to the teaching of the Triune God, with Jesus as the Savior. It is interesting that in the Celtic languages and in much modern music, He is worshiped as "Yesu" instead of in the English, Greek, Roman, or Hebrew forms of His Name!

The Druid hope for a future life made the Celts especially receptive. Their speculative hope of reincarnation, which Pythagoras had derived from ancient Hindu sources, could not compete with the Christian hope based on the historical Resurrection, with its promise of sharing eternal life in Christ, glorified in God's eternal Kingdom. So the Druids never resisted Christianity strongly. The Roman state religion was the common enemy in Britain of the Druidic faith driven underground, and of the Christ Way being spread under persecution. If there was one first-century martyr, Welsh tradition claims Aristobulus, (Arystli-hen) saying he was mistakenly mistrusted as a Roman at the time of Boadicea's revolt. The martyrs of the third century were executed by Roman persecutors. Later tales about Patrick in Ireland tell of violent confrontations, but the reported violence, at Slane, was on the side of Patrick's God! Christ's Way offered really a still higher morality, and inspiration of Divine Love to motivate it. The philosophical Druids had been tolerant of many gods, and were willing to listen to an intelligent presentation of the incarnation of the great Triune God of the Universe in Jesus Christ, when their own Trinity had been so similar. Religious truth was not something to fight over, but to consider and think through. Tradition says the Druids' slogan was "The Truth against the world." May the greater truth win! Jesus said he was born to bear witness to the truth, and would not use force to protect himself in advancing it. Truth is not served by coercion. Truth must be freely acknowledged and embraced by the mind. So the Celts did not martyr Christians. Their own religious heritage offered what was almost another Old Testament background for the Christian faith, with prophetic features similar to those in the Jewish Scriptures. Columba of Iona was said to have prayed in battle to Christ as "My Druid, Son of God."[11]

That the Druid faith continued to exist underground in Britain after the destruction of their former headquarters on the Isle of Anglesey is evident from the account in Nennius of an act of Vortigern, the Welsh leader of the Celtic nobles after the departure of the Romans in the fifth century. After being excommunicated by Germanus, he reverted to paganism and invited twelve Druids to assist him. There were still unconverted Druids after 400 years! Yet, most of these suppressed, underground Celtic religious leaders had in time accepted Christ, and had become leaders in the Church in Britain as they later did in Ireland, having welcomed this other spiritual underground, sharing the same tolerant attitude. Not that the followers of Christ would ever compromise their personal loyalty to Him by idolatrous eclecticism. Still, they resented with the Druids all attempts to force conformity to emperor worship, and would not welcome, when the empire embraced Christianity, any intolerant means of promoting their own faith. So Constantine's edict of 319 proscribing heathen sacrifices was never enforced in Britain. The building of the large Temple of Nodens at Lydney in the Severn Valley so near Caerleon in 364 shows that Christians were not pushing their restored legal preferment after the death of Julian the Apostate reestablished governmental promotion of their faith. So association with the Druids maintained and stressed religious toleration as an essential of Christianity and a condition of its true evangelism, and toleration, or better, religious freedom, became an indelible part of the heritage of the Celtic churches. In the Westminster Confession of Faith, a Constitutional Document of all modern Presbyterians, it appears in the memorable words:

God alone is Lord of the conscience, and hath left it free from the doctrines and commandments of men which are in anything contrary to His Word, or beside it, in matters of faith and worship. So that to believe such doctrines, or to obey such commandments out of conscience, is to betray true liberty of conscience; and the requiring of an implicit faith, and an absolute and blind obedience, is to destroy liberty of conscience and reason also.[12]

Evangelical faith in the British Celtic Church was eagerly

shared, but by graciously commending Christ in word and deed to free minds, that they might abide in His word, become truly His disciples, and so know the truth that makes and keeps men free.[13]

2. Biblical Education—Obtaining, Studying, and Interpreting the Scriptures

"Pussy-Cat, Pussy Cat, where have you been?"
"I've been to London to visit the Queen!"
"Pussy-Cat, Pussy-Cat, what did you there?"
"I frightened a little mouse under the chair."

Let the wisdom of this Mother Goose gem illumine and warn us as we seek to appreciate how Celtic Christians in Britain interpreted the Scriptures. Christians in every age, visiting the King of Kings by means of the written Word, have seen only what their capacity to appreciate and their previous interests and political and cultural biases prepare them to discern of the infinite greatness and truth there. Even in our modern time, with all of the evidence of historical Bible study available, Bruce Barton, an American advertising executive, wrote a popular book describing Jesus as *The Man Nobody Knows* as a go-getter, self-advertising businessman, and Sarah Cleghorn said poetically:

Comrade Jesus hath his red card.

Scholarly New Testament interpreters show their predilections by the way they pounce upon Judas Iscariot, as Pussy Cat did the little mouse. Modern scholarly tradition has often seen Judas as an eager radical zealot, hopeful that Jesus' promised Messianic rule in Jerusalem would catapult him into the role of World Treasurer, but disillusioned by Jesus' seeming conservatism in His refusal to use his evident miraculous power to set up the Kingdom. Recently Professor James Smart has insisted that Judas was an arch-conservative, driven to betray Jesus to the conservative Pharisees because the Master was too liberal for him![14] What did the ancient British Christians find in the Scriptures, and how can we safeguard against assumptions from our own biases in trying to interpret their responses? Two constants safeguard the process: the plain truth of the Scriptures themselves in most important moral and spiritual concerns, and the promised personal help of the Holy Spirit illuminating the sacred page as

> The Spirit breathes upon the Word,
> And brings the truth to sight.

Coming upon the riches of Holy Writ with fresh eyes, unencumbered by too much divisive scholarly tradition, new converts in Britain had these two advantages, however simple and untutored they were.

That they studied and devoured all the Scriptures they could get is evidenced by the few writings that have survived. The homily of Fastidius, the lament of Gildas, and both writings of Patrick are so packed with Scriptural language that we cannot escape the impression that their minds were saturated with Bible truth from avid reading, study, copying, and memorizing. In those days of parchment, hand-written publication, they had few other books, and Scriptures themselves were so scarce and expensive that few had access to the whole Bible. What portions they acquired, they cherished and shared carefully. As late as the mid-sixth century, Columba's teacher was so jealous of his possession of a good copy of Jerome's Vulgate translation of the Psalms that he would not let Columba copy it! Through the third century, the Scriptures and liturgy were in the original *koine* Greek, the common trade language of the Mediterranean, translations to Latin coming largely in the fourth century after the empire became nominally Christian and promoted the faith for state purposes. If parts of the Scriptures were translated into the native Celtic tongue, no evidence survives. When Pelagius, as a British Christian scholar went to Rome and the East around 400, he was proficient and fluent in both Greek and Latin. When Patrick reflected in his *Confession* upon his feelings of inadequacy because he had neglected his Latin studies as a boy, he remarked upon the pride in learning of his colleagues, when he was receiving his missionary training in Britain. Every evidence points to a scholarly tradition of Christian education in the Scriptures in the British Church.

Yet we must remember the simple conditions under which this education in the Scriptures was maintained. Roman cities in Britain were few and far between, and, in the country, churches were not usually housed in villas like the one excavated at Lullingstone in Kent. The more common situation is suggested by the Welsh syllable "Llan" meaning "Church," or Christian settlement. To have Christian fellowship, Christian families gathered together for their living. Llandaff was the Church settlement on the River Taff. Llanilltyd was the Church of Illtyd. This did not mean a large church building, nor a set of monastic buildings like the Medieval abbeys. Diana Leatham in her delightful book, *Celtic Sunrise*, has helped us to visualize the little Christian settlements scattered over Wales, Scotland, Ireland, and Brittany, forming the focus of religious and cultural life for these pastoral and agricultural people without cities from the fifth to ninth centuries, a custom from earlier country areas in Britain. People who had formerly lived in scattered farmsteads or in little hovels of wattle and thatch around the local chieftain's dun now gathered in a "Llan," as a group of Christian families housed in a village of huts, or later as monastics in little beehive cells. Prior to the sixth century, there was no regulated celibacy: families lived there with their children, along with the bishop or presbyter with his wife and children. The huts were grouped about a somewhat larger structure that served for common worship, taking the central place of the former chieftain's dun. The people continued to go out to till their fields or pasture their animals for sustenance, but there was time for common life. Each Llan was a worshiping and learning community. Christians had much to learn: how to read, the strange tongue of the Scriptures and Litany, the wonderful teachings of the Bible, Christian doctrine. Their chief pursuits were the studying and copying of the precious Scriptures and worship. Converts had to be taught the sacred traditions. A well-educated clergy had to be maintained, and larger bishops' Llans became gatherings of students for the ministry.

Amid this simplicity, the interpretation of Scripture was not all primitive. The Scriptures spoke to them more naturally because their culture was still very similar to that in pastoral Palestine. When they read "The Lord is my shepherd," or Jesus' words, "I am the good shepherd," they understood. Most Bible reading and homiletical interpretation would be personal and devotional, as the Bible speaks so directly to the moral and spiritual needs of all people everywhere. Being Celts of Druidic religious background, however,they approached the Scriptures with a traditional moralistic awareness prone to encourage the emphasis Pelagius brought to Rome. Yet, the corrective was in the Scriptures themselves and in the teaching of Irenaeus from the Mother Church in Gaul.

Much New Testament teaching safeguards against a simple Scriptural literalism which would accept everything in the Old and New Testaments as equally authoritative and inspired. In His Sermon on the Mount, Jesus repeatedly improved Old Testament teachings saying, "You have heard that it has been said . . . but I say to you."[15] Jesus had set the example of knowing His Bible so well that he could draw upon its truth to sustain him in the crises of his life, quoting Scripture to answer the Devil in each of his three temptations, and to sustain his soul during his suffering on the Cross.[16] Yet He had been selective, as when he read the prophecy of his Messiahship from Isaiah in the Nazareth Synagogue, he stopped reading and cut off the closing words of the sentence, "and the day of vengeance of our God."[17] He taught that Old Testament ceremonial law was subordinate to human need,[18] and said that in His Kingdom, the Temple worship would be obsolete.[19] He selected two love commandments from the Pentateuch and said they encompassed the whole law and the prophets. He was so selective of the eternal truth from the passing cultural matrix of Old Testament Scripture that He could say, "Heaven and earth will pass away, but my words will not pass away." Paul shared his Master's inspired spiritual judgment in interpreting the old written code:

We are ministers of the New Covenant, not in the written code, but in the Spirit, for the written code kills, but the Spirit gives life.[20]

The British Church would have a critical awareness of this difference between the Old Testament Law and the Gospel, not only from these passages and Paul's clear teaching in Romans 6-9 and Galatians 3-5, but also from Irenaeus' *Proof of the Apostolic Preaching*:

. . . our belief in Him was well-grounded, and true to the tradition of the preaching, that is, the witness of the apostles, who, sent by the Lord, preached to the whole world that the Son of God was come unto sufferings, undergone for the destruction of death and the giving of life to the flesh; that by casting out hostilities to God, that is, iniquities, we should receive peace with Him, doing what is acceptable to Him . . .

And that men were to be saved not according to the wordiness of the law, but according to the brevity of faith and charity, Isaias says thus: "a word shortened and cut short in justice; because a short word shall God make upon all the earth." And therefore also the Apostle Paul says, "love is the fulfillment of the law."

That He does not wish those who are to be redeemed to be brought again under the Mosaic legislation—for the law has been fulfilled by Christ—but to go free in newness by the Word, through faith and love towards the Son of God . . . And He has poured forth rivers in abundance, to disseminate the Holy Spirit upon the earth, as He had promised through the prophets to pour forth the Spirit on the earth in the end of days.

So our calling is in newness of Spirit and not in the oldness of the letter.[21]

They knew that in Christ we are new creations, and Christ is Lord, even of the Scriptures!

3. Piety: Public Worship, Private Prayer, and Charity

That the practice of personal piety in private prayer and devotion was rich and helpful in the spiritual life of the Church in Celtic Britain is evident from the few glimpses into that life which have come down to us. Patrick had misspent his boyhood, but when he was carried into slavery in Ireland, and was suffering loneliness and cold, out keeping his master's cattle in every weather, he could remember his rejected Christian training, and turned to prayer, many times night and day. When Alban of Verulam sheltered the fugitive priest in his home, it was when he observed the depth and devotion of his sincere piety that his heart was opened to the Gospel, and he received instruction and was converted to the faith for which he willingly endured martyrdom. Our only literary evidence of the piety of the British Church is the little book *On The Christian Life* by Fastidius, a British bishop who wrote sometime between 420 and 432. This was the time when Agricola was bringing the Pelagian heresy to Britain, and because of the ethical emphasis of his little book, Fastidius has been dubbed "Pelagian." It is a simple pastoral homily, addressed to a Christian widow, Fatalis, and written for the encouragement and instruction of grieving widows. It pictures widowhood as a noble vocation in piety and charitable works, showing how highly widowhood was regarded in the early Church. He summons Fatalis to be quiet and humble, to perform deeds of mercy and righteousness unceasingly, and to busy herself with reading and prayer. To be accounted a Christian, one must imitate the example of Christ:

A Christian is one who shows pity to all, who is not in any way troubled by injury, and who does not allow a poor man to be oppressed if he is present.

Free of rancor or fanaticism, with no evidence of controversy, yet humane, pious, and cultured in tone, this attractive book represents the commendable type of Christianity common in Britain at the time.

With no written evidence remaining of the British Celtic Church's order of common worship, we may assume it followed liturgical patterns common in the Church of the first two centuries on the Continent, as some of these rites continue later in Ireland. The pattern of worship in the early Church developed from the tradition in the Jewish Synagogue:

The opening Benedictions—two fixed adorations of Adonai.
The Shema ('Hear O Israel . . . ')
Six Precomposed Prayers for the living and the faithful departed.
Free Prayer
The Lessons: (with a blessing asked before each)
    One of 150 sections of the Torah (Standing)
    The Prophets.
Expository Address
Aaronic Benediction ('The Lord bless you and keep you . . . ')

Our Lord Himself customarily attended this worship,[22] so his Church early adapted it. From the worship materials of the Didache, the writings of Ignatius, Justin Martyr, Clement, Cyprian, and Pliny's letter to Trajan, we know the early worship included:

The Lessons (Old and New Testaments)
Sermon in exposition of what had been read.
Prayer for All the People
The Kiss of Peace
The Offertory of Bread and Wine and Water by the Deacons
The Eucharistic Prayer (Thanksgiving)
The Consecration by the Words of the Institution.
Intercession for the Living and Faithful Departed
Communion.[23]

Much of our exact knowledge of worship and customs in the Church of the first two centuries we owe to a quarrel between Hippolytus, bishop of the Port of Rome, and Callistus, liberal bishop of Rome in 217. Hippolytus led his church to declare Callistus morally apostate because of his lax policies. Hippolytus had hoped his scholarship would win him the Roman bishopric. In the midst of the controversy, to preserve knowledge of the Church as it had been in the first 200 years, Hippolytus wrote his account of *The Apostolic Tradition*. Suppressed in the West for obvious reasons, this priceless source has been found in the Arabic and Ethiopic versions. This and *Charismatic Gifts*, by the same author, help us to see what the Church had been as seen by one who was resisting change early in the third century.

The Church Hippolytus describes is threatened by persecution and worships in private homes. Liturgic practice is simple. The pattern of the Eucharist was: Thanksgiving, Recitation of the Institution, The Act of Remembrance, Invocation, and Final Doxology. Sexes were segregated in the Church service. Infants were admitted to baptism. There were offerings of cheese, olives, and fruit, but not of vegetables.

Hippolytus describes how converts were prepared for baptism and received into the Church from paganism. Viewed as former slaves of the Devil and his principalities and powers, the demons, they were ransomed by Christ, and transferred transformed from the kingdom of Satan to the Kingdom of Christ. So baptism was the dramatic portrayal of the mighty act of God in Jesus Christ, who by His death and resurrection freed men from the grip of Satan. He restored them to fellowship with Himself through the gift of the Holy Spirit, who enables us to die with Christ and rise with Him to newness of life. Whereas Satan has led people into sin, resulting in spiritual blindness and death of the soul, Christ's victory has overcome sin for us, and brought life and immortality to light. The light shines anew, illuminating for us the immortal way of obedience to the Father. So with the central theme of ransom from the Devil were combined other atonement experiences: death and resurrection in Christ; forgiveness and erasing of past sins; regeneration and rebirth; and illumination.

So the ancient Church had developed a realistic theology, and expressed what was experienced in impressive ceremonies for receiving new members. Hippolytus lists four stages in the yearly observances for Catechumens:

1. *The Preliminary Inquiry*—questioning the applicant's motives, sharing elemental facts of the history of salvation from Genesis to Revelation, and determining whether he is ready to become a Catechuman.

2. *Pre-Baptismal Instruction*—in the Scriptures, Theology, Prayer life, and Christian Living. They attended the fore part of weekly worship. This instruction might last three years. Forty days before Easter, the Teacher or Bishop decided on the basis of upright living, examplary piety and charitable care of the poor which Catechumens were ready for final preparation for Baptism.

3. *Lenten Preparation*—special instruction in the meaning of Baptism and the Eucharist. They received the Laying on of Hands, were "sealed" with the sign of the Cross on their foreheads, and "salted," all signs that they no longer belonged to the Devil but to Christ. Until they were baptized, there were daily instructions and exorcisms to drive out the satanic hosts holding them in thrall. On the Thursday before Easter, there was preparatory washing and cleansing. Friday and Saturday they fasted, with a final exorcism and the sealing of the sign of the Cross by the Bishop and an all-night vigil Saturday night.

4. *Easter Dawn Sacramental Rites:*

Prayer over the Water of Baptism, that the Holy Spirit might empower it.
Removal of clothing for nude baptism
Blessing of the oils of thanksgiving and exorcism
Renunciation of "Satan, his pomp and his services," facing West.
Anointing with the oil of exorcism over entire body by Presbyter.
Acknowledgment of Christ or of The Trinity, facing East.
Triune immersion upon confession of the Father, Son and Holy Spirit.
Anointing with the oil of Thanksgiving over entire body by Presbyter.
Reclothing and entering of the Assembly—sometimes footwashing.
Laying on of Hands of the Bishop, invoking Grace of the Holy Spirit.
Anointing with consecrated oil, sealing on the forehead, and giving of the Kiss of Peace by the Bishop.
Prayers by the whole Assembly, and exchanging of the Kiss of Peace.
The Partaking of the Milk and Honey, food of the Promised Land.
The Eucharist, partaking of the Bread and Cup with the faithful.

This elaborate initiation process was designed to strengthen the new convert for his continuing but now victorious battle with the Evil Tempter, who now no longer holds dominion over the Christian, but whose continued assaults may be expected.[24]

Actually, the Roman rites were somewhat simpler than the ritual used in Gaul and Britain. Stemming from the Orient through Northern Italy, the Gallican liturgy tended to be more free and florid. Saint Gemian of Paris (576) left an account of it.

1. Antiphon at entry of officiating Bishop like an Introit: "Alleluia, Blessed is He that cometh in the Name of the Lord.
   God is our Lord and Light.
   Response: "In the Name of the Lord."
   "Glory and Honor to the Father and to the Son and to the Holy Spirit unto all ages."
   Response: "In the Name of the Lord." [Deacons enjoin silence.]
2. Introductory Canticles:
   "Holy, Holy, Holy" intoned by the Bishop first in Greek, then in Latin.
   "Benedictus."
   [The Kyrie Eleison was added sometime after the Council of Vaison in Gaul.]
   The Prophecy (Luke 1:68-79), and Collect by the Bishop.
3. The Lections and the Psalms.
   1st from the Old Testament, 2nd from the Epistles.
   Hymn of Three Children (acc. to St. Gemian)
4. The Gospel with the Trisagion chanted going and coming.
5. The Homily. Though this preaching was denounced by Pope Celestine, it was confirmed and extended even to rural parishes by the Second Council of Vaison in 529 as St. Caesarius of Arles was a zealous advocate of preaching, his homilies having clarity and simplicity. The Church in Britain followed Gallican patterns.
6. The Prayers. The Prayer of the Faithful begins with a deaconal litany. All translations were from Greek texts of Oriental Litanies.
7. The Dismissal of the Catechumens.
8. Procession of the Oblation. Bread and Wine brought in in vessels, three veils, one linen and one silk to cover the oblation.
9. The Prayer of the Veils.
10. The Reading of the Diptychs.
11. The Kiss of Peace.
12. The Eucharistic Prayer.
13. The Epiclesis.
14. The Fraction, arranging particles of the Host upon the paten in the form of a Cross.

15. The Benediction.
16. The Communion. [In Gaul the faithful entered the sanctuary and came up to the Altar.]
17. The Thanksgiving. The Communion being ended the Bishop calls upon the Congregation to thank God, he himself reciting the prayer of Thanksgiving. followed by the final Benediction. "Missa acla est—in pace."[25]

Worship would have been simpler in the smaller churches in Britain than in Saint Gemian's sixth-century Cathedral Church in Paris, but they were in the the Gallican tradition, emphasizing beauty in liturgy and song.

Piety found its practical expression in good works of charity and service. Deacons led in the care of the sick and the poor. Christians cared for the aged and orphans. Widows were given opportunities to serve and were supported. Christians out-thought, out-prayed, and outloved all others, with a wholesome piety that attracted others to the Gospel.

Finally, we may deduce that the British Church early shared the strong disciplinary practice of the Church of the first three centuries, requiring obvious penitence of sinners. Discipline around the year 200 was reflected in two treatises, *On Penitence* and *On Purity* by the North African theologian, Tertullian. Like Hippolytus, Tertullian broke with the Church of Rome about 212 because of the laxness of the Roman Church under Callistus. The *Homily on Penitence* preceded this break, and may be accepted as an accurate picture of general practice.[26] Christians guilty of serious sins were not allowed at the Lord's Table until they had made their true penitence evident by a public demonstration called "Exomologesis."

Exomologesis, then, is a discipline which leads man to prostrate and humble himself. It prescribes a way of life, which, even in the matter of food and clothing appeals to pity. It bids him to lie in sackcloth and ashes, to cover his body with filthy rags, to plunge his soul into sorrow, to exchange sin for suffering . . . It requires that you habitually nourish prayer by fasting, that you sigh and weep and groan day and night to the Lord your God, that you prostrate yourself at the feet of the priests and kneel before the beloved of God (i.e., the Congregation) making all the brethren commissioned ambassadors of your prayer for pardon.[27]

That penitence was taken seriously in the Celtic Church in Britain is shown by the adoption of the strict Penitential Discipline by the Welsh Synod of Menevia in the year 560. Each soul's personal relationship to the Holy and Merciful and Righteous God and Father of our Savior was taken seriously in the deep piety of early Christianity, maintained in the Celtic Churches.

4. Charismatic Inspiration: Gifts and Works of the Holy Spirit

We have slight written evidence of the degree of activity of the Holy Spirit in the British Celtic Church. These disciples of The Way were orthodox Trinitarians in doctrine, always professing to believe in the Holy Spirit, but charismatic faith and practice are something more. Charismatic Christians are those whose faiths and dispositions and activities give evidence of the active inspiration, power, and grace of the living Spirit of God in their lives. This is a very personal occurrence, and certainly not under human control. Jesus told Nicodemus the wind blows where it wills without our knowledge of its source or destination, and so is everyone born of the Spirit.[28] The Holy Spirit works where, when, and how He pleases! So the charismatic richness characteristic of Patrick and the later Irish and Scottish churches need not have been inherited from or learned in Britain. Our one literary source, Gildas the Wise's remark about the early reception of the Gospel, "The rays of light were received with lukewarm minds by the inhabitants" would seem to deny any fervor or ecstatic activity. The absence of any tradition of an outstanding leader, preacher, healer, or missionary through those 350 years of real presence and growth of Christianity in Britain would point similarly. The tardiness of missionary activity, sending no missionary to the Picts until Ninian in the late fourth century, and Patrick's difficulty in getting the British Church to sponsor his missionary call until prodded by Rome's sending of Palladius to the Scots in Ireland, give a similar impression. Finally, there was the refusal of the British bishops to cooperate with Augustine in the evangelizing of the Anglo-Saxons in 603. The early Apostles had to wait in Jerusalem for the power of the Holy Spirit to come upon them before they could be Christ's effective missionary witnesses to the ends of the earth! Was this a lack in Britain?

As a Scripturally informed Church, the Celtic Britons could not miss reading about the importance of receiving the grace and power and Presence of the Holy Spirit in the New Testament. Every believer was supposed to receive the Holy Spirit when he was baptized, and there was one special prayer by the bishop for this in the ancient Easter Dawn Sacramental Rite for Catechumens.[29] Yet the New Testament tells of the Holy Spirit inspiring people in so many different ways that it was easy for converts and for the Church to become satisfied with a less than fulfilling result from that prayer.

The original outpouring of the Holy Spirit at Pentecost was a very special occasion hardly to be repeated, and the seeming description there of speaking in unknown foreign languages was apparently never witnessed again.[30] The power to witness to the ends of the earth might be interpreted as meant for only special Apostles.[31] Besides, there was the Scriptural distinction between the common and special gifts of the Holy Spirit. The common gifts of the Holy Spirit to all believers were a saving faith,[32] the illumination of the conscience, and the nine fruits of the Holy Spirit in Christian character: love, joy, peace, patience, kindness, goodness, faithfulness, gentleness, and self-control.[33] There was also the illumination that came when reading the Holy Scriptures. These common gifts were not lacking.

From the New Testament times on, the special gifts of the Holy Spirit were at His discretion and bestowed upon special people: wisdom, talent to teach, gifts of healing, administration, prophecy (preaching or predictive), miracles, speaking with tongues, ability to interpret tongues, the ability to distinguish between spirits (empathy), knowledge (scholarship), apostleship (missionary), helpers.[34] Everyone could be a helper, but all of the rest were special callings. One, speaking in tongues in the form of incomprehensible glossolalia, had proved to be a disturbing embarrassment in the Church at Corinth, where Paul had to advise its curtailment and subordination to sensible prophecy and teaching.[35]

The Celtic Churches, through Irenaeus of Lyons and other contacts through Gaul with Asia Minor, were of the Johannine tradition from Ephesus. In the Gospel according to John, Jesus, after the Resurrection, breathed the Holy Spirit upon the Apostles gathered in the Upper Room, to confer upon them the power to absolve guilt by granting forgiveness of sins.[36] The Master promised the common gift of the Holy Spirit to all disciples as "The Spirit of Truth," the Counselor who would guide His followers into all the truth after he departed, even into new truth those original disciples were not ready to bear.[37] He would become their Teacher, bringing Jesus' teachings to their remembrance, interpreting them so as to glorify Christ, and convicting the world of sin, of righteousness and of judgment.[38] So, in John's tradition, the most important work of the Holy Spirit is inner guidance, illumination, and enlightening of the conscience. The Spirit witnesses that Jesus is the Son of God.[39] When we love in deed and truth, and so abide in Him, we know it by the Spirit.[40] So Paul also said the greatest gift of the Spirit to be desired is love, even above ecstatic speaking, knowledge, faith, or sacrifice.[41] These common or generally bestowed gifts of the Holy Spirit, available to all Christians, are the most essential.

Another historical circumstance which may have affected the Church in Britain, through Irenaeus, was the Montanist controversy in Asia Minor. In 156, in Ardabau in Phrygia, a Presbyter named Montanus proclaimed himself the passive instrument through whom the Holy Spirit spoke, announced that the end of the world was at hand, and that the Lord would return soon to set up His Kingdom in little Pepuza, in Phrygia. He enjoined all to rigid asceticism in expectation. Two prophetesses joined him in this prophecy. Thousands sold their property and joined them expectantly. The bishops of Asia Minor in Synods held soon after 160 condemned Montanism as a heresy, but it spread widely nevertheless. At this time, Irenaeus, born around 140, was a young student cleric in Smyrna. There he had known the aged martyred Bishop Polycarp, the disciple of John who died around 155. Irenaeus knew of Montanus' misguided enthusiasm and became an early advocate of looking to the bishops of the major churches who were direct successors of the Apostles for guardianship of the Apostolic truth against heresies. The Bishops overreacted in this controversy, enhancing their own office and stifling the special gifts of the Holy Spirit in others. The emphasis in Irenaeus's *Proof of the Apostolic Preaching* is upon the common gift of a saving faith, and upon the special gifts associated with scholarship. Describing the work of the Holy Spirit in charismatic rebirth, he writes:

> For those who are bearers of the Spirit of God are led to the Word, that is to the Son; but the Son takes them and presents them to the Father; and the Father confers incorruptibility. So without the

Spirit there is no seeing the Word of God, and without the Son there is no approaching the Father, for the Son is knowledge of the Father, and knowledge of the Son is through the Holy Spirit. But the Son according to the Father's good pleasure administers the Spirit *charismatically* as the Father will to those to whom He will.[42]

In a later paragraph, he stresses the charismata prophesied for the "Shoot from the stump of Jesse," in Isaiah 11:

... the spirit of wisdom and understanding,
  the spirit of counsel and might,
the spirit of knowledge and the fear of the Lord.[43]

Certainly the Holy Spirit was in Jesus. This suggests that the vagaries of unbridled claims of Holy Spirit inspiration may have been prevented among the Celts by the Christ-centeredness of their spiritual experience. The Apostle Paul recognized that, experientially, there is no distinguishing our fellowship in the Spirit and our fellowship in Christ:

Now the Lord is the Spirit, and where the Spirit of the Lord is there is freedom.[44]

With their love of freedom, the British Celtic Church welcomed this promise.

5. Realistic Trinitarian Doctrine—The Truth That Makes Men Free

Irenaeus and Pelagius

All of our evidence points to the conclusion that the doctrine of the Celtic Church in Britain was realistic, in contrast to the yielding of Continental theology to Greek philosophical idealism; that it was orthodoxly Trinitarian; and that it stressed God's gift of freedom of will to mankind over against theories of Divine determinism. In all these respects, the churches in Gaul and Britain followed the teaching of the greatest theologian of the Ante-Nicene Fathers, Irenaeus of Lyons.

From the time of the Apostle Paul until Irenaeus wrote toward the end of the second century, the great successful in-

tellectual struggle of the Old Catholic Church was to resist the
inroads of Gnostic heresy, whose various proponents tried to
twist the realistic Gospel into some form of Greek idealistic
speculative philosophy. The Apostles' Creed, formulated to be
recited in the Church of Rome by Catechumen candidates for
baptism, was phrased to safeguard them against these unreal
notions, and has rightly been called the graveyard of Gnostic
heresies. The one real and true God created the heavens and
the earth, and saw that his material creation was good—it was
not the work of an imagined, evil Demi-urge. Jesus Christ our
Lord was truly human, conceived in and born of a real human
mother, with a physical body that suffered, died, and was
buried while He was under the power of death until God raised
Him the third day. He was not just a Divine phantom, only
seeming to be human, parading in what appeared to be a
human body but safeguarded from contamination with such
dross. God in all his three Personal manifestations as Creator,
Redeemer, and Inspirer is consciously real Spirit, thinking, willing, hating evil, loving His children, not just abstract Idea, the
highest Good in the structural pyramid of Plato's general concepts, remote, unapproachable, unfeeling, inactive, the con-
struct of proud philosophical contemplation!

The first three books of Irenaeus's great work *Against
Heresies* are largely taken up with detailed answers to these
heresies. In his *Proof of Apostolic Preaching,* he says:

Faith rests upon reality, for we shall believe what really is as it is
forever, keep a firm hold on our assent to it. Since then it is faith that
maintains our salvation, one must take great care of this sustenance,
to have a true perception of reality.[45]

In his orthodox description of the Trinity, he says of the Son,

He also, in the end of times, for the recapitulation of all things, is
become a man among men, visible and tangible, in order to abolish
death and bring to light life, and bring about the communion of God
with man.[46]

In that same summary of apostolic preaching, he says of the
freedom of man, "He was free and his own master, having been
made by God in order to be master of everything on earth."[47]
In Irenaeus's greater tome, *Against Heresies,* is this classic definitive argument for the responsible freedom of the human will:

God made man a free agent from the beginning, possessing his own power, even as he does his own soul, to obey the behests of God voluntarily, and not by compulsion of God. For there is no coercion with God, but a good will towards us is present with Him continually. And therefore does He give good counsel to all. And in men as well as in angels, He has placed the power of choice, so that those who had yielded obedience might justly possess what is good, given indeed by God, but preserved by themselves. On the other hand, they who have not obeyed shall with justice be not found in possession of the good, and shall receive condign punishment.

But if some had been made by nature bad and others good, these latter would not be deserving of praise for being good, for such were they created, nor would the former be reprehensible, for thus they were made originally. But since all men are of the same nature, able both to hold fast and to do what is good; and on the other hand having the power to cast it from them and not do it, some do justly receive praise even among men who are under control of good laws ... but the others are blamed and receive a just condemnation because of their rejection of what is fair and good....

No doubt, if any one is unwilling to follow the Gospel itself, it is in his power to reject it, but it is not expedient. For it is in man's power to disobey God, and to forfeit what is good, but such conduct brings no small amount of injury and mischief....

And not merely in works, but also in faith has God preserved the will of man free and under his own control.[48]

So Irenaeus was the great theologian of the human free will, and his whole teaching was consonant with this conviction. When God created mankind, he made Adam and Eve like innocent young children, and unredeemed in order that upon earth they might grow toward maturity, a process requiring conscious human participation. Man has to learn how to use his freedom through life in earth's historical process. Even Adam and Eve had to learn through experience. God deals with people according to the way they act in history.

Since man would be overwhelmed by a direct manifestation of God, and so unable to decide for himself, God must deal with us indirectly through His Word. He did this through the Prophets, and especially in His Son, Jesus Christ, the Word of God incarnate, who was before Creation, awaiting sufficient maturity of man on earth for Him, helpfully, to be born. Even if there had been no sin, the incarnation would have been necessary to surmount human limitation with an adequate revelation of God. Jesus came as the first fully human person. As

Irenaeus said it, "We become by grace what He is by nature." So we cannot become fully human without God and His redemption.

Redemption is more than forgiveness of human sin. Yet, because mankind has sinned, we have come under the power of Satan, a fallen angel. Satan has only the limited power God allows, of temptation, death, and Hades. Jesus Christ, on the Cross, by vicarious sacrificial love, was victor over Satan's power, conquered death, ransomed our souls, and went to break down the doors of Hell, then up to throw open Heaven's doors.

When we repent in response to God's love in Christ's Cross, we turn from sin, and see for the first time that life has a better option than death. The old self dies. We see the futility of the life of sin, and the beauty of the redemption experience. In recapitulation, Christ, the Second Adam, has undone for us the failure of the First Adam, beginning the growth of our second, mature humanity, as Adam in his innocence had begun immature humanity. In Christ, we are a new creation. Through all this, our freedom of choice is necessary, that we may respond to God's redeeming grace by a faith that is not just belief, but also willing trust and obedience.

This is a realistic personal theology, in direct contrast to the later speculative philosophical theology of Platonic idealism which engulfed the thinking of the Church around the Mediterranean from the teaching of Clement of Alexandria in the East, followed by Origen, and from the writings of Augustine of Hippo in the West. While these abstruse philosophical theologians compromised to bridge the gap to the educated Greco-Roman mind, and helped to make Christianity popular in that world, the more practical and ethical theology of Irenaeus served the newly evangelized, practical-minded Christians in Gaul and Britain, keeping the former realism and moral urgency of the New Testament and the Old Catholic Church. God and Satan are real, personal beings, and not just abstract ideas. Man confronts real choices with real, eternal consequences. How much of this theology was taught in Britain we must gauge from the results 150 years and more later in the thinking of Pelagius, Patrick, Fastidius, and Faustus of Riez.

It was natural for Irenaeus's emphasis on moral freedom to become popular and be exaggerated among the Celts of Britain. Their former Druid belief had been strongly moral, as demonstrated in the moral fervor of revulsion that spurred Boadicea's revolt. Pythagoras had been a great ethical reformer, and his philosophical descendants maintained the strong moral tradition. The result was the moral emphasis and drive of the greatest scholar produced by the British Church, Pelagius. Eloquent in both Latin and Greek, ably tilting intellectually with the two greatest minds of the Church of his day, Jerome and Augustine, initially accepted as orthodox in both Rome and in the East, he was ultimately condemned by the Bishop of Rome as a heretic, the more is the pity.

Born around 360, Pelagius was a mature monk and scholar when he arrived in Rome about the year 395. There is no certainty of where he came from in Britain. Later Welsh tradition claims he was the twentieth abbot of the great Abbey of Bangor Iscoed on Dee, south of Chester, and had been condemned for his heresy by a British Synod at Winchester before going abroad. Such a tradition would satisfy both Welsh pride and the desire to be free from the taint of heresy, but has no ancient foundations. The Monastery of Bangor on Dee was founded by Maelgwen in the sixth century, over a hundred years after Pelagius left Britain.

Pelagius had probably studied law before turning to theological ethics. When he arrived in Rome, he was shocked at the low level of morals in both church and society. It was more than two generations since Constantine had made Christianity the state religion. The Church, now wealthy from imperial favors, had lowered its standards to accommodate the millions who flocked in. The bishopric of Rome was now a prize to be won. The pagan Praetextatus had remarked, "Make me Bishop of the Church of Rome and I will become a Christian without delay." The year 367 had seen the unedifying spectacle of civil war over the coveted office between partisans of Damasus and Ursinus, with 127 deaths in one day! Ammianus Marcellinus, recording the incident, thought it only natural for men to compete for the opportunity of becoming rich from the offerings of the wealthy ladies of Rome, of riding in sumptuous raiment through the streets, and of giving kingly banquets. Pelagius, of excellent repute, much learning, and great moral concern, set himself to labor earnestly for more strenuous ethical standards in keeping with his more rustic background of the British-Druidic Christian tradition, loyal to the New Testament.

He found the practical teaching of sexual morality made

difficult by the impossibly idealistic celibate attack upon marriage in Jerome's treatise *Against Jovinian.* So he attacked Jerome's teaching. A friend of Jerome in Rome named Domnio wrote to that scholar in Bethlehem, telling him of the activity of this certain monk who was stirring up controversy. Jerome was a great scholar, but he had a vile temper and a mean disposition. In his *50th Letter to Domnio,* Jerome informs us that Pelagius had been intent upon a career in law before turning to theology. He attacks Pelagius' personal appearance, as "towering above with the shoulders of a Milo (a wrestler) he plods along at the pace of a turtle," and is "a huge dolt grown wide and thick with Scottish porridge," like "an Alpine dog, enormous and 'corpulentus'." In attacking Jovinian's teaching that no difference in merit attaches to the estate of the Christian virgin, widow, or married woman, Jerome had described the marital union as 'bad' (malus) and had written of the dirtiness of nuptials not being washed away even by the blood of martyrdom. He said that sexual union makes one unfit for prayer and prevents obedience to the apostolic injunction to pray without ceasing.

Pelagius taught that Divine generosity has given to everyone the privilege of following his own free will in the matter of marriage or abstaining from marriage, and one's will may go in either direction without fear of opposing the Divine will. Thereupon, Jerome accused Pelagius of being a disciple of *Jovinian.* This writer had also taught, "Those who with full faith had been born again in baptism cannot be overthrown by the Devil." Pelagius, concerned with the Christian's growth toward perfection, was convinced that God's gift of free will to man is important from the beginning of the Christian life to its final consummation, and that any doctrine of baptism or of faith which does not allow that the Christian, after baptism, is continually winning and meriting by works of righteousness that which he does not yet surely possess, i.e., eternal life, is to be rejected. In the Confession of Faith which he sent to Pope Innocent in 417, he took pains to denounce "those who assert with Jovinian that man is not able to sin."[49]

The fundamental difference between Pelagius and Augustine is largely traceable to different religious experiences from early childhood. We know Augustine's story in detail from his own *Confessions* written in 397. He was the spoiled son of a pagan father and a doting Christian mother in Tagaste, a small town in North Africa. Ambitious for their bright lad, his parents were willing to spend more for their son's education in rhetoric than his freedman father could well afford. Later, as a Christian, he blamed his parents for not having him early baptized, as though that would magically have saved him from his sins. He cheated on his teachers, resented discipline, lied, and stole. He stole from his parents to buy the companionship of other boys in play. He joined in their lusts, and at seventeen took a concubine. When his long continued resistance to the will of God and his mother's prayers was finally overcome in his cataclysmic conversion in Milan, it was to him completely an act of God's grace. Augustine therefore stressed the universal complete sovereignty of God; the total depravity of human nature; ever since Adam's fall; predestination of some to salvation and others to damnation according/to God's election; and the irresistable grace of God towards those he elects to save. His experience of God's grace and power after such a misspent youth had been overwhelming.

Pelagius on the other hand had been, relatively speaking, a good boy. He had resisted most of the temptations of his youth in honor of his parents. As an overgrown lad, people had expected him to act mature beyond his years, and he had tried to live up to their expectations. He had loved his parents, and had no mind to fault the Christian nuptials that had produced him. What second birth he had came gradually with good early Christian training, without rebellion or the need of a cataclysmic conversion. As long as he could remember, he had loved Christ's example, and had received His grace to use the moral freedom God had given him wisely, willing to do God's will and resisting the snares of the Devil on most occasions. His only major departure from parental guidance, after their death, was to abandon the law for theology and avidly pursue perfection as a monk, a life they could only approve from heaven. Granted that this picture is constructed from only partial evidence, yet it is true to life and to type. It is the other major variety of Christian experience, prevalent at least since Jesus told the parable of *The Father and His Two Sons*. Pelagius's tendencies to sin were more like the Elder Brother's. He had little patience with seeming cheap grace!

So Pelagius emphasized free will and personal responsibility. God in fairness could not require of us the impossible: "If I ought I can!" He denied any inherited original sin from Adam, and affirmed that all men now have the power not to sin, in this latter echoing Irenaeus. Adam's sin and other men's sins have set us a bad example, but God in His grace has given us willpower and a good example in Jesus Christ. All do sin and need to be set right. This is accomplished by our being justified, by faith alone, in the redeeming work of Jesus Christ who was victor over Satan, ransoming us from the power of sin and death. This is sealed to us in baptism, after which we have full power and duty to keep the Divine law. Augustine's teaching that by God's predestined decree some are elected to salvation and others assigned to condemnation; that people since Adam and Eve are totally depraved and incapable of willing and doing good; and that free choice of right conduct has little to do with eternal destiny since it is all in God's hands in prevenient election and grace, was in his view too lenient upon people's moral laxity. It excused them in sin. People needed to be encouraged to exercise their own willpower, freely to decide for Christ and then to do right.

When Alaric and his Visigoths invaded Italy, and in 410 captured and plundered Rome, among the refugees to North Africa were Pelagius and a young friend named Coelestius. They went out to Hippo to call on Augustine, but were not welcomed. Coelestius was an Irishman who had been a lawyer in Rome. He stayed on in Carthage and sought ordination as a presbyter at the hands of Bishop Aurelius. But that bishop received from one Paulinus, a deacon of Milan, a letter charging Coelestius with six theological errors:

1. Adam was made mortal, and would have died whether he had sinned or not sinned.
2. The sin of Adam injured himself alone, and not the human race.
3. New-born children are in that state in which Adam was before his fall.
4. Neither by the death and sin of Adam does the whole race die, nor by the resurrection of Christ does the whole race rise.
5. The law leads to the Kingdom of Heaven as well as the Gospel.
6. Even before the coming of the Lord there were men without sin.

The letter was unfriendly, but Coelestius did not reject its statements of his views, which were more radical than those of Pelagius. An advisory Synod of Carthage decided against his ordination, so he journeyed on to Ephesus, and there was ordained. Augustine was not present, but when he was informed of the matter, began his long literary polemic against what he called "Pelagianism."

In the East, where the Church was engaged in Christological controversy, Pelagius's views of Christ were quite acceptable, and he found considerable support for his emphasis upon the freedom of the will. Early in 415, Augustine sent Orosius to Jerome to enlist his collaboration. Jerome readily accused Pelagius before Bishop John of Jerusalem. Yet Pelagius was approved by that bishop, and a Synod held at Lydda declared him orthodox. He was helped by his scholarly fluency in Greek, speaking before the Synod of his own beliefs, while his Western accusers were poor in that language.

Augustine and his colleagues then called two North African Synods, one in Carthage and one in Mileve for Numidia, both condemning the "Pelagian" opinions and appealing to Bishop Innocent of Rome for confirmation. Innocent, pleased with this early recognition of Roman authority, did their bidding but died soon thereafter. When he was succeeded by Zosimus in 417, Coelestius appealed to him in person. Zosimus, a Greek with no special sympathy with the North African position, declared that the North African synods had been too hasty and considered Coelestius orthodox.

The Africans called for a new Synod of Carthage in 418, persisting that Pelagius must be compelled to acknowledge that the grace of God through Christ is required for every single good human action. They made another more offensive move, and more effective! They convinced the Western Emperor, Honorius, that the peace of the Empire required his action in the case, and Honorius, in April, issued a rescript condemning Pelagianism, and ordering its adherents into exile. Emperors had been so interfering in church affairs ever since Constantine. After all, the state religion had to be applicable to the masses of the people, with salvation made easy through profession of orthodox doctrine and the magic of the sacraments. This was possible under Augustine's definitions, but difficult and disturbing under Pelagius' emphasis upon morals. Christianity could not be placed above the average man's reach! Pelagius disappeared. Meanwhile, the Carthage Synod met in May, deciding that Adam became mortal by sin; that grace was necessary for right living; and that sinlessness is impossible in this life. Moved by all of these actions, possibly more by the emperor's rescript, Zosimus of Rome now issued a circular letter condemning

Pelagius and Coelestius. Pelagianism was formally condemned by the Council of Ephesus in 431.

In the heat of debate, both sides had overstated their cases. Augustine answered more questions than Pelagius had raised, and it is obvious that his too great emphasis upon unaided Divine initiative, predestination, and effectual calling deprives Christians of their incentive to do their best, and would cut the nerve of all evangelism and missionary endeavor. Unfortunately, John Calvin, when he was looking for an ally among the early Church fathers, found him in Augustine and agreed with his emphasis upon Divine Sovereignty, and hyper-Calvinism repeated Augustine's worst excesses. An early enthusiast of the great Missionary Awakening of the late eighteenth century was badgered by hyper-Calvinists saying, "If God wants to convert the heathen he can do it without your help!"

Meanwhile, exaggerated Pelagianism denies the Gospel. The Gospel does begin with the recognition that everyone is sinful and needs to be redeemed, not just informed, in a way we cannot accomplish ourselves. Christ gives us a new-life possibility men never had before. Jesus is our Redeemer, not just a teacher or model. The Cross was necessary. Augustine was right when he asked Pelagius, "If infants inherit no sinful character, why don't you deny infant baptism?"

The anti-Pelagian writings of Augustine and others aroused a tremendous controversy, both in the East and in the Celtic West. John Cassian of Lerins Monastery on an Isle near Marseilles was a leading thinker of what came to be called the "Semi-Pelagian" position. He refused to accept the doctrine of Pelagius that human nature is essentially uncorrupted. He maintained the freedom of the human will, and the non-irresistibility of Divine grace, i.e., that people can resist the grace of God if they choose. He saw the essential antinomy for human thought in the logical contradiction between Divine omnipotence and human freedom, and admitted that it is not possible to define the relation between free will and grace exactly, while both are necessary in the work of salvation. The Apostle Paul had put it well:

Work out your own salvation with fear and trembling, for God is at work in you, both to will and to work for His good pleasure.[50]

Cassian denied the Augustinian doctrine of prevenient grace

and predestination, and declared that a man could take the first step toward his salvation without awaiting the motive power of grace.

Meanwhile, the condemnation of Pelagianism had scattered its advocates, and one Agricola, the son of an Italian Bishop named Severianus, traveled to Britain preaching the heresy in its worst form. There he stirred up a great controversy, winning many adherents in an atmosphere still partly informed by the ancient Druid moral tradition, and where many would be proud of their famous fellow-countryman. The British Church leaders were unable to refute Agricola's plausible arguments, and wisely decided to ask for help. It is significant that they did not turn to Rome, but to their Mother Church in Gaul. The Venerable Bede tells us that the church in Gaul summoned a synod in 429, to consult together about whom they should send to support the faith, and unanimously chose Bishops Germanus of Auxerre and Lupus of Troyes.

That same year Prosper of Aquitaine in Southern Gaul sent a letter to Augustine, telling him of the widespread antagonism toward his writings in Gaul. Augustine, who had admired John Cassian, replied trying to explain his position in *On Perseverance of the Saints.* This gives evidence that the two men chosen to go to Britain and answer the Pelagian heretics were not Augustinians, but sensible Semi-Pelagians from Gaul, who would irenically resolve the disturbance to the satisfaction of most Britons. This they did, though the heresy broke out afresh later, and Germanus and Severus came on a second expedition to combat it sometime between 430 and 434.[51]

Further evidence of this Semi-Pelagian theological climate in Gaul and Britain is shown in the works of two other Britons of the same fifth century, Fastidius and Faustus. We have already considered Fastidius's little homily, *On The Christian Life,* written sometime between 420 and 432, at the very time Agricola was stirring up Britain, and sometimes accused of being Pelagian, when it is not at all controversial unless one considers anything mildly moralistic controversial. More active in the controversy was Faustus of Riez in Gaul, who came from a fine Christian family in Britain with an exceptionally devout mother. He was chosen abbot of Lerins in 433, remaining there twenty-seven years. In 462, he was called to be bishop of Riez in the Northern Gaul province of Aix. There he had a wide reputation for learning, and served until his death in 490. Afterwards, he was regarded in some circles as somewhat heretical because of his outspoken Semi-Pelagianism. He led two local synods in 472 and 475, in which the doctrine of predestination was condemned. One, at Arles, declared the following opinions denied, and those who hold them anathema:

1. That the labor of human obedience is not to be linked with the grace of God.
2. That Christ has not undergone death for the salvation of *all* men.

Faustus was opposed by the very Augustinian Fulgentius of Ruspe in North Africa.

This illustrates the closeness of the British Church to her Mother Church in Gaul, and their common Celtic emphasis upon doctrines emphasizing human freedom and voluntary obedience to the will of God. Call it Semi-Pelagian or whatever, this is in harmony with the major emphasis of the Scriptures of both the Old and the New Testaments, especially the Psalms and the Gospels and the practical appeals with which Paul balanced the abstruse doctrinal portions of his Epistles, as in Romans 12. Certainly, it was a mature and responsible interpretation of the ethical appeals of our Lord, and is still assumed in every evangelistic appeal for decision for Christ. Little wonder that Liberty under Divine Law became a major emphasis in the heritage of the Celtic Churches. People who exercise and cherish this religious freedom under God also insist upon civil liberty under constitutionally limited governors and laws in the body politic. So Celtic Christians, in both church and state, have advocated the liberties of representative democracy, and have been staunch defenders of freedom against all forms of tyranny. They also make good citizens, for without citizens who are thus freely and voluntarily law abiding, from inner moral convictions and willingness to do the will of God, democracy has nowhere been successful and enduring. Realistic Christian doctrine makes a real difference.

6. Faithful Missionary Outreach

We have already seen, under our discussion of the degree of charismatic activity in the Celtic Church in Britain that in the latter years of that 350-year span, they were not greatly empowered or enthused about missionary outreach. Of course, in the earlier second and third centuries, under the heel of Roman persecution, when they could have little overt activity of their own and were trying to evangelize their own part of the empire, they could hardly be expected to send missions abroad. Yet after the empire became nominally Christian in the early fourth century, the awareness of their duty to the marauding Irish, Scots, and Picts beyond their empire boundaries was slow in arriving. What was wrong? They were Bible-believing Christians, and the message of the New Testament with the Risen Christ's great commission to go forth and teach all nations, to carry the Gospel into all the world to every creature, was always there. Their tardy sending of Ninian to the Picts and of Patrick to Ireland was an acknowledgment that they recognized the obligation.

There is one indication in the attitude of Patrick himself toward the people he served in Ireland that is illuminating. Patrick never completely identified himself with the people of Ireland, though he lived there and served them lovingly for many years. They were still to him foreigners, outside the bounds of Roman civilization. The indication is that as and when Christianity gained status and popularity in Britain from becoming the empire religion early in the fourth century, it became identified with Roman civilization and culture, so that to be a Christian and to be a Roman citizen were almost identical in the general public mind. This all but engulfed the Church, so that it became difficult to conceive of taking the faith alone to the barbarians beyond the bounds of empire peace and culture. Even Patrick, after his Divine call to go back and serve where he had suffered as a slave, and his eagerness while training to obey, could not shake the prejudice, and the feeling of being exiled from civilization while he remained in Ireland. Is it not a warning that the Church too readily becomes acculturated and accommodated to some comfortable part of the world it has helped to civilize, to become "of the world" it is in, and to neglect those parts of the world that need it most?

7. Strict and Steadfast Personal Ethics—Gildas the Wise's Lament

To describe and gauge the personal morality for laity and clergy taught and practiced in the Celtic Church in Britain from 180 to 560 with our limited indigenous written sources, and to gain any help for our thesis therefrom might seem a fruitless endeavor. Yet its duty of educating and inspiring people to do the righteous will of God and to grow in Christlike goodness is one of the major functions of any church as it serves the Gospel of Christ; and its accomplishment therein is one measure of a true church, and a major attraction to those who would look to her for salvation. How did the church of the Celtic Britons measure up ethically?

She had the high moral teachings of the Old and New Testaments, and the inspiration of the Holy Spirit toward obeying them. This meant the Ten Commandments with their righteous conduct commended and expanded in the Psalms and the Prophets, and fulfilled and deepened in the teaching of Jesus in His Sermon on the Mount, His Golden Rule, and His Rule of Love for God and neighbor. So they had goals no one can reach without the help of Divine Grace, to keep them humble and striving.

Planted as part of the early Old Catholic Church while she was still persecuted and pure, the British Church inherited her strong ethical tradition. A vivid nursery rhyme can help to describe her:

> There was an old woman who lived in a shoe,
> She had so many children she didn't know what to do;
> She gave them some broth without any bread,
> And whipped them all soundly and sent them to bed.

In all but transient domicile Mother Church moved over the ancient world, accumulating such a large family so swiftly she had problems to feed them adequately with the strong meat of the Gospel and the Bread of Life, and had to concentrate on behavior and discipline. Moral issues became paramount. This has disappointed some scholars, who think the faith of the second century inferior to that of Paul and John. Theological understanding of salvation by faith alone through the grace of God in Christ seemed forsaken for preoccupation with good works. They fail to reckon with the changed situation. Out in the Greco-Roman world, even among the Jews of the Dispersion, the main issue was no longer freedom from the legalism of the Pharisees, but conflict with philosophical idealism and moral laxity. The strong temptation was to accommodate to the Greek thought world and its common corruption. Gnostics, despising the flesh as part of the material world, could either punish it as ascetics, or indulge it with impunity, as it was of no consequence. Scholars now say that this heresy was rife in the scattered Jewish synagogues of the Dispersion, among the Hellenist Jews and their partial converts, the God-fearers among the Gentiles who were prime prospects for Christian conversion. Accepting the Way in Christ meant a stringent moral change for the self-indulgent majority, and maintaining Christian standards of conduct in the growing churches meant careful attention to discipline, as we saw in Tertullian's definition of exomologesis.

Two writers from the second-century represent its emphasis: *The Epistle to Diognetus* was written by an intelligent Christian to an earnest Gentile inquirer describing "The Manner of Christians" soon after 100:

They display to us their wonderful and confessedly striking method of life. They dwell in their own countries but simply as sojourners ... They marry, as do all others, they beget children; but they do not destroy their offspring. They have a common table but not a common bed. They are in the flesh but do not live after the flesh. They pass their days on earth but as citizens of heaven. They obey the prescribed laws, and at the same time surpass the laws by their lives. They love all men and are persecuted by all .... repay insult with honor. They do good and yet are punished as evil-doers.

To sum up all in one word,—what the soul is to the body, that are Christians in the world ... The soul dwells in the body, yet it is not of the body. The Christians dwell in the world, yet are not of the world.[52]

Justin Martyr had accepted in turn Stoicism, Aristotelianism, Pythagoreanism, and Platonism before finding in Christianity "the oldest, truest and most divine of philosophies." In 153, he addressed his *Apology* to the Emperor Antoninus Pius, seeking to defend The Way from persecution:

We ... after being persuaded by the Word ... now follow the only unbegotten God through His Son. Those who once rejoiced in fornication now rejoice in continence; those who made use of magic arts have dedicated themselves to the good and unbegotten God; we who valued above all things the acquisition of wealth and possessions, now bring what we have into the common stock and communicate to everyone in need; we who hated and destroyed one another on account of their different manners, and would not use the same hearth and fire with men of a different tribe, now, since the coming of Christ, live familiarly with them and pray for our enemies.[53]

Justin was scourged and martyred. Despite such treatment, the Church grew, actually because of it, for "the blood of the martyrs was the seed of the Church." So long as discipleship was costly, being a Christian was heroically moral and required real faith.

One early reaction against this strongly moral emphasis was repulsed. Marcion, son of a bishop in Pontus and a wealthy shipbuilder, was excommunicated by his father for "polluting a virgin"—not literally, for the virgin was the Church. Marcion was advocating heresy. He wanted to cut out of the Scriptures the whole Old Testament and all of the New, except the Gospel of Luke and Paul's writings emphasizing grace and not obedience. He attempted to form the first-defined Canon of the New Testament on this basis. In 139, he came to Rome and gave that church a great sum, over $250,000. When they suspected his purpose and learned of his Gnostic notions, denying the real, fleshly incarnation of Christ, the Roman Church excommunicated him and returned the money. These were the days before Bishop Dionnysius of Rome began to urge that the Church be less rigorous in discipline, and take more account of the weakness of the majority of the people, and especially before the corruption under Callistus against which Hippolytus and Tertullian revolted in disgust. Faith in Christ issued in strenuous moral endeavor. Salvation by grace rather than by works of law did not mean the abolition of the moral law, but its fulfillment in willing obedience from the heart. Irenaeus of Lyons, writing, *Against Heresies,* between 182 and 188 said:

> The Lord did not abrogate the natural precepts of the law, but rather fulfilled and extended them. He removed the yoke of bondage of the old law, so that mankind, being now set free might serve God with that trustful piety which becometh sons.[54]
> The Decalogue however was not cancelled by Christ, but is always in force. Men were never released from its commandments.[55]

This was the heritage of Christian ethical rectitude taken to Britain from the Mother Church in Gaul. It would be readily accepted by people whose highest religion, driven underground, was the strongly moral Druid heritage from the ethical reformer Pythagoras. So long as the Church was threatened by intermittent Roman persecution, the real dedication of its members and clergy and their moral steadfastness would be secure.

It was when the Emperor Constantine made Christianity the state religion of the empire that the moral climate began to change, its leadership spoiled by numerical and monetary prosperity under state coddling. The Edicts of Constantine, offering Christians toleration and freedom in 313, and soon thereafter exempting clergy from taxation and onerous civic duties, granting subsidies for church buildings, payment of travel costs for synod and council gatherings, the right to receive legacies, and the forbidding of all work on Sundays to encourage attendance at worship, ushered in for British Christianity an era of rapid growth and church-building. People were admitted into the churches in such numbers there was too little time to train them, or even to gauge how many claimed conversions were sincere. All at once, the Church needed many new presbyters and bishops, and there were insufficient dedicated candidates, with little time to train them. Meanwhile, the increase in prestige and emoluments of ecclesiastical office made positions of religious leadership never before coveted now plums indeed. Aristocratic families, now flocking into the churches, looked upon bishoprics as proper seats of preferment to be purchased for younger sons not needed for the management of family estates. The door was wide open for simony. Purchased religious office means the loss of morally dedicated leadership and the corruption of the church.

We are speaking now of a period of nearly 250 years, from the Edict of Toleration until the writing of Gildas's lament, *De Excidio et Conquestu Britanniae,* in 560. This long period contained first 100 years of prosperous peace under protection of the Roman legions, then their withdrawal and the hiring of treacherous Saxon mercenaries under the inept and morally corrupt leadership of Vortigern. There followed the decades of increasing battles against Saxons and Picts invading the land until Ambrosius Aurelianus and/or Arthur won the respite of a whole generation of peace and prosperity after the Battle of Badon Hill. Then came the horror of the yellow plague, and the final deadly onslaught of the Saxons, driving the Britons completely out of what was to become England, back into Wales and Cornwall and across the channel into Brittany, and the fury of the barbarians was sated.

It was in view of this tragic history that Gildas the Wise wrote his book, *Of Annihilation and Conquest of Britain.* He was a monk trained at Llanilltyd in Wales, who spent some time at Glastonbury, traveled to Ireland, and to Brittany to escape the yellow plague. While his book attempts to be a history, it is really a lament over the tragic fate of Britain and an attempt to account for it in the Providence of God. It was sometimes called *Liber Querolus.* Five-sixths of it is lamentation over the wickedness of the British princes and clergy, justifying God's darker Providence in the destruction of this once-flourishing Church. Like the Old Testament Prophets, Gildas is convinced it was a just Divine judgment upon their many sins.

Gildas gives a vivid, rhetorical account of the Saxon assaults:

The conflagration blazed over cities and regions, and did not cease until almost the entire island had been devastated, it licking the western seas with its ruddy tongue ... They came like the assault of the Assyrians on Judea. . . . so that all the columns were levelled with the ground with the frequent stroke of the battering ram, all the husbandmen routed together with their bishops, priests and people, whilst the sword gleamed and the flames crackled round them on every side. The people were slain along with their priests and the altars polluted. The fugitives reached the hills only to be overtaken and slain in heaps. Others gave themselves up as slaves when overcome with hunger. Others found refuge overseas, chanting in their misery beneath the swelling sails, "Thou hast given us up as sheep to the slaughter and scattered us among the Gentiles."[56]

He is convinced the judgment was deserved because even still, in his own time, the wickedness has not abated, and men readily forget and return to their evil ways even as the Israelites did of old:

And yet neither to this day are the cities of our own country inhabited, as before, but being forsaken and overthrown, still lie desolate; our foreign wars have ceased, but our civil troubles still remaining. For as well the remembrance of such a terrible desolation of the island, as also the unexpected recovery of the same remained in the minds of those who were the eye-witnesses of the wonderful events of both, and in regard thereof the kings, public magistrates and private persons with priests and clergymen did all and every one of them live orderly according to their several vocations. But when these had departed out of the world, and a new race succeeded, who were ignorant of this troublesome time and had only experience of the present prosperity, all the laws of truth and justice were so shaken and subverted, and not so much as a vestige of remembrance of those virtues remained among the above named orders of men, except among a very few, who, compared with the great multitude which are daily rushing headlong down to hell, are accounted so small a number that our reverend mother, the Church scarcely beholds them.[57]

Note in passing that for Gildas in 560 in Britain, "our reverend Mother" is the Church and not Mary.

In Part III, Gildas gets down to specific attacks upon the sins of all the kings in the remaining parts of Britain in his time. First, he spells out and condemns the sins of the king of Damnonia (Cornwall), then of the four kings of Wales, in lurid detail. Then, after an exhaustive recounting of prophecies of doom from the Old Testament, and threats of Divine judgment from the New, to gain perspective that still another terrible doom is deserved, Gildas comes to the climax of his Lamentation in condemnation of the clergy, who have shared the sinfulness that deserves the holocaust:

Britain hath priests, but they are unwise; very many that minister but many of them impudent; clerks she hath but certain of them are deceitful raveners; pastors as they are called, but rather wolves prepared for the slaughter of souls. For they provide not for the food of the common people, but covet rather the gluttony of their own bellies, possessing the houses of the Church, but obtaining them for filthy lucre's sake; instructing the laity but showing withal most depraved examples, vices and evil manners, seldom sacrificing and seldom with clean hearts, standing at the altars not correcting the commonality of their offenses while they commit the same sins themselves; despising the commandments of Christ, and being careful with their whole hearts to fulfil their own lustful desires, some of them with unclean feet usurping the seat of the Apostle Peter, but for the demerit of their covetousness falling down into the pestilent chair of the traitor Judas . . . debasing themselves into such bad creatures, and after all these seeking rather ambitiously for ecclesiastical dignities than for the kingdom of heaven, and defending after a tyrannical fashion their achieved preferments.[58]

The reference to "usurping the seat of the Apostle Peter," referring to Rome, implies that bishoprics have been claimed with improper authority, perhaps by forging appointments as though from that See. Higher dignities than the bishop's office were beginning to be claimed and defended with tyrannous abuse of power.

For what is so wicked and so sinful as after the example of Simon Magus (even with other faults he had not been defiled before) for any man with earthly price to purchase the office of a bishop or priest, which with holiness and righteous life alone ought lawfully to be obtained, but herein they do more wilfully and desperately err, in that they buy the deceitful and unprofitable ecclesiastical degrees, not of the Apostles or their successors, but of tyrannical princes, and their father the Devil, yea rather they raise this as a certain proof and covering of all offenses over the frame of their former serious life, that being protected under the shadow thereof, no man should lightly lay to their charge their old and new wickednesses, and hereupon they build their desires for covetousness and gluttony, for that now being the rulers of many they may more freely make havoc at their pleasure.[59]

Here the purchase of bishoprics has been from tyrannical civil rulers under whose protection they batten. Gildas accuses them of crossing seas to buy ecclesiastical offices. They are enemies of God, and not priests. "O ye traders of wickedness and not bishops!" Gildas concludes by conceding that there are a few worthy clergy:

And may the same Almighty God of all consolation and mercy preserve his few good pastors from all evil, and (the common enemy being overcome) make them free inhabitants of the Heavenly City of Jerusalem which is the congregation of all saints.[60]

Since bishops were the highest clergy criticized, it is clear there are still no higher ranks in Britain in 560. Yet, the bitter fruit of the establishment of the Church under Roman and later under British civil rulers is clear: abuse in conferring ecclesiastical offices, such as bishops of churches in major towns, so corrupting the clergy and with them the morals of the commonwealth that the horrible destruction was deserved.

But now, Gildas is seeking desperately to reverse the trend. Like the Prophets of old, he is daring to be explicit in condemning the sins of both kings and clergy in his own time, proving that he at least is not a corrupt kept priest. He has dared to assert religious independence from all establishments. He has set the example again of the prophets of old which the Church must ever heed or be in peril. Not all bishops had been time-servers. Patrick, when he went to Ireland, stood his ground, to the High King, and in writing to Coroticus in Glasgow. Gildas was called "The Wise" because his lesson was remembered in the Celtic churches. Too close alignment with civil rulers and acceptance of civil favors spells corruption. So Celtic monastic sites in later days were placed, wherever possible, on separate islands off the coast like Iona and Lindisfarne, symbols and examples of the morally and spiritually superior detachment of the Holy Church from mundane controls and contamination. It was a hard lesson to learn and keep. Separation of church and state, of the Kingdom of God from the world's culture, in the world yet not of the world, is still a difficult position to maintain, yet necessary for the Church's soul.

8. Constructive but Relativistic and Independent Social Ethics

The responsible impact of the Christian Church upon society, and especially the relationship of Christians to the civil government has been problematic ever since Jesus was born and Herod reacted with fear and violence. We should not be surprised that the experience of the Church in Celtic Britain raised the question of social action in a new setting those early Christians were hard put to assess.

Of course, they had the New Testament social teaching for guidance, as well as the Old Testament Law and Prophets. Until the early fourth century, under oppression of the Roman Empire, their situation was little different than that of Palestine in Jesus' day, and the New Testament setting remained easily understandable.

Jesus had come proclaiming the Kingdom of God at hand on earth for all who would follow Him. He taught His disciples to pray for that Kingdom's increase, that more of the will of God might be done on earth as in Heaven, and that His followers must be willing to serve humbly and sacrifice, taking up daily crosses to further its coming. Works of compassion and reconciliation, making for justice and peace, fulfilling the message of the Hebrew Prophets, were clearly in the line of Christian duty when followers of The Way gave their lives in faith to Christ.

Yet, in some ways, Jesus' earthly ministry had disappointed

Israel's social and political hopes of the Messiah.[61] John the Baptist and Jesus' zealot disciples, probably including Judas, expected more immediate and effective social action. It was hard for them to learn that He was then only the world's Prince of Peace, and not yet its King![62] He mounted no social movement challenging the most flagrant injustice in the Roman world, slavery; he only taught how to undercut its stigma by serving others willingly without being forced.[63] There were social implications in much that He taught, but they were not always clear.[64] For the simplest social unit, the family, He taught a higher ethic of unending faithfulness in marriage with no divorce, but when challenged by the Pharisees allowed that the use of Moses' divorce provisions would continue to be necessary because widespread unregenerate hardness of heart would make the Christian standard legally unenforceable.[65] He seemed in no hurry about the Kingdom's coming. It would grow like a mustard tree from a tiny seed, and spread in the world like leaven in bread-dough.[66] But when the wheat-seed was sown in God's field, and the fruit of the word began to sprout, there would be weeds found growing amid the wheat, sown by the Devil, until the final harvest at the end of the age.[67]

There was a practical realism about his teaching often disturbing to impatient idealists. It is expedient not to assay the impossible, as a king doesn't go to war with only 10,000 soldiers against 20,000, and a person who begins to build a tower without the means to finish it only looks foolish.[68] He taught a higher ethic for His Church than can be expected of the world. His disciples were to keep the higher way among themselves, being in the world yet not of it.[69] In His own Temptation, pondering the means of establishing His Kingdom, he rejected the lower means of this world: buying followers with bread; startling them with miraculous stunts; winning nations by compromise with the Devil's ways in military aggression and political coercion.[70] His Kingdom would be a pearl of great price for all who would value it freely to choose at some cost. It would be fulfilled only at the end of time, when the evil would be sorted from the righteous as a fisherman separates valuable fish from the worthless dragged up in his net.[71] Plainly, Jesus knew His Kingdom would never be fully organized in this age upon earth, by enacting external laws, as in Plato's utopian Republic, nor brought about by persuading people to keep legal minutia, the impossible burden laid upon folks by the Pharisees.

His disciples would be the "*ec-clesia*," "called out" of the world to be His Church, a colony of Heaven on earth, a fellowship of persons already with higher citizenship in Heaven.[72] They would be the salt of the earth and the light of the world,[73] yet be discommoded with a continuing dual allegiance, rendering to Caesar the things that are Caesar's, and to God the things that are God's, yet being ready to suffer the Cross when Caesar may usurp God's sovereignty over us.[74] Paul and Peter had made the Christian duty to honor and obey civil rulers more explicit in earlier New Testament days when Roman laws protected Christians, and before the Roman rulers required people to worship them.[75] The situation had changed by the time the author of *Revelation* celebrated the impending fall of "Babylon" when Christians were being martyred for refusing to burn incense to the emperor, and the corrupt state had to be resisted.[76]

How much of this New Testament social teaching the British Christians of the second and third centuries understood is an unanswerable question. Christians still have difficulty agreeing about the present social implications of the Gospel. Since, for two hundred years, the British Church was too small a minority to command great social influence anywhere, the question is somewhat academic. Yet, everywhere and always, Christian compassion and charity, gathering and rearing babies exposed to die by pagan parents, caring for the aged, the sick, the poor, the widows and orphans, could not help making some impact by example throughout the empire. People said, "How those Christians love one another!"

Yet in the early fourth century, the Celtic Church in Britain shared in projecting the most significant and seemingly successful program of social strategy ever launched in all Christian history, before or since. There were such dire consequences that this participation has been largely buried and unrecognized. This British Church participation in the victorious crusade of Constantine the Great has been obscured and ignored by secular historians. Yet they were only following the lead of Roman and Anglican writers from the time of the Venerable Bede. For although Constantine freed Christianity from persecution throughout the Roman Empire, and then made it the state religion, Bede merely mentions him as a comment upon his erroneous assertion that the Arian heresy, sweeping the world, infected Britain (see quote, page 29). Bede writes not a word about the Edict of Milan, nor about who crowned Constantine at York, so near Jarrow where Bede lived. He was carefully avoiding giving any credit to the non-conforming Celtic Church, though he also probably lacked access to the pertinent histories of Lactantius and Eusebius.[77]

This writer was re-alerted to the much debated historical problem of how Constantine was motivated to so favor Christianity by the dramatic reenactment of his crowning by his troops at York, depicted in the 1900th Anniversary Pageant at that city in 1971. Who were those troops? What was their motive? When did Constantine become a Christian? Unhampered by secular or Romanist-Anglican biases, let us try to piece together the well-known historical facts and a bit of seldom recognized documentary evidence to find an answer to these questions.

The problem arises because Constantine the Great, despite the eulogizing biography of Eusebius, was not a Christian even formally until after he had won the battles that made him emperor, and after the Edict of Toleration that freed the Christian Church from further persecution. Even then, there is doubt that he ever made a true, heart-changing surrender of faith, though he certainly thought of himself as a great Christian late in life. He was too much an ambitious, self-willed, power-hungry egotist. There was an element of cruelty in his nature that was never conquered. After his crowning at York, when he had crossed to Gaul and was pacifying the Rhine frontier, he condemned his prisoners to mortal combat with wild beasts in the amphitheaters of Trier and Colmar. After four years in Gaul, wisely biding his time, he had his first vision of power, but the promise of victory and long life was the pagan god Apollo at his shrine at Autun. The Sun-God then became his patron. His coins, the only means then open to a government to proclaim its policy to the masses, bore, instead of the inscription of the former Tetrarchy, "To The Genius of the Roman People," his own devise, "Soli Invicto Comiti" (To the Unconquered Sun my Companion). This device was still on coins struck to mark the occasion of his meeting with Licinius to draw up the Edict of Milan in 313, while the symbols on the Arch of Constantine in Rome, built to celebrate his victory over Maxentius in 312 before Rome, when his soldiers wore Christian symbols on their shields, remained those of the patron divinity of the Empire.[78] The first Christian symbols appeared upon Constantine's coinage in 315, but a decade later, he executed his eldest son, his second wife, his favorite sister's husband, and many others on a variety of doubtful charges. He used force against the Donatist Christians in North Africa to compel a unified church to provide unified morale for his empire. He may have told Eusebius, as that Christian historian reports, that he considered himself a tremendous Christian instrument in the hands of God, and that he had seen a great vision in the clouds with the words by a Cross saying, "By This Sign Conquer," and Eusebius may have seen the jeweled "Labarum" made to copy this vision which he carried as an omen of victory in his later battles, but his slaughter of the Donatist Christians, and his banishment and imprisonment of Arians after the Council of Nicea to force Christianity as a tool of empire showed where his god really was. He was not baptized until he was on his deathbed. Then how can we account for his sending his troops into battle at the Milvian Bridge over the Tiber with Chi-Rho symbols on their shields, and his elevation of Christianity to supremacy among religions in the empire? Was it all that vision of a dazzling Cross in the clouds as Eusebius' history has led the Church to believe?

The facts indicate two major collaborating factors: the tremendous growth in social and political importance of the sheer increase in the membership of the Church throughout the empire; and the crusading zeal of a large contingent of Christian troops in the army he inherited from his father. By the beginning of the fourth century, the Christians had out-thought, out-lived, out-died, and out-loved the pagans and their religious heritage throughout the empire. There had been no active persecution for over a generation, and the Church had grown rapidly to include many aristocratic Roman families. Some Eastern areas, notably Asia Minor, had a majority of Christians. Curiously, Asia Minor, with its Galatian Celtic heartland, was also one of the best recruiting areas for the army. Protecting the frontiers of civilization could be justified as an acceptable vocation for a Christian, and there were increasing numbers of Christians in the legions.[79] Many other Christians, feeling the now-popular Church was becoming too worldly and losing its sacrificial challenge, were entering the new ascetic monastic movement.

Yet to discern what happened in that army, as a spiritual

movement, calls for some spiritual discernment.[80] We are here dealing with what German Christian scholars have called "Heilsgeschichte," often translated "Salvation History," or "History of Salvation," but really meaning "History understood in depth in the light of Salvation." What occurred in the motivation of Constantine was one of the outstanding events in human history in the advance of freedom. Literally, we are plumbing "the truth that makes men free."[81] Jesus told the uncomprehending Pharisees at the Feast of Tabernacles that one must abide in His word and become truly his disciple to know the truth that makes one free. In the historical situation that produced freedom for Christianity throughout the empire, we are confronting an important event in "Heilsgeschichte," and it requires inner understanding of such an event from evangelical Christian experience to interpret how those Christians acted. For they were practically all twice-born, enthusiastic evangelical Christians, as most Christians had to be before the Edict of Toleration, under threat of Roman persecution.

To shore up the weakening empire, Diocletian had reorganized it as a tetrarchy, with four imperial generals, himself, and Galerius as Augustus and Caesar in the East, and Maximian and Constantius Chlorus with similar titles in the West. Diocletian and Galerius were agreed that one major cause for the crumbling of the empire was the forsaking of the worship of the spirit of Augustus, and of the ceremonies of Jupiter and the ancient Pantheon, as these had supported patriotism. As part of the scheme of succession for the tetrarchy, Constantius Chlorus had been required to divorce his wife, Helena, the mother of Constantine, and marry Theodora, the stepdaughter of Maximian. Constantine was provided for by having him trained as an aide-de-camp and possible successor in training on Diocletian's staff at Nicomedia, in Bithynia, the Eastern capital in Asia Minor, at the age of nineteen. For twelve years, Constantine saw empire administration firsthand, meanwhile improving his Latin with a famous teacher of rhetoric from North Africa, Lactantius, who had a school in Nicomedia. Constantine accompanied Diocletian on the Persian campaign, and later watched the onslaught of the Diocletian persecution of Christians, remaining discreetly quiet as his father's son.

The Eastern Caesar, Galerius, known as "The Beast," had the most livid hatred of Christianity. In 298, General Veturius, Galerius's master of soldiers in the Danubian provinces, required of all troops the "Adoratio," which was a ceremonial genuflection to the emperor, or be stripped of their rank. Officers resigned their commissions and Christian soldiers accepted ignominious discharge rather than comply. Nine died as martyrs. Eusebius reports this early outbreak of the Diocletian persecution five years early in the army, and expresses guilt on the part of the Church for doing nothing about it. Since it was widely known that Constantius Chlorus, Caesar in the West, had a different attitude toward Christians, it would be natural for these unemployed Christian soldiers to migrate quietly out to Gaul and reenlist where they were wanted. Eusebius's report that Constantius Chlorus refused to persecute Christians in his realms of Gaul and Britain, and that he actually preferred them, as their loyalty to God made them more loyal servants in his household force and in his army, has been dismissed by some scholars as an exaggeration motivated by Eusebius's basking in the friendship of Constantine, as he wrote his *Life of Constantine* with its untrustworthy adulation of the "Christian Emperor." We found, however, definitive confirmatory evidence from an earlier documentary source which has not had due recognition. In 313, the Donatists in North Africa published an "Appeal to Constantine," pleading with the emperor to allow the bishops of Gaul to judge their case with the following explanation:

Most Excellent Emperor Constantine:
Whereas there are disputes between us and the other bishops of Africa, we pray you—since you are of just stock, inasmuch as your father did not prosecute the persecutions with the other Emperors, and Gaul is free from this crime—we pray you that Your Piety may command that judges be given us from Gaul.[82]

The result of this request was the very Council of Arles of 314 which we saw was attended by three British bishops, including a bishop from York. This proves not only Constantius Chlorus's favorable disposition toward Christianity, but also that there was a strong enough church in York to send their bishop at Constantine's invitation to Gaul in 314, and that Constantine remembered that bishop and invited him! Was Constantius Chlorus a Christian? Not enough to admit it. He was a monotheist, a believer in the Summus Deus. He and his second wife, Theodora, named their second daughter "Anastasia," Greek for "Resurrection."

After the purge of the army in the East, nothing was done to pursue the persecution for several years. Then Galerius goaded Diocletian to further measures. Looking forward to the planned retirement of Diocletian and the Western Augustus, Maximian, due in 305, Galerius saw that he, then becoming Augustus in the East, would be outranked in seniority and ability by Constantius Chlorus, who would become Augustus in the West; and worse still for him, if Maximian's son Maxentius, and Constantius Chlorus's son Constantine became the two new Caesars, as seemed most probable in the planned succession, he would be boxed. The majority of the tetrarchy Diocletian had planned would then favor Christianity. The time to strike was passing. Galerius goaded Diocletian into active persecution of the Church as total empire policy.

On February 24, 303, a decree was posted in Nicomedia ordering suspension of all Christian worship, destruction of church buildings, surrender of Scriptures, confiscation of properties, dismissal of Christians from all posts of authority, making suspects liable to torture if they would not sacrifice to the gods, returning Christian freedmen to slavery, and denying Christians access to the courts. The first pagan move was the dismantling of the newly completed Cathedral Church in Nicomedia, which had been erected provocatively opposite the palace gates. A Christian tore down the posted edict in Nicomedia, and was executed. The same day, the Imperial Palace caught fire twice, the second blaze raging through the Sacred Bedchamber. Galerius ostentatiously removed himself from the city, saying he had no intention of being burned alive. Christians charged he had been slyly responsible.

Diocletian, furiously aroused, issued decrees causing the grievous persecution executed throughout three-fourths of the empire, with churches destroyed, Scriptures and archives burned, bishops arrested and many martyred, and prisons filled to overflowing. Only Constantius Chlorus withheld his hand, disarming critics by allowing the destruction of a few church buildings. Constantine remained quiet in Nicomedia.

Then in 305 one morning, he was in obvious personal jeopardy. At military parade, Diocletian announced that he and Maximian were retiring as Augusti, and that the new Caesars would be Severus and Maximin Daia. Severus, a general, everyone knew as one of Galerius's friends. But who was Maximin Daia? There stood Constantine, straight and tall, groomed for the office. Was this his new official name? Maximin Daia was Galerius's nephew! "The Beast" had persuaded Diocletian, now fatigued to the point of neurosis, to accept his new scheme for succession. Maxentius and Constantine were out. Then any move of protest by Constantine or his friends would have been just what Galerius wanted.

When the other new Augustus, Constantius Chlorus, far away in Gaul, received the news, he knew better than to spring that trap on his son. He simply sent word through his son to Galerius, saying he was old and dying, and would Galerius permit his son to see him before his demise? Constantine wisely waited to present the request after dinner, when Galerius and his fellow officials were mellow in their cups. In that company, Galerius could not refuse such a request. He signed the travel papers Constantine foresightedly had ready at hand, meaning to revoke them on some excuse when Constantine would come to bid him farewell in the morning. Constantine didn't wait. Next morning, Galerius was furious to learn that Constantine was already fifteen hours ahead of any pursuit on the road! He was riding the post-horses, and Zozimus the historian says he cut the fetlocks of the horses behind him to prevent any use of them in pursuit. He rode the 1600 miles from the Asiatic south shore of the Black Sea to Boulogne just in time to catch his father setting sail for Britain. With what joy they greeted each other after years of separation and that record ride!

They sailed for an expedition to clear the Picts out of an area threatening the wall north of Eboracum (York), then settled down in that fortress city to plan. Constantine had nearly a year with his father before Constantius died in York on July 25, 306.

Constantine found another atmosphere in Britain: complete religious toleration, and actual favor shown by his father to loyal Christians among his household servants and the officer corps of his army, trusted as they were so loyal to their God. This was true in the Striking Force, the troops especially loyal to the Augustus who had succeeded the abolition of the old Roman Praetorian Guard. Some were the Christian officers Constantine had known in the East, driven out seven years earlier by the beginning persecution in Galerius's army. There was a Christian church in York, with a bishop whose worship services and fellowship were immediately sought out by the Christians in Constantius's servant staff and army. Greek- and

Celtic-tongued Christian soldiers from Galatia in Asia Minor would be doubly at home in that church. There were troops from the British Auxiliary recruits in that Christian fellowship also. There must have been active evangelizing going on in that favored atmosphere.

It was an open secret that Constantine would likely have to succeed his father in the not-too-distant future, if their part of the empire was to remain free from persecution. British, Gallic, and Galatian Christians, there with the Bishop of York, couldn't help dreaming that with a leader like Constantine, his father's policy might be extended to the whole empire. Hopefully, they might help him to power. Then he might lead the army to put an end to the grievous suffering of fellow Christians throughout the Roman world. From what followed, we cannot help concluding that the first great world-history-changing adventure in Church-inspired political strategy had its beginning there in York!

When his father died in 306, Constantine was coy. He did not seize the loose reins of the Western Empire obviously, but waited for his father's army to take the initiative. A panegyrist claimed he rode away and had to be brought back. According to Aurelius Victor, the acclaim for the new Augustus first came from King Crocus of the Alemanni, commander of the Auxiliary Frankish Cavalry during the Pictish campaign, and the other legions took up the cry. Clothing him in purple, they hailed Constantine as imperator, Caesar, and Augustus.[83] This was rebellion! The leaders of the Striking Force allowed the foreign auxiliary leader to have the public honor of acclaiming him first. Christian leaders in the Striking Force would be in character wisely not to show their hand. When the news reached the other parts of Britain and the Continent, all of his old dominions except Spain immediately declared for Constantine, preferring him to Severus, the legal heir to the Herculean Augustus. As Constantine rode south from York to Dover, collecting other troops on the way, to cross with the Striking Force into Gaul, what was a rebel move became a grand crusade.

In Gaul, Constantine wisely bided his time, testing his own leadership and honing his troops' fighting spirit with expeditions against the barbarians along the Rhine. For his sixteen-year-old son, Crispus, he secured the services as tutor of his own former teacher Lactantius who had been converted to Christ in Nicomedia, impressed by the heroism of Christians under the Diocletian persecution. So Lactantius joined the growing Christian movement.

In 308, the Spanish bishops decided to desert Maxentius, for whose rebellion against Severus they had earlier opted, and led their people to Constantine's side in the upcoming contest for empire. Bishop Hosius of Cordoba permanently left his city church, won Constantine's confidence, and became his first fully informed adviser on Christian concerns. He would also serve as chaplain for the Christian troops.

Constantine built his fences in the East, marrying his sister to Licinius who had replaced Maximin Daia, with an agreement that resulted in Licinius persuading the now deathly sick and superstitious Galerius to issue the first Edict of Toleration in 311. Then, the time being ripe, he rounded out his Striking Force with picked men to make 40,000, and conducted a whirlwind campaign through Northern Italy, defeating Maxentius' generals, and swept down upon Rome with brilliant military strategy. Maxentius, with a much larger army, was waiting for him nine miles north of Rome before the Milvian Bridge over the Tiber.

Lactantius's word may be trusted when he wrote:

Constantine was directed in a dream to mark the Heavenly Sign of God on the shields of his soldiers, and thus to join the battle. He did as he was ordered, and with the cross-shaped letter X with its top bent over he marked Christ on the shields. Armed with this device he engaged the enemy.

By evening, Maxentius's army was routed, and Maxentius drowned in the Tiber. The next day, Constantine entered Rome in triumph. The conquering symbol was the Chi Rho emblem. This was not the same vision which Constantine reported later to Eusebius, of seeing a Cross of light in the heavens above the sun bearing the inscription *In Hoc Vinces*, then dreaming at night that Christ appeared to him and commanded him to make a likeness of that sign to carry in his battles.[84] There would have been no time to fashion an elaborate jewel-studded "Labarum," made the day after that vision, during the whirlwind marches of the Italian campaign. That was a later vision. When Lactantius says that Constantine marked the Chi Rho on his soldiers' shields before the fateful battle for Empire, he could not have meant that Constantine personally marked those 40,000 shields. Of course, the men themselves did the marking. With what feelings?

There were two good reasons for the use of that emblem: to advertise to Constantine's opponents that his army came to liberate Christians everywhere, and to build up Constantine's own troops' morale. Certainly, no intelligent commander would send his men into battle to win an empire confused with new symbolic devices in which they had no faith. If the Chi Rho on their shields gave extra courage and valor and eagerness to triumph to those 40,000 picked men, it was because most of them were already believers, and the rest now willing to put their trust in that sign. The leading Christian cadres from Constantius Chlorus's army, from Galatia, Gaul, and Britain, men who had flocked to his banners because he favored Christians and elevated them to officership, had finally convinced Constantine. He had his dream and they had their desire. The meaning of Constantine's order was, "All right boys, you have been wanting to make this your Christian crusade for religious freedom under your God Christ ever since York. Now is the time! I got the Edict of Toleration for you from Galerius through Licinius last year. Now I share your dream. So paint the Chi-Rho emblem on your shields, men, and with the power of your God, get in there and fight!" The battle for the freedom of the church and universal religious toleration throughout the empire was won by an army of mostly Christian Celts from Galatia, Britain, and Gaul.

Subsequent events strongly support this interpretation. From that moment, Constantine's policy openly supported Christianity. In 313, with Licinius, he issued the Edict of Milan, granting religious freedom to all, but mentioning Christians first. Yet the most telling evidence is the popular precedent it set in Britain for generations to come. Imagine those British troops finally reaching home after twenty years, returning to the church that had furnished their zeal, telling their tales of the glorious battles by which they had won freedom for the Christian faith throughout the world. That church itself had grown by leaps and bounds in the intervening years, now with support from the Roman State. This was well remembered in 383, when the Arian heresy on the Continent threatened the freedom of orthodox Athanasian Trinitarians. Magnus Maximus, the Roman governor of Spanish origin in Britain, was converted by the British Christians to the orthodox faith, then shortly after his baptism promised to lead another army of British troops to Gaul and Rome on an orthodox Christian crusade. They were sure they were called to do it again, and the young Christian men of Britain flocked to his banners. Then again, in 407, when the Empire was overrun by the barbarian hordes, and Christian Roman civilization was in jeopardy, the British army acclaimed a mere commoner who happened to be named Constantine their emperor, as the Roman legions were withdrawn, and away they went to Gaul again, another crusading Celtic army to save the world for Christianity. Christian idealism and enthusiasm twice thought it could repeat the glorious pattern of victory, only twice to suffer terrible disillusionment. Both of those leaders were slain, their armies defeated, and most of those British men never came home. This left their island weak and denuded of fighting men, facing the savage inroads of Picts and Anglo-Saxons.

Meanwhile, what resulted in the compromise of Christianity with purposes of empire, in the loss of spiritual integrity in the churches as a result of prospering playing Constantine's game, was not really understood until Gildas wrote his lament. The British Church finally learned some bitter lessons from all this. Not every movement men call a Christian cause, no matter how much idealistic enthusiasm it engenders, or how relevant it seems at the moment, has the Providential blessing of God! It ill becomes the Church of Jesus Christ to stir men to warring crusades of foreign adventure, and neglect the duty of defending their own homeland. Even successful political alliances may tragically harm the Church's spirit, as the Church under Constantine found itself unable to protest the slaughter of the Donatists. The very favors the Church received from the empire resulted in a loss of moral integrity for the Church, Church offices becoming plums to be fought over and bought, with simony resulting in a corrupted Church leadership. So league with the state involves compromise with Satan, as Jesus' third temptation in the wilderness warned. It is not the business of the Church to make war or to become entangled in worldly policies of governments. This compromises her with evil and spoils her ability to witness to Jesus Christ and His Kingdom. Jesus would not allow Peter to use his sword to defend him in the Garden of Gethsemene, for the Church cannot use violent means to achieve its ends. In God's Kingdom, a worthy end never justifies evil means, for the means always shape the ultimate nature of the end. So the Church and her clergy have different and higher ethical standards than the laws of civil governments can require. This was the later conviction of the Irish Church, at the time Columba started a just but bloody war and was censured by his synod for conduct unbecoming a clergyman. The state may use the sword to defend order and protect its people, but it is not the proper instrument for the Church in extending the Kingdom of Christ. Maximus's son came home from Gaul, peaceably to found a monastic mission in Wales. The Kingdom of God suffers violence when well-meaning men of violence try to take it by force.[85] Ours is a spiritual conquest achieved by spiritual means. Yet the temptation is ever recurrent for the Church to risk getting into the toils of statecraft and political compromise to achieve what look like immediate great results for humanity, and seemingly ideal causes promoted by civil rulers so often approach the Church wanting her goodwill and morale. Christians need to heed the pertinent nursery jingle:

"Will you walk into my parlour?" said the Spider to the Fly,
"You will find it bright and airy, and the place is clean and dry."
"No thank you," said the wary Fly, "I've heard those webs you spin;
I won't take your apartment for I might get taken in!"

9. Humbly Ordered Polity—Government Maintaining a Spiritually Minded Clergy

Since church government is a quite objective and easily observed characteristic which changes very slowly, we can be quite certain of the polity of the Celtic Church in Britain from its antecedents on the Continent before the fourth century, and from the similar orders Patrick took to Ireland and the later fleeing Britons took to Brittany. As it was a Scripture-saturated Church, uncorrupted by worldly success for over a century, we may be assured it took New Testament teachings about the offices and qualifications of Church leaders seriously.

The New Testament taught a simply ordered Church government, with a humble, non-hierarchical, non-authoritative, servant leadership. Jesus was more interested in the spirit of those who would be responsible for His Church than in giving them detailed job-descriptions, and though His own office would ever be higher than theirs, he gave them a living example of that humble servitude. Paul told how Christ Jesus, though He was in the form of God, did not hold on to equality with God, but emptied himself, taking the form of a servant in His incarnation, and then in human form humbled himself in obedience even to death on a cross.[86] John's Gospel said that when the Word became flesh, His glory was that he was full of grace and truth. Grace is humble self-giving, bestowing unmerited favor. Truth is honest subjection to reality, with no pretensions, and an eagerness to know and to share worthy knowledge. When churchmen make Jesus their example, they are kept forever humble, for we forever fall short of His grace and truth.

Jesus plainly warned his disciples against corruption, as leaders are tempted to exercise undue power and authority and covet honored position. James and John hoped to be leaders in a Messianic Kingdom of worldly power and glory, and asked for special seats of honor at His right hand and left therein. Other disciples were jealous. Jesus called them all together and said,

You know that those who are supposed to rule over the Gentiles lord it over them, and their great ones exercise authority over them. But it shall not be so among you; but whoever would be great among you must be your servant, and whoever would be first among you must be the slave of all. For the Son of Man also came not to be served, but to serve, and to give his life as a ransom for many.[87]

So he specifically warned against the inherent moral danger in the hierarchical, authoritarian pattern of government in the Roman state and army, as destructive of the humility and unselfish service which must remain prime virtues in His Church and Kingdom.

Giving final training to his future leaders at the Last Supper, Jesus dramatized this humble service unforgettably when the disciples all disdained the servant role and rushed to get the best places at the table with unwashed feet. Knowing that He had all power from On High, came from God and was going to God, Jesus arose from the table, removed his clothing, wrapped a towel around him, and washed their feet. Then resuming his place of reclining at the table, He said,

If I then, your Lord and Teacher, have washed your feet, you also ought to wash one another's feet. For I have given you an example . . . [88]

The illustration on page viii is an amateur attempt to depict this scene with more accurate historical realism, to correct the romantic idealizations of more accomplished artists. Someone has quipped that Leonardo daVinci assumed an unrecorded saying of Jesus at the Last Supper: "All of you fellows wanting to get into the picture, come on one side of the table!" Seriously, I have tried to capture the Master's real challenge so often ignored. It was also given in the First Beatitude, "Blessed are the poor in spirit...." When Paul spelled out the high character qualifications for elder-bishops and deacons in his letters to Timothy and Titus, he warned that recent converts should not be quickly elected to office, lest they be puffed up with conceit and fall into the Devil's condemnation.[89] The warning was clear enough in Scripture.

Jesus gave little specific instruction for the organization of his Church. Its rock foundation would be faith in Him as the Messiah, the Son of the Living God.[90] The traditional organization of the Jewish Synagogue, with its representative democracy of a council of elders was assumed at first. So there was a council of "presbyters" (elders) or "overseers" (bishops) in each little church, the two names used interchangeably for the same office, as Paul's letter was addressed to several "bishops" with no mention of elders in Philippi.[91] Jesus had trained twelve original Apostles, symbolic of the Twelve Tribes of Israel, as his Church would be the new Israel of the New Covenant. They were to be missionary messengers, and they ordained "bishops" or "elders" to serve as leaders locally when they moved on. Early, in Jerusalem, the Apostles found it necessary to ordain helpers for non-teaching services, and their office of deacon became general.[92]

During the first 200 years, before the Church was planted in Britain, there was only one minor change in this organization. In the early second century, under Ignatius of Antioch's promotion, the offices of bishop and presbyter were differentiated in the local church, the one bishop presiding over the council of presbyters, and having the power of ordaining other bishops and deacons. There had been no further elevation in office a hundred years later when Hippolytus of the Port of Rome wrote his account of *The Apostolic Tradition*. Here clerical offices are classified as those requiring ordination: bishops, presbyters and deacons, and those not requiring ordination: widows, readers, and sub-deacons. There is no higher office than bishop in the Church and all bishops are equal. The presbyters rule, and lay hands in blessing at the ordination of other presbyters. Bishops alone ordain deacons and other bishops. Bishops are "chosen by all of the people," then approved and ordained by at least three neighboring bishops, while presbyters stand by in silence. The Prayer for the Consecration of a Bishop reads:

And now pour forth that power which is from Thee of "the princely Spirit," which Thou didst deliver to Thy beloved Child Jesus Christ, which He bestowed on Thy Holy Apostles who established in Church which hallows Thee in every place to the endless glory and praise of Thy Name.

Father who knowest the hearts of all, grant upon this Thy Servant whom Thou hast chosen for the episcopate to feed Thy holy flock and serve as their high priest, that he may minister blamelessly by night and day, and that he may unceasingly propitiate Thy Countenance, and offer to Thee the gifts of Thy Holy Church, and that by the high priestly Spirit he may have authority "to forgive sins" according to Thy command, "to assign lots," according to Thy bidding, "to loose every bond" according to the authority Thou gavest to the Apostles, and that he may please Thee in meekness and a pure heart, offering to Thee a sweet-smelling savour.[93]

Continued equality of all bishops was still evident after the middle of the third century in actions of synods in North Africa called by Cyprian of Carthage. There was a problem whether brethren whose faith had lapsed in the Decian persecution needed to be rebaptized to be restored. Stephen, bishop of Rome said baptism was once for all. In 255, a synod of Carthage approved rebaptism. In 256, a Carthagenian council again decided for rebaptism, claiming their right to differ in a letter to Stephen:

" . . . since each prelate has in the administration of the Church the exercise of his own free will, and he shall give account of his conduct to the Lord."[94]

At the Second Council of Carthage, Cyprian said of the equality of bishops:

It remains that upon the same manner (the rebaptizing of heretics and schismatics) each of us should bring forward what we think, judging no men, nor rejecting anyone from the rite of communion if he should think differently from us. For neither does any of us set himself up as a bishop of bishops, nor by tyrannical terror does any compel his colleagues to the necessity of obedience; since every bishop according to the allowance of his liberty and power, has his own proper right of judgment, and can no more be judged by another than he himself can judge another. But let us wait for the judgment of our Lord Jesus Christ, who is the only one who has the power, both of preferring us in the government of His Church, and of judging us in our conduct there.[95]

Other bishops followed with statements of their opinions, statements being recorded for 85 of the 87 bishops present, all from the Carthage area of North Africa. Evidently, each local church had its bishop, so there were many bishops in one synod area, and all were equal and free in their administrative decisions, with neither the bishop in Carthage nor in Rome having any superior power. This was the governmental tradition received by the church in Britain.

We have seen that Gildas in his condemnation of the clergy in Britain in the sixth century could point to no higher office than that of bishop. He said that promotions to that office were sometimes sought abroad, whereby then there were metropolitans and archbishops, probably in Gaul, or even by some falsely ambitious clergy, in Rome, as he twice mentions the See of Peter. This plainly underlines the very unique characteristic of the Celtic churches in the Isles from the fourth to the eighth century. They kept the earlier organization of the Old Catholic Church. There was complete absence of hierarchy among the secular clergy, no diocesan organization, and when the monasteries grew, many bishops were willing to be subservient to abbots, even if the abbot were not a bishop, having the special power of ordination, but serving as simple monks under abbot's orders in monastic communities. Dom Gougaud, the French Benedictine scholar, writing about the conflict which developed between the emigrant Breton church and the Metropolitan See of Tours in the sixth century over the ordination of bishops in Brittany, quotes the Ninth Canon of the Council of Tours, in 567, seven years after Gildas wrote in Wales:

Let no Pontiff presume to give episcopal confirmation in Armorica, either to a Breton or a Roman, without the sanction of the Metropolitan or the Bishops of the province, otherwise he shall hold himself excommunicate.

Gougaud states that the Bretons had not grown accustomed to the institution of metropolitan sees, having known nothing of the sort in Britain, where even the notion of a diocese was foreign to them. So their episcopal organization, their abbot-bishops, their monastic clergy, their tonsure and the date of their Easter were reprehensible irregularities in the eyes of the Franks, demanding urgent and radical reform.[96] Later, commenting how the Venerable Bede did not note the sees of the seven bishops from Wales who met with Augustine in 603, Gougaud says, "In Celtic Britain there were no definite territories ruled by diocesan bishops."[97] Irish bishops without diocese roaming the Continent as itinerant missionaries in the seventh and eighth centuries were a trial and a nuisance in the eyes of their then ecclesiastically legal neighbors. Meanwhile, in sixth-century Ireland, Columba was never ordained a bishop. It was intended that he be given episcopal orders, but when by mistake he was ordained a presbyter, he accepted it as providential, ruled his monasteries as their abbot, and let bishops under him attend to ordinations.

It is difficult to imagine British bishops so willingly accepting subservience to abbots if they ever had held diocesan authority. That the diocesan pattern, which became common throughout Continental and North African Christendom after Constantine, never was adopted in Britain may be laid to several historical causes. The young Church in Britain, while it may have won a majority of the populace in the fourth and fifth centuries, was largely in the cities and in scattered villas, still interspersed with tolerated pagans. With so much of the countryside unconverted, the partitioning of the whole country into dioceses would have been premature. Celts were not systematic or organization-minded by temperament and disposition anyway. With their strongly moral tradition, humility in religious leaders continued to be considered an essential virtue among the Briton Celts. Finally, the British Church remained very biblical in teaching and practice, and there were no officers other than bishop, presbyter, and deacon mentioned in the Scriptures, and no hint of diocesan rule. So the Church in Britain must have had a firmly rooted early start, and could exist quite independently without looking to higher authorities. On the rare occasion when they needed help against the Pelagian heresy, the appeal was from a synod to a synod in Gaul.

So orderly transfer of hierarchical Roman religious authority seating bishops where flamens had sat, and archbishops in arch-flamen's sees, imagined in Geoffrey of Monmouth's *Historia Regum Brittaniae* as having occurred after the second century conversion under the fabled King Lucius, just never occurred at any time in Celtic Britain, wherever else it may be occurred after Constantine's victory in the rest of his empire. Though latterly, according to Gildas, some bishops had corruptly sought appointment by civil rulers, and so the Church was corrupted by state favors, the British Church had no formal relationship to civil rulers until the coming of Augustine to Canterbury. Before then, the whole Celtic Church had already recoiled from its sad experience with worldly ways when Gildas's interpretation of the Saxon holocaust as Divine retribution was accepted, his writing alone preserved as the wisdom of "Gildas the Wise." So when Augustine came from Rome in 597, allied himself to a Saxon king, and sported his archbishop's pallium at the Severn River to the Celtic bishops, these Welshmen were less than impressed.

The importance of this was more than a difference in polity. Jesus' spiritual purpose for his Church and its clergy was at stake. Charismatically called, spiritually discerning leadership does not survive under hierarchically organized polity subservient to civil rulers. If the clergy are to remain deeply inspired "in Christ," they must remain humble, and subject to the call of the sincerely worshiping laity as the Holy Spirit works at the Church's grass roots. High office, power, authority, and political manipulation are full of grievous temptations to pride, the deadliest of the seven deadly sins. Therefore, in the Church of Christ, all clergy must remain equal, and the Church remain separate from the state. We must continue the heritage of humble, spiritually vital, equal, free leadership from the Celtic Church!

10. Broadly Tolerant Spiritual Ecumenicity

That the Church of Jesus Christ was one Church throughout the world was never questioned by the Christians of the Celtic Church in Britain. They had received their faith from the church in Gaul, with its great teacher, Irenaeus of Lyons, only two generations removed, through Polycarp of Smyrna, from the Apostle John. They had the Holy Scriptures accepted as inspired teaching by the whole Church. The whole Church had, according to the Scriptures, "one body and one Spirit, . . . one hope . . . one Lord, one faith, one baptism, one God and Father of us all, who is above all and through all and in all."[98] So, "with all lowliness and meekness, with patience forbearing one another in love," Christians should be eager to "maintain the unity of the Spirit in the bond of peace."[99]

John had told how Jesus had prayed, that night after He and the Disciples had left the Upper Room, probably in the temple as the true High Priest of the Holy Place before the Altar, for the unity of His Church throughout all generations:

> I do not pray for these only, but also for those who are to believe in me through their word, that they all may be one; even as Thou, Father, art in me, and I in Thee, that they also may be in us, so that the world may believe that Thou hast sent me.[100]

Christ's unity with the Father is a spiritual unity, of oneness in nature, in love, in purposed good, in the will to serve unselfishly, and we who are one body in Christ throughout the whole world share this same Holy Spirit in oneness with Christ and the Father.

This did not call for a complete uniformity in every teaching or practice. Even Paul and Peter in the New Testament had differences of opinion, Paul thinking Peter should forsake his Jewish eating restrictions at once before everybody;[101] Peter saying there were some things written by Paul according to his wisdom but difficult to understand.[102] There was no requirement in the New Testament to force uniformity of belief in complicated, detailed philosophical doctrines never mentioned by Jesus. There was nothing requiring uniformity of political opinion as to the practicability of this or that idealistic social scheme. There was no conception of a hierarchical church government ruled by metropolitans, archbishops, or popes. These developments might prevent believing souls from experiencing their oneness in Christ, substituting unities more tangible but less real and never fully realizable.

Yet it was necessary to have basic agreement in some doctrines, so that when a rampant Pelagianism threatened belief in the need of Christ's salvation, the British Church called on the church of Gaul for wise help; and when the Arian heresy seemed to dominate the Continent denying the full Deity of

Christ, the British Christians sent an army under Magnus Maximus, using the wrong means but with the right purpose, to seek to preserve the Trinitarian faith. When the Monastic movement spread in the Church, with its strange appeal to exaggerated asceticism, the church in Britain had many who responded with great enthusiasm while others remained in local churches with secular clergy who still married and had children like Patrick's parents. Where the Spirit of the Lord is, there is freedom. The glorious liberty of the sons of God in Christ allowed for rich diversity in one Church universal when Christians remained one in the Spirit, one in the Lord.

Yet before we follow that Church into Patrick's Ireland, we must glimpse why the churches on the Continent lost that Spirit largely, and forfeited the ability to be fruitfully missionary and evangelize the barbarians.

Chapter III

FALSE WAYS THE BRITISH CHURCH ESCAPED

Humpty Dumpty sat on a wall,
  Humpty Dumpty had a great fall.
Not all the King's horses, Not all the King's men
  Could ever lift Humpty Dumpty again.[1]

Even when with childish glee we shouted, "An egg!" and proved to our own pride and satisfaction we were not fooled by such simple conundrums, we suspected that Humpty Dumpty was more than a hen's egg. He was dressed up and had a funny face. He also pictured fragile, foolish human life, poised in pride for a fall, as

Pride goeth before destruction,
And a haughty spirit before a fall![2]

But what if we dress Humpty in clericals and make him a bishop? We don't have to do this. History has done it for us long ago. It was the king's men who always helped such Humpty Dumpties up on proud walls, but all the king's horses and men couldn't lift them again when they fell. Between the third and sixth centuries of the Christian Era, the bishops, bent on enforcing unity, built up three different walls, from which proud heights they fell, and the emperor's power, which had helped them up on all three of them, could neither put the Church, so broken, "together again," as the more familiar version of the jingle has it, or "ever lift Humpty Dumpty again" from moral and spiritual degradation suggested by the Scottish version quoted above. Seeking to build dogmatic unity for the emperor, they perched on walls of intellectual pride and theological division. Seeking to serve social and political unity, they scaled a crumbling wall of secular power which for them held all of the temptation of Jesus' high mountain vision. Seeking to enforce ecclesiastical unity, they climbed the temple pinnacle of proud authority in churchly office, which ever since has divided Christ's Church.

It will not excuse them to say they were men of their times, that they couldn't help it under the circumstances, that they had to exercise such power to combat the heresies, or that since history went this way, it must have been the will of God. The fact is that in all three respects, they departed from the teaching and example of their Lord, yielding to the Tempter's wiles. Their own monistic Neo-Platonic philosophical theology has rationalized it with the un-Christ-like doctrine of complete predestined determinism ever since. We are under no obligation to honor the resulting continuing sins. These have dogged the churches, whether Roman or Orthodox, nationally Established or Reformed to this day. The humble, self-limiting, self-effacing, self-sacrificing, self-abnegating God whom Jesus revealed as His Father, whom Irenaeus had understood in His educative process of granting moral freedom to His wayward children, never willed what those bishops did. Else He is not the God whom John proclaimed from Jesus' authority: " . . . that God is Light, and in Him is no darkness at all."[3]

We must now sketch these three historic developments in the church of the Roman Empire on the Continent which the church in Britain escaped: partly by being on the distant insular frontier; partly by being stubbornly conservative and independent in disposition; partly because her Mother Church in Gaul all but disappeared in the barbarian destruction, partly because she was nearly destroyed herself and cut off by the Anglo-Saxon invaders, and probably because she learned some grievous, needed lessons through tragic experience. On the Continent, the stronger, older churches largely lost their evangelistic and missionary zeal, and their ability to propagate The Way in Christ. It was a varied, uneven process, of course, and always, by worldly standards seemed quite justified. Yet it was all the result of yielding to the Tempter's lure of the First Cardinal Sin.

1. The Pride of Philosopher-Theologians

Pride in their intellectual attainments perched many bishops on walls that divided the Church. Burdened with the odious problems involved in the discipline and the pastoral care of their flocks, they would welcome escape into their scholarly pursuits. It was necessary to meet the intellectual challenge of pagan philosophers and various heretics. Since the route to election to the bishopric was most often through capable teaching in the school for catechumens, presbyters with human ambition for ecclesiastical preferment showed their talents by lecturing the catechumens, and by writing treatises against all the heresies and pagan philosophies. Hippolytus did this as bishop of the Port of Rome, hoping to be elected bishop of Rome itself. Irenaeus as bishop of Lyons and other Ante-Nicene fathers became prodigious scholars, outthinking the pagan philosophers and rhetoricians, conducting schools competing with them for the intellectual leadership of their cities. Men like Tertullian, Cyprian, Clement of Alexandria, Origen, and Augustine of Hippo became intellectual giants. Their literary works are astounding. Their successors were hard put to maintain the tradition. The result eventually was a theology more philosophical than Christian, more oriented to intellectual speculation than to Scriptural truth and real Christian experience, with a tendency to engage in proud theological controversy. This both split the Church and cut the nerve of moral determination and evangelical missionary zeal.

Let us confine ourselves to one major example: the most influential of all upon subsequent Church history, both Roman Catholic and Protestant, Augustine, Bishop of Hippo in North Africa at the time of the fall of Rome. We have Augustine's theological writings, his philosophy of history, hundreds of sermons, and his own spiritual autobiography. Among them all the latter, the *Confessions* is the most revealing. Herein, he discloses not only his personal experiences, but also the sources and nature of his thinking. It is not primarily biblical, but philosophical, not chiefly concerned with moral rightness with God or the teachings of Jesus Christ, but with a Neo-Platonic interpretation of ontology, the being of Truth.

We need not deny the vivid reality of Augustine's conversion experience: only the adequacy and balance of its Christian content. Resisting his Christian mother's prayers, he had gone to Rome, then to Milan to teach Rhetoric, taking with him his concubine and his son Adeodatus, rationalizing his resistance to Christian faith and morals with a Manichaean philosophy. This over-simple dualism of good and evil allowed him to blame his faults on the Devil:

> For I still thought that it was not we that sin, but that I know not what other nature sinned in us, and it delighted my pride to be free from blame.[4]

His widowed mother followed him to Italy, praying for his soul and arranging for his betrothal to a young girl two years too young for marriage. Augustine sent his faithful concubine of many years back to Africa, then still unable to contain his lust, took another for the interim. Meanwhile, he was tired of teaching the tricks of rhetoric, and weak with some lung ailment. In Milan he came under the influence of Bishop Ambrose, first admiring his rhetoric, then captivated by the truth of his preaching. Yet the content of what he took to be the Christian alternative to his Manichaeanism and lustful self-indulgence, which built up in his divided mind until he was in a weeping fit of inner conflict in the garden, was not Christ's truth from the New Testament, but a Neo-platonic philosophy and a celibate asceticism. He heard a child's voice saying, "Take up and read!" and, seizing a New Testament, opened, by Divine Providence he was sure, to the verse, " . . . not in chambering and wantonness . . . but put ye on the Lord Jesus Christ and make not provision for the flesh." Such a surrender required not only no concubine or marriage, but also a complete philosophical switch. The mental alternative he saw is revealed in the *Confessions* where, of his Manichaean period he wrote:

> I had not known or learned that neither was evil a substance, nor our soul that chief and unchangeable good.[5]

> . . . because as yet I knew not that evil was nothing but a privation of good, until at last a thing ceases altogether to be.[6]

Of his new Christian conviction, he wrote:

> . . . all which is corrupted is deprived of good . . . Therefore if they shall be deprived of all good they shall no longer be. So long therefore as they are they are good. Therefore whatever is is good. That evil then, which I sought whence it is, is not any substance: for if

it were a substance it should be good . . . Thou madest all things good, nor is there any substance at all which Thou madest not.[7]

Augustine here sounds like Mary Baker Eddy and other modern disciples of Platonic and Hegelian idealism!

And to Thee is nothing whatsoever evil; yea, not only to Thee, but also to Thy creation as a whole, because there is nothing without, which may break in, and corrupt that order which Thou hast appointed it.[8]

All things are true so far as they be; nor is there any falsehood, unless when it is thought to be, which is not.[9]

So Augustine was converting to a Platonic, semi-Christian philosophy with little room for moral struggle with real evil in it. He would of course use the traditional Christian language about Christian victory over the Devil, meaning it in a figurative sense. If evil has no reality, and whatever is is good, and nothing is evil to God, then opposition to evil becomes unnecessary shadow-boxing, and Christ's victory on Calvary as a ransom from the Devil becomes a figure of speech. Augustine never seems to realize that we are always free to resist the Devil and responsible for yielding to his temptations. His conversion away from Manichaeism with its irresponsible moral dualism made it difficult for him to embrace the moral realism of the New Testament. His Platonic idea of God, emphasizing His impassive eternal unchangeable knowledge and purpose ruled out any really active free will on man's part. Man's abuse of free will might require God to act provisionally:

Will you affirm that to be false which, with a strong voice Truth tells me in my inner ear, concerning the eternity of the Creator, that His substance is no ways changed by time, nor His will separate from His substance. Wherefore He willeth not one thing now, another anon, but once, and at once, and always He willeth all things that He willeth.[10]

Commenting on Psalm 105, Augustine wrote:

In God all things are ordered and fixed; nor doth He anything as by a sudden counsel, which He did not from eternity foreknow that He should do; but in the movements of the creature, which He wonderfully governeth, Himself not moved in time, in time is said to have done, as by a sudden will, what He disposed through the ordered causes of things in the unchangeableness of His most hidden counsels, whereby each several thing, which in its appointed time comes to (our) knowledge, He both makes, when present, and when future had already made.[11]

This was the philosophical basis of Augustine's doctrine of predestination, in Plato's idea of God as the unmoved mover of all things: the Absolute.

While in his *Confessions*, Augustine admits three of his own sins, even at great length, "the lust of the flesh, the lust of the eyes (idle curiosity), and ambition of the world (desire for fame), he is peculiarly blind to his own intellectual pride. He readily accuses others of this sin:

> For they being high minded sought Thee by the pride of learning, swelling out rather than smiting upon their breasts,[12]

and accuses others who do not agree with his farfetched philosophical interpretation of Genesis I:1 to be guilty of rashness, over-boldness and vanity, which he does not like or love.[13] God is Truth, but as Augustine the brilliant Platonic philosopher now sees it. A Scripture passage may have multiple meanings, just so Augustine's neo-Platonic philosophical meaning, on the highest level of intelligence is included![14]

That this teaching of Augustine should supersede that of Irenaeus as the most influential upon later Church history in the West, and that Origen of of Alexandria should have a similar influence in the Eastern Church, should argue against the very doctrine of the Divine determinism of all things which Augustine fostered. It might convince us that since sin can take such a high polish, we cannot assume that whatever triumphs for awhile in history is necessarily true and good. With so much palpable evil, how can whatever is be good? If Patrick and the Celtic missionaries after him had believed that to God nothing whatsoever is evil, they would have had small incentive to go forth as missionaries.

We need not trace here all of the doctrinal battles between Athanasians and Arians, between Monophysites and Cappadocians, etc. over the definition of the Person of Christ in hairsplitting Greek philosophical terms, which drove the Nestorians, the Coptic Churches, and the Jacobites out of fellowship with the majority of Christians. Pride in learning, and the notion that all must be forced to agree to one set of complicated ideas to be saved, were joined to the demands of the Roman state for complete unity in doctrine to serve to unify the empire. The result was division and corruption in the Church. Orthodoxy drove out orthopraxy. The Spirit of Jesus, and His simple request that men follow Him as Lord, the Son of God Messiah, could have kept spiritual unity, while tolerating minor theological differences in speculative matters. Pride of mind exalted the learned bishops and divided the Church.

2. The Pride of Political Importance

The second height to which the bishops were tempted, like the high mountain in Jesus' temptation from which, in imagination, He could see all the kingdoms of the world, was the eventual opportunity to participate in Roman political preferment and power. During the first three centuries of persecution, Christians were political non-entities, often charged with being enemies of the state, opposing and sapping the spirit of empire, and distracting people from their citizenship duties. Tertullian, writing in Carthage around 200, answered this criticism in his *Letter to Scapula,* the Roman pro-consul. He said Christians believe the emperor to have been appointed by God. So they desire his well-being. Christians were becoming a majority in many cities. Their quiet, law-abiding conduct was an asset. Remarkable for the reformation of their former vices, Christians were the better citizens thereby.

Before the time of Constantine, the Christians were becoming another kind of political force. The Edict of Toleration and other edicts favoring Christians were responses of would-be rulers who saw the growing Church as the coming majority to be placated and courted throughout the empire. That the bishops were politicking is clear from the way they brought Spain over to Constantine's side against Maxentius, and sent Bishop Hosius of Cordoba to join his staff as a religious adviser.

When Constantine won the whole empire, using Christian symbols, and made Christianity its state religion, Christians became responsible for the social order of the state in a new way. The bishops and the lesser clergy gained a social influence and political relevance of which they had never dreamed. It was the greatest opportunity for social action in Christian history, and the way they embraced the accommodations involved was the ruination of most of the Church! Constantine had to have Church unity to use Christianity as a morale-builder. The controversy between the Donatists and the Catholic bishops in North Africa over how severely the lapsed in the Diocletian persecution should be penalized in repentance threatened this unity. He called upon Italian bishops to settle it, then summoned the larger Council of Arles in Gaul in 314, then decided the issue against the unyielding Donatists himself in 315, and finally took state measures against them, closing their churches, banishing their bishops, and shedding Christian blood to enforce Christian unity for his state. The Catholic churchmen, profiting in their new position, accepted this without protest.

The more serious disunity broke out in the East over the theology of the Person of Christ, between the followers of Athanasius and Arius. To preserve unity, Constantine called the Council of Nicaea in 325, and though he had not yet been baptized, he was welcomed there as "a Bishop of Bishops." He entered into the proceedings, and actually proposed the compromising formula which ruled the definition of the Person of Christ in the resulting Nicene Creed. To be promoted throughout the empire by the state, this new religion had to be clearly defined in the doctrines that would be required.

Now the bishops became officials of the empire. It seemed a grand improvement, to be elevated from hunted and persecuted outlaws to high official position in the now officially Christian community, elected no longer by a small Christian minority, but by the whole citizenry. Now great Church buildings, in Rome, in Bethlehem, Jerusalem, Constantinople, and elsewhere were erected under imperial bounty. By imperial order all clergy were released from other public offices and services other than their religious duties.[15] The historian and celebrator of all this was Eusebius, the bishop of Caesarea, who became a friend of Constantine, took a leading part in the Council of Nicaea, and wrote his *Ecclesiastical History* and a eulogizing *Life of Constantine* in priase of the new order. Included in the latter work are two letters written by Constantine to Eusebius personally, which the good bishop proudly quotes.

Eusebius was aware of the spiritual danger of pride. He cites it as the sin of the previous prosperous peace of the Church in the latter decades of the third century:

. . . with our greater freedom a change came over us. We yielded to pride and sloth. We yielded to mutual envy and abuse. We warred upon ourselves as occasion offered, and we used the weapons and the spears of words. Leaders fought with leaders and laity formed factions against laity. Unspeakable hypocrisy and dissimulation travelled to the farthest limits of evil.

Then the judgment of God, with unaccustomed lenience and because the congregations were still crowded, embarked upon the quiet and measured exercise of its dominion. Persecution began among the brethren in the army. And we were so blind that we took no care to secure the benevolence and friendly disposition of God.[16]

So the Diocletian persecution, beginning in 297 in the army, and descending with crushing force upon the Church in 303, was to Eusebius God's judgment upon their former pride. Strange he could not see it in his own generation under the favor of Constantine.

Not all of the use of the new power by the bishops was evil. Many bishops did great good, dispensing public charity. Leo I of Rome, left as the most conspicuous official in the West by the transfer of the political government to Constantinople, stopped Attila the Hun from sacking Rome in 452. Yet the flocking of the people everywhere into the Church for other reasons than a vital faith resulted in a sad change in the moral and spiritual caliber of the average "Christian." Salvation now had to be guaranteed to the multitudes who claimed they believed in Christ. Yet the Christ in whom they believed was no longer the humble servant Lord of the New Testament. He was the conquering Christ who had strengthened Constantine's sword, the Lord of Power at the Right Hand of God, the "Christus Pantocrator" or Christ Almighty. His image, similar in appearance to the traditional Olympian Jupiter, began to appear in the new churches, majestic in colored, inlaid tile in a commanding position high in the apse. Faith in Christ became intellectual assent to the authoritative doctrine of His Deity as defined by the Nicene and other creeds, whether understood or not, rather than the belief-plus-trust-plus-obedience it had meant when the surrender of faith to His Lordship was costly and morally demanding. Discipline became impractical to enforce. The Church guaranteed salvation to all who said they believed and who submitted to the Sacraments. The latter now became magic rites, efficacious in the performance, *"ex opere operato."*

So the experience of the Holy Spirit was practically forgotten. In place of an inner awareness of God, there was the superstitious veneration of the relics of the martyrs. To fill the void left by the loss of the many pagan gods, there was now adulation of the Saints. To satisfy the desire for compassion in the Divine, now that Christ was seen mostly as an Almighty Commander and Judge, someone else had to take the place of the pagan mother goddess, variously worshiped as Cybele, Isis, Ishtar, or Artemus of Ephesus (Diana of the Ephesians). So the Council of Ephesus in 431, significantly held where the great Temple of Artemus had flourished, prescribed prayers to Mary as "Theotokos," Mother of God. The resultant adoration of the Virgin is graphically seen in Michelangelo's great painting, *The Last Judgment,* in the Sistine Chapel of the Vatican. There Christ, the implacable heartless Judge, is consigning the souls of the damned to everlasting torment, and Mother Mary is piteously pleading with Him for mercy.

Being a Christian became accepting the authority and mediation of the clergy. If a soul wanted more, the frequent route was the complete celibate dedication of the monastery or nunnery. For the average layman, there was little difference between being a Christian and being a part of the civilized culture of the Roman empire.

Just because the Church and State had become so interdependent and merged, the shock was greater when the barbarians finally overran the defenses of the corrupt and weakened empire, and Rome fell. How could God have allowed that to happen? The fall of Rome to Alaric the Visigoth in 410 shook the faith of Christendom. It drove the Church's foremost theologian of the time, Augustine of Hippo, to write his great philosophy of history, *De Civitate Dei* (Of the City of God). This book dominated the political thinking of the West in the Holy Roman Empire, the papacy, and in the institutions of feudalism for the next thousand years.

Augustine claimed that far from blaming Christianity for the fall of Rome, its citizens ought to thank God for Christianity, which had softened Alaric's heart and caused him to allow all who claimed to be believers to find sanctuary in the churches. Rome was not the City of God, but an earthly city of sin which deserved its punishment. There have been two cities all through history, from the time of Abel and Cain, one of God, the other of the earth, mixed together in this world's history. Those who live in the love of God and in contempt of self are in the City of God. Those who live by love of self in contempt of God inhabit the earthly city.

In his historical development of this theme, we might expect Augustine to trace the growth of Israel's social faith through Moses and the Prophets, praising the advantages of the City of God. Instead, he merely asserts that the City of God could not attain its proper destiny in the life of the Saints were it not a social life, and then proceeds to enumerate the great grievances with which human society on earth abounds in the misery of this mortal state, in family life, in city life, and in the world community endlessly at war.[17] The only unalloyed blessing of the Saints is in the peace of the final blessedness:

> The city of the saints above, though it have citizens here upon the earth wherein it lives as a pilgrim until the time of the Kingdom come and then it gather all the citizens together in the resurrection of the body.[18]

Strangely, though Augustine identifies the Kingdom of Heaven taught by Jesus with the City of God,[19] he completely ignores the Master's parables of the Kingdom, and gives no exposition of the Way of the Kingdom in the Sermon on the Mount. Where this would logically come in his historical development, there is only a bare mention in three pages of the birth, life, death, resurrection, and message of the Master,[20] with scattered incidental references to particular teachings elsewhere. In contrast, the opinions of Marcus Varro, a first-century B.C. Roman scholar and his book *De Philosophia* receive eight pages of exposition and argument.[21] Augustine's speculative interest in rationalizing his celibacy is evidenced in a six-page unintentionally funny detailed description of how Adam and Eve might have begotten children without sinful passion in compliance with the Divine order to be fruitful and multiply, if they had never sinned and had remained in Paradise, by controlling their organs of reproduction with pure willpower.[22]

Although in Augustine's own thinking, the climax and end result of the City of God is the Beatific Vision of Heaven,[23] the most influential thought in the book in its results upon history was his identification of the Catholic Church with the City of God on earth. He found prophecy of the Church in the Song of Hannah, the mother of Samuel. Hannah speaks of the number seven, which to Augustine signifies the "perfection of the universal Church."[24] To this, John had witnessed in writing to the seven churches of Asia. The Church is not morally perfect, he admits, yet "the Church even now is the Kingdom of Christ and the Kingdom of Heaven."[25] So Augustine teaches the supranatural character of the Church, and Christians, who have two allegiances, united under God in the Church and under the obligations of earthly citizenship, must obey God rather than men. Their allegiance to the City of God takes precedence. This became the root of the medieval conception of society, differentiating itself into civil and ecclesiastical functions, and subordinating the former to the latter as superior. So *De Civitate Dei* became the authority for the papal rule of kings.

The Holy Roman Empire concept grew out of the misuse of *De Civitate Dei* by Charlemagne, who mistakenly thought his state to be the realization of Augustine's plan for a holy society, the "Holy Roman Empire." Pope Gregory VII, Hildebrand (1073-1085) conducted his papal throne by the extreme interpretation of Augustine's principles, viewing the papacy as the Divinely appointed universal sovereignty, spiritual, and civil, crowning and uncrowning kings and emperors, judged by no one and absolving subjects from fealty to wicked men, himself determining who is wicked. When he made Henry IV of the Holy Roman Empire stand barefoot before the castle door in the snow at Canossa on three successive days before he would release him from excommunication and restore his crown, the world knew where ultimate power resided!

3. Scaling the High Walls of Ecclesiastical Hierarchy

The third type of pride which corrupted the Continental church in a manner not shared by the early Celtic Church in Britain was involved in the growth of power and authority in adding higher Church offices. This came so gradually, and seemed so practical and necessary for efficient order, and so valuable to stamp out heresy, and so natural as the Church grew rapidly in numbers, in a social environment so under the influence of the hierarchical power structures of the Roman political system and the efficient Roman army, that its heresy was seldom noticed. It was not doctrinal heresy, and that was what was feared. If anyone recalled Jesus' plain words of warning against the way "the rulers of the Gentiles Lord it over them, and their great ones exercise authority," it was not recorded. The reminder in Hippolytus' *Apostolic Tradition* of the way Church government used to be could be suppressed or ignored. Conservative diehards like Hippolytus could be dismissed as petulant schismatics. The times, especially after the Church had become the established religion of the empire, demanded more and better organization, and the bishops of the now great leading city churches, whose own vanity would be tickled by the innovations, readily acquiesced.

It began long before the time of Constantine. The first step away from the New Testament pattern of a college of equal Presbyter-bishops in each local church, had been taken around the beginning of the second century under the leadership of Ignatius of Antioch. Around 100, Clement of Rome was still writing in a way that assumed the old pattern, but Ignatius, having become a monarchical bishop over the presbyters in his church, wrote to the Smyrnaeans:

> Let all things therefore be done by you with good order in Christ. Let the laity be subject to the deacons, the deacons to the presbyters, the presbyters to the bishop, the bishop to Christ even as He is to the Father.[26]

In defense of Ignatius's position, we may recognize value in the office of one pastor-bishop in each church. Someone had to preside over the presbytery in session. Someone had a larger home with rooms for the prescribed hospitality for itinerating saints. Someone was best at leading in worship, at giving instruction in sound doctrine, and in confuting heretics. Besides, when the original twelve Apostles and the larger group of seventy who had known the Lord passed off the scene, others had to carry on their tradition. Paul trained younger men like Timothy, Linus, and Titus for just such leadership. So long as they were humble, spiritually minded, faithful disciples, answerable to the trust of congregations, and checked by the presbyters, there was no great hazard of spiritual loss, and considerable gain in effectiveness by having one bishop. He could give full time to the leadership, freed from the necessity of earning any other living by the support of the church's giving. We have seen that these bishops remained equal in power and station until after the mid-third century.

Yet their authority was growing before that. It was given

stimulus by the Montanist heresy. Montanus was from Ardabau near Phrygia in Asia Minor, a region long noted for its ecstatic religion. The Apostle Philip's daughters had prophesied there. Jerome records a tradition that before his conversion Montanus had been a priest of Cybele. Around 156, he proclaimed that the Age of the Holy Spirit had dawned, as promised by Jesus in John 15:26, with himself as the passive instrument of the Spirit's speaking. Two prophetesses, Prisca and Maximilla, joined him. They claimed inspired revelations calling for strenuous asceticism, celibacy, fastings, and abstinence from meat. They taught the priesthood of all believers, men and women. Any Christian was permitted to perform the ministries of the Church, since ministers are ordained by God, not by human ordination. They prophesied the immediate Second Coming of Christ, with the Millennial Kingdom to be set up at little Pepuza in Phrygia. They opposed the growth of authoritative Church organization, and were a direct threat to the growing power of the bishops. They aimed at the cultivation of the higher reaches of Christian piety.

That their movement rapidly gained a popular Christian following gave evidence of current discontent with the growing worldliness of the Church, the neglect of charismatic faith, and the hope of the millennium. The bishops in Asia Minor, feeling their authority threatened, held synods soon after 160 in which Montanus was condemned. His movement spread nevertheless, to Rome around 170, and Tertullian of Carthage, attracted by its asceticism, embraced it to defect from the moral laxity of such bishops as Callistus in Rome in 207. It was gradually suppressed by the bishops of the Orthodox Catholic Church, but in doing so, they took a position in opposition to the general experience of charismatic gifts which practically quenched the Holy Spirit in the Church. For the average believer, the work of the Holy Spirit was thenceforth confined to the gift of saving faith and an enlightened Christian conscience. Any more spectacular gifts were said to have been confined to the closed Apostolic Age, or reserved for the inspiration of the bishops. A charismatic Church is more difficult to rule.

Montanist prophecies of the end of the world were soon proved false by the mere passing of time, and the tendency to asceticism was absorbed into the monastic movement. Had the bishops been less authoritative, and trusted more in Providence, false prophets would have been culled from the true. Those who grab for power never really believe in God, or they would heed the Scriptural advice of Gamaliel:

So, in the present case I tell you, keep away from these men, and let them alone; for if this plan or this undertaking is of men, it will fail; but if it is of God, you will not be able to overthrow them. You might even be found opposing God.[27]

By 220, Callistus of Rome was acting like a metropolitan archbishop over other bishops in Central Italy, and defending himself against the charge of too readily readmitting sinners to communion by claiming the authority of the keys of the Kingdom given by Christ to Peter, his Apostolic predecessor.

During the latter decades of the third century, Christianity grew apace, raising a problem for the bishop of each "Civitas" or leading city church: how to train bishops and presbyters to staff congregations in the small villages round about. We learn of "Chorepiscopi"—country bishops, responsible for a group of rural communities. Bishops in the provincial capitals asserted precedence over their lesser colleagues. Regardless of former theories of episcopal freedom and equality, as in the writings of Cyprian, and of the teachings of Jesus, the authority of the metropolitan bishops grew. In Egypt, the "pope" of Alexandria gained undisputed primacy over the other bishops, including those of Cyrenaica, who served as his suffragens. By 314, Rome's See had acquired rights of jurisdiction over the churches of Italy south of the Po. Antioch ruled the churches of Syria and eastward to the Euphrates. When the Council of Nicaea in 325 gave official patriarchal rights and honors to Rome, Antioch, Alexandria, and Jerusalem, it formalized a system which had been becoming actual during the previous half-century.[28] Canon four directed that the bishop be appointed by all the bishops of the province, (eparchy), or if the many cannot assemble, at least three shall consecrate the bishop with the consent of those absent in writing, and "The confirmation of what is done belongs by right in each Eparchy to the Metropolitan."

Even before this, the Synod of Ancyra in 314 forbade *chorepiscopi* to ordain presbyters and deacons, confining that right to metropolitan bishops. The Synod of Caesarea in 324-25 prohibited country priests from serving at the altar in the city church when the bishop and presbyters were present, though they might be invited to serve in the absence of such brethren of greater dignity. Country bishops might serve at any altar. The Synod of Antioch in Encaeniis in 341 decreed that "The bishops of every province must be aware that the Bishop presiding in the Metropolis has charge of the whole province.[29] The Council of Sardica in 347 gave Rome the preeminence of appeal. Canon two states:

If a bishop has been deposed by sentence of those bishops who are in the neighborhood, and he desires to defend himself, no other shall be appointed to his see until the Bishop of Rome has judged and decided thereupon.[30]

The Council of Laodicea in 363, Canon twelve, decreed that bishops must be appointed by the decision of the metropolitan and the surrounding bishops.[31]

So, by the mid-fourth century, as a result of the power accrued to the Church since Constantine, it was organizing itself into a diocesan system, with larger areas coterminous with Roman provinces, and the hierarchical pattern of Church governmental authority conformed to the civil government pattern of the Roman Empire. It was the very authoritarian rule Jesus had warned His disciples against. The only remaining anomaly was for the Roman bishop to become officially "Pope." The 381 Council of Constantinople reflected the futile attempt of the bishopric of the newer capital to equal Rome in status. Canon two reads:

The Bishop of Constantinople shall hold the first rank after the Bishop of Rome because Constantinople is the new Rome.[32]

Strong bishops of Rome soon advanced the claims of that See. Innocent I (402-417) claimed for the Roman Church the foundation of all Western Christianity, utterly ignoring the heritage of the Celtic churches from John of Ephesus through Polycarp of Smyrna and Irenaeus of Lyons, and ascribed the decision of the Council of Sardica to the Council of Nicaea, basing thereon claim to universal jurisdiction for Roman bishops. Leo I (440-461) procured an edict from the Western Emperor-Valentinian III ordering all to obey the Roman bishop, as having the primacy of Peter. Yet in 451, the Council of Chalcedon placed Constantinople on a practical equality with Rome. During the Monophysite Controversy of 519, Gelasius of Rome wrote a letter to the Emperor Anastasius in the East, claiming:

there are two by whom principally the world is ruled: the sacred authority of the pontiffs and the royal power. Of these the importance of the priests is so much greater, as even for kings of men they will have to give an account to the divine judgment.

The title "Pope," or Universal Bishop was first bestowed upon the Roman bishop in 610. The Emperor Phocus had been excommunicated by Bishop Ciriacus of Constantinople for having caused the assassination of his predecessor, the Emperor Mauritius. So, to spite Ciriacus, the emperor tried to elevate the Roman See. Gregory the Great, already acting like a universal bishop in the West, refused the title, dubious under the circumstances, as too proud, preferring to call himself "servant of the servants of God." His third successor, Boniface IV, accepted it. Somewhere in this sad departure from Christ's Way, the bishop's seat became a papal throne, the popes took the title "Pontifex Maximus," former religious title of the emperors in Rome, and took to wearing the former emperors' triple tiara crown.

So the heresy of ecclesiology was complete. The third wall on which the bishops climbed involved a fall from the grace of humility which no political prerogative could help. Both authoritarian power and subservience to that power block the Holy Spirit's access to the soul. The spontaneity of an inspired ministry is banned when organizational interests become primary. Serving as or under an archbishop is either way a hazard to spiritual integrity.

Then why did the Continental Church lose its spiritual vitality? Simply because these three forms of pride involved idolatries which displaced the rule of the all-encompassing Lord Christ Jesus. When church leaders rationalize their prior allegiance to their own intellectual preeminence, or to their worldly sociopolitical importance, or to their prerogatives of ecclesiastical power, they thereby cut themselves off from the guidance and power of the Holy Spirit. He takes the things of Christ and declares them anew in present relevance to any yielded spirit rich in humble faith.

Out on the Western fringe of civilization, the Celtic Church of Britain largely escaped these three desecrations of the Christian Spirit. In respect to the second, they escaped after having been burned quite badly, as by fire, warned by Gildas the Wise, as we saw in Chapter II, section 7. Somehow, they never succumbed to the third until after, in God's Providence, their great missionary work had been accomplished. For centuries, they preserved the organization of the Old Catholic Church, in which all bishops were equal and did not even have dioceses to rule. The first pallium of an archbishop or metropolitan to arrive in Britain was bestowed upon Augustine of Canterbury by Gregory the Great of Rome, some years after 597.

Chapter IV

THE WAY IN IRELAND

We have now reached the crux of our research into the faith that renewed the Church after the Dark Ages. Unfortunately, we do not have much writing of Columba and other missionaries of the sixth and seventh centuries to give us the spiritual evidence in depth we need. What we do have is contemporary written evidence of great value from Ireland where that faith was eminently fruitful in the ministry of Patrick and the succeeding two centuries: *The Deer's Cry* or *Lorica,* the *Hymn of Sechnall* and especially Patrick's own two important writings, the *Letter to Coroticus* and his *Confession.* The first mentioned is probably the latest written, and of mixed value, but we quote it here that the reader may share the flavor of some Irish prayer poetry in use a century after Patrick and before the time of Columba.

The Deer's Cry

(Known as Patrick's *Lorica* or Breastplate)

I

I arise today:
> through a mighty strength, invocation of the Trinity;
> through belief in the Threeness;
> through confession of the Oneness;
> towards the Creator.

Map: Early Christian Sites in Ireland

II

I arise today:
> through the strength of Christ's Birth and His Baptism;
> through the strength of His Crucifixion and Burial;
> through the strength of His Resurrection and Ascension;
> through the strength of His descent to the Judgment of Doom.

III

I arise today:
> through the strength of the order of Cherubim;
> through the obedience of Angels;
> through the ministration of Archangels;
> through the hope of resurrection for the sake of reward;
> through prayers of Patriarchs;
> through predictions of Prophets;
> through preachings of Apostles;
> through faiths of Confessors;
> through innocence of holy Virgins;
> through deeds of righteous men.

IV

I arise today:
> through the might of Heaven;
>> brightness of Sun; whiteness of Snow;
>> splendor of Fire; speed of Lightning;
>> swiftness of Wind; depth of Sea;
>> stability of Earth; firmness of Rock.

V

I arise today:
> through God's Strength to guide me,
> God's Might to uphold me,
> God's Wisdom to lead me,
> God's Eye to look before me,
> God's Ear to hear me,
> God's Word to speak for me,
> God's Hand to guard me,
> God's Way to lie before me,
> God's host to defend me
>> against snares of demons,
>> against allurements of vices
>> against lusts of nature,
>> against all who wish me harm, far and near,
>>> alone or in a crowd.

VI

I invoke therefore all these forces:
 against every fierce merciless power
  that may assail my body and my soul;
 against incantations of false prophets,
 against black laws of paganism,
 against false laws of heresy,
 against deceit of idolatry,
 against spells of women and smiths and druids,
 against all knowledge forbidden the human soul.

VII

Christ protect me today:
 against poison, against burning,
 against drowning, against wounding,
  that I may receive abundant reward;
Christ with me, Christ before me,
Christ behind me, Christ in me,
Christ beneath me, Christ above me,
Christ to right of me, Christ to left of me,
Christ where I lie, Christ where I sit, Christ where I arise,
Christ in the heart of every person who thinks of me!
Christ in the mouth of every person who speaks to me!
Christ in every eye that sees me!
Christ in every ear that hears me!

VIII

I arise today
 through a mighty strength, the invocation of the Trinity;
 through belief in the Threeness;
 through confession of the Oneness;
 towards the Creator.

Salvation is of the Lord;
Salvation is of the Lord;
Salvation is of Christ;
May Thy Salvation, O Lord, ever be with me.

The *Lorica* is a sixth-century expression of the faith of some Irish followers of The Way, early ascribed to Patrick. Some parts of it may have come from The Apostle of Ireland, particularly most of Stanzas V and VII. Its heart and soul is in the prayer for Christ's enveloping Presence, and His immanence effective in personal relationships in the last nine lines of Stanza VII. The "Breastplate" protection motif seems to have been superimposed upon this core of more deeply personal prayer which sounds more like Patrick. Much of the rest sounds like semi-pagan incantation obsessed with fear. Yet, the whole reveals a basic faith in the Triune God and in prayer. It is from Patrick's life and his own unquestioned writings that we must glean the saving characteristics of The Way in Christ, later brought by Columba to Iona and the Northern Picts of Scotland; by Aidan to Northumbria; and by Columbanus, Willibrord, and the hundreds of scholarly evangelical missionaries who took the Gospel to the devastated Continent. So we also may recover the essentials of The Way in Christ to renew our churches in this time.

Patrick's roots were in Britain. He was born there. He was trained for his ministry and ordained there. He was sent as a missionary and supported from there for a quarter century by colleagues in Britain who later questioned and investigated and attacked his laborious ministry in Ireland, greatly distressing Patrick, and moving him to write his *Confession*. Modern scholarship has disproved the legend about Patrick believed for many centuries: that Patrick was trained under Germanus of Auxerre in Gaul; that he was appointed as a missionary in 432 by Pope Celestine after the death of Palladius; that he was consecrated a bishop by Bishop Amator in Gaul, and that in 441 his mission was "approved in the Catholic Faith" by Pope Leo I. We now conclude that the spiritual succession of Irish Christianity was from the British Church. The French Benedictine specialist on Celtic Christian history, Dom Louis Gougaud in his *Christianity in Celtic Lands* wrote, "The Christian Faith was first propagated in the insular Celtic countries from Roman Britain as a base."[1] R. P. C. Hanson, after exhaustive review of the historical evidence in his *St. Patrick, His Origins and Career* concludes that it is "the plain verdict of Patrick's own writings, unobscured by later tradition, that Patrick came from there too (Britain)."[2] John T. McNeill in his latest book, *The Celtic Churches,* says,

It seems highly probable that after some twenty years of training and service as a British cleric, and following the inner dedication associated with the vision of Victorinus and the pleading Irish, he received his commission and episcopal consecration from some British Church authority.[3]

Therefore, we went to such lengths to fill in the unique British background.

It is unnecessary here to recount the scholarly debates which have cleared away the legendary overgrowth. Even approved Roman Catholic biographies now reject the biographies written over two centuries after Patrick's death by Muirchu and Tirechan, preserved in the *Book of Armagh* and all the later works based upon them. Paul Gallico in his popular modern account, *The Steadfast Man,* has a chapter on "The Legendary Figure" beginning, "Probably never has a man been quite so falsified by legend, pseudo-history and propagandizing biographers as St. Patrick." Two centuries of oral traditions built up by a garrulous, superstitious, half-pagan nation of blarney-artist storytellers were reported uncritically by ecclesiastical politicans bent on gaining popular attention and support for the raising of Armagh to an arch-episcopal see. The result was a picture of a grim, savage Ireland with treacherous and murderous kings thirsting for Christian blood, and blasphemous Druid magicians casting their spells to destroy Patrick; and the portrayal of Patrick as no humble, sensitive, conscientious, love-inspiring Christian and Roman gentleman, but as an irritable, vindictive, vengeful, old curmudgeon, going about killing people with ghastly miracles, anathematizing, burning, sterilizing, pronouncing maledictions upon families for generations to come, cursing the unborn child in its mother's womb, and in high dudgeon ordering a chariot to be driven thrice over the body of his own sister in punishment for her sins. With such an ungoverned temper, he never could have won anyone to Christ!

Nor need we be concerned at length with the theory of *The Two Patricks* of Prof. Thomas F. O'Rahilly, based on a remark in Tirechan, "Palladius who is called by the other name 'Patrick'." Thereby, Palladius is made the Patrick who converted Ireland, and was called "Old Patrick," and a later namesake fulfilled some of the later legends. Scholarship has not taken this lead. The note in the *Chronicle of Prosper of Aquitaine* for the year 431, "Palladius ordained by Pope Celestine is sent to the Scots who believe in Christ as their first bishop," has general acceptance, together with the tradition in Muirchu that he withdrew after a brief ministry among the Scots in Ireland and died among the Picts in Britain. The Patrick who wrote the *Confession* had no such papal appointment, or else he would have claimed it in reply to his carping critics when his ministry was assailed. There could have been a later Patrick than the founding missionary of the Irish Church, who served after the death of the original saint, and died toward the end of the fifth century at Glaston-bury Abbey, giving rise to the legend that Patrick, like Moses, lived 120 years. If so, he has no importance in our history.

Providentially, we have two unassailable literary works of the saint himself, the *Confession* and the *Letter to Coroticus,* on which to base our main knowledge of Patrick's life, character, work in Ireland, and the content of his faith. The *Letter* un-doubtedly was written first. When he wrote it, Patrick was still in the midst of his active ministry, organizing a new church and baptizing converts. The very day after their baptism, a group of his Irish converts were assaulted by a British raiding party of Coroticus, or Ceretic, king of Ail-Cluaide (Rock of Clyde), that is, of Dumbarton. Some of the Christians were killed. Most, in-cluding virgin women, were captured and sold in slavery to the heathen Picts. Coroticus was pretending to carry on Roman culture after the breakup of the empire, and was a nominal Christian. Patrick sent a letter of open vehement protest, meant to be read before the kinglet's soldiers and clerical subjects, ex-communicating Coroticus and his soldiers, and calling upon his Christian subjects to shun them. In order to identify himself and his position to Coroticus and his followers, Patrick included some valuable autobiographical data.

The *Confession,* written toward the end of Patrick's life when he was in semi-retirement, is not an act of penance. Its title uses the Latin "confiteor" meaning a witness of thankful testimony for God's personal help. The main purpose, however, is to defend his ministry in Ireland against derogatory charges and rumors which had been made public against him in Britain, possibly triggered by his *Letter to Coroticus,* but digging up old doubts of his qualifications as a bishop. In justifying his minis-try, Patrick tells much of the story of his life in a curious, dis-connected manner, and reveals the depths of his spiritual ex-perience and motives of his Christian service. He writes for his "Brethren and kinfolk" and clerical colleagues in Britain, but also for his Irish converts who may have heard of the charges against him. He wants all to understand. They must judge whether his ministry in Ireland was "in accordance with God's good pleasure" and "let it be most truly believed that it was the gift of God. And this is my confession before I die." So Patrick concludes his apologia.

With the *Letter to Coroticus* and the *Confession* as our primary sources, and some knowledge of the social, political, and religious conditions in Britain and Ireland from other historical evidence, and some carefully sifted, untainted clues from the late seventh century biographies, we may derive a quite understandable account of the life and ministry of the Apostle to the Irish. Magonus Sucatus Patricius, his Celtic name was Sucat. Scholars of nearly all persuasions would agree to a birthdate within the five years A.D. 385-390, probably 387.

Then Patrick grew up in a relatively prosperous, peaceful, civilized Roman Britain, still protected by the Roman legions, harassed only occasionally by Irish and Pictish raiders. The coming of the first Saxons, hired as mercenaries against the Picts, was later in 449, well after the last Roman legions withdrew in 410. It was nearly three generations since British Christians had helped crown Constantine the Great at York, and had seen their religious toleration shared with the whole empire. Christianity had become the imperial religion. Favored and coddled, the Church had grown by leaps and bounds, only to become secularized and corrupted. Religious toleration was never abolished in Britain. Paganism had a brief renaissance under Emperor Julian the Apostate in 361-63. Shortly thereafter, the temple to the Celtic God Nodens was built and flourished in the Severn Valley near Patrick's home during his boyhood. Yet Christianity was the official faith, and to many, being a Christian and being a civilized Roman were largely synonymous.

It was a few years before Patrick was born that Magus Clemens Maximus, the Roman governor from Spain, newly baptized in the Orthodox Christian faith, led his troops to fight against the Arians in Gaul. The defeat of his army by Theodosius in Italy in 388 did not prevent another similar attempt under Constantine in 408, when the British learned of the invasion of Gaul by the barbarians. This later excitement and draining of troops to the Continent took place when Patrick was enslaved in Ireland after he was sixteen. So his capture by the Irish may have saved the lad from being lost with Constantine's demolished army. If there was an enthusiastic, militant, activist party in the Church during Patrick's boyhood, it did not affect him, for he was not religiously interested.

Patrick's home was well supplied with creature-comforts, such as central heating, glass windows, hot and cold running water for baths, warm woolen clothing, many tools and utensils, and as ample and cultured a table from a culinary standpoint as

Britain has ever enjoyed. There were plenty of servants. Life in Roman towns in Britain and in the large country villas was somewhat like the aristocratic county seat and plantation culture in the South before the American Civil War. There were good roads for easy, safe travel by foot, horseback, or chariot, and sturdy sailing ships for sea travel. Britain had been under the Romans for 350 years, with no organized center for developing insular patriotism. Patrick thought of himself as a Roman citizen, heir of Roman civilization and its official Christian religion. Outside the empire were barbarians, like the Irish and the Picts. All of this was in Patrick's world before he knew God. Patrick says of himself:

> I was freeborn according to the flesh; I was born of a father who was a decurion; but I sold my noble rank—I blush not to state it nor am I sorry—for the profit of others;[4]
>
> My father was Calpurnius, a deacon, one of the sons of Potitus, a presbyter, who belonged to the village of Banavem Taberniae. Now he had a small farm (villula) hard by, where I was taken captive.[5]

Banavem Taberniae has never been located. Most scholars think it was somewhere along the shore of the Bristol Channel near the mouth of the Severn, chiefly because the ownership of a villa with many maidservants and manservants[6] fits better into the opulence of that part of Roman Britain. Also, the Church had been there for at least two generations, whereas it was newer up farther north where Ninian began his work in 396.

Obviously, the British clergy at this time were not celibate, but were cohabiting normally with their wives and bearing children. During Calpurnius's later life, two Roman bishops made pronouncements against this. Siricius (384-399) in a decretal letter to the Spanish bishop of Tarragon forbade the clergy to have sexual intercourse with their wives, and Innocent I (402-417) in a letter of 404, addressed to Victricius of Rouen in Northern Gaul, applies his predecessor's rule to Gaul. However, we have seen that as late as 603, the Welsh bishops, in refusing the authority of Augustine of Canterbury, were not recognizing any papal rule from Rome.

The more significant indication in what Patrick wrote about his father lies in the fact that Calpurnius was both a deacon of the Church and a decurion, and at the same time owned a villa. A decurion, a member of the town council, having the rank of *curialis* under Roman law, incurred certain civic duties and burdens. Since Patrick received no religious instruction from his father, and had no real faith at the age of sixteen, we may assume that Calpurnius became a deacon simply to evade the tax burden which would have fallen upon his property as a curialis.[7] In 313, Constantine I, in his early favoritism toward the Church, had exempted all clergy from curial duties. This opened too large a loophole for tax evaders. Later, he ruled that all men of curial rank could not be ordained. Still later, he allowed them to be ordained, but ruled that upon ordination they must surrender their property to a kinsman. By 365, these rules were so slackly observed that Valentinian and Valens reenacted them. After 388, Theodosius did likewise, and in 398, Arcadius, an Eastern emperor, reimposed an absolute ban on the ordination of curials. Honorius in the West did not follow suit, and it was not enforced in the West until much later, by Valentinian III in 439 or 452. Generally, higher clergy who were curials could retain their orders if they surrendered two-thirds of their property. The two Roman bishops quoted above disapproved of the ordination of curials on the ground that the duties of public officials involved functioning at games and public exhibitions embarrassing to the Church. Apparently, when Patrick was a lad, these rules were not being enforced in Britain, and his father took advantage of the laxity. So we may judge his deaconate had little religious significance.

After telling about being taken captive, Patrick continues:

I was then about sixteen years of age. I knew not the true God; and I went into captivity to Ireland with many thousands of persons, according to our deserts, because we departed away from God, and kept not his commandments, and were not obedient to our priests, who used to admonish us for our salvation.[8]

So faithful Christian instruction was available from the local presbyters, but Patrick, in Calpurnius's family, did not heed. At this time, he committed a sin which later caused him serious conscientious scruples:

... things that I had done in my youth one day, nay, in one hour, because I had not yet overcome. I cannot tell, God knoweth, if I was then fifteen years old; and I did not believe in the living God, nor had I since my infancy; but I remained in death and in unbelief until I had been chastened exceedingly, and humbled in truth by hunger and nakedness and that daily.[9]

Note that his later conversion encompassed overcoming his sinful disposition. The slave-taking raid was a large operation, capturing thousands from the unprotected countryside, but apparently did not include Patrick's parents. The captives were sold as slaves in the North of Ireland. There, for six years, Patrick was poorly treated, exposed to the elements, keeping the flocks of his master. Ireland was much less developed than Britain. There were no towns. Cattle and sheep farming was the chief industry.

Now after I came to Ireland, tending flocks was my daily occupation; and constantly I used to pray in the day time. Love of God and the fear of Him increased more and more, and faith grew, and the spirit was moved, so that in one day (I would say) as many as a hundred prayers, and at night nearly as many, so that I used to stay even in the woods and on the mountain (to the end). And after daybreak I used to be roused to prayer, in snow, in frost, in rain; and I felt no hurt; nor was there any sluggishness in me.[10]

Alone at prayer, he was converted:

And there the Lord opened the understanding of my unbelief, that, even though late, I might call my faults to remembrance, and that I might turn with all my heart to the Lord my God, who regarded my low estate, and pitied the youth of my ignorance, and kept me before I knew Him, and before I had discernment, or could distinguish between good and evil, and protected me and comforted me as a father does his son.[11]

Patrick experienced both judgment and mercy:

Wherefore then I cannot keep silence—nor would it be fitting—concerning such great benefits and such great grace as the Lord hath vouchsafed to bestow on me in the land of my captivity; because this is what we can render unto Him, namely, that after we have been chastened, and have come to the knowledge of God, we shall exalt and praise His wondrous works before every nation which is under the whole heaven.[12]

No one knows exactly where Patrick endured this service and was spiritually reborn. He was "in the woods and on the mountain." Tradition says that the ships carrying the captives landed at Larne, north of today's Belfast, and that the mount was Slemish nearby. Later, when he was called in a vision in the night to come back to Ireland, he "heard the voice of them who lived beside the Wood of Foclut which is nigh unto the Western Sea" crying to him "We beseech thee, holy youth, to come and walk among us once more." Tirechan, though he accepts Mount Slemish as the place of Patrick's captivity, identifies the Wood of Foclut as his own birthplace, Tirawly, near Kilala Bay on the Atlantic. Was Patrick in his vision hearing the people he had known during his enslavement, or was his dream colored by the apocalyptic conviction that he was "predestined to preach the Gospel even to the ends of the earth"?[13] He felt he was "in the last days," undertaking "such a holy and wonderful work, imitating those who were sent to preach the Gospel for a testimony to all nations before the end of the world." Later, he preached the Gospel "to the limit beyond which no man dwells," the Western Sea.[14]

Six years of slavery and spiritual awakening were ended by God's guidance in prayer. A voice in the night directed Patrick where to flee, 200 miles to a waiting ship:

And there verily one night I heard in my sleep a voice saying, to me, "Thou fastest to good purpose, thou who art soon to go to thy fatherland." And again, after a very short time, I heard the answer (of God) saying to me, "Lo, thy ship is ready." And it was not near at hand, but was distant perhaps two hundred miles. And I had never been there, nor did I know anyone there. And thereupon I shortly took flight, and left the man with whom I had been for six years, and I came in the strength of God who prospered my way for good, and I met with nothing to alarm me until I reached that ship.[15]

Two hundred miles must have brought him to the south coast of Ireland, to Wicklow or Weckford harbor. There was the ship ready to sail. When he said he must sail with them, the shipmaster, annoyed, roughly refused. Now it was time for more prayer as Patrick, wondering, started back. But before he finished praying, one of the ship's company came shouting for him to return. They even offered to let him choose the terms of their friendship in the company. So he refused to participate in the heathen custom of sucking their breasts as a ritual of loyalty, and hoped he would be able to lead some of them into the faith of Jesus Christ.[16]

Setting sail, after three days, they reached land. A big question for scholars has been, "Which land?" Patrick had been promised he would soon go to his fatherland, but he says they "journeyed for twenty-eight days through a desert; and food failed them, and hunger overcame them." Halfway along, the shipmaster chided Patrick: if his God was almighty, now was the time to prove it. Patrick told them to pray in good faith, and lo, a herd of swine appeared in the way before their eyes:

... and they killed many of them; and in that place they remained two nights; and they were well refreshed, and their dogs were sated, for many of them had fainted and were left half dead by the way.[17]

This was the first mention of dogs, "canes." Professor Carney found a manuscript in which the word was *"carne"* (sic) meaning "flesh." So he decided it was only the men who had been left half dead and now were stuffed with pork. Patrick says Satan assailed him mightily that night, falling upon him like a huge rock. Too much pork after many days of hunger! In his dream, his limbs were paralyzed and he woke up shouting "Helias!" with all his might, as though invoking the pagan sun-god. When the warming rays of the rising sun awakened and relieved him, he was sure it had been Christ his Lord who had made the sun, who had helped him by the power of His Spirit in quite orthodox terms. Now, refreshed, they traveled fourteen more days, finding some food, firewood and dry quarters, but no people every day until they reached human habitations just as their last food ran out.[18]

Where could all this have taken place? Many prefer the "carne" reading as original, and dismiss the story of the dogs as having an air of improbability, if not to say of absurdity, concluding that the ship took Patrick near his native place, and they wandered through some sparsely inhabited part of Northern Wales or Cambria or Strathclyde.[19] To account for the twenty-eight days, they think the journey might have been fourteen days inland, and fourteen back to coastal habitation near the ship.

The earlier interpretation has more to commend it. They landed on the coast of Gaul, and journeyed southwestward toward the Mediterranean through territory recently destroyed by the Vandals and the Suevi and left deserted and largely without food supplies for the first 250 miles, except for the strayed herd of swine. Accepting the "canes" reading in most manuscripts, scholars have elaborated that Patrick was signed on by the shipmaster because he knew how to handle animals, and that the cargo of the ship was a load of Irish wolfhounds destined for the Mediterranean market. Though starving, they had not eaten the dogs as these were their valuable merchandise, and it was easier to consider them leaving the dogs half dead along the latter miles than the men. When the dogs were sold, Patrick was released from the terms of his passage far from home, to make his way back the best he could from the Mediterranean.

It has seemed to scholars that the whole subsequent career of Patrick might be involved in these alternatives. Did Patrick have contacts in Gaul, in Lerins on its Island of the Mediterranean Sea, or even in Rome? This was the obvious propaganda intent of the seventh century biographers who claimed his authority for the Romanist takeover in Ireland. So they had him go back for all of his training in Gaul.

There are three disjointed sentences, with the title "Dicta Patrici" in the Book of Armagh:

1. I had the fear of God as the guide of my journey through Gaul and Italy and, moreover, in the Islands which are in the Tyrrhene Sea.
2. Ye departed from the world to Paradise. Thanks be to God.
3. Church of the Scots! nay of the Romans! In order that ye be Christians as well as Romans ye must chant in your churches at every hour of prayer that glorious word, "Kyrie eleison, Christi eleison." Let every church that follows me chant "Kyrie eleison, Christi eleison!" Thanks be to God.

The third of these sayings is obviously propaganda, proven to be of later origin since the "Christi eleison" phrase was first introduced into the liturgy of the Western Church by Pope Gelasius (492-496).[20] The attitude of constantly begging for mercy is not characteristic of Patrick's spirit. Commending it was a bid for Roman conformity. The second "saying" is simply a quotation from paragraph seventeen of the *Letter to Coroticus.* The first has obviously been useful to those who wanted to link Patrick with Rome, yet its very indefiniteness regarding where he went in Italy suggests it may be genuine.

On the basis of what Patrick wrote in the *Confession,* and of simple geography, the journey through Gaul seems more probable. Britain had not yet been invaded by the Anglo-Saxons in 409, and Irish and Pictish raids had left no large areas of the country deserted of population. Even if the journey is interpreted as fourteen days in and fourteen back out, there is nowhere in Britain that such wandering could be done without meeting up with people, even with inhabited towns. At a leisurely pace afoot, men travel at least twenty miles a day. In fourteen days, that would be nearly 300 miles. From Anglesey to London is less than that.

On the Continent, the Vandals, Alans, and Suevi had crossed the Rhine at Mainz on the last day of 406. Beaten by the Franks, they had swarmed southwestward. Stopped by the Pyrenees, they had fanned out East and West, driving out and slaughtering the inhabitants and reducing the land to a deserted waste. When Flavius Claudius Constantinus and his poorly led army crossed from Britain, they only added to the melee. Constantine set up his capital at Arles and sent his son Constans after the Vandals, whose second leader, Prince Gunderic, led through the Pyrenees into Spain in 409 with Constans and his troops at their heels. If Patrick and his companions traveled through that year, after the Vandals and their pursuers had left, there would have been just such a condition as Patrick describes for nearly 500 miles. If they sold the dogs in Northern Italy, Patrick, released from his duty in payment for the passage, would take some time getting home. He says, "And again, after a few years, I was in Britain with my kindred." With his vitalized faith, he would seek out the hospitality of the Church wherever he journeyed, skirting the devastated area on the way. With conscientious scruple, he would insist upon working to pay for his keep. His only skill was in caring for animals, lowly work worth small wages. He could speak only Welsh, Irish, and a bit of vulgar Latin as it was spoken in Britain, such as he remembered from six years before when he had been so neglectful of his studies. He would hardly visit Lerins, for Honoratus founded his monastery on that isle in 410.[21] If he came through Auxerre, it was years before Germanus became bishop in 418. Patrick had not yet received his call to be a missionary, and as yet had no interest in holy orders. On such a journey, the young rustic would pick up precious little more literary Latin. He might have learned of how the Roman Gauls had redeemed baptized captives from the Franks and other heathen across the Rhine,[22] and might have gained the basis for the later desire he expresses, to travel to Gaul "in order to visit the brethren and to behold the face of the Saints of my Lord—God knoweth that I used to desire it exceedingly."[23] If Patrick made his journey through Gaul with his shipmates in

409, he would not go on to Rome in 410, for that was the year of the invasion of the Visigoths and the fall of Rome. If he was twenty-two in 409, he was born in 387.

When Patrick reached home and told his kinfolk the tribulations he had suffered, they implored him never to leave again. They had thought him dead. But soon he saw in night visions a man named Victoricus from Ireland bringing him a letter entitled, "The Voice of the Irish," and heard the call of the people living beside the Wood of Foclut that he walk among them once more.[24] Another night he heard someone praying within or beside him, exalted words he could not understand except the last: "He who laid down His life for thee, He it is who speaketh in thee."[25] Awaking rejoicing, he knew he must make any sacrifice to serve Christ. Still he was just an ignorant, uneducated, young man. To be a missionary to the Irish, he must study the Scriptures and learn churchmanship. To be Christ's Apostle to the Irish with the power to ordain, he should be a bishop. He needed training. It took twenty years.

The whereabouts of his schooling and service as a deacon and possibly as a presbyter can only be guessed. The preponderant evidence from what he wrote in the *Confession*, his unscholarly Latin style, and the locale of the derogatory charges against him all dictate that it was in Britain. It could have been in the monastery at Glastonbury, as Hanson suggests, or possibly in a bishop's *familia* for the training of clergy at Caerleon-on-Usk. Wherever it was, his colleagues were far more scholarly than Patrick, more skilled in Latin literature, rhetoric, and law. They deprecated his rustic manner, made fun of his halting Latin, and discouraged his hope to become the British Church's Apostle to the Irish. Years later, when they had attacked his Irish mission, the memory of it spilled over in his *Confession:*

Wherefore then be ye astonied, ye that fear God, both small and great, and ye clever sirs, ye rhetoricians, hear therefore and search it out. Who was it that called up me, fool though I be, out of the midst of those who seem to be wise and skilled in the law, and powerful in word, and in everything? And me, moreover, the abhorred of this world, did He inspire beyond others—if such I were—only that with reverence and Godly fear and unblameably I should faithfully be of service to the nation to whom the love of Christ conveyed me, and presented me, as long as I live, if I should be worthy; in fine, that I should with humility and in truth diligently do them service.[26]

So it was the love of Christ that called him to faithful humble ministry. For that service, Patrick prepared diligently in all things needful. He studied the Scriptures until he thought in biblical terms, and his Latin was mostly in Scripture quotations. He learned to conduct worship, to bring people to Christ, and to be a shepherd of souls. He had one friend among the clerics who encouraged him. Deeply conscientious, scrupulously preparing his soul for his ordination as a deacon, he confessed to his friend the serious sin that had marred his misspent youth before his captivity.[27] This friend later raised his highest hopes by saying, "Lo, thou art to be raised to the rank of bishop."[28]

We have seen in Chapter II, Section 3, how the scholarship of this period in Britain produced Pelagius, Fastidius, and Faustus. Surely the most exciting intellectual ferment of Patrick's years of clerical training was the Pelagian controversy. Agricola's spreading of the heresy, and the debates of the Pelagians with Bishops Germanus and Lupus from Gaul aroused tremendous interest and drew great crowds in Eastern Britain from Eboracum (York) to Saint Albans near London.[29] There is no record that they came out West to Caerleon, and there is no mention in Patrick's writings of his going East to hear the debates. With his vivid experience of God's initiative in his own conversion, Patrick would not be attracted to Pelagianism's extremes. He would have agreed wholeheartedly with the moderate orthodox teaching of Germanus.

Yet the bishops' coming may have had a great indirect influence upon Patrick's destiny. With Germanus and Lupus was a deacon from Auxerre named Palladius. They learned that Ireland, the land of the Scots who had been raiding Britain's shores, had some Christian believers: slaves, traders, and wives of chieftains. These believers needed leadership. Ireland would normally be looked upon as the mission territory of the British bishops. Rather than being chargeable with invading their domain, Germanus sent Palladius to Rome, asking agreement to sending a mission there. Pope Celestine ordained Palladius "Bishop to the Scots who believe in Christ," and sent him to serve them in 431. The news would cause some heart-searching among the British bishops. They had not sent out a significant missionary since Ninian went from North Wales to the Southern Picts a whole generation before. The news of Palladius would concern Patrick, whose call to just such a mission had been discouraged so long. Palladius went to central Ireland and established a few churches. then, learning that there were Scots in Pictland, an emigration that later grew into the Kingdom of Dalriada, he sailed there, and unexpectedly taking sick, died. Later rumors that his ministry in Ireland was unsuccessful are superfluous. He had been commissioned to the Scots, and some of them lived in Albion among the Picts.

The news of Palladius's death aroused the British bishops. Now they must make up for the dereliction of duty for which the Roman bishop's action had been a mild rebuke. They would call a synod meeting, for the funds to support such a mission should come from all the churches, and the ordination of a bishop-apostle to the Irish required as many bishops as possible for the laying on of hands. Whom should they elect and send?

To poor, long-frustrated Patrick, waiting for the fulfillment of his Divine call, it seemed that this must be the Will and Providence of God for him. He says:

I was ready, but that I did not know through these revelations what I should do about my position, because many were forbidding this embassage. Moreover they used to talk amongst themselves behind my back and say, "Why does this fellow thrust himself into danger amongst hostile people who know not God?" They did not say this out of malice; but it did not seem meet in their eyes, on account of my illiteracy, as I myself witness that I have understood.[30]

Yet his good friend and confidant of many years assured him that he would be so elevated and agreed to plead for him. He might not be very learned or polished, but the people to whom he would be sent were barbarians. Best of all, he knew their language, and was acquainted with their customs, and even might still find some old friends among them. Twenty years before he had received just this Divine call! Still with some misgivings, the synod agreed, and Patrick was ordained missionary bishop to the Irish people, and sailed with a small company in the year 432. Patrick was forty-five.

The Ireland to which he sailed was as simple and primitive, if not more so, than Britain had been when the Romans arrived four centuries earlier. There were no cities or towns. The duns of the ruling princes were their private dwellings. It was a herdsman's economy, with cattle and sheep, and very little agriculture. Monetary terms were expressed in cattle. The law made kinfolk responsible for the conduct of every member of the clan. Irish society was aristocratic and heroic, with graded status from kings down to slaves. Though there were higher kings over lesser chieftains, there was no all-powerful monarch ruling the whole of Ireland. Ireland had never been invaded from abroad since the Goedelic Celts came centuries B.C., so there was no outward threat to compel unity from such an independent-minded people. The High King of Tara had limited power over northern Irish clans in times of certain crises, but his status was that of head of the noble grades. The nobility had special privileges, but were not a consolidated class with group influence like the English barons of the Middle Ages. Each king or clan chief headed his own kin group, keeping a retinue, receiving higher compensation for offenses against his person, and having defined responsibilities. There were no crimes against the state. Injuries to private persons were to be compensated by the guilty person or his kin, according to the seriousness of the injury and the status of the injured party. Contracts were guaranteed by a surety system, by treasures given in pledge or by guarantors. In each clan, there was a representative who guaranteed the duties to which his kinsmen were bound. Any man who did not keep faith was degraded and lost his honor-price. A wounded person could claim sick maintenance as well as a fine for his injury. The aged and the sick were protected by law within the clan.

Children of noble and freeborn families were usually sent away from home to be fostered in another home during childhood, with special laws regulating the costs and obligations of fosterage, and the teaching they received according to class. There were laws of hospitality. According to status, men of free or noble grade had the right to demand hospitality from their equals or superiors, for themselves and retinue, and obligation to provide the same. We shall see how Patrick established his status and took advantage of this hospitality code. One class of wealthy free men gained an honor-price equal to that of the king by promising similar universal hospitality. Patrick knew of the Christian tradition of the universal hospitality of bishops.

Learning was prized in Irish society, and there were special schools for training in law and literature. Every king needed a "*brehon*" to elucidate the law, and a "*fili*" or bard to entertain his household and guests. The brehons or Druids advised the kings and maintained the legal traditions of society; the bards remembered the poems, epic tales, and genealogies of the clans, and composed more of them after each epic occasion. By their frequent repetition, the bard maintained the public morale, and when war with neighboring clans threatened, inspired the warriors for battle with recollections of their heroic past. The Druids and bards maintained the religious lore of the culture as well. The mythological cycles, not written down until the eighth century and much later, were then too greatly influenced by Christian ideas to preserve any basis for a clear exposition of their beliefs. They had sacred groves, and an ancient tradition of human sacrifice and the cult of the severed head, but any knowledge of the religious significance of these practices is lost.[31] They were inordinate braggarts, with a tradition of boasting of prowess at feasts, celebrating their heroic deeds which guaranteed bumptious exaggeration.

Providentially, Patrick had lived six impressionable years in Ireland, spoke the language, and had some understanding of the culture and social customs of the people he was called to serve. He also had an avidly studied knowledge of the New Testament methods of evangelism, and a tremendous faith in the guiding Providence of God, and the inner inspiration of the Holy Spirit. So prepared, and with a supply of Scriptures, and breviaries for conducting worship and vessels for the celebration of the sacraments, Patrick and his little company sailed through Strangford Lough to the mouth of the Quoile River at what is now Downpatrick in County Down.

We wish Patrick had not been quite so modest and had told us more of his ministry in Ireland in his *Confession.* At the point where he might have done so, he wrote:

Now it were a tedious task to declare particularly the whole of my toil, or even partially. I shall briefly say in what manner the most righteous God often delivered me from slavery and from twelve perils whereby my soul was endangered, besides many plots and things which I am not able to express in words. Nor shall I weary my readers. But I have as my voucher God who knoweth all things even before they come to pass, as the answer of God frequently warned me, the poor, unlearned orphan.[32]

In scattered passages, he says:

Whence came to me this wisdom, which was not in me? . . . Because I am debtor exceedingly to God, who granted me such a great grace that many peoples through me should be regenerated to God and afterwards confirmed, and that clergy should everywhere be ordained for them, for a people newly come to belief, which the Lord took from the ends of the earth.[33]

Wherefore then in Ireland they who never had the knowledge of God, but until now only worshipped idols and abominations—how has there lately been prepared a people of the Lord, and they are called children of God? Sons and daughters of Scottic chieftans are seen to become monks and virgins of Christ.[34]

And so it is proper that according to the rule of faith in the Trinity I should define doctrine, and make known the gift of God and everlasting consolation, without being held back by danger, and spread everywhere the name of God without fear, confidently; so that even after my decease I may leave a legacy to my brethren and sons whom I baptized in the Lord, many thousands of persons.[35]

Patrick was not giving a story of his ministry. He was testifying what God had done through him to justify his ministry under serious criticism. In the opening paragraph of his *Letter to Coroticus,* he gives a curious insight into his feelings about himself and his ministry in Ireland, where he never really felt at home, or identified himself with the Irish people, even though he loved his friends and sons and daughters in the faith there:

Patrick the sinner, unlearned verily:—I confess that I am a bishop, appointed by God to Ireland. Most surely I deem that from God I have received what I am. And so I dwell in the midst of barbarians, a stranger and an exile for the love of God. He is witness if this is so. Not that I desired to utter from my mouth anything so harshly and so roughly; but I am compelled by zeal for God; and the truth of Christ roused me, for the love of my nearest friends and sons, for whom I have not regarded my fatherland and kindred, yea not my life even unto death, if I am worthy. I have vowed to my God to teach the heathen, though I be despised by some.[36]

Kathleen Hughes, author of *The Church in Early Irish Society,* on the basis of this passage, thinks that Patrick's whole mission was distinctly unconventional, that it is doubtful whether it was even officially recognized, that his opponents always thought him unfit to hold orders, and that his only episcopacy was conferred upon him by God without Church sanction.[37] This is taking his words too literally. With Patrick's keen sense of God's over-arching Providence engineering his ordination, despite the misgivings of his human superiors in Britain, and Patrick's inner knowledge that God had ordained it when Christ called him twenty years earlier, these words expressed the major truth regardless of lesser human instrumentality.

Lacking any other sources for details of Patrick's mission, we wish we could give more credence to the stories and traditions in the seventh century biographies of Muirchu and Tirechan. Especially picturesque is the legend of his bout with High King Laoghaire (pronounced Leary) and his Druids on the Hill of Slane in Meath, and in the king's banqueting hall at Tara. Were there truth in much of this tale, another way than Christ's conquered Ireland in one fell battle.

On the night when the king with his chieftains, Druids, and bards, were feasting at Tara, at the spring solstice, when by royal decree no fire was to be lit until after the King's holy fire blazed from Tara's hill, Patrick challenged the religion of the king and the Druids by lighting an Easter Fire on Slane. When the king in high dudgeon consulted his Druids, they prophesied with amazing accuracy:

O High King, unless this fire which you see be quenched this same night it will never be quenched; and the kindler thereof will overcome us all and seduce all the folk of your realm.

In nine chariots, the king, queen, and magicians drove the ten miles to Slane. There they paused outside the dread magic of Patrick's blaze and summoned Patrick and his little band of unarmed clerics. Lochru, a chief Druid, began to blaspheme the Christian faith. Therupon Patrick, transfixing him with a stern look, prayed to God to raise him aloft and fling him to the ground. Instantly, an unseen hand lifted Lochru into the sky and flung him to earth, dashing out his brains. The king ordered Patrick killed, but the Saint prayed, "Let God arise and His enemies be scattered." Muirchu narrates:

Then straightway darkness came down, and a terrible commotion arose, and the ungodly men fought amongst themselves, one rising up against another and there was a great earthquake. And he bound the axles of the chariots, and drove them with violence, and they rushed in headlong flight, both chariots and horses over the level ground of the great plain till at last only a few of them escaped half-alive to the mountain of Monduirn, and at the curse of Patrick seven times seven men were laid low by this stroke in the presence of the King and his elders, until there remained only himself and his wife, and two others of his companions, and they were sore afraid. So the queen approached Patrick and said to him, "O man, righteous and mighty, do not destroy the King, for the King will come and kneel and worship thy Lord." And the King, compelled by fear, came and knelt before the Saint and feigned to worship Him whom he did not wish to worship.

And when they had parted one from another, the King went a little way, and called St. Patrick by feigned words minding to slay him by some means. But St. Patrick, knowing the thoughts of the villainous King, blessed his companions, (eight men and a lad) in the Name of Jesus Christ, and came to the King. The King counted them as they came; and straightway they were nowhere to be seen, taken away from the King's sight, but the heathen folk saw naught but eight stags and a fawn. (The lad was Patrick's boy disciple, Benighus or Benen) going as it were to the wilderness. And King Laoghaire with the few that had escaped return at dawn to Temoria, sad, cowed and humiliated.

His humiliation didn't last. Saturday night's sleep restored him and he was feasting with his assembly as usual on Easter Sunday when Patrick and five companions entered Tara's Hall through closed doors (like Jesus). Only Dubthach-maccu-Lugir, the Chief-Bard rose to honor him. The king invited them to the table, and the other chief Druid, Lucetmael, uncowed by his partner's death the night before, proposed a further trial of powers. Lucetmael spiked Patrick's cup with a drop of poison. Patrick detected the trick, prayed, and the liquor was turned to ice, so when the Saint inverted the cup, only the drop of poison fell out. When Patrick then blessed the cup, it was a safe drink. Lucetmael conjured up a waist-deep snow on the plain, but couldn't melt it away. Pointing up the moral, Patrick said, "Thou art able to do evil but not good; I am not of that sort," blessed the plain and the snow vanished. The wizard incanted a thick darkness; Patrick blessed it away. Laoghaire suggested they test which one's books would be unharmed if thrown into the water, but Lucetmael, having heard of baptism, opined that water was Patrick's god, and refused. He also refused a similar trial by fire, though one might presume that might have given him the advantage. In the ancient Pythagorean philosophy of the Druids, fire was the chief element. Patrick's Easter Fire claimed it for his God too. A trial by fire was final.

Patrick then suggested a test loaded against himself. A hut was to be built with two sections, one of green wood, the other of dry. Lucetmael in Patrick's mantle was to enter the green end, Benen in Lucetmael's Druid cloak the dry, and the house set alight to let the Most High judge. It sounded like Elijah on Mount Carmel with the Prophets of Baal. The house of green twigs and Lucetmael were completely consumed by the fire, leaving only Patrick's cloak unsinged, while Benen in his tinderbox survived unharmed, only the Druid's garment being burned to ashes. The king, enraged at the death of his second Druid, lunged at Patrick, but the Saint, praying, brought the wrath of God upon many of the company, slaying them, thereby compelling Laoghaire's conversion.

Actually, the king never was converted. Irish history records that Laoghaire was buried standing upright, pagan fashion, his weapons to hand facing his old enemies, the men of Lienster who had killed him in battle—so he never was really high king of all Ireland, but only of Patrick's North, and he never embraced the faith of Patrick's God, but still hoped in a Druidic immortality. Then Patrick's mission was a gradual victory, one chieftain and his Tuath at a time, through most of the twenty-nine years of his arduous service. Perhaps he did confront Laoghaire bravely, at some early date after he had won a strong following, and gain the right to proselyte anywhere in his realm. Undoubtedly, there were brave confrontations with Kinglets and Druids.

Patrick tells of two incidents in which he was captured and imprisoned:

And again, after many years, I went into captivity once more. And so on that first night I remained with them. Now I heard the answer of God saying to me, "For two months thou shalt be with them." And so it came to pass. On the sixtieth night after, the Lord delivered me out of their hands.[38]

His account of the second imprisonment throws real light upon Patrick's gradual progress across the island, spending precious mission funds to buy his way, an entourage of converted young men from the previously evangelized Tuath with him to claim hospitality and give him status and needed protection:

... Wherever I journeyed for your sake, through many perils, even to outlying regions beyond which no man dwelt, and where never had anyone come to baptize, or ordain clergy, or confirm the people, I have, by the bounty of the Lord, initiated everything, carefully and gladly for your salvation.

On occasion I used to give presents to the Kings, besides the hire that I gave to their sons who accompany me; and nevertheless they seized me with my companions. And on that day they most eagerly desired to kill me; but my time had not yet come. And everything they found with us they plundered, and me myself they bound with irons. And on the fourteenth day the Lord delivered us from their power; and whatever was ours was restored to us for the sake of God and the near friends whom we had provided beforehand.[39]

This would have been impossible if Patrick had had the backing of a converted High King of all Ireland, and was accustomed to praying for another kind of miraculous protection. God worked through Patrick's previous converts in the nearest neighboring Tuath, bringing the needed peaceful pressure to release Patrick and their sons.

There are some of the stories in Muirchu's and Tirechan's biographies and in the later *Tri-Partite Life of Patrick* which impress us as bearing the inherent truth, and at the same time affording precious insights. One is the tale of Dichu's barn.

When Dichu's swineherd spied the strangely clad and tonsured men in their long cloaks and with the forehalfs of their heads shaved from ear to ear, landing from their boat, he took them for raiders and ran to alert his master. Dichu whistled for his savage wolfhound, grabbed his sword and shield, and ran out to meet the danger.

One man, unarmed, advanced up the hillside to greet him. He was chanting a strange verse from the Psalms, and his voice quieted the wolf-hound: *Ne tradas Domine, bestiis animas confitentis tibi.* Then the two men faced each other, and all suspicion and fear vanished from Dichu. Immediately, they liked each other and knew they would be friends. The Triparte Life says:

When he beheld the countenance of St. Patrick, the Lord turned his thoughts to good.

Muirchu says:

. . . when Dichu saw Patrick, grief of heart seized him, and he believed, and Patrick baptized him.

Grateful, Dichu presented to Patrick a barn which stood on a rise near his home, and Patrick consecrated it as his first church in Ireland. This is the site at Saul near Downpatrick where a chaste new church was built by the Episcopal Church of Ireland in 1933 to commemorate the 1500th Anniversary of Dichu's gift in 432. In gratitude, Patrick is said to have responded:

God's blessing on Dichu,
  Who gave us the barn;
May he have afterwards,
  A heavenly home, bright, pure, great!
God's blessing on Dichu,
  Dichu and all his children,
No child, grandchild, or descendant of him
  Shall die but after a long life!

The strategy of Patrick's mission in approaching kings and chieftains through their young people and wives is illustrated in the founding legend of the Christian community at Trim, west of Tara at the ford of the Alder on the River Boyne. *The Tripartite Life* tells how Patrick left a companion, Lomman, to mind their ship there while he visited Tara, probably knowing that the wife of the nearby prince was a Briton who had either been a Christian or was well-disposed to the faith.

Ath Truimm was at that time the stronghold of Fedilmid, son of Laoghaire, son of Niall. In the morning Fortchern, son of Fedilmid, went and found Lomman with his Gospel before him. A marvel to him (Fortchern) was the doctrine he heard. He believed and was baptized by Lomman, and Fortchern was listening to the doctrine until his mother came a-seeking him. She made welcome to the clerics, for of the Britons was she, namely Scoth, daughter of the King of the Britons. Fedelmid himself came to have speech of Lomman, and he believed and offered Ath Truimm to God and to Patrick and to Lomman and to Fortchern—(the latter probably becoming its Deacon-Priest after due instruction!)

Patrick's aplomb and steadfastness of purpose in securing donations of sites for his churches is shown in Muirchu's story of Daire, chieftain of Armagh:

There was in the country of Airthir a certain rich and honorable man named Daire. To him Patrick made request that he would grant him some place for the exercise of religion. And the rich man said to the Saint, "What place dost thou desire?" "I desire," said the Saint, "that thou grant me that high ground that is called the Ridge of the Willow, and I shall build there a place." But he was unwilling to give the Saint that high ground; but gave him another place on lower ground, where is now the Church of the Relics near Ardd-Machae: and there St. Patrick dwelt with his people. . . .

And after these things Daire came to pay his respects to St. Patrick, bringing with him a wonderful bronze pot holding three gallons that had come from beyond the seas. And Daire said to the Saint, "Lo, this bronze pot is for thee." And St. Patrick said, "Grazacham!" (So sounded the colloquial expression of the Latin "Gratias agamus": "Let us give thanks!") And when Daire returned to his own house he said, "That stupid man, who said nothing more civil than "Grazacham" in return for that wonderful bronze three-gallon pot!" And Daire then proceeded to say to his servants, "Go and bring us back our pot." So they went and said to Patrick, "We are going to take away the pot." Nevertheless Patrick that time too said, "Grazacham! Take it away." And they took it away. And Daire questioned his companions and said, "What did the Christian say when ye took back the pot?" And they answered, "He just said 'Grazacham'!" Daire answered and said, " 'Grazacham' when it is given, 'Grazacham' when it is taken away! His expression is so good that his pot must be brought back to him with his 'Grazacham!' " And Daire came himself this time and brought the pot to Patrick saying, "Thy pot must remain with thee; for thou art a steadfast and unchangeable man; moreover as for that parcel of ground which thou didst once desire, I give it to thee now, insofar as I possess it, and do thou dwell there."

If this is trustworthy tradition, Patrick was steadfast and more. He was also a canny person, with sensitive insight into personal motives, and a realistic appraiser of social situations. He was humble and meek, but never obsequious. Like Moses, to whom he was often compared, he was of the terrible meek who inherit the earth.

We may now, on the basis of these traditions and especially from the analysis of the fifty-first and fifty-second chapters of the *Confession* quoted above (pp. 142-43), attempt to visualize the realistic method Patrick used for his evangelism. Since he had observed the aristocratic society in Ireland before his call and education, he would study the Scriptures with this situation in view. Particularly, Jesus' instruction to his twelve disciples for their first apostolic mission would seem pertinent:

. . . preach as you go, saying, "The kingdom of heaven is at hand." Heal the sick, raise the dead, cleanse lepers, cast out demons. You received without pay, give without pay . . . and whatever town or village you enter, find out who is worthy in it, and stay with him until you depart. As you enter the house, salute it. And if the house is worthy, let your peace come upon it; but if it is not worthy, let your peace return to you. And if anyone will not receive you or listen to your words, shake off the dust from your feet as you leave that house . . . " (Matt. 10:7-14)

In Ireland's heroic aristocratic society, the most worthy man was the king or chieftain with the highest honor price. Since he ruled the common people of the clan, it would be a waste of time to try to reach them without the clan leader's goodwill and permission. Patrick knew how to approach the top men through their younger sons and wives, but he also knew how to demand and get the king's hospitality. He was the representative of the King of Kings and Lord of Lords, and must meet any king on an equal footing. So he traveled with as large a retinue as he could gather, claiming an honor status of a chief Druid, equal to a king, demanding hospitality according to the common law of Ireland and getting it. It was costly. He made presents to judges (Druids) and kings befitting his rank, and then asked the right to preach to the people, and when he had made converts, asked for the most commanding hilltop property not too far from the most worthy man's dun as a worthy gift from the king, chieftain or other wealthy man, where he had them help him build his church. One tradition says Patrick included a cowherd in his entourage. This was his banker. In Irish economy, the cow was the medium of monetary exchange, and people contributed cows toward the construction of the church to be built in every Tuath or Rath.

As Patrick moved on to the dun of the next worthy chieftain, he took a number of enthusiastic new youthful converts from the last newly organized church as part of his retinue, to interest the young people of the next Tuath, to impress the king, and make it difficult under Irish custom to refuse them hospitality. Once he had that, Patrick with his knowledge of the language and of the Bible, and his own experience of the living Christ to witness about, and the young people of his retinue to exhibit the joy and enthusiasm of the new life in Christ, was a persuasive evangelistic preacher. It was not as though the Christian Gospel were a complete novelty. It had been the accepted faith of the Roman world, the civilized peoples, for over a hundred years. Traders, captured slaves, and wives of kings and nobles from neighboring Britain had brought some of its message in. There were churches established down in Leinster by the brief mission of Palladius before Patrick came. The Druids knew that the British Druids had largely found this faith a superior one and converted long ago. When they heard Patrick preach, and saw the kinglets and chieftains being converted, and learned that they could become trained and effective leaders in this more helpful and higher faith, they too embraced it. The opposition of the Druids has been exaggerated in later corrupted Irish tradition. Some opposed Patrick at first, of course, as their position was threatened, but he was never harmed, and there were no martyrdoms, and most of the country was converted and dotted with churches within twenty-five years.

Every church required an intensive educational program. Christianity was a literate faith, whereas Irish religious tradition had been practically all oral. Ogam writing was scant. Now Christians had to learn to read and write Latin so they could read the Bible and understand Christian worship with its Scripture lessons and Latin chants and hymns. The bards with their heritage of poetry and literary skill were natural native leaders to be trained for this task, and from the first were ready converts, as the story of Dubthach-maccu-Lugir's welcome at Tara signifies. Patrick, with his own feelings of inadequacy about his lack of scholarly Latin and rhetoric, was in his element training Irish bards in the rudiments of biblical Latin and the reading of the Scriptures, the better adapted to it just because his own learning was nearer their beginning level. Ireland became literate for the first time in Patrick's generation, and the leading Druids and bards carried their best cultural heritage over into the new Christian catechetical schools. Patrick as bishop ordained them as soon as possible as presbyters and deacons for his growing churches.

Through all of this, Patrick took no pay from his converts, continuing to be supported by his synod in Britain. Had not Jesus said, "You received without pay; give without pay?" Had not Paul as a missionary preferred not to receive support from his converts? Patrick was so happy and busy with his fruitful labors that he did not realize the misunderstanding building up back in Britain, the questioning about the airs he was reputed to be putting on, with large retinues of servants, while still receiving mission aid. Helpers had been sent out, badly needed, but none of his seniors had ever come to Ireland to see his work.

Then something precipitated the shameful open criticism

of his whole missionary episcopate in an open synod meeting back in Britain. Perhaps it was the *Letter to Coroticus*. Patrick had been so incensed at the British king of Dumbarton, killing and enslaving his new converts when the oil of anointing of their Easter baptism wasn't dry on their foreheads. Selling those sweet, dedicated virgin girls to the heathen Picts as concubines! He had excommunicated Coroticus, and told in no uncertain terms just where he and his soldiers and anyone who ate at his corrupt table were going!

What shall I do, O Lord? I am exceedingly despised. Lo, around me are Thy sheep torn to pieces and spoiled, and that too by the robbers aforesaid, by the orders of Coroticus with hostile disposition.

Far from the love of God is he who betrays Christians into the hands of Scots and Picts. Ravening wolves have swallowed up the flock of the Lord which verily in Ireland was growing up excellently with the greatest care. And the sons and daughters of Scottic Chieftans who were monks and virgins of Christ I cannot reckon. Wherefore be not pleased with the wrong done to the just; even unto hell it shall not please thee.

Which of the saints would not shudder to jest and feast with such men? They have filled their houses with the spoil of dead Christians. They live by plunder. Wretched men, they know not that it is poison; they offer the deadly food to their friends and sons; just as Eve did not understand that verily it was death she handed to her husband. So are all they that do wrong; they work death as their eternal punishment.

... Thou handest over the members of Christ as it were to a brothel. What manner of hope in God hast thou, or has he who consents with thee, or who holds converse with thee in words of flattery? God will judge; for it is written, "Not only those who commit evil but those that consent with them shall be damned."

Imagine that letter being read, as it was intended, in Coroticus's court in the presence of his clerics, and these worthies hearing themselves consigned to hell for eating at Coroticus's table, then sending a hot protest to the synod down in Wales about their renegade bishop in Ireland taking it upon himself to excommunicate a ruler and his subjects in another country entirely outside his ecclesiastical jurisdiction! What disciplinary action did the Welsh synod intend to take? Perhaps they could not openly criticize Patrick's righteous wrath about his virgins' plight without arousing undue sympathetic support for Patrick in their constituents. But then there were still those who had opposed the ordination of that rustic, uncouth bumpkin in the first place. There was criticism of his putting on airs, riding around with a retinue of noble princelings in his pay, squandering the synod's funds, never sufficiently developing the stewardship of his field, so that by now it should support him and relieve the synod of still raising benevolences for him after over twenty-five years! Patrick's one old friend came to his defense, and they turned on him, made him admit that in some ways Patrick had been a poor candidate for Episcopal orders. And then, without intending to do it, in the midst of the argument, this dear old friend had let it out: the sin Patrick had confessed to him with conscientious scruple before he took Deacon's Orders thirty years before. They didn't want to hear what he was trying to say when he unwisely betrayed Patrick's confession, namely that Patrick mustn't be judged for his early faults. Some of them, quite avid Pelagian moralists, had little understanding of Divine grace.

They sent a deputation of clerics out to Ireland to inform him of the criticism leveled against his right to hold Episcopal office:

And when I was assailed by not a few of my elders, who came and urged my sins against my laborious episcopate—certainly on that day I was sore thrust at that I might fall, both here and in eternity. But the Lord graciously spared the stranger and sojourner for His name's sake; and He helped me exceedingly, when I was thus trampled on, so that I did not come badly into disgrace and reproach. I pray God that it may not be laid to their charge as sin.

After the lapse of thirty years they found, as an occasion against me, a matter which I had confessed before I was a deacon. Because of anxiety, with sorrowful mind, I disclosed to my dearest friend things I had done in my youth one day . . . [40]

But rather I am grieved for my dearest friend, that we should have merited to hear such an answer as that; a man to whom I had even entrusted my soul! And I ascertained from not a few of the brethren before that contention—it was at a time when I was not present, nor was I in Britain, nor will the story originate with me—that he too had fought for me in my absence. Even he had said with his own lips, "Lo, thou art to be raised to the rank of bishop"; of which I was not worthy. But how did it occur to him afterwards to put me to shame publicly before everyone, good and bad, in respect to an office which before that he had of his own accord and gladly conceded to me and the Lord too, who is greater than all.[41]

Yet Patrick in his grief and anxiety for his work was comforted by the Lord:

And so on that day on which I was rejected by the aforesaid persons whom I have mentioned, in that night I saw in the night visions:—there was a writing void of honor over against my face. And meanwhile I heard the answer of God saying to me, "We have seen with anger the face of the person designated, (the same being expressed)." Nor did he say, "Thou hast seen with anger," but "We have seen with anger," as if in that matter He had joined Himself with me, As He said, "He that toucheth you is as he that toucheth the apple of mine eye."

Therefore I thank Him who hath enabled me in all things, because He did not hinder me from the journey on which I had resolved, and from my labour which I had learnt from Christ my Lord . . . [42]

The approved Roman Catholic scholars who still accept Muirchu's account of Patrick's major education in Auxerre under Germanus have a quite different theory regarding the time and circumstances of the meeting in Britain against Patrick's episcopate. They figure the thirty years from the time Patrick committed the sin at the age of fifteen to the time he was first being considered for episcopal orders in Britain around 430, prior to Palladius's appointment. Then Patrick, they claim, was still in Gaul, where his elders came and told him of his disgrace and rejection. In this tradition, Patrick was on his way to assist Palladius in 432 when news came to him in Northern Gaul of Palladius's death, and he was quickly ordained there as Palladius's successor by a Gallic Bishop Amatore.

Four considerations render this construction most improbable:

1. The sentence in the *Confession* in which the thirty years' lapse of time is mentioned, definitely measures it from the time of the confession to his friend before he became a deacon: "After the lapse of thirty years they found, as an occasion against me, a matter which I had confessed before I was a deacon."[43]

2. The deputation of his elders who came to confront him with the charges ("came and urged my sins against my laborious episcopate")[44] accused him of more than one sin, and the episcopate had already been "laborious."

3. Had Patrick spent years of training in Gaul, he would have gained a facile use of the Latin language, whereas his style of writing, and his own many apologies for it indicate otherwise:[45]

... I had long since thought of writing; but I hesitated until now; for I feared lest I should fall under the censure of men's tongues, and because I have not studied as have others, who in the most approved fashion have drunk in both law and the Holy Scriptures alike, and have never changed their speech from their infancy, but rather have been always rendering it more perfect. For my speech and language is translated into a tongue not my own, as can be easily proved from the savor of my writing, in what fashion I have been taught and am learned in speech; for saith the wise man, "By the tongue will be discovered understanding and knowledge and the teaching of the truth,"[46]

... And so today I blush and am exceedingly afraid to lay bare my lack of education; because I am unable to make my meaning plain in a few words to the learned.[47]

There are at least four more expressions of Patrick's feeling of inadequacy about his Latin in the *Confession,* and they are far more than polite affectations of modesty.[48-51]

4. The other serious charge his seniors came to investigate was his use of the mission funds in Ireland, which he goes to great pains to answer in the *Confession,* a charge impossible at the time of his ordination! He tells how he conscientiously refused to accept gifts from his people:

Moreover, as regards those heathen amongst whom I dwelt, I have kept faith with them, and will keep it. God knoweth I have defrauded none of them, nor do I think of doing it, for the sake of God and His Church ...[52]

But though I be rude in all things, nevertheless I have endeavored in some sort to keep myself, both for the Christian brethren, and the virgins of Christ, and the devout women who used of their own accord to present me with their little gifts, and would cast of their ornaments upon the altar; and I returned them again to them. And they were scandalized at my doing so. But I did it on account of the hope of immortality, so as to keep myself warily in all things; for this reason, namely, that the heathen might receive me and the ministry of my service on any grounds, and that I should not, even in the smallest matter, give occasion to the unbelievers to defame or disparage.

Perchance then when I baptized so many thousands of men, I hoped from any one of them even so much as the half of a scruple. Tell me and I shall restore it to you. Or when the Lord ordained clergy everywhere by means of my mediocrity, and I imparted my service to them for nothing, if I demanded from one of them even the price of my shoe, tell it against me and I shall restore you more.

I spent for you that they might receive me; and both amongst you and wherever I journeyed for your sake, through many perils . . . I have, by the bounty of the Lord, initiated everything carefully and very gladly for your salvation.

On occasion, I used to give presents to Kings, besides the hire that I gave to their sons who accompany me . . . Moreover ye know by proof how much I paid to those who were judges throughout all the districts which I more frequently visited; for I reckon that I distributed to them not less than the price of fifteen men, so that ye might enjoy me, and I might ever enjoy you in God. I do not regret it, nor is it enough for me. Still I spend and will spend more. The Lord is mighty to grant me afterwards to be myself spent for your souls.

Behold I call God for a record upon my soul that I lie not; nor would I write to you that there may be an occasion for flattering words or covetousness, nor that I hope for honour from any of you. Sufficient to me is the honour which is not seen as yet, but is believed on in the heart. And faithful is He that promised; never does He lie.[53]

When Patrick's *Confession* was made into many copies in the Irish schools, and sent to all the churches in Britain who had sent him funds through the years, where the rumors of the disgraceful synod meeting had raised doubts of the worth of his ministry, and of mission benevolences, with what burnings of heart they realized the truth! The charges against Patrick all proved unworthy. The Lord helped him when he was "trampled on," so that he "did not come badly into disgrace and reproach."[54]

What Patrick studiedly refused to tell in his *Confession,* though he had let it be known in the *Letter To Coroticus* was that he had spent far more on his mission than the synod mission funds. He had sold his own noble rank as decurion, inherited from his father, his whole family inheritance, and poured all his private resources, without regret, into the mission.[55]

There has been much claim that Patrick had a special see, an arch-episcopal seat in Armagh. What is the evidence? Patrick began his *Letter to Coroticus* claiming, "I confess that I am a Bishop, appointed by God in Ireland." In the night vision of his call, a man named Victoricus came from Ireland with a letter beginning, "The Voice of the Irish." He ended his *Confession* telling that it was "composed in Ireland," without mentioning where. He thought of his mission as to the whole island, and there is no place in his writings to indicate that he thought of any place as his special seat. In contrast, later tradition made Armagh very definitely his arch-episcopal see.

We need not doubt that he founded churches in Armagh. Muirchu's legend of Daire's donations tells of two. It not only shows Patrick's ability to beg for land. The hill-top site became of historic importance as the site of the present Episcopal cathedral.

The epilogue of the Daire story also tells sweetly of the gentler side of Patrick's nature. After the donation, Daire and Patrick are said to have gone out to view the high ground of the Ridge of the Willows, and found there a hind with her little fawn lying on the spot where the altars of later cathedrals were built. Patrick's companions were minded to kill the fawn, but Patrick halted their intent by taking it up gently upon his shoulders and carrying it, with the hind following him like a tame sheep, to another wood on the North side of Ardd-Machae, and putting it down where the Roman Catholic cathedral was eventually built.

This story is called in serious question by an archaeological find recently dug up on that hilltop site which belies its tradition as a silvan willow-grove. The obliging sexton of the Episcopal Cathedral of Armagh showed us in a side room three ancient images, carved of stone, each about two feet in height, most likely from a heathen worship shrine on that high place which preceded its dedication to Christian use. One is obviously an idol of the goddess of fertility, the second a sun-god, and the third a god of war. The crudity of their artistry might indicate that they represented a still earlier religion replaced and buried by the Druids, except that the Druids were wont to tolerate the idolatry of earlier cultures. They were probably buried when Patrick converted the people of Ardd-Machae, and built his church on their traditionally most sacred hilltop. Patrick is reputed to have been hated in some quarters because he abolished idols wherever his faith triumphed. So the wooded condition of the hilltop of the Daire legends at Armagh is dubious.

Even less believable is the tradition still promoted in Armagh that Patrick and his sister Lupita were buried by the Church of the Relics on the lower land first given by Daire to Patrick, the site being identified on Scotch Street where the Georgian building of the Bank of Ireland now stands. Because two centuries later, Ardd-Machae or Armagh was promoting itself as the chief ecclesiastical city and seat of learning in Ireland, much about Patrick was invented to obtain his sanction for the development. To this day, the city with two vying cathedrals does not express his humble spirit.

Patrick's last days of semi-retirement and death were not in Armagh. The explanation was that the warriors from Tara in Meath defeated the Ulstermen, driving them eastward into Antrim and Down Counties, and Patrick went along. Yet this assumes a narrower political alignment of Patrick's church than ever he desired. If he spent his old age in County Down, it was probably because there he had more contacts with the beloved Britain from which he always felt exiled, and more friends like Dichu who gave him the barn. Patrick never was an archbishop with a cathedral. His own writings clearly indicate that to the end of his life he was the only bishop in Ireland after the withdrawal of Palladius. When he sent his *Letter to Coroticus,* he would entrust it to the most prestigious emissary he had, and that was a presbyter he had taught from his childhood, other clergy accompanying him.[56] In the *Confession,* he says he longs to visit in Britain and in Gaul, but must stay in Ireland until the end of his life for fear his great labor might be undone, for as yet there were no successor bishops who could be trusted to take over the charismatic leadership Christ had entrusted to him:

> Yet "I am bound in the Spirit," who "witnesseth to me" that if I should do this (make a trip abroad) He would note me guilty; and I fear to lose the labour which I began; and yet not I, but Christ the Lord who commanded me to come and be with them for the remainder of my life, if the Lord will, and if He should keep me from every evil way, so that I may not sin in His sight.[57]

Here it seems obvious that Patrick has been alone in his episcopal leadership throughout his Irish ministry.[58] Else why could he not call upon fellow Irish bishops for support when his ministry was questioned? All clergy sent to help him were promoted to bishop status in the imaginations of the later glorifiers of the history, or later-known bishops were imagined to have been ordained earlier in Patrick's time. So Saint Sechnall (Secundinus) who traditionally wrote the splendid *Hymn in Praise of Patrick,* was said to have died in 447, and to have arrived in 439 with two other bishops, Iserninus and Auxilius, Benignus arriving later. The Hymn of Saint Sechnall, by its style and contents, was most likely written in the late sixth century, representing the best heritage of faith from Patrick as it was remembered and practiced at that time. If Patrick had other bishops with him to share in the responsibility of converting the Irish, and confirming them, and ordaining the new Irish clergy, he could not have written as he did claiming to have done it all himself in defense of his ministry.[59] All of the converts and ordinations were glorious proof that God had blessed his Irish ministry beyond criticism. In this assurance, Patrick died in County Down in 461, and was buried in Saul. His remains were later removed to be buried beneath the great slab marked with his name and the Celtic Cross in the churchyard of the Cathedral of the Holy Trinity, Down.

TEN ESSENTIAL CHARACTERISTICS OF THE WAY FOR PATRICK

We have labored to understand the historical background of the Celtic Church in Britain, and to know Patrick who came from that background, in order to appraise the essential, repeatable characteristics of the Way in Christ which enabled the missionaries from Iona and Northern Ireland to be God's instruments of renewal for England and for the Continent after the first Dark Ages in Christian history. Therefore, our chief interest in this chapter is not the biography of Patrick nor the history of the church in Ireland, but a careful analysis of the Christianity Patrick lived and taught as it became a transmissable heritage through the Irish Church. Of course, the main inspiration of this Way in Christ is the continuing Presence of the Living Lord, and His indwelling Spirit in the consciousness of all faithful Christians. Yet it is always an historical heritage from the incarnate Jesus of Nazareth transmitted in Scripture and traditions also, with a complex nature essential to the living of the Way in Christ. We may make our analysis of the Irish Church of Patrick in depth because, providentially, we have two such revealing writings of Patrick himself, and also evidence of the faith and practice of his successors several generations later in Ireland, as they remembered Patrick, especially in the *Hymn of Sechnall.*

For our use, this *Hymn In Praise of Patrick* need not be contemporary, or even close to the time of Patrick in origin. Since there is obvious literary dependence between the *Confession* and the *Hymn*, the *Hymn* could not have been written first, for then we should have the impossible situation of Patrick borrowing eulogistic words from a hymn written in praise of him by his friend during his lifetime. The *Hymn* first appears in the *Bangor Antiphony* (680-91) with no ascription to Sechnall. It is ascribed to Sechnall in the *Martyrology of Cengus* and the *Vita Tripartita*, ninth century sources, but was probably written in the sixth century. We regard it, with scholars Binchy and Hanson as "the earliest extant testimony to a cult of Patrick."[60] It is an alphabetical hymn, like the 119th Psalm in Hebrew, with twenty-three stanzas of eight lines each (translated into four line stanzas), the key word of each stanza beginning with a letter of the Latin alphabet. Despite this artificiality, it contains considerable Christian insight, and is greatly helpful to our purpose as it shows what the Irish Church prized in Patrick's life.

We arrived at the "Ten Characteristics" from careful consideration of Patrick's own writings and of this Hymn. In the following analysis, each of the Ten Characteristics is introduced by the cognate stanzas of the *Hymn,* and as far as possible, Patrick's own writings are allowed to illustrate these essentials of The Way In Christ. Even if the Saint's expressions are sometimes quaint, the living eternal truth speaks through his words.

1. Evangelical Faith

i: Audite

Hear, all ye who love God, the holy merits
of Patrick the bishop, a man blessed in Christ;
how, for his good deeds, he is likened unto the angels,
and, for his perfect life, is compared to the apostles.

xiii:Nomen

He proclaimeth boldly to the tribes the name of the Lord,
to whom he giveth the eternal grace of the laver of salvation,
for their offenses he prayeth daily unto God;
for them also he offers up to God worthy sacrifices.

We have already quoted (pp. 128, 129) the passages from the *Confession* in which Patrick tells of his own conversion: how as a lad he "knew not the true God," and later accepted his captivity and enslavement as due desert for his sins. God in His Grace pitied Patrick's ignorance, kept him before he knew Him, protected and comforted him as a father does his son, and in prayer opened his understanding so that he might "turn with all his heart to God" and so come to an experiential knowledge of Him:

I was like a stone lying deep in the mire, and He that is mighty came, and in His mercy lifted me up, and verily raised me aloft, and placed me on the top of the wall. And therefore I ought to cry aloud, that I may also "render somewhat to the Lord" for His benefits which are so great both here and in eternity, the value of which the mind of men cannot estimate.[61]

He therefore had to share the life-changing grace of God he had received:

I am debtor exceedingly to God, who granted me such great grace that many people through me should be regenerated to God and afterwards confirmed.[62]

believers will come from all parts of the world . . . therefore we ought to fish well and diligently, as the Lord forewarns and teaches saying, "Come ye after me and I will make you to become fishers of men" . . . [63]

Wherefore then, it was exceedingly necessary that we should spread our nets so that a "great multitude" and a throng should be taken for God . . . Wherefore then in Ireland they who never had the knowledge of God, but until now only worshipped idols and abominations—how has there been lately "prepared a people" of the Lord, and they are called children of God?[64]

He defines his salvation in terms of complete self-surrender:

I have cast myself into the hands of God Almighty, for He rules everywhere.[65]

Behold, now "I commit the keeping of my soul to my most faithful" God, "for whom I am an ambassador" in my ignoble state, only because he accepteth no man's person, and chose me for this duty that I should be one of His least ministers.[66]

He fitted me, so that I should today be something which was once far from me, that I should care for, and be busy about, the salvation of others, whereas then I did not even think about myself.[67]

I pray God to give me perseverance, and to vouchsafe that I bear

Him faithful witness, until my passing hence for the sake of my God.[68]

Lo, again and again I shall briefly set forth the words of my confession: I testify in truth and in exultation of heart "before God and His holy angels," that I never had any cause except the Gospel, and His promises for ever returning to that nation from whence previously I scarcely escaped.[69]

In his *Letter to Coroticus,* Patrick further reveals his evangelical passion and describes himself in evangelism as "a slave in Christ."

Woe to those who fill themselves with what is not their own," and "What is a man profited if he shall gain the whole world and lose his own soul?"[70]

Was it without God, or according to the flesh, that I came to Ireland? Who compelled me? "I am bound in the Spirit" not to see any one of my kinsfolk. Is it from me that springs that godly compassion which I exercise towards that nation who once took me captive, and made havoc of the menservants and maidservants of my father's house? . . . for the profit of others I am *a slave in Christ* to a foreign nation for the unspeakable glory of *the eternal life which is in Christ Jesus our Lord.*[71]

It is not any grace in me, but God that "put His earnest care into my heart" that I should be one of his "hunters" or "fishers" whom long ago God foreshowed would come "in the last days."[72]

Wherefore then, where shall Coroticus with his accursed followers, rebels against Christ, where shall they see themselves?—they who distribute damsels as rewards, and that for the sake of a wretched temporal kingdom, which verily passes away in a moment like a cloud of "smoke which is verily dispersed by the wind." "So shall the deceitful wicked perish at the presence of the Lord; but let the righteous feast" in great *constancy with Christ* . . . The words are not mine but of God . . . " He that believeth shall be saved, but he that believeth not shall be damned." God hath spoken.[73]

Was ever evangelism undertaken under a greater sense of urgency? "Constancy with Christ" or damnation were the alternatives.

In Patrick's call to become a missionary to the Irish, the second night's revelation ended with the understandable words, "He who laid down his life for thee, He it is who speaketh in thee." We wish we had a sample of Patrick's evangelistic preaching to supplement our two sources, neither of which was evangelistic in immediate purpose. In the *Hymn in Praise of Pat-*

rick, he is "a man blessed in Christ," "after Christ's example he disregardeth his life."[74] In the *Lorica,* Stanzas II and VII a Christ-piety is deeply expressed. Patrick's witness to his own faith *in Christ* converted thousands.

2. Biblical Inspiration

ix: Impeger

Unwearied he feedeth believers with celestial repasts,
lest those who are seen in Christ's company should faint by the way:
to these he distributeth as loaves, Gospel words;
and he doth offer it to God, as a living and acceptable sacrifice.

xviii: Sacrum

In the Sacred Volume sacred treasure he findeth;
and in the Savior's flesh discerneth Deity:
this treasure he buyeth with his holy and perfect merits
"Israel" is his soul's name, as "seeing God."

It is unnecessary to quote examples of Patrick's constant use of the Scriptures, not only to prove his points, but to express almost everything he wanted to say, as his Latin was largely learned from immersing himself in the Bible. His theology is biblical theology, his ethics are biblical ethics. His missionary approach is biblically directed. He quotes the Bible 54 times in his *Letter to Coroticus* and 135 times in the *Confession,* often unconsciously, quoting from 23 out of the 27 books of the New Testament, 12 books of the Old Testament, and 3 of the Apocrypha. He quoted most from the Psalms, Romans, Acts, Corinthians, and Matthew in that order. Patrick was not a Christian of just one book, as some have claimed, for his theology shows the influence of a pre-Nicean doctrine of the Trinity identified with Victorinus, bishop of Pettau who was martyred in the Diocletian persecution, and he probably knew of Sulpicius Severus' *Life of St. Martin of Tours.* His quotation of the Scripture is not literalistic and argumentatively dogmatic, but natural and with spiritual insight. He does not scurry for proof-texts, but trusts his experiential knowledge of the Trinity as a basis for testing beliefs:

And so it is proper that according to "the rule of faith" in the Trinity I should define doctrine, and make known the gift of God and "everlasting consolation" "without being held back" by danger, and spread everywhere the name of God without fear.[75]

Here the first Scripture reference is Romans 12:3 " . . . to think with sober judgment, each according to the measure of faith which God has assigned to him." His practice seems that commended by Paul in 2 Corinthians 3:3-6:

 . . . written in your hearts, not with ink, but with the Spirit of the living God.[76]
 . . . our sufficiency is from God, who also made us sufficient as ministers of a new covenant; not of the letter but of the Spirit: for the letter killeth but the Spirit giveth life.

3. Practice of Personal Piety

xxiii: Zona

Girded with the Lord's girdle, day and night,
without intermission he prayeth unto God, the Lord;
hereafter to receive the reward of his mighty labour,
as a saint, he shall reign with the Apostles over Israel.

So Patrick's was an eager life of prayer. We saw how his conversion came when he prayed many times each day and night while alone out in every weather, keeping the flocks of his master. When turned away by the shipmaster, he prayed, and was called back. When they were starving in the deserted land, he told them to pray, and a drove of pigs appeared. In prayer, he heard his call. When in captivity again after many years, he prayed and God gave him assurance he would be released in two months.[77] When his ministry was assailed by his seniors, he sought help in prayer and received it.[78] He prayed for perseverance to drink the martyr's cup:

 . . . more than enough do I desire and was ready, that He should grant me to drink of His cup, as He granted to others who also love Him. On which account let it not happen to me from my God that I should ever part with His "people which He purchased" in the ends of the earth. I pray God to give me perseverance, and to vouchsafe

that I bear to Him faithful witness, until my passing hence, for the
sake of my God.[79]

viii: Humilis

Humble in spirit and body through the fear of God,
upon him, for his good deeds, the Lord resteth:
in his righteous flesh he beareth the stigmata of Christ;
and in His cross alone doth glory, staying himself thereon.

xiv: Omnem

All the glory of the world he spurneth for the law divine;
all things compared with His table he counteth as chaff:
nor is he moved by the violent thunderbolt of this world
but rejoiceth in afflictions when he doth suffer for Christ.

With humility, Patrick begins his *Confession*, "I Patrick the
sinner, am the most illiterate and the least of all the faithful."
We have seen how overconscious he was of his rustic lack of
facility in Latin, of his failure to study as a lad, of how he put
off writing because he blushed to lay bare his lack of refined
education.[80] He is astonished that God could use his unworthiness:

... me, moreover, the abhorred of this world, did He inspire beyond others—if such I were—only that with reverence and Godly fear
and unblamably I should faithfully be of service to the nation to
whom the love of Christ conveyed me, and presented me, as long as I
live, if I should be worthy, in fine, that I should with humility and in
truth diligently do them service.[81]

He sums up his accomplishment: "Whatever trifling matter I
did . . . it was the gift of God."[82]

vi: Fidelis

The faithful servant and eminent messenger of God,
he sheweth good men an apostolic example and pattern:
To God's folk he preacheth by acts as well as by words,
that he may stir up by good deeds the man whom he converteth
by speech.

His piety was not esoteric or ingrown. He did not seek eremetic escape and seclusion. He loved the fellowship of the faithful, "his own folk," and everywhere produced the pious communion of the living Church, the Body of Christ:

xv: Pastor

The good and faithful shepherd of the Gospel-flock,
him hath God chosen to guard the people of God:
to feed with divine doctrines his own folk,
for whose sake, after Christ's example, he disregardeth his life.

Patrick set the example of a praying, faithful humble pastor, willing to spend himself unstintingly and sacrifice anything to life itself for his flock. Pouring all of his patrimony into his mission, he became a slave to Christ in a foreign land for the glory of eternal life in Christ Jesus our Lord.[83]

4. Charismatic Ministry

xx: Verus

The true and eminent tiller of the Gospel-field,
his seeds are seen to be the Gospels of Christ:
these, with divine mouth, he soweth in the ears of the prudent,
whose hearts and minds he ploweth up with the Holy Spirit.

People sensed the Presence of God when they were with Patrick, because he was a Holy-Spirit-possessed Christian. We have told of his repeated experiences of Divine Guidance, to escape from Ireland, to prepare to become a missionary to the Irish, to be comforted when assailed. Two chapters from the *Confession* will bear repeating here as they intimately describe his inner experiences of inspiration:

And another night, whether within me or beside me, I cannot tell, God knoweth, in most admirable words which I heard and could not understand, except that at the end of the prayer He thus affirmed, "He who laid down His life for thee, He it is who speaketh in thee." And so I awoke, rejoicing.[84]

And another time I saw Him praying within me, and I was as it were within my body; and I heard One praying over me, that is, over "the inner man"; and there He was praying mightily with groanings. And meanwhile I was astonied, and was marvelling and thinking who it could be that was praying within me; but at the end of the prayer He affirmed that He was the Spirit. And so I awoke, and I remembered how the Apostle saith, "The Spirit helpeth the infirmities of our prayer, for we know not what we should pray for as we ought; but the Spirit Himself maketh intercession for us with groanings which cannot be uttered, which cannot be expressed in words." And again, "The Lord our Advocate maketh intercession for us."[85]

This is the closest Patrick comes to the experience of glossolalia. There is no reference to "speaking with tongues" in all of the Celtic literature I have read, even though the Holy Spirit's inspiration was claimed, and the gifts and fruits of the Spirit were manifest. Though many miracles were claimed in later biographies, they were chiefly of the wonder-working, bizarre sort we must doubt. Patrick claims no miracles except those of guidance, prophecy, and inner conviction, inspiration, regeneration, and strength to do God's will, even as Jesus promised the Counsellor would do. If Patrick healed the sick miraculously, he does not mention it:

Nevertheless I ought not to hide the gift of God which He bestoweth upon us in the land of my captivity; because then I earnestly sought Him, and there I found Him, and He kept me from all iniquities,—this is my belief—"because of His indwelling Spirit" who hath worked in me until this day.[86]

Hence therefore I render unwearied thanks to my God; who kept me faithful in the day of my temptation, so that today I can confidently offer to Him a sacrifice, as a living victim, my soul to Christ my Lord who saved me out of all my troubles so that I may say, "Who am I, O Lord, or what is my calling, that Thou hast worked together with me with such divine power?"[87]

It was the regenerating of people's lives by the power of God's Spirit working through him that was to Patrick the greatest and most important miracle:

Because I am a debtor exceedingly to God, who granted me such great grace that many people through me should be regenerated to God and afterwards confirmed, and that clergy should everywhere be ordained for them for a people newly come to belief, which the Lord took from the ends of the earth, as He had in times past promised through His prophets.[88]

5. A Realistic Trinitarian Bi-Worldly Theology

iii: Constans

Steadfast in the fear of God, and in faith immovable,
upon him, as upon Peter, the Church is built:
and he hath been allotted his apostleship by God;
against him the gates of hell prevail not.

iv: Dominus

The Lord chose him to teach the barbarous
nations and to fish with the nets of doctrine:
from the world to draw believers unto grace,
who should follow the Lord to the eternal abode.

The doctrine which Patrick taught was the early orthodox
Trinitarian theology of the ancient Church which found its first
Scriptural formulation in the Apostolic Benediction. The reader
may wish to turn again to pages 119-122 to observe the theology
of the *Breastplate* Prayer, which, though of later composition, reflects some of Patrick's theological teaching. The first Stanza
and the Conclusion are invocations of the Trinity. Stanza IV is
an invocation of the Father-Creator through the wonders of His
creation. Stanzas II and VII are invocations of the Son-
Redeemer, historically and in his risen, current, omnipresent
availability. Stanza V is an invocation of the Holy Spirit—
Inspirer for all the kinds of inner help our Indwelling God
gives us. This "Threeness" is a "Oneness," meeting in the
Creator, of whom is our salvation. The *Hymn of Sechnall* also
expresses it:

xxii: Ymnos

Hymns, with the Apocalypse and Psalms of God, he singeth
and doth expound the same for the edifying of God's people:
this law he holdeth in the Trinity of the Sacred Name,
and teacheth One Substance in Three Persons.

In the *Confession,* Patrick's Trinitarian creed is carefully defined:

Because there is no other God, nor was there ever any in times past, nor shall there be hereafter, except God the Father unbegotten, without beginning, from whom all things take their beginning, holding all things (i.e. Almighty), as we say, and His Son Jesus Christ, whom we affirm verily to have always existed with the Father before the creation of the world, with the Father after the manner of a spiritual existence, begotten ineffably before the beginning of anything. And 'by Him' were made 'things visible and invisible'. He was made man, and having overcome death, He was received up into heaven to the Father. And 'He gave to Him all power above every name of things in heaven and things in earth and things under the earth; and let every tongue confess to Him that Jesus Christ is Lord and God.' in whom we believe. And we look for His coming soon to be; He the judge of the quick and the dead, 'who will render to every man according to his deeds'. And 'He shed on us abundantly the Holy Ghost', the gift and earnest of immortality, who makes those who believe and obey to become 'children of God' the Father and 'joint heirs with Christ,' whom we confess and adore as one God in the Trinity of the Holy Name.[89]

There may be a reflection of an oft-repeated sermonic teaching to pagan sun-worshipers in this paragraph:

For that sun which we behold, by the command of God rises daily for our sakes; but it will never reign, nor will its splendor endure; but all those who worship it shall—wretched men—come badly to punishment. We, on the other hand, who believe in and worship the true sun, Christ—who will never perish, nor will anyone who "doeth His will"; but He "will abide forever," who reigneth with God the Father Almighty and with the Holy Spirit, before the worlds and now, and for ever and ever. Amen.[90]

Patrick closes his *Letter to Coroticus* with what must have been one of his accustomed benedictions:

Peace—to the Father, and to the Son, and to the Holy Ghost. Amen.

In Patrick's theology, God punishes people with grievous sufferings in this world to redeem them, as He did in sending Patrick into slavery in Ireland. He knows all things before they come to pass.[91] The living Christ is a present, experiential Savior[92] who saves us out of all our troubles.[93] The Holy Spirit strengthens and illumines the conscience, as Patrick was "bound in the Spirit" to stay in Ireland.[94]

The ethical realism of Patrick's theology, as he knows that

he is in a constant battle with the Tempter, is reflected in the *Lorica* or *Breastplate*. It is a prayer meditation obeying Paul's admonition:

Put on the whole armor of God, that you may be able to stand against the wiles of the Devil . . . Stand therefore . . . having put on the breastplate of righteousness . . . (Eph. 6:11, 14)

The *Hymn of Sechnall* has the same theological realism:

xxi: Xtus

Christ hath chosen him for himself to be his vicar on earth;
from twofold slavery he doth set captives free:
very many he hath redeemed from slavery to men;
countless numbers he releaseth from the Devil's thrall.

Patrick confesses his own continuing warfare in the flesh:

I do not trust myself as long as I am in the body of this death, because he (the Devil) is strong who daily endeavors to turn me away from the faith, and from the chastity of unfeigned religion which I have purposed to keep to the end of my life for Christ my Lord. But the flesh, the enemy, is ever dragging us unto death, that is, to enticements to do that which is forbidden. And "I know in part" wherein I have not lived a perfect life as have other believers; but I confess to my Lord, and I do not blush in His Presence, for I lie not:—from the time that I knew Him, from my youth, there grew in me the love of God and the fear of Him; and unto this hour, the Lord being gracious to me, "I have kept the faith."[95]

Finally, Patrick's doctrine stresses the everlasting hope of reward:

v: Electa

He tradeth with Christ's choice Gospel-talents,
which among the Irish tribes he doth require with interest:
hereafter, as a reward for the pains of his labor of voyaging
he shall possess the joy of the heavenly kingdom with Christ.

Patrick teaches that on the Judgment Day we shall be called upon to give an account of every idle word,[96] when none of us shall be able to absent ourselves or hide from the dread sentence. Yet he has a sure hope of his eternal reward and has no fear of martyrdom:

Most surely do I deem that if this should happen to me, I have gained my soul as well as my body, because without any doubt we shall rise on that day in the clear shining of the sun, that is in the glory of Christ Jesus our Redeemer, as "sons of the living God," and "joint heirs with Christ," and "conformed to His image" that will be; since "of Him and through Him and in Him" we shall reign.[97]

Yet the despicable soldiers of Coroticus await a terrible fate:

Whom the devil grievously ensnared. In everlasting punishment they will become slaves of hell along with him; for verily "whosoever committeth sin is a bondservant of sin," and is called "a son of the devil."[98]
Without are dogs and sorcerers and murderers; and liars and false-swearers shall have their part in the lake of everlasting fire.[99]

Patrick comforts himself in the death of his converts:

Thanks be to God it was as baptized believers that ye departed from the world to Paradise. I can see you. Ye have begun to remove to where "there shall be no night nor sorrow nor death any more"; but "ye shall leap like calves loosened from their bands, and ye shall tread down the wicked, and they shall be ashes under your feet."[100]

6. Missionary Dedication

xi: Lumenque

And he is the great, burning Gospel-light of the world; (mundi)
raised upon a candlestick, shining through the whole world (Saeculo);
the King's fortified city, set on a hill;
wherein is much store which the Lord doth possess.

See also above iv *Dominus* p. 164
Patrick considers himself "an Epistle of Christ for salvation to the ends of the earth."[101] When he was called to be a missionary, his home folks offered him many gifts endeavoring to

persuade him to stay, and his elders in the Church also tried to discourage his divinely inspired purpose:

> Whence afterwards came to me that gift so great, so salutary, the knowledge of the love of God, but only that I might part with fatherland and kindred.
> And many gifts were proffered me with weeping and tears. And I displeased them, and also, against my wish, not a few of my elders; but God being my guide, in no way did I consent to yield to them. It was not any grace in me, but God who overcometh in me; and He withstood them all, so that I came to the heathen Irish to preach the Gospel, and to endure insults from unbelievers, so as to "hear the reproach of my going abroad," and endure many persecutions, "even unto bonds," and that I should give up my free condition for the profit of others. And if I should be worthy, I am ready to give even my life for His name's sake unhesitatingly and very gladly, and there I desire to spend it even unto death if the Lord would grant it to me.[102]

Patrick felt that he alone was called to take the Gospel to the far bounds of the West in preparation for the end of this age when Christ would return. All of the great eschatological missionary passages of Scripture he took to heart and applied to his own mission:

> And again, "I have set thee to be a light to the Gentiles, that thou shouldest be for salvation unto the ends of the earth."
> And there I wish to "wait for His promise" who verily never disappoints. As He promises in the Gospel, "They shall come from the east and west, and from the south and from the north, and shall sit down with Abraham and Isaac and Jacob"; as we believe that believers will come from all parts of the world.
> . . . As the Lord in the Gospel forewarns and teaches saying, "Go ye therefore now and teach all nations, baptizing them in the name of the Father and of the Son and of the Holy Ghost, teaching them to observe all things whatsoever I have commanded you, and lo, I am with you alway, even unto the end of the world! And again He saith, "Go ye therefore into all the world, and preach the Gospel to every creature. He that believeth and is baptized shall be saved; but he that believeth not shall be damned!" And again, "This Gospel of the Kingdom shall be preached in all the world, for a witness unto all nations: and then shall the end come."
> . . . And Hosea saith, "I will call them my people; which were not my people and her one that obtained mercy which had not obtained mercy. And it shall come to pass, that in the place where it was said,

'Ye are not my people'; there shall they be called children of the living God."[103]

From Patrick's example and teaching, these passages became the inspiration of the missionary zeal of the Scots-Irish.

7. Steadfast Faithfulness in Personal Morality

ii: Beata

In all things he keepeth Christ's blessed commandments;
his works shine forth brightly among men:
and these follow his holy, wonderful example;
whence also they magnify the Lord, the Father in heaven.

xii: Maximus

For greatest in the kingdom of heaven shall he be called
who fulfilleth in good actions what by sacred words he teacheth:
he excelleth as a good example and pattern to the faithful
and in a pure heart he hath confidence toward God.

We have already quoted under other headings many passages from the *Confession,* illustrating Patrick's steadfast faithfulness in battling the temptations of the Devil, and his assurance that since his conversion as a youth, he had remained faithful in obedience to his Lord by God's grace. He had a most sensitive conscience, with a scrupulosity that made him confess, in preparation for ordination as a deacon, the sin of his youth before his conversion. When he boarded the ship to sail from Ireland, he refused to compromise himself by "sucking the breasts" of the sailors. When they had been starving and the men found honey, and offered some to Patrick, with the information that it had been dedicated to their heathen gods, he would taste none of it for fear of seeming to be idolatrous too.[104] He scrupulously refused to accept any fees for baptisms or ordinations, to prevent the heathen from thinking his ministry was for gain. He even returned little presents women gave him out of gratitude, and their ornaments they had cast upon the altar, despite the fact that he knew it upset them.[105] He could write in his old age:

You know, and God also, in what manner I have lived from my youth with you, in the faith of truth and in sincerity of heart. Moreover, as regards those heathen amongst whom I dwell, I have kept faith with them, and will keep it. God knoweth I have defrauded none of them, nor do I think of doing it, for the sake of God and His Church, lest I should raise persecution against them and all of us, and lest through me the name of the Lord should be blasphemed; for it is written, "Woe to the man through whom the name of the Lord is blasphemed."[106]

The moral corruption prevalent in the Church in Rome which had aroused the ire of Pelagius had not yet penetrated Britain, and it would not have affected Patrick in any event, because he served the Christ he knew in his heart and in the Scriptures. The grace of God he had experienced kept him from being either a Pelagian or a legalist, but his combined love and fear of God also prevented him from any least tendency to moral laxness or anti-nomianism. The ethical heritage he left in Ireland was a background of the strict penitentials of the later monastic period.

This raises the question of whether Patrick was a monk. He was personally celibate:

x: Kastam

For the love of the Lord he keepeth chaste his flesh;
which flesh he hath prepared as a temple of the Holy Spirit;
by whom, in pure activities, it is continually possessed;
and he doth offer it to God as a living and acceptable sacrifice.

This stanza from the *Hymnus In Laudem Sancti Patrici* very evidently comes from a later century in which a celibate priesthood had become the accepted ideal. In Patrick's time, and even later in the time of Gildas, when monasticism was burgeoning, the Scriptural requirement for bishops, "the husband of one wife," was still being quoted. Patrick did not require celibacy of the clerics he trained and ordained for his Irish churches. It was sufficiently difficult to require a biblical chastity, with no divorce and no concubines, in that first generation from heathenism. Yet Jesus had taught that some would elect to live as eunuchs for the sake of the Kingdom of God, and our Lord had remained single in his sacrificial calling. Ninian had established Whithorn with a cenobitic monastic settlement, following the pattern of St. Martin of Tours, and there is some evidence that Patrick welcomed a daughter establishment on Strangford Lough. Still, Patrick was never a member of a monastic foundation. The churches he founded, in every Tuath and Rath he could penetrate, were secular churches, served by secular presbyters, and would later have secular bishops. He repeated the ecclesiastical pattern into which he had been trained in Britain. His presbyters married. Personally, however, he remained voluntarily celibate. The love he expresses for his virgin converts and his vehement anger at their violation under Coroticus evidence no abnormality in his sexuality. As a normal man, he continued to be tempted by the flesh, according to his *Confession*. Yet he was enough influenced by the growing popularity of celibacy in his time to rejoice when some of his Irish converts proved the depth of their devotion by electing to take vows of virginity against the wishes of their families:

Sons and daughters of Scottic chieftans are seen to become monks and virgins for Christ.[107]

In especial there was one blessed lady of Scottic birth, of noble rank, most beautiful, grown up, whom I baptized; and after a few days she came to us for a certain cause. She disclosed to us that she had been warned by an angel of God, and that he counselled her to become a virgin of Christ, and live closer to God. Thanks be to God, six days after, most admirably and eagerly she seized on that which all virgins of God do in like manner; not with the consent of their fathers; but they endure persecution and lying reproaches from their kindred; and nevertheless their number increases more and more— and as for those of our race who are born there, we know not the number of them—besides widows and continent persons.

But the women who are kept in slavery suffer especially; they constantly endure even unto terrors and threats. But the Lord gave grace to many of his handmaidens, for although they are forbidden, they earnestly follow the example (set them).[108]

Obviously, Patrick was not popular with owners of these women slaves whose concubinage rights under Irish law were so denied them!

8. A Positive but Relative Social Ethic, Separating Church Standards from Tribal Law

xiii: Nomen

He proclaimeth boldly to the tribes the Name of the Lord,
to whom he giveth the eternal grace of the laver of salvation:
for their offenses he prayeth daily unto God
for them he offers up to the Lord worthy sacrifices.

xiv: Omnem

All the glory of the world he spurneth for the law divine;
all things, compared with God's table, he counteth as chaff,
nor is he moved by the violent thunderbolt of this world,
but rejoiceth in afflictions when he doth suffer for Christ.

xvii: Regis

As the King's messenger bidding believers to the marriage,
he is adorned, clad in a wedding garment:
in heavenly vessels he draweth out heavenly wine;
offering drink to God's folk in the spiritual cup.

These three stanzas of the *Hymn* reflect the continuing strain a hundred years later between the tribal secular Irish society and the Christian Church. Boldly seeking to convert the people, from chieftain on down, to Christ's salvation, Patrick daily prays for their still sinful ways. He cannot share their world's glory, or wealth, or heroic nobility, or prowess in arms. He presides with a different honor over the Lord's Table, clad in the garments of the spiritual wedding feast of Christ with His bride, the Church, sharing the wine of the Eucharist with all the faithful. Note there was no reservation of the Cup to the clergy! The Lord's Table, where only professing Christians are served, draws the line of separation between the divine colony of heaven and the secular society. At the Lord's Table, Patrick presides as the messenger of the King of Kings.

Behind Patrick, as he came to Ireland, was the sad experience of the establishment of the Christian Church as the state religion of the Roman Empire. Now Rome had fallen. Her culture was still synonymous with civilization in Patrick's home world, but the Church of necessity now had to adjust to the sovereignties of local kinglets, and, as a world-wide institution with other-worldly standards, it had difficulties.

Coming to Ireland, Patrick faced a simple, heroic, barbarous culture fully integrated with an inadequate but traditional Druidic religion. Some of the laws and customs of this culture, such as the pledges under the surety system to keep contracts, and the tribal kinship responsibilities to redress wrongs, and care for the sick, the injured, and the aged were good. Customs of tribal warfare, feuding, raiding of other shores to capture slaves, the ownership of slaves, of divorce and concubinage could not be challenged or changed very soon, except as converted individuals came under the conviction of the love of Christ. There were tribal ceremonies with ancient rituals of the idolatrous religion that had served for centuries. Only at the points of idolatrous worship versus worship of the true God alone for his converts to Christ, and monogamy for his converts, could Patrick make definite issues. He must in each place gain recognition of his converts' rights to exclusive worship of God by securing the grant of a worship site from the kinglet who owned the most land. There he conducted the rituals of his faith, with independent freedom and mutual toleration with continuing paganism. Even when the chieftain and his Druid *brehon* and bard were converted, leading their people to Christ, it would be a long time before most social customs were affected by Christian ideals. We must remember that it would be 1400 years before slavery was abolished in the nominally Christian Western world, including America.

It is in this setting that we must view the protest of Patrick in the *Letter to Coroticus*. Here Patrick does not deny the professing Christian kinglet's right to wage war on the Irish, or even to capture foreign people, or to own and sell slaves. In the secular culture, all this was still fair game. It is because Coroticus and his soldiers have gorged themselves with the blood of innocent Christians that they are to be condemned.[109]

True, there are general Christian principles of ethics by which they might stand accused in their consciences:

"Woe to those who fill themselves with what is not their own," and "What is a man profited, if he gain the whole world and lose his own soul."

It would be tedious to discuss or declare their deeds one by one and to gather from the whole law testimonies concerning such greed. Avarice is a deadly sin; "Thou shalt not covet thy neighbor's goods"; "Thou shalt do no murder; a murderer cannot be with Christ; he that hateth his brother is reckoned as a murderer."[110]

But the much greater sin is the disregard of the special Christian brotherhood:

And again, "He that loveth not his brother abideth in death." How much more guilty is he that hath stained his hands with the blood of the sons of God whom He recently purchased in the ends of the earth through the exhortation of our littleness . . . [111]

So he tells how God has sent him to Ireland, and though he was a free-born Roman citizen of noble rank, he sold his father's decurion status to finance the mission to convert these foreign Irish. Now his own British countrymen have made what he told the Irish about Christian conduct seem false:

And if my own know me not, "a prophet hath no honour in his own country." Perchance we are not of "the one fold," nor have "one God and Father." As He saith, "He that is not with me is against me, and he that gathereth not with me scattereth abroad." It is not meet that "one pulleth down and another buildeth up" . . .

Men look askance at me. What shall I do O Lord? I am exceedingly despised. Lo, around me are thy sheep torn to pieces and spoiled, and that too by the robbers aforesaid, by the orders of Coroticus and his hostile disposition.

Far from the love of God is he who betrays Christians into the hands of Scots and Picts. "Ravening wolves" have swallowed up the flock of the Lord which verily in Ireland was growing up excellently with the greatest care. And the sons and daughters of Scottic chieftans who were monks and virgins of Christ I cannot reckon. They have filled their houses with the spoil of dead Christians . . . Thou handest over "the members of Christ" as it were to a brothel.[112]

So the "body of Christ" meant something sacred to Patrick and different from ordinary people of the secular world. What could not be required of common society in the world outside the Church, even of Christian believers participating in that society, must be required of Christians under God within the Church's brotherhood and sisterhood. Patrick had Scriptural ground for this distinction. In the *Epistle To Philemon*, the Apostle Paul had not denied Philemon's right in this world to continue to own claves, even as a Christian. He sent his runaway slave Onesimus back to him. But "no longer as a slave, but more than a slave, as a beloved brother" now that they both were Christians! Christians living "in the world" are not "of the world." They have one foot on earth and the other in heaven. They are "of" the Body of Christ, the kingdom of God, the colony of God in this world foreshadowing the way life will be when Christ is Lord of all.

As an ordained cleric of Christ's Church, Patrick knew he must be doubly careful to live the Christian Way in Christ fully, and not compromise with the world. We have seen how scrupulously he avoided accepting gifts for his services, and any semblance of fraud. There were civic duties in Irish society, as there were in Roman culture, which an ordained clergyman had to be freed from, such as bearing arms and participating in heathen festivals.

There are extant some canons of Church law attributed to Patrick, Auxilius, and Isernus, assuming that these later bishops had been Patrick's contemporaries, which were most likely promulgated in the early sixth century. Among them is a canon which defines how a cleric may go surety for another man's obligation under a contract, but not exercise all of a secular surety's methods of recourse in case of default. Secular law recognized that a cleric might act as a "*naidm*," i.e., as a surety who stakes his honor on the principal's performance of his obligation. Should the principal then fail of performance, secular law allows the "naidm" who had to pay it, to recover by compelling the principal to pay him, even using physical force to the extent of wounding or slaying the one in default. Canon eight of the collection ascribed to Patrick, Auxilius, and Isernus reads:

> If a cleric has given surety for a pagan in whatsoever amount and it so happen—as well it might—that the pagan by some ruse defaults upon the cleric, the cleric must pay the debt from his own means; should he contend with him in arms let him be reckoned to be outside the church as he deserves.[113]

So a clergyman may act as surety, but not use force of arms to compel recovery. Clergy by their rights and limitations must demonstrate the separation and difference between Church and secular society. The laymen's voluntary endeavor to live The Way In Christ is never so clearly defined.

In the late Roman Empire, the establishment of Christianity gave the Church a responsibility it could not adequately discharge, resulting in the Church accommodating to the secular culture and losing its soul. In Ireland, the Church started by Patrick had to be beholden to rulers for gifts of property for churches, and for protection. But the maintenance of its purity of worship and its allegiance to Christ in the confrontation with paganism guaranteed an early separation of Church and State, and insistence upon liberty by Patrick's Church from dominance by civil rulers. At the same time, there were limits to what the Church could achieve in bringing about social change. There was no utopian idealism insisting that Irish society as a whole conform to Christian standards. That had to be approached realistically and relatively, with a bit of leaven to grow in the lump.

9. A Humble Non-Authoritarian Church Polity

xvi: Quem

Him, for his merits, hath the Savior advanced to be pontiff,
to exhort the clergy in their heavenly warfare;
to them he distributeth heavenly food with clothing
and this is supplied in his divine and sacred discourses.

The term "pontiff" here means "bishop." Rome at the time was in process of elevation to become the see of the supreme pontiff, but the title had earlier been claimed for all bishops. The Council of Sardica in 347 gave Rome the preeminence of appeal over other metropolitan patriarchates, making Rome first among equals (*Primus inter pares*), and Leo I during Patrick's latter ministry in Ireland procured the edict of Valentinian III, ordering all churches to obey the Roman bishop as having the primacy of Peter, but somehow these maneuvers for power were not heeded out on the Western frontier in Britain and Ireland. The older tradition defined in the third century at the Second Council of Carthage: "For neither does any of us set himself up as a bishop of bishops, nor by tyrannical terror does any compel his colleagues to the necessity of obedience; since every bishop, according to the allowance of his liberty and power has his own proper right of judgment," had long been set in British usage.

But note what this office of "pontiff" means in the *Hymn:* "to exhort the clergy"—not "command" or "direct" or "order" the clergy. Patrick's leadership was remembered as persuasive, not compelling. His "divine and sacred discourses" were "food and clothing" for all those whom he had converted, confirmed, baptized, and ordained as deacons and presbyters. We have seen from the evidence of the *Letter* and the *Confession* that there were no other bishops in Ireland, even when he was in semi-retirement toward the close of his ministry. When bishops were later elected and ordained in Ireland for the churches in every Tuath, they were mostly from among the former presbyters Patrick had ordained, and were imbued with his ideals of independence and humble service. They were never diocesan bishops, ruling a given territory. Some, like Patrick, were ordained to be missionary bishops with no fixed sees. Such Irish bishops later became the plague of the Continental hierarchy.

That the early Irish bishops never became covetous of ecclesiastical power is proved by the generally acknowledged fact that they did not resist the growth of the power of the abbots in the seventh century. They were only too willing to relinquish all temporal powers in the Irish Church to the heads of the monasteries and their larger "paruchiae" orders until finally Leinster and Armagh took counter action, as we shall see. Bishops continued to serve secular Tuath churches, or often served as humble monks under abbots in monasteries. They were the charismatic bearers of the grace imparted in ordination, and confirmed the election of other bishops together in council, and dedicated churches. So they were held in honor, but usually they did not care to rule. Later, some abbots became bishops, and vice-versa. Only after Armagh in the seventh century encouraged the Romanist party for the elevation of its own abbot-bishop to metropolitan-archbishop status do we begin to observe the spiritual decline that always follows the corrupting influence of power.[114]

10. Ecumenical Unity In Christ's Spirit

xix: Testis

The Lord's faithful witness in the Catholic law,
his words are seasoned with the divine oracles:
lest human flesh decay, and of worms be eaten;
but with heavenly savour be salted as a sacrifice.

Patrick's teaching was that of the Catholic or Universal Church of Jesus Christ. His Gospel was meant for all mankind everywhere:

We shall exalt and praise His wondrous works before every nation which is under the whole heaven.[115]

So that I might imitate in some degree those to whom the Lord long ago foretold, when forshewing that the Gospel would be for a witness unto all the nations before the end of the world.[116]

His argument with Coroticus is that, in murdering Irish Christians and selling them into slavery, the King of Dumbarton and his soldiers had denied the ecumenical faith. Patrick says he is an exile in Ireland for the love of God, an ambassador there for Christ his God,[117] called and predestined to preach the Gospel "even unto the ends of the earth."[118] If "we are all members of Christ's body," then "if one member suffer, let all the members suffer with it." When Coroticus and his soldiers reject the rights of Christians from Ireland, they cut themselves off from God. With telling sarcasm, he says, "Perchance we are not of the one fold, nor have one God and Father."[119]

So Christians are of one universal family in the love of God in Christ, regardless of race or nationality or where they live on earth.

It was essential for Patrick that the spiritual unity of the Church be maintained, so he was deeply disturbed when his synod in Britian, which had ordained him and supported his mission for years, called his character and ministry into question. If they cut him off, it would not destroy the work God had done through him in Ireland, but it would damage the relationship between the British and Irish churches which needed to continue in the unity of the Spirit and the bonds of peace. So his *Confession* was written primarily as an ecumenical endeavor. The "Seniors" who had come to Ireland to report the synod action and to investigate had not been able to harm his "laborious episcopate":

But the Lord graciously spared the stranger and sojourner for His name's sake; and He helped me exceedingly when I was thus trampled on so that I did not come badly into disgrace and reproach. I pray God that it may not be held to their charge as sin.[120]

In that spirit, Patrick pled to be understood by his brethren and kinsfolk at home, that ecumenical unity might be preserved.

It was not the only time in Church history that a Church council has erred. Judging our brother man is a risky business, whether done by individuals or by an ecclesiastical establishment. When it is done administratively by those with higher ecclesiastical power, it can be even more abused. Forced ecclesiastical unity for purposes of efficient administration ultimately is abused and becomes divisive. The true unity of the Church is in the hearts of the people who are "one in the Spirit, one in the Lord."

Patrick was in all respects loyal to The Way In Christ. All ten of these essential characteristics of The Way he brought to Ireland were rooted and grounded in the life and teaching of Jesus portrayed in the New Testament, as we have seen in Chapter II. Also remarkable in Patrick's writings is the complete absence of later, non-biblical superstitions. There is no mariolotry, no praying to saints or apostles as intermediaries, no reference to purgatory, no veneration of relics, no use of incredible miracle tales, no setting up of shrines in commemoration of special miraculous events, no special holy places. His was a truly spiritual faith, so real and direct in access to the living Christ, the Holy Spirit in prayer, so one with God and with others in Christ, that none of the later substitutes for these basic spiritual realities were wanted.

THE IRISH CHURCH AFTER PATRICK

Anyone who has observed pioneer work on the mission field can imagine what had to happen after Patrick's death in

461. So long as he lived, his church went on as he had established it. His presbyters and deacons, loyal in Christian love to Patrick, carried on under his charismatic leadership even though he was semi-retired in Saul. If difficulties and disputes arose, they could take their problems to him, and he itinerated and ordained as long as he could. Yet the time came when the growing churches needed more and stronger local leadership. After Patrick's death, an embassage of bishops from Britain came, and found that Patrick had anticipated the need in his last will and testament:

Riagail Padruic

Here is what the testament of Patrick contains for the souls of the men of Ireland: Every Tuath should have a chief Bishop (Prim-escop) to ordain its clergy, to consecrate its churches, to give direction to its chiefs and nobles, and to sanctify and bless the children after baptism. For the Tuath and territory which have no bishops to discharge these functions see the law of their faith and belief perish.

Yet in contrast to this, a century or more later, the Irish Church which sent forth the missionaries to convert the Picts of Scotland, the Anglo-Saxons of England, and the barbarians ruling the Continent after the fall of the Roman Empire, in the late sixth, seventh, and eighth centuries, was largely monastic, ruled by abbots. Somehow, in the two centuries after Patrick's death, the monastic movement gained a great ascendancy in Ireland, as it did also in Wales.

Two ancient sources help us to measure this growth. The first is by an unknown author of the ninth century who disliked the development, and claims the gradually increasing asceticism brought on a decline of faith. He divides the reigns from 428 to 666 into three periods: 428 to 544; 544 to 599; and 599 to 666, each having four reigns, and entitles his work *The Catalogue of the Saints of Ireland according to their Diverse Periods*. In the first period of Patrick and immediately thereafter, there were all bishops in leadership, 350 of them, non-ascetic, "They disdained not the service of women," and they were most holy. The second period had few bishops and 300 presbyters ruling as abbots, and refused the service of women, separating them from the monasteries. They were holy of holies. The third period was characterized by "holy presbyters and few bishops, in number 100, who dwelt in desert places," i.e., in extreme asceticism, these he called just "holy." The descent in spirituality he compares to the waning in brilliance from the sun to the pale moon, then to the *aurora borealis*. This is an artificial and biased appraisal, as no historical development was ever so cut and dried, and hermit monasticism never did so completely displace the monasteries. There is witness in this source to a tolerance of different worship rituals and different rules of conduct. Kathleen Hughes, who made a detailed study of Irish law, says that sixth-century legislation reveals some monasticism in Ireland, analyzing the Annals of Ireland to show:

Before 549, of 28 Irish clerics:	25 bishops,	1 abbot
550—600, of 33 Irish clerics:	13 bishops,	17 abbots
601—664, of 97 Irish clerics:	24 bishops,	48 abbots[121]

Secular churches with bishops continued to exist with relatively shrinking numbers and importance. In the late sixth and seventh centuries, abbots were preponderant.

A number of causes may be discerned for this growth in ascetic monasticism. Its roots were not primarily Christian, but more from the Orient and from Neo-Platonic Greek philosophy, with its emphasis upon the mind and denigration of the flesh. The Christian retreat to the desert began in Egypt in the late third century, as soon as the Church in the East began to be popular among the aristocracy, and to let down its moral stringency. The more earnest, devoted Christians, wanting to sacrifice everything for Christ, seemingly freed from the threat of martyrdom, withdrew from the world and its temptations, crucifying the flesh and the lusts thereof. The movement spread westward, popularized by Sulpicius Severus' *Life of St. Martin of Tours*. The intense devotion to Christ taught by Patrick found abundant expression for a few generations in overcoming paganism and winning Ireland to Christ. Then with much encouragement from Wales, where the movement slightly preceded the Irish development, Irish desire to express complete surrender and devotion to Christ found more and more satisfaction in the monastic movement. Another cause was the heroic alternative it offered young men to the former popularity of heroism in battle and training for fighting with broadswords. As this fighting became less popular, young men could honorably take up the spiritual warfare of the monastery with its strenuous self-discipline and sacrifice. The popular *Lorica* or *Breastplate* prayer is evidence of the strength of this motif.

Another cause of growing monasteries in Ireland was the demand for Christian schools to replace the training of the former schools of the Druids and bards. Much Druid training was incorporated into the schooling for young men offered by a number of monasteries. Some scholars from the Continent were driven by the barbarian invasions to join in the teaching. We read of huge schools of 4,000 monks at Bangor, 3,000 at Clonmacnois, with many coming from Britain and the Continent, so that there was a Saxon Quarter for foreign students at Armagh, using a third of the city area. Aldhelm reports that English students went to Ireland in flocks, swarming to Irish schools like bees gathering honey.[122] Bede says:

> At this period there were many English nobles and lesser folk in Ireland who had left their own land during the episcopates of Bishop Finan and Colman, either to pursue religious studies or to lead a life of stricter discipline. Some of these soon devoted themselves to the monastic life, while others preferred to travel, studying under various teachers in turn. The Scots welcomed them all kindly, and without asking for any payment, provided them with daily food, books and instruction.[123]

This may be a bit exaggerated!

Another cause of monastic growth was socioeconomic. Monasteries learned to attract huge endowments of land by offering a peculiar inducement to deeply religious aristocratic families. They could give land to found a monastery without alienating it from their kinship holding and control, if the whole family turned to the religious life with the founding saint, with the right to continue to furnish abbots from their kinship group. This was the "coarb right." In Wales, the nephew of Saint Illtyd claimed the right to succeed his uncle as abbot at Llanilltyd. At Iona, Columba was succeeded by his cousin Bathene, and until the death of the ninth abbot, Adomnan in 704, all but one were descendants of Columba's great-grandfather, Conall Gulban. By the eighth century, not all abbots of Irish monastic settlements were celibate, and the abbatical succession could pass directly from father to son.[124] While monasticism was so courting lay interest and donations, the tribal bishops were discouraging lay influence and authority, insisting that they must consecrate churches before they could be used for worship, and enacting canons stating that anyone who looks to a layman for permission to build a church shall be "alienus," an outsider. Yet there was no opposition from tribal bishops to the establishing of several monasteries by outstanding monastic leaders such as Columba, Ciaran, and Brigit, and continuing to rule them as monastic *paruchiae* (larger parishes). They ordained humble monk-bishops who served in these monasteries under abbots.

Yet beyond all of these causes of growing monasticism was the tremendous Christian dedication of the monks and nuns during this flowering period, with their ability through charismatic inspiration, strenuous discipline, and worthy scholarship to attract the idealistic youth of Ireland and the whole of Western Europe. They continued the true spiritual heritage left by Patrick for over 200 years. All ten of the essential characteristics of Jesus' Way, which we discerned in Patrick's witness, could be expressed in monastic life, even to a positive though detached social ethic, as we shall see in the life of Columba.

Meanwhile, the monastic organization offered a peculiarly useful vehicle for projecting foreign missions. Small groups of thirteen monks, trained in survival and self-sufficiency, including a smith, a carpenter-builder, some farmers, fishermen, and herdsmen to support the cleric scholars, could travel anywhere in the world and shortly be economically independent, with none of the problems of home-base support Patrick had known.

We should like more real knowledge of the lives of the saints in sixth-century Ireland. Even John Ryan's official Roman Catholic history, *Irish Monasticism, Origins and Early Development* (1972) affords little real biographical information for most of them, for the authors of the ninth-century "Lives" were mostly interested in miracle stories. If the reader wishes to gain a more living glimpse of this important period, the reading of a modern historical novel of the life of Columba, *Isle of Glory* by the Scottish novelist Jane Oliver is warmly recommended.[125]

Candida Casa at Whithorn in Galloway, founded by Ninian a century earlier, was rejuvenated in the late fifth century as a training school for the monastic life. Irish tradition calls it Rosnat, or "The Great Monastery." There Enda of Aran, Tigernach of Cluain Eois, Eogan of Ars Sratha, Finnian of Moville, and Coirpre of Cuil Raithin are said to have trained.[126]

The first, Enda of Aran, started a settlement on the largest of the Aran Islands with an astonishingly severe rule of discipline, including complete seclusion. He alone of the Candida Casa fathers remained a presbyter, the others eventually becoming bishop-abbots.

Finnian of Clonard received his training under Gildas the Wise of Wales, whose contempt for the low performance of most of the secular clergy in Britain we have previously noted. Gildas's exaltation of the monastic life probably was the inspiration of Finnian's leadership in the amazing extension of monastic institutions in Ireland in the sixth century.[127] At Clonard in Meath, disciples flocked in large numbers to group themselves around Finnian's cell to learn from the great saint-teacher. His twelve leading disciples were called "The Twelve Apostles of Ireland": Ciaran of Saigher, Ciaran of Clonmacnois, Columba of Iona, Derry and Durrow, Brendan of Clonfert, the famous navigator, Brendan of Birr, Colman of Tir-da-glas, Molaisse of Daiminis, Cainech (Kenneth) of Achad Bo, Ruadan of Lothra, Mobi of Glas Noiden, Senell of Cluain Inis, and Nannid of Inis Maige Sam.

There were other great sixth-century monastic founders, chief among them Comgall of Bangor, whose monastery, founded in 588, was reputedly the largest and the greatest supplier of Irish missionaries to the Continent. Another was Kevin, who was trained by Saint Petrock near Dublin. Fleeing the advances of an amorous girl, he fled to beautiful Glendalough in County Wicklow. There his purpose to live as a hermit was soon interrupted by hosts of young monastic admirers, and his monastery, set between the upper and lower lakes, became a lasting institution, while his grotto, "Saint Kevin's Bed" by the upper lake where he would retire for solitude with God, is still a place of pilgrimage.

Women prominent in Irish monasticism were Saint Ita with her nunnery at Kileedy, with its school for boys where Brendan of Clonfert was a pupil; Brigid of Kildare, a great leader in the Irish Church of her time, who modeled her double monastery with anchorite monks in an adjacent site on what she saw at Candida Casa; and Moninne of Killeavey, who is said to have received the veil of virginity from Patrick's own hand.

Monastic life in Ireland in the sixth century was severe and strictly disciplined. The Penitential Of Finnian reflects a general increase in ascetic rigor from the earlier canons ascribed to Patrick, Auxilius, and Iserninus. Those of Columbanus are similarly severe. Monks could not leave the monastery without the abbot's sanction. They gave him implicit obedience without murmuring. They ate little, slept little, worked hard, studied hard, and prayed long hours. By their austerities, studies, and prayers, they hoped to win eternal bliss, and to commend a better life to the Irish people.

Yet it would be an unbalanced picture if we stressed only austerity. Many abbots were less strict than Finnian of Moville and Columbanus. Worship in the chapel with its singing and chanting was a time of rejoicing in the beauty of holiness several times each day. The Celtic love of nature found greater expression in celebrating its beauty as the artistry of the Creator. *The St. Gall Priscian Manuscript,* copied in Ireland and later taken to the Continent, has this verse written by a happy monk on its margin:

> A hedge of trees surrounds me;
> a blackbird's lay sings to me—
> praise which I will not hide.
> Above my booklet, the lined one,
> the trilling of the bird sings to me;
> In the grey mantle the cuckoo's beautiful chant
> sings to me from the tops of the bushes:
> May the Lord protect me from doom!
> I write well under the greenwood.

Celtic artistry found beautiful expression in the gloriously illuminated manuscripts of the Scriptures with their intricately designed, colored initial letters and paintings of biblical characters, as may be seen in the *Book of Kells* in the Library of Trinity College, Dublin, all labor of love done to the glory of God. Another major artistic legacy are the beautifully carved standing crosses of stone, once used as a focal point of worship before there was any church building, then kept as an outdoor location for evangelistic preaching, by the market place. They were never crucifixes, the superimposed circle symbolizing the eternal life in the Risen Christ with victory over the Evil One, while the carved illustrations of biblical stories were visual aids to preaching, as the illiterate crowds came to market.

THE DECLINE OF FAITH IN IRELAND

The faith Ireland shared abroad, she shortly lost at home. Eventually, the very popularity and success of monasticism helped cause the decay and spiritual decline. Monastic *paruchiae* became wealthy through the gifts of the faithful, and abbots became rich and powerful. Farmers on monastic lands might be called "monach" without taking vows of celibacy and poverty. Abbots became hereditary feudal lords. The loss of true spirituality may be measured in the quality of the religion in the biographies of the saints, who were honored and used superstitiously, celebrated for their traditional miracles, and no longer followed in their true sainthood. So the legendary lives of Patrick actually defame his character, and the *Life of Columba* by Adomnan, written a century after his death makes him a plaster-saint miracle worker with no missionary zeal.

The power of the monastic paruchiae finally stirred the envy of some of the bishops into building paruchiae of their own, combining many former Tuath churches, creating archbishoprics in Kildare and Armagh. Conforming to the power of Rome became a useful tool toward this end, for Rome wanted to rule through archbishops. The *Book of Armagh* is evidence of the collaboration of that community with the Romanist party, its two *Lives of Patrick* by Muirchu and Tirechan, written just before 700, and the *Book of the Angel* written shortly after 800, revealing the machination. *The Book of the Angel* defines the parish area immediately subject to the abbot-bishop of Armagh, yet also claims for Patrick and his assumed Armagh successors a much wider judicial and financial control. Tirechan makes specific the churches granted to Patrick and therefore subject to Armagh over the whole North of Ireland, and a few in the Southern half. So the Bishop of Armagh was trying to assert overlordship of a widespread paruchia. In the *Additions to Tirechan* Aed, bishop of Sletty in the South, accepts Segene, bishop of Armagh as his overlord because Armagh is willing to conform to the Roman date of Easter. Muirchu's *Life of Patrick* was written by a disciple of Bishop Aed at his request in the campaign to persuade the North of Ireland to become Roman in its polity, with Armagh as the center. So the made-up story of Patrick's triumph over King Laoghaire with his Easter fire at Slane, transferring the ancient pagan Mayday fire observance of the Feast of Beltane to Easter around the Spring Solstice and having Patrick assert authority over the High King was propaganda for Armagh. Embarrassed by Patrick's retirement in County Down, and his burial there, the Armagh lawyers needed to have grounds on which to assert Patrick's authority for their grasp of widespread power. The Roman cause would be furthered by having Patrick represent authority for a "doctrine brought from a long distance across the seas," regarding an observance at Easter time. Also Patrick needed to be sent by Rome! So all of these documents in the *Book of Armagh* were helps toward the elevation of Armagh to a Roman archepiscopal see.

The Armagh lawyers were successful, and the North of Ireland, except for the Paruchia Columbae, conformed to the Roman date of Easter shortly before Adomnan's death in 704. Armagh acquired relics from the city of Rome of "Peter and Paul, Stephen, Lawrence et cetera," and in *The Book of the Angel* claimed appellate authority immediately under Rome in the judgment of disputes. Disputes which cannot be settled at home must be referred "to the apostolic see, that is to the chair of the apostle Peter which has authority in the city of Rome." But to Armagh as the highest Irish court of appeal:

Whatever difficult cause shall arise, one unknown to all the judges of the tribes of the Irish, it shall rightly be referred to the cathedra of the Irish archbishop, i.e. Patrick, and to the examination of that bishop.[128]

The result of this grasping for power was the loss of the soul of the Irish Church. Abbots at the head of the monastic paruchiae and abbot-archbishops of the paruchiae of Kildare and Armagh became worldly, powerful officials who wanted men of their kind under them in the administration and leadership of the monasteries and churches. Those who pleased the authorities were preferred and charismatic leadership was lost. Superstitious practices were substituted. Moral standards sagged. Abbots were often not celibate and their sons inherited the abbacies, sometimes ruling more than one monastic house. When there were outbreaks of disease or drought or famine, they would make a circuit with relics to ward off the evils. Otherwise, the circuit of the relics meant the imposition of the "cana," the tribute collected for the promulgation of the saints' "law."

To compare the faith of the ninth century with that of the fifth or sixth, we may quote a Lorica prayer dated 800-850. A certain Colman Moccu Cluasaig, lector of Cork, is said to have composed it for protection against the yellow plague:

God's blessing lead us, help us. May Mary's Son cover us!
May we be under His safeguard tonight.
John the Baptist we invoke,
May he be a safeguard to us, a protection!
May Jesus with His Apostles be for me help against danger;
May Mary and Joseph herd us, and the spirit of Stephen;
From every strait may the commemoration of Ignatius' name now
        release us;
May every martyr, every hermit, every saint that has been in chastity,
Be a shield to us for our protection,
Be a dart from us against the devils!

Compare this with the Breastplate ascribed to Patrick 300 years earlier.

Rival monasteries became involved in physical violence. In 760, there was a pitched battle between the households of Clonmacnois and Birr, followed in 764 by a major battle between Clonmacnois and Durrow, won by Clonmacnois when 200 men of the familia of Durrow were slain. The monasteries involved themselves in secular wars also. In a battle at Emain Macha near Armagh in 759, the king of Ulster was victorious over the Southern Ui Neill, and the Annals of Tigernach report believably that "the battle was at the will of Airechtach priest of Armagh through discord with abbot Fer-da-chrich." Synods ceased to be held to settle disputes, the abbots looking more to kings for their support.

In reaction to this corruption, many retreated to the hermit's life, the number of anchorites increasing in the eighth and ninth centuries. Also, in the late eighth century, there was an ascetic revival with a new reforming order calling themselves the "Celi De," "Vassals of God," whose successors in Scotland were known as the "Culdees." The churches popularly supported the reformers, but there was never a sufficient recovery of spiritual and moral soundness, for the power structure was never changed. The power of prelacy and a wealthy Church offer too many manipulative handles to the Evil One. When the Church ignores the warning of her Lord about lording it over and authority, sincere spiritual endeavors of many faithful souls in humble devotion cannot prevail. An ill-prepared Irish Church came under the scourge of the Vikings.

Still, some of Patrick's spirit survived. The following prayer poem from the tenth or eleventh century has been translated into one of the splendid hymns which is still inspiring for twentieth-century congregations:

May Thou be my vision
O God of my heart;
No one else is anything
But the King of the seven heavens.

May Thou be my meditation
By day and by night;
May it be Thou I see
Ever in my sleep.

May Thou be my speech,
May Thou be my understanding;
May Thou be to me,
May I be to Thee.

May Thou be my Father
May I be Thy son;
May Thou be mine,
May I be Thine.

May Thou be my battle-shield,
May Thou be my sword;
May Thou be my honour,
May Thou be my joy.

May Thou be my protection,
May Thou be my fortress;
May it be Thou who will raise me,
To the assembly of the angels.

May Thou be every good,
To my body, to my soul;
May Thou be my kingdom
In heaven and on earth.

May Thou alone
Be the special love of my heart;
May it be no one else
But the High King of Heaven.[129]

Map: Britain—Sixth to Eighth Centuries

Chapter V

THE WAY IN SCOTLAND: IONA

Prayer of Columba

Almighty Father, Son and Holy Ghost,
Eternal, ever-blessed gracious God,
To me, the least of saints, to me, allow
That I may keep a door in Paradise;
The furthest door, the darkest coldest door,
The door that is least used, the stiffest door,
If so it be but in thine house, O God!
Even afar and hear Thy Voice, O God!
And know that I am with Thee—
Thee, O God!

After deep probings into the long historical backgrounds, we now return to where our quest began: to the Holy Isle which for a century and a half made a spirited bid to dispute with Rome for the leadership of the West in the Christian Church.

Iona was not the first missionary center in the northern part of Britain which eventually became Scotland. We have seen how Ninian, a generation before Patrick, built his stone church and monastery at Whithorn, Candida Casa, the center from which he evangelized the Britons of Galloway and Strathclyde, and the Southern Picts to the east and north as far as the Grampians. From the *Letter to Coroticus,* who was king of Strathclyde, we also learned that the Christianity Ninian planted had suffered some relapse. *The Pictish Chronicle,* a twelfth century document, says that Nechtan Morbet, king of the Southern

Picts from 457 to 481, offered up his capital, Abernethy, to God and to Saint Brigit of Ireland in the presence of Darlugdach, the abbess of Kildare, who was then in exile from her country. Thus, there was Irish mission work in that land shortly after the time of Patrick. Saint Cadoc of Wales, after founding the monastery at Llancarven, built a monastery of stone among the Southern Picts "on this side of Mons Bannauc" (the Peaked Hill Range), probably at Cambuslang.[1] Better known was Saint Kentigern (Saint Mungo) who reawakened the church in Strathclyde, and serving his "beloved family" there became the founder of the City of Glasgow. Yet all of these earlier lights were outshone by the monastic mission from Northern Ireland to the Kingdom of Dalriada and the Northern Picts in the latter half of the sixth century. This was primarily because of the Christian personality and faith of its leader, Columba, who, after Patrick, was the outstanding representative of Celtic Christianity.

Disappointingly, we do not have any writings of Columba comparable to Patrick's *Confession* and *Letter*: only a few poems and prayers of no certain authorship ascribed to him. We do have a biography: Adomnan's *Life of Columba,* written by his Coarb kinsman, the ninth Abbot of Iona less than a century after Columba's death, around 690. Sadly, it represents the benighted hagiography of the faith's decline only somewhat less pitifully than Muirchu's and Tirechan's lives of Patrick of the same period. This is not to say that it is poorly written, for Adomnan was a leading scholar of his period, a great storyteller, and a masterful stylist of beautiful, simple Latin. His *Life of Columba* is a classic in hagiography. It follows the literary model of the lives of saints from continental sources. This model had begun in commemorative sermons preached on saints' days, such as that preached by Hilary of Arles in memory of Saint Honoratus, founder of the island monastery of Lérins in Southern Gaul. Adomnan's biography's three books are composed almost entirely of wonder stories: I Prophecies, II Miracles of Power, III Visions of Angels. These tales are in no chronological sequence, and tell very little of the actual life and work of Columba. There is a brief preface, containing a few biographical facts, and a touching description of Columba's last day and death toward the close, from which some facts about life on Iona may be gleaned. The usual purpose of writing the life of a saint was to prove his sanctity by telling of the miraculous occurrences with which God rewarded his merit. Adomnan claims strict veracity:

> Let not anyone suppose that I will write concerning this so memorable man either falshood or things that might be doubtful or unsure: but let him understand that I shall relate what has come to my knowledge through the tradition passed on by our predecessors, and by trustworthy men who knew the facts; and that I shall set it down unequivocally, and either from among those things that we have been able to find put in writing before our time, or else from among those things that we have learned after diligent inquiry by hearing from the lips of certain informed and trustworthy aged men who related them without any hesitation.[2]

Adomnan had some written tales by Cummeme, his second predecessor in the abbacy, who had succeeded Columba sixty years after his death, but Cummeme also was not a direct witness, and may also have been similarly uncritical in his acceptance of superstitious tales. Although Bede says Columba's life and sayings were said to have been recorded by his disciples,[3] Adomnan claims such a source for only one story, a vision on the night of Columba's death. Apparently, Adomnan believed any story the monks told. There are miracle tales to match most of the Old and New Testament wonders. Columba got water from a rock to baptize a baby, raised the dead like Elishah, multiplied the cows of his friends instead of loaves and fishes, told his monks to cast their net into the river once more to catch a huge salmon, turned water into wine, healed a woman far away in Ireland, and made winds blow contrary or favorably for ships many miles away, according to his will. That he had charismatic gifts of prophecy and healing we can believe, but here there are no limits!

A.O. and M.O. Anderson, in the Introduction to their 1961 Edition of *Adomnan's Life of Columba,* claim that Adomnan's value is less for the history of Columba than for Adomnan's own ideas and the circumstances of his time. He had too little genuine tradition to copy, and filled in with passages derived from well-known books at hand, namely the *Dialogues of Gregory I*; Evagrius's Latin translation of Athanasius's *Life of Anthony*; Sulpicius Severus's *Life of Martin, Epistles,* and *Dialogues*; Constantius's *Life of Germanus* and *The Actus Silvestri.* He further improvised from his knowledge of conditions in his own time.[4] In his description of the last moments of Columba's life, claimed to be learned from those present, the words are partly derived from Evagrius's *Life of Anthony*.[5] Especially disappointing is the discovery that Adomnan's double account of the Saint's own description of his prophetic consciousness is likewise derived. In one account, Lugbe mocu-Blai begs to know how Columba received his prophetic knowledge of things not present to him. Columba, after extracting a promise that the secret will be kept, answers:

There are some, although few indeed, on whom divine favour has bestowed the gift of contemplating, clearly and very distinctly, with scope of mind miraculously enlarged in one and the same moment, as though under one ray of the sun, even the whole circle of the whole earth, with the ocean and sky about it.[6]

The other account is in Adomnan's Introduction. Columba, questioned by a few brothers who were not sworn to secrecy, "admitted . . . in some speculations made with divine favour the scope of his mind was miraculously enlarged and he saw plainly, and contemplated, even the whole world as it were caught up in one ray of the sun."[7] Both replies, the second more accurately, were copied from the *Dialogues of Pope Gregory I* whose papacy (590-604) bracketed Columba's death.[8] Most damaging to its usefulness as an accurate reflection of Columba's life and ministry is the fact that Adomnan wrote the *Life of Columba* between 688 and 692, just when, as a convert to the Romani and a traitor to the liberty of the Celtic Church, he was attempting to bring the Columban paruchiae into conformity with Northumbria, Canterbury, and Rome.

Adomnan tells of a journey " . . . in England when we visited our friend King Aldfrith, while the pestilence still continued and devastated many villages on all sides." This was the plague of 686, described in the anonymous *Life of Abbot Ceolfrid* (or Ceolfrith) as sweeping away all the choir monks at Jarrow but the abbot and one boy he was rearing. Almost certainly, the lad was Bede, who was fifteen at the time.[9] Ceolfrid is the source of the information that, in 686, Adomnan went to Northumbria as an ambassador of Ireland to Aldfrith, to conduct sixty Irish captives, taken by Ecgfrith in 684 from Mag-Breg, back to Ireland. Two years later, he visited Northumbria again, went to see Ceolfrid's monastery of Wearmouth and Jarrow, and after seeing the relationship of the bishop to the king of Northumbria, and the courtly honor accorded the bishop, and having been instructed regarding their customs and practices regarding the date of Easter and the tonsure of the monks, he was persuaded.[10]

Returning to his monks on Iona, though he was their abbot, Adomnan failed to convince them to convert and forsake their Celtic traditions. So he left them for Ireland in 692, where he had more success persuading Irish monks not under the dominion of Iona. Southern Irish monks had already accepted the Roman date of Easter years before. Now he joined with the Romani party recently embraced by Armagh. He could not celebrate Easter with his own monks, and remained away from Iona most of twelve years, possibly founding another work on the mainland at Forglen in Banffshire. Thence, he returned to Ireland in 697, to have adopted at Birr some laws in defense of women and children which Columba had proposed a century earlier.[11] In the last year of his life, he made one more attempt, after Easter, to persuade his monks, and failing, died on Iona in 704.[12] Iona held out against the change until 716.

From all this, we are persuaded that Adomnan had little leadership ability, as he could not persuade his own monks. It was, therefore, a big moment for him when the Irish government sent him on an official mission to Northumbria and he could claim King Aldfrith as his friend. Such a man would be impressed with the advantages in terms of dignity of office and the glory of human acclaim to be gained from a closer link of Church and Crown. Date of Easter and tonsure of monks seemed small differences to stand in the way of such advantages. As Bede says:

. . . he observed the rites of the Church canonically performed. He was earnestly advised by many who were more learned than himself not to presume to act contrary to the universal customs of the Church, whether in keeping of Easter or in any other observances, seeing that his following was very small and situated in a remote corner of the world.

Adomnan returned to Iona and set up a bishop's chair in his monastery. In the years before he departed for Ireland, he wrote his *Life of Columba*. Had this exercise something to do with his purpose to persuade the brethren? Might the writing of the biography of their great founder with the cooperation of the monks help to raise his stature in their eyes, and perhaps convince them that he did treasure their traditions, and was not being a traitor in advocating submission to Rome as the price of unity and peace? If that was his purpose, evidences of the current conflict must not be too obvious in the biography, though there might be subtle slants and emphases in the way he depicted Columba favorable to his own conceptions. So, while we must use Adomnan's *Life* along with all other ancient references and traditions in our attempt to understand Columba, we may be on our guard to discount his over-adulation, superstitions, and bias.

THE LIFE OF COLUMBA

There is a ruined prehistoric cairn in a meadow near Gartan Lough in northern Donegal in Ulster, which is famous in local legend as the birthplace of Columba. The Lough lies in a deeply wooded glen amid the bare hills, the "thousand hills" among which lived the Northern Ui Neill from whom the O'Donnells descended. Here on December 7, 521, Aethne, the wife of Fedilmidh, bore a son.[13] Fedilmidh was the son of Fergus, son of Conall Gulban, son of Niall of the Nine Hostages, the famous high king of Northern Ireland. This is the same king who conducted a heavy raid on Britain around A.D. 400, possibly the same raid in which Patrick was captured. Aethne, also of royal descent, had an ancestor, Cathair Mór, king of Leinster. So the child was a potential heir to the kingship of Tara, according to the law of Irish succession. His royal blood counted in his later life amid that aristocratic society sensitive to human breeding, even though he forsook the possible royal office for humble service to Christ in the Church. Apparently, such high selectivity is also used by the Creator, whose Son was "of the house and lineage of David."

Also significantly, his parents were devoted Christians. His original name was said to have been "Crimthann" (a fox), but his parents destined him for the priesthood, and he was christened Colum (Latin Columba, "dove") for the Holy Spirit descended "sicut columbam" (Matt. 3:16). Tradition says his mother Aethne had a vision of an angel who promised her son would lead numberless souls to heaven. So when they gave him in fosterage, as was the custom among families of high rank, it was to Cruithnechan, the priest who baptized him, and who therefore gave him the elements of Christian teaching. It is said that his affectionate name, Columcille "Colum of the Church" was given him at this early time by his boyhood companions, who noticed his frequent emergence from the little church where he would go to read the Psalms. While he was still quite young, he chose the monastic life, and studied with Finnian (Finbar) at Moville Abbey. This abbey was founded in 540 at what is now Newtownards, at the head of Strangford Lough, east of Belfast. Finnian of Moville was an alumnus of Candida Casa, at Whithorn in Britain. Under him, Columba studied the Scriptures and was ordained a deacon. Sometime before he was thirty, he also studied with Finnian of Clonard (d. 550), becoming one of his famous "Twelve Apostles of Ireland." When he was a young deacon, he also spent some time at Lagin in Leinster with an aged Christian bard named Gemman, from whom he learned Irish wisdom and imbibed an early love of poetry and music.

Columba's ability drew special attention from Finnian of Clonard, and some of his fellows apparently complained about the preferred treatment. Finnian wished to advance him to bishop's orders, so that he might be attached to a monastery with that office, and, for this purpose, sent him to Etchen, bishop of Comfled in Meath to be consecrated. Through some misunderstanding, Etchen ordained him a presbyter. Columba accepted this as an intervention of Providence to keep him humble, and declared that he would always remain a presbyter. In the eleventh century, a writer referred to him as "the arch-presbyter of the Island of the Gael."

Among the company of Finnian's disciples at Clonard, he formed friendships with Kenneth (Cainnech) and with Comgall, who were both to be associated with him at Iona, and with Brendan the Voyager. Another chum, Mobhi, left Clonard to found a monastery at Glasnevin on the Liffey, where both Comgall and Columba followed him, but the plague of 543, taking the life of the founder, caused this monastery to be abandoned. Columba returned to Ulster and founded his own first monastery at Derry on Lough Foyle, receiving the ground from Aedh, son of Aimmere in 546.

Of his early years, Adomnan wrote in his biography:

Devoted even from boyhood to the Christian novitiate and the study of philosophy, preserving by God's favour integrity of body and purity of soul, he showed himself, though placed on earth, ready for the life of heaven; for he was angelic in aspect, refined in speech, holy in work, excellent in ability, great in counsel.[14]

This is gilding the lily in the description of any young man, not to mention denying the doctrine of universal human depravity. That Columba was devoted, able, attractive in Christian leadership, and able to inspire others to sacrificial Christian devotion is proved by his early record of founding monasteries. Later legend multiplied the number he founded in Ireland before leaving for Iona to a hundred. We may be certain of two more after his beloved Derry: Kells in Meath and Durrow in Offaly.[15] What he did do throughout the land, obscured by later monastic-centered traditions, was evangelistic preaching. Columba early preached in almost every county in Ireland.[16] He also developed his lifelong habit of copying the Scriptures. The Book of Kells, brought to Kells from Iona in 874, may or may not have been from his own pen, yet it represents his example of careful and artistic inscription.

Yet his unreadiness for the life of heaven was proved by the major offense of which he repented just before he left Ireland. Even Adomnan had difficulty maintaining his saint's innocence. At the place in his Second Preface or Introduction, where it would have been jeopardized by a full disclosure, he writes:

In the second year after the battle of Cul-debrene, the forty-second year of his age, Columba sailed away from Ireland to Britain, wishing to be a pilgrim for Christ.

"A pilgrim for Christ," that is all. No word about being a missionary to win others for Christ. No mention of the connection between Columba's leaving and the battle of Cul-debrene.

Yet there was something told about Columba which called for more defense, which Adomnan felt constrained to undertake in his Book III. There he carefully prepares for the main issue by telling how when Columba was a little lad, his foster-father Cruithnechan had seen a ball of fire standing over the sleeping child, lighting the whole house, indicating the special grace of the Holy Spirit. Then:

After many years had passed, when on a charge of offenses that were trivial and very pardonable, Saint Columba was excommunicated by a certain Synod (improperly, as afterwards became known in the end), he came to the assembly that had been convoked against him.[17]

Only Saint Brendan arose, bowed to Columba, and kissed him as he approached, while some of the elders remonstrated, "Why do you not refuse to rise in the presence of an excommunicated person, and to kiss him?" Then Brendan told of seeing a similar vision of a fiery pillar going before Columba, portending how he would lead nations into life. So they quashed the excommunication, honored the saint with great reverence, and the story closes:

This utterance was made in Telltown.
In those same days the saint sailed over to Britain, with twelve disciples as his fellow-soldiers.

So the excommunication by the Synod of Telltown, which the elders considered a serious matter, took place after the battle of Cul-debrene, and the cause was sufficient to require two miracle stories to counteract it! Then what were the offenses Adomnan called "trivial" and "very pardonable"?

We gain some understanding from various ancient sources. According to an account from the ancient *Black Book of Molaga*, now lost, given in O'Donnell, *Betha Colain Chille* (pp. 167-77), and in Keating's *History of Ireland* (iii, 88), and by Duke's *History of the Church of Scotland to the Reformation* (p. 25), the battle fought at Cuil Dreimmne near Sligo in the year 461 was stirred up by Columba as he was incensed by a double injustice perpetrated against him by Diarmaid, the high king!

Finnian of Moville, Columba's old teacher, had gone on pilgrimage to Rome, and brought back an exceptionally fine codex of Jerome's Vulgate Psalter, placing it for reading in his church. Columba begged the privilege of copying it, but was refused. Nothing daunted, he stole into the church by night, and had almost finished transcribing it by candlelight when Finnian caught him. Finnian demanded the copy. Columba refused to give it up. When the dispute was referred to King Diarmaid, he pronounced his judgment: "To every cow her little calf; to every book its little book," favoring Finnian. There is a hastily copied, almost completed very ancient Psalter called "The Cattach" in the Royal Irish Academy in Dublin, believed by many to be Columba's clandestine work.

According to Tigernach's *Annals* and the *Chronica Scottorum*, shortly after this, the same king wrongly invaded Columba's tribal sanctuary. A young son of the king of Connaught had inadvertently killed another young man at the king's court in Tara, and had sought sanctuary in Columba's protection. By command of the king, he was dragged from Columba's presence and put to death. In high indignation over the double affront, Columba aroused the O'Donnells to willing battle, and the king of Connaught readily joined them against the high king. As Columba was praying and fasting the night before the battle, Michael the Archangel came to him and assured him his prayer was heard, but because he had asked such a worldly thing from God, he must afterwards go into permanent exile from Ireland.

In the ensuing battle, Columba praying for one side and Finnian for the other, the O'Donnells, with the help of Saint Michael, defeated the forces of High King Diarmaid, but three thousand men were slain. At a synod of the Church called in 562 at Tailte (Teltown), Columba was excommunicated for his responsibility for the slaughter, though the penalty was afterwards revoked.

The *Altus Prositor,* a Latin hymn attributed to Columba was said to have been composed by the saint to beg for forgiveness. In the Latin *Life of Laisran,* abbot of Daminis, who was Columba's "Soul-Friend" (*anmchara*), we learn that Columba went to Laisran as his confessor, and asked how he could best show repentance to obtain remission of his sins and gain God's favor after he had caused so many deaths in battle. Laisran said that he must release from torment by conversion as many souls as those whose perdition he had caused, and must accomplish this mission in perpetual exile from Ireland. If this last stricture was growth of legend current by Adomnan's time, he deliberately helped to contradict it. He made much of the glorious reception Columba received when he went back to Ireland to attend the Council of Druimm-cete in 575, and although Bede and others tell of his founding the monastery of Durrow before going to Iona, Adomnan makes him spend months in Ireland on this project as late as 585.[18]

Scholars differ on the tradition of Columba's culpability and repentance, according to their predilections. Nora K. Chadwick in the fourteenth centenary pamphlet, *St. Columba,* upholds Adomnan's position. John T. McNeill omits the account of the killing of the son of the king of Connaught, tells the story of the copied Psalter as the possible invention of a hundred and thirty years of Irish imagination, but says that close studies of the "Cathach" of St. Columba leave us with the possibility that it is a genuine product of the saint's pen. The name "Cathach," meaning "battler," refers to its use as a protective talisman by the O'Donnell chiefs in their battles. More than half of the original nine-by-six leaves have been lost. Already so mutilated, it was encased in a wooden box in the eleventh century, and much later enclosed within a silver case. When opened in 1813, its leaves were stuck together, but it was made legible, its fifty-eight pages of the Psalter in majuscule script, with a few illuminated large initial letters being now preserved in the Royal Irish Academy, Dublin.[19] James Bulloch, in *The Life of the Celtic Church,* tells favorably of the controversy of the copied Psalter. Duke, in his *History of the Church of Scotland to the Reformation* (1937), favors the truth of the complete double legend. A.O. and M.O. Anderson, in their *Introduction* to their edition of *Adomnan's Life of Columba,* tell the tradition about the death of Curnan, the son of the king of Connaught, as the basis for Columba's stirring up the battle, and tell of the penance imposed by Laisran in the Latin life of that saint, but do not mention the controversy over the copied Psalter. C.J. Godfrey, in his excellent chapter on "Christianity Among the Celts" in *The Church in Anglo-Saxon England* (1962),[20] says that there is no reason to suppose the traditional and picturesque causes of the saint's departure from Ireland are not substantially true. Modern Christians who find it difficult to believe that a responsible forty-year-old monk would deliberately stir up such a war in the sixth century should reflect upon the fighting Irish in Ulster in the twentieth, and upon the widespread tendency among modern Protestants to confer martyred sainthood upon Dietrich Bonhöffer after his participation as a cleric in a politically justified murder attempt in World War II. Of course, historians are reluctant to believe ill of great saints. The Andersons reflect that some rumors adverse to Columba appear to have reached Bede, but he regarded them with caution and preferred to ascribe to him the merit he had known in Columba's successors.[21] Viewed objectively, these are not the sort of stories easily made up. Like the account of the Cross of Jesus, there is slight possibility they would ever have been told about a marvelous person, were they not true.

Yet even if it is all true, this does not deny Columba's positive motivation as he sailed away from Ireland in 563, sharing with his twelve companions his desire "to be a pilgrim for Christ." Their chief purpose was to enlarge the Kingdom of Christ by winning disciples in Dalriada and the Kingdom of the

Picts. Their leader, a tall man of forty-two years, of noble bearing and unusual strength and endurance, one of the best educated men of his age, and trained in the finest, unspoiled heritage of the Christian Church, was now humbled to a new contrite devotion. Now he would hold his imperious temper in closer rein. Now he would determine never again to yield to the "Crimthann" of his original worldly nature which the foxy Devil had so easily aroused, and would cultivate the saintly gentleness which from then on endeared him to his younger associates and caused him to be remembered with such peculiar affection in the Celtic Churches. "Columcille," the peaceful "Dove of the Church." Now he would use his unmistakeable ability to influence earthly powers for peace. Of the twelve with him, three were relatives, Ernan, his uncle and two cousins. Mochonna was the son of a king. To be freed from the nostalgia to return to his beloved homeland, they must find a site for their Christian enterprise beyond any distant view of the hills of Ireland.

First, however, they must visit Columba's royal cousin Connall, ruler of Dalriada in Britain at his fortified capital, Dunadd, near the coast of Kintyre at the head of the Sound of Jura. Connall was in trouble. The Irish expansion at the expense of the Picts, started a century earlier by invaders from Dalriada in Ulster, had recently been checked by a revived Pictish power under King Brude macMaelchon who ruled at Inverness, and whom Bede calls "a very powerful king." Brude had reduced Connall to vassalage after regaining some territory from Dalriada's northern frontier. Columba would want to know about this whole situation from his cousin before making any attempt to convert Brude and his subjects. He might also be useful in improving the peace.

After leaving Dunadd, Columba and his companions scouted the larger islands of Islay and Jura, and perhaps sailing through the Sound of Islay, are said to have landed on Colonsay. Climbing a hill on the neighboring islet of Oronsay, he found the hills of Ireland were still visible. A cairn on Oronsay called "Cul-re-Erind," "Back to Ireland," still marks the spot where he took his last backward-longing look.

The coracle of wicker and hides in which they sailed must have been quite large, for along with thirteen men were carried supplies and implements to begin a settlement. This was no fly-by-night whimsy, like Brendan's voyages, but a well-planned enterprise. It was on the eve of Pentecost, the twelfth of May, that the northward sailing vessel reached the little Isle of Iona, then called Hy, located "seaward from the westernmost projection of Mull," across half a mile of sometimes turbulent sound. The terraced beach, shining with many-colored pebbles where they drew their boat ashore, is now called Port a Churiach, the Port of the Coracle. From this island's highest point, Ireland could no longer be seen. By its eastern shore, across from Mull, an ancient Druid stone circle stood, for Hy was a place of Druid worship, and also sacred for the burial of kings, before Columba came. On this place, he must build his church, displacing heathendom's shrine.

That the island was renamed Ioua, later Iona, the Hebrew word for "a dove," which was Colum in Latin, is evidence for the scholarship the Irish monks took with them, including Greek and Hebrew of the Scriptures and Celtic and Classical philosophy and letters. But now, they must become economically self-supporting, with fishing first, then agriculture. The isle is three miles long, one-and-a-half wide at its broadest part, with roughly 500 of its 2,000 acres arable land. If, as is probable, there were already Scottish farmers and fishermen on the island, there is no record that they either welcomed or opposed the new settlers. Men in monks' garb had come there before, for the Reilig Oran, the sacred burial ground of the kings of Dalriada had been given Christian sanctity and dedicated by or to Saint Oran, who died in 549. More significantly, it was an ideal place for a mission center in those free-sailing days, within easy reach of the Scots of Dalriada to the East, the Britons of Strathclyde to the South, and the Picts to the North on the mainland and in the Outer Hebrides.

If Columba's only motive in the choice of Iona had been to live a hermit life, it was a strange location. Other islands would have been less accessible. From Adomnan's emphasis, we might gain the impression that withdrawal for the conservative life was Columba's prime objective. His subsequent use of the island as a base for the evangelization of the Picts and the development of the Columban paruchiae shows a more active purpose.

How did Columba gain the right to settle upon Iona? The *Annals of Ulster* later state, in the entry recording the death of King Connall of Dalriada, that he gave the island of Ia to Columcille as an offering. Adomnan does not say this, but assumes that it was in Connall's domain. Bede, a generation later, says the island "long ago was resigned by gift of the Picts who inhabit those parts of Britain to monks of the Irish through whose teaching they had received the faith of Christ," and

Columba came to Britain while Bridius Mailochon's son, a most powerful king, reigned over the Picts in the ninth year of his reign; and by word and example he brought that nation to the faith of Christ. Therefore he received from them that island, to hold it for the making of a monastery.

Bede was in correspondence with Nechtan, king of the Picts in his day, and may have received his information from Nechtan's messengers. Both accounts may be partly accurate. Connall was Brude's vassal at the time, and Columba may have received permission to settle from Connall, but wisely also asked for title from Brude at the time of his successful mission to his court. This, however, was after his monks were settled on the Holy Isle.

The monastic settlement they built was simple. Each had his own tiny hut, arranged irregularly about that of their abbot which crowned a small rocky eminence, Tor Abb. There was a small church, a guest house, a refectory with a kitchen, a scriptorium with library attached. Above stone foundations, the walls were of wood and wattle and the roofs of thatch. These buildings were surrounded by a thick earthen wall or cashel, outside of which were a smithy, kiln, mill, and two barns.

The original band was soon increased in numbers with eager recruits from Ireland, and later from among the Britons and even the Saxons, so that it became necessary to supplement supplies from the neighboring islands of Tyree and Mull. When the number reached 150, additional recruits were discouraged. Adomnan says of the activity of the Abbot:

Living as an island soldier for thirty-four years, he would not pass even the space of a single hour without applying himself to prayer, or to reading, or to writing, or some kind of work. Also by day and by night, without any intermission, he was so occupied with unwearying labors of fasts and vigils that the burden of each several work seemed beyond the strength of man. And with all this he was loving to every one, his holy face ever showed gladness, and he was happy in his inmost heart with the joy of the Holy Spirit.[22]

He divided his monks into three classifications. There were the "Seniors" who were engaged in intellectual activities, the conduct of worship, and the copying of manuscripts in the scriptorium. The "Working Brothers" performed and taught the outdoor farm labor, fishing, and sealing on the shore of Erraid, a nearby island where seals congregated. The "Juniors" were young learners or novices, candidates for monastic vows. All had to work hard, and participate in all the hours of worship.

They were all dressed in the cowl, a long hooded cloak of undyed wool, a white tunic almost as long, and leather sandals. They slept in their habits, ready to go to the church promptly to keep the night hours of praise. They were tonsured, shaving their foreheads from a line over the cranium from ear to ear. Meals were scant and beds were hard. Adomnan tells with admiration how Columba used "for straw mattress a bare rock and for pillow a stone." That helped to keep his sleeping time to a minimum! In 1957, the Tor Abb was excavated and the austerity corroborated. On the highest point, a slot in the stone was a socket for a small cross, probably erected later to mark the site of the holy man's cell. Beside it, slightly to the south, is a circle of "bluish" cut stones, the base of the original foundation walls. Stones in the center which look like an open-air fireplace were the base of his seat, a wooden board extending across the two granite ends. Beneath this, on the inlaid stone base, he kept thepigments for his missals dry. The slanting gray rock to one side was his couch. Adomnan tells of seeing his stone pillow, faithfully preserved beside his grave.[23] An oval slab of granite, one foot seven inches long, found nearby, is thought to be this precious relic and is shown in the museum at Iona. Columba, like his Lord, liked to go apart for periods of more intensive prayer and meditation. For this, he had a lonely spot within a mile of the community. His more distant retreat was on the island of Hinba (Elachnave), one of the Graveloch islands in the Firth of Lorne. There he soon built another monastery, closer to Connall's court of Dunadd, but still apart. It appears on the old maps as Insula Ailechi.

Columba's great mission to the Northern Picts was begun in 564 by his visit to King Brude's court near Inverness, nearly 150 miles to the northeast. The journey was chiefly by boat, with short portages, by Loch Linnhe, Loch Lochy, Loch Oich, and Loch Ness in the long straight cleft of Glen More. Columba had interpreters with him, as he did not yet trust himself with the Pictish dialect. Other sources than Adomnan say he took with him his friends, Abbot Comgall of Bangor and Kenneth, later abbot of Agaboe.

Adomnan's tale of a miraculous incident on the way is the earliest written account of an encounter with a Loch Ness monster. On the bank of the River Ness, Columba saw a man being buried who had been savagely bitten while swimming by a "water beast." Despite this danger, Columba ordered Lugne, his companion, to swim across the infested water and sail back a boat on the opposite bank. Lugne obeyed, and the "monster," lurking in the depths, its appetite whetted and frustrated by being deprived of the previous prey, surfaced and made for Lugne with gaping mouth and a great roaring. While the rest froze with terror, Columba calmly drew the sign of the Cross in the empty air, invoked the name of God, and commanded the savage beast: "You will go no further. Do not touch the man; turn backward speedily!" At this, "the beast, as if pulled back with ropes, fled terrified in swift retreat." Lugne swam on to sail back in the boat, and the brethren and the pagan barbarians glorified God.

When, after a tiring climb, they reached the high-built fortress of King Brude, that haughty monarch would not open the gates. Columba again made the sign of the Cross, "and immediately the bars were forcibly drawn back and the doors opened of themselves." The alarmed king then hurried out to receive the blessed man with due reverence, and greatly honored him thenceforth.[24] In an account parallel to Adomnan's in the Latin *Life of Comgall*, it was Comgall who made the sign of the Cross to break open the locked gates, Columba forced the door of the king's house in the same manner, and when the king threatened them with a sword, Kenneth caused the king's hand to wither until he believed in God.

Unfortunately, none of the accounts tell us much we would like to know about Columba's successful mission, the real conversion of King Brude, the securing of the deed to Iona, and the favor of Brude upon the evangelizing of his kingdom. In Adomnan's eyes, it was all a big contest of magic between Columba and Brude's court Druid, Broichan. A well had been notorious as bewitched, causing all who drank of it to be crippled or blinded. Broichan and his magicians hoped Columba would be so stricken, but he blessed the water, causing the demons to depart, washed in it, drank of it, and it became a healing shrine.[25] The son of a family which had recently been converted and baptized through Columba's preaching at Brude's court, sickened and died, and the court magicians taunted the bereaved parents for forsaking their gods. Thereupon, Columba raised the boy from the dead, praying, his face suffused with tears, to Christ the Lord.[26] Columba then asked Broichan to release an Irish slave-girl as an act of human kindness, and, when he obstinately refused, threatened him with death on the coming day of their departure. When that day came, Columba waited at the River Ness for the expected king's emissary, who galloped up on horseback to report Broichan stricken and ready to release the slave-girl. Columba sent back a little white stone which floated on water like a nut and made of the water a healing drink that healed Broichan.[27] Even so, when they did sail away, Broichan raised an adverse wind against them, but Columba ordered the sail raised, and sailed away down Loch Ness with extraordinary speed against the contrary wind.[28] One semi-miracle may contain some truth. While the monks were singing vespers beside Brude's fortress, the Druids tried to outshout them to keep the heathen peoples from hearing the sound of divine praise, whereupon Columba drowned their din by singing the forty-fifth Psalm "like a terrible peal of thunder" filling the king and people with an intolerable dread.[29] Columba had a powerful voice! But if we depended upon Adomnan, we would have only glimpses of Columba's missionary travels, noted only because of accompanying wonders. On a visit to Skye, Columba prophesies that an aged Pict will sail to the island, be baptized, die, and be buried, whereupon within an hour, his ship comes and all this transpires.[30] Another time, on the Isle of Skye, he is alone praying in a dense wood when he is nearly attacked by a huge wild boar. Raising his hand in prayer, Columba tells it to die and it falls dead on the spot.[31] When we visited Skye in search of traces of Columba's missionary activity, we were shown the site of the ancient Loch Columcille monastery founded by Columba, beyond the now silted-up Lock near Kilmuir Church. The Episcopal Church in Portree is called "Columba Church," and the Church of Scotland minister of Portree, the Rev. Gillespie I. McMillan, told us of a small islet in Portree Bay associated with Columba in local tradition. There I found the crumbled remains of the rectangular foundations of a very ancient chapel, about 25' by 15', called through the centuries by Columba's name.

In a list compiled by Reeves, who did an earlier monumental work on Adomnan's *Life of Columba,* there are names of ninety churches and monasteries associated with Columba's name. Thirty-seven of these are in Ireland, fifty-three in Scotland and the Western Isles. Even if allowance for error is made, the number of his foundations, especially in the Western Isles and on the western coast, is tremendous, from Wigton in the south to Butt of Lewis in the north and as far west as Saint Kilda. From these Christian colonies, the light of the Gospel spread far and wide throughout the area, preparing for the union of the Picts and Scots under Christian faith that laid the foundation of the united Scottish nation.[32]

Some of the work often credited to Iona was done by other monks of Pictish race from Dalaradia in the district of Ulster, later called County Down. The best known of them, Comgall, worked with Columba. Comgall founded the church on Tyree and others in the Hebrides. Saint Moluag, another Pict, settled on Lismore Island in Loch Linnhe, planting there an important monastery. Saint Maelrubha from Bangor served for nearly fifty years, 673-722, founding Applecross in Banffshire, while Saint Drostan is the alleged founder of the monastery of the Deer in Aberdeenshire.[33] Yet it was all one missionary movement, from the same unspoiled source in the North of Ireland during those marvelous centuries of the fruitfulness of the Celtic Church.

In the year 574, King Conall of Dalriada died. Adomnan tells us that Columba, then living on the Island of Hinba, saw a vision on three successive nights of an angel with a glass book of the ordination of kings in his hand, showing him he must ordain Aidan, Conall's cousin, as king, though he was second in line to Iogenan, his elder brother, whom Columba loved and preferred. When the saint refused, the angel scourged him, leaving a scar for the rest of his life. After the third vision, the saint submitted to the word of the Lord, sailed to Iona and there ordained Aidan king. The story tells us that by Columba's prayer-inspired advice Aidan, though not the rightful heir, was chosen to succeed Conall, a choice which proved eminently wise.[34]

The next year, 575, saw the calling of the great convention at Drumceatt near Londonderry, summoned by Aedh, high king of Ireland, which Columba and the new King Aidan of Dalriada attended together. It was the first time Columba had set foot in his homeland in twelve years, and Columba went with an imposing retinue of twenty bishops and other clergy. He was received with all honor, and not as a banished and excommunicated vagabond. Important in the business was the claim of Dalriada in Ulster to exemption from tribute to the Tara kings. The important part played by Columba in the debate is indication of the position he held in the regard of his countrymen and the influence he wielded in affairs of state. Another issue was the proposed suppression of the old order of bards, who had aroused hostility by their frequent damaging satires and exorbitant fees. In spite of opposition from King Aed mac Ainmere of Tara, Columba won substantially the argument for the Dalriadans. He also prevented the loss of the bards as an essential element in Irish society. He did propose that they be regulated, and commanded to attend to their teaching duties. Thereupon, the chief bard of Ireland, Dallan Forghaill, composed in his honor the poem still preserved, *The Praise of Columcille*, which is useful for some details about his life. It tells how 1200 bards entered the meeting, and so lauded him in song as to embarrass the saint, who covered his head with his cowl. Adomnan tells of his visit on the way home to Clonmacnois, where Alither had succeeded Ciaran in the abbacy. Hearing of his approach, all of the monks ran from the fields to greet him, together with their abbot, hailing him "as if he had been an angel of the Lord," and led him into the church with hymns and praises.[35]

When King Brude of the Northern Picts died in 584, he was followed by Gartnaidh, a Southern Pict and a Christian. The union of Northern and Southern Picts resulting made the whole Pictish area cooperative with Columba's mission, and Iona became the spiritual capital of practically the whole area which is now Scotland.

The kindly, helpful spirit of Columba is illustrated in an incident Adomnan tells of his visit to Clonmacnois. An unprepossessing lad, rather discounted by the monks, slipped behind him to touch the hem of his coat. Columba stopped, reached around and pulled the boy before him by the neck. The monks shouted, "Send him away," but Columba said to the trembling boy, "Open your mouth and put out your tongue." Touching his tongue, the saint blessed it, and prophesied his gradual growth from a seemingly contemptible boy of little worth to a man of great goodness and virtue of soul, and of eminence in their community, his tongue eloquent from God with healthful doctrine. This was Ernene, Crasen's son, later famous among all the churches of Ireland.[36]

His love of God's creatures is witnessed by the story of his prophecy of the coming of a storm-tossed crane from Ireland, which would fall exhausted on the shore. He told one of the brothers that when it came, he was to lift it tenderly and care for it as a guest for three days in the house nearby, waiting upon it and feeding it with anxious care, until, revived, it would fly back to the sweet district in Ireland from which it came. All this came to pass precisely as the saint foretold, and he commended the brother, "God bless you my son, because you have tended well the pilgrim guest."

Earnest and constant in prayer, he was ever the spiritual leader of his brethren. Adomnan says:

By virtue of prayers, and in the name of the Lord Jesus Christ, he healed people who endured the attacks of various diseases. He, one man alone, with God's aid repulsed innumerable hostile bands of demons making war against him, visible to his bodily eyes and preparing to inflict deadly diseases upon his community of monks and they were thrust back from this our principal island.[37]

Ever Columba was the singing poet who rejoiced in the beauty of God's world. God was with him everywhere. One ancient verse ascribed to him records him as saying:

Christ, Son of Mary, greater than every assembly,
Father, Son and Holy Spirit,
With me in Ceanannus of the Kings,
In Sord and Doire equally.

An Irish poem, possibly of Columba's writing, sings of the outlook from Iona, the sea, the waves, the sandy beaches, the wheeling birds, and the queer creatures of the ocean, even of whales frequenting their waters at times, and the author, varying his occupation from prayer and contemplation and Psalm-singing to give food to the poor, catching fish, and picking dulse (edible seaweed) off the rocks:

That I might bless the Lord who conserves all,
Heaven with its countless bright orders,
Land, strand and flood. . . .
The King whose servant I am
Will not let anything deceive me,

In the seventy-seventh year of his life, after several years in which he had premonitions of death but was sustained by the prayers of his beloved community, Columba knew that his last day upon earth had come. It was Saturday, the Sabbath on Iona, the sixth day of June 597. Taking his faithful servant Diormit with him, he went out to bless the nearest barn. Finding two heaps of grain in store, he thanked God there would be enough bread for the year after his departure. Diormit, hearing this, was apprehensive and asked what the abbot meant. Sworn to secrecy, he was told that the Lord in the middle of the night had revealed to Columba that he would be invited to depart. Diormit wept, and the saint comforted him.

Halfway back to the monastery, the saint sat down to rest, and the white horse, who used to carry the milk from the cowpasture to the monastery, came and put his head on Columcille's bosom and sobbed, and he was blessed too!

Then, climbing the small hill overlooking the monastery, he raised his hands and blessed it, saying:

On this place, small and mean though it be, not only the kings of the Irish with their peoples, but also the rulers of the barbarians and foreign nations, with their subjects, will bestow great and especial honour; and especial reverence will be bestowed by saints even of other churches.[38]

Returning to his cell, he resumed his current scribal task, transcribing a Psalter. When he finished the words of the Thirty-Fourth Psalm, "They that serve the Lord shall not want any good thing," he said, "Here at the end of the page I must stop. Let Baithene write what follows." He attended vespers, then went to his cell, and reclining, told Diormit his last message to the brethren. They should have mutual and unfeigned charity with peace, and he would pray in Heaven that God would help them. When the bell tolled at midnight, summoning all to the church, he ran and entered before the brethren alone, and bowing his knees in prayer, sank down before the altar. The faithful Diormit, following, saw the whole church aglow with angelic light from a distance, but entered to grope in the dark and find his master lying before the altar. As the brothers came in with lights, Diormit had the saint's head in his lap, and they lamented as they saw he was dying. Speech had already departed. Diormit lifted his hand, and the saint moved it in the sign of the benediction. With wonderful joy and gladness of countenance—as seeing the welcoming angels—he breathed out his spirit. So passed the greatly human and lovable person, worthy to stand as the beginning of the history of Scotland, laying the foundation of that nation's religion, which still offers its light to the Christians of the world.

COLUMBA'S FAITHFULNESS TO THE WAY ETERNAL

From the story of his life, it is not difficult to review Columba's faithful living of the ten essential expressions of The Way, as we discovered them in the life of Patrick.

1. His evangelistic message and zeal we must gauge from the number of his converts and his ability to found new churches, for poor Adomnan had so far departed from evangelical fervor that he tells us practically nothing of his preaching and cure of souls. Only incidentally, as in a section where he describes how Columba dealt with the worthiness and unworthiness of people bringing gifts as offerings, does he reveal the way Columba labored to bring life-changing power into people's lives. So he said he would taste nothing of the gift of an avaricious man until he first would show true repentance for his sin of avarice, and while he commended one rich man for his mercies to the poor and his generosity, when that donor asked a special prayer, Columba first brought him to profess repentance for certain sins he had, and promise he would thenceforth amend and be corrected of his particular faults.[39]

A charming incident is related in a sixteenth century *Life of St. Columcille* compiled by Maghnes Ua Domhnaill from ancient sources:

When Columcille was going into exile in Scotland, Mochonna, this holy child of whom we have spoken, said that he would go with him. "Do not go," said Columcille, "but remain with your father and mother in your own country." "You are my father," said Mochonna, "and the church is my mother, and the place in which I can give most service to God is my country," said he. "And since it is you, Columcille, who has bound me to Christ, I will follow you till you bring me to where He is." And then he took the vow of pilgrimage.

2. Columba's eagerness for Scripture truth is evident from his avid boyhood reading of the Psalms in Cruithnechan's church, from his eagerness to copy Finnian's Psalter, and from his last

labor of love, scribal copying his last day. The Christ he served was the Lord he knew through the New Testament. The illuminated beauty of the *Book of Kells* and the *Book of Durrow* came from his monasteries.

3. His devotional life in prayer and humble service needs little further comment. In the rigors of the monastic life on Iona and Hinba, he set the pace, and all the others depended upon him to lead them in the way of prayer and contemplative devotion. His own humility of spirit, so difficult to attain by one so highly born, and so difficult to keep when human adulation of one so able was too readily profuse, is attested by his great acts of self-abnegation, his refusal to take higher orders than that of presbyter, his sharing of humble labor to his last day, and the rigor of his daily discipline to the last. He who could have been high king of Ireland wanted only to serve the Heavenly King to the best of his ability. Read again the Prayer of Columba heading this Chapter.

4. Of his charismatic gifts from the Holy Spirit, there is no doubt. Though we may discount Adomnan's exaggerations, and uncritical recounting from superstitious sources, there is enough evidence to substantiate that Columba had the gifts of healing and prophecy: what the Scots call "second sight." We who know of faith healings during our own ministries may have little doubt when we read the stories of God's healing of Columba's servant Diormit and many others through Columba's prayers. Adomnan in his introductory summary says:

. . . along with miracles, that, by the gift of God, this man of the Lord performed while he lived in mortal flesh, he began from his youthful years to be strong also in the spirit of prophecy; to foretell future events; to declare absent things to those present, because although absent in the body he was present in spirit, and able to observe what took place far away.[40]

5. There is no evidence that Columba was involved in any doctrinal controversy. The Irish Church was without question orthodox in its theology, sharing a rich belief in all three Persons of the Trinity and a realistic awareness of battling with the Devil, sustained by a lively hope of eternal life in Heaven. Columba's doctrine of the atonement was that of the ancient Church given classic expression by Irenaeus: that the victory of the Cross and Resurrection of Jesus ransoms and frees us from the thralldom of Satan. The hymn in the Irish *Liber Hymnorum*, at-

tributed to Columba, has been translated freely but faithfully to Columba's spirit by Duncan MacGregor:

> Down in the realm of darkness
> He lay a captive bound;
> But at the hour appointed
> He rose a victor crowned;
> And now to heaven ascended
> He sits upon the Throne;
> In glorious dominion
> His Father's and His own.

The other poems we have quoted, traditionally ascribed to Columba, are all expressive of a clear doctrinal conviction of our faith. Yet his was a broad and tolerant faith, as witness his defense of the ancient order of the bards.

6. The sixth essential, participation in missionary zeal, taking the Gospel to all nations to the ends of the earth, was his passion from the time he left Ireland. If it had been only penitential exile, suffered because of his guilt for the losses he had caused in battle, he could have stopped early in his career when the three thousand specified had been won for Christ. We shall see how the true missionary spirit continued in his inspired successors, when through men like Aidan, they took The Way to Northumbria and far beyond.

7. The seventh characteristic of The Way, an uncompromisingly high personal morality, Columba both taught and exemplified. In his account of Columba's prophecy concerning Libran of the Reed Plot, Adomnan reveals the conditions under which a candidate was accepted for monkhood on Iona. Libran, a layman came to Iona from the district of Connachta in Ireland, seeking to expiate his sins in pilgrimage. Columba described to him the hard and heavy discipline of monastic life, and the man said, "I am ready for any commands you may wish to impose upon me, though they be very hard, though they be humiliating." When he had confessed all of his sins, the saint said, "Rise and sit. You are required to complete a penance of seven years in the land of Tyree." After the seven years, he sent him back to square accounts on a false oath of servitude he had given and broken, and to give the service due to his parents. Then he returned to Columba, and was sent to serve the remainder of his days on Tyree. There was no moral softness in the Christian life as interpreted and exemplified by Columba.

Yet Columcille was no killjoy, and no advocate of universal asceticism. Contrary to the Eastern ascetics, such as Jerome and Origen, and to many western celibates, he did not consider sexuality sinful for those who chose normal family life, but taught the Scriptural obligation to be true to marriage vows. A layman came to Columba complaining that his wife had taken an aversion to him and would not allow him to enter into marital relations. Columba told the wife how Christ said, "The two shall be one flesh." She said she would do anything the saint might enjoin, except sleeping with her husband, hoping the willingness to go on religious pilgrimage or become a nun might substitute. Columba said God had forbidden the separation of those lawfully joined, and proposed that all three of them should fast and pray about it for three days. That night, the saint prayed for them, and the next day, when he asked the woman if she still wanted to become a nun, she said that, in the night, her heart had been changed by his prayers from hatred to love for her husband.

8. It is in the realm of social ethics that Columba's example is most instructive to us. He had a positive, realistic social concern, and saw clearly the Celtic Church heritage of the separation of Church and State. If he didn't understand it clearly at the early age when he elected to forego his birthright opportunity as candidate for the high kingship for humble obedience and service in the monastic life, he had the lesson brought home to him unmistakeably when he stirred up the Battle of Culdebrene.

Columba was particularly prone to temptation to the mistake he made in that tragic event. His doubly royal blood, his engaging, commanding personality, his high intelligence, and his holy life developing a high sense of justice and a strongly persuasive conscience all made the role he took seem natural and inevitable. Meanwhile, from this world's viewpoint, Columba was fully in the right. He had no peaceful legal recourse. He had already taken his dispute with Finnian to law before the same King Diarmaid, who had now invaded his tribal sanctuary to kill the lad under his sworn protection, and had been rendered an injustice. If Columba had not been a monk, a priest, or an abbot, thus a representative professionally of the Church, the colony of Heaven upon earth, but had been acting as a prince according to his worldly birthright, and had called his tribe to battle for the same causes in that heroic society, it would have been no sin at all. It would have been a glorious deed, no matter how costly in human lives. Then he would have led his kinsmen in the battle, and the inevitable result of that victory would have been his crowning as the high king of Ireland, with all the glory such a deed and his blood lines would have deserved. If he had done it as an abbot a century or more later, after Irish acceptance of the Roman Church compromise with the world, in the agreed relationship of the Church as the handmaiden of secular governments, and when abbots led their monks into battle as feudal lords, and bishops acted as agents for kings and popes, drumming up bloody crusades against the Muslims, there would have been no church-imposed culpability. This was exactly the basis of Adomnan's appraisal of what Columba did. As a traitor to the higher heritage of the Celtic Church, and a leading advocate of the Romani position when writing his *Life of Columba*, what Columba had done was "trivial" and "very pardonable" in his eyes. This very point of view took over with the triumph of the Rome-Canterbury hierarchy over the Celtic Church tradition 150 years later. But that was no excuse for Columba and his contemporary churchmen in the Synod of Teltown. They knew from Jesus' temptation that the Kingdom of God served by the Church is not built by bowing down to Satan to win kingdoms of this world. As Bible-taught Christians, they knew Jesus would not defend himself with a sword, nor allow Peter to defend him that way, no matter how just the cause! From Patrick's *Letter to Coroticus*, they had learned that the churchman's weapons must be persuasive appeals to moral conviction through truth from the Word of God. From Gildas, they may have learned of the terrible corruption that descended upon the British clergy in the two-and-a-half centuries after Constantine. Then, too-close alignment with the Roman government and too much meddling in military crusades, however nobly conceived, had corrupted the clergy and deprived the country of protection against the Saxons. It had destroyed the morale of both nation and church after the crushing defeats of the British armies under Maximus and the other Constantine in the days of Patrick. With this history in their heritage, and with the training they had from Patrick and the New Testament, there would have been no excuse if the reality of his sin as a churchman had been overlooked.

For the Church and the secular governments of this world must keep their policies separate because they have different purposes and different standards. The Church, preparing men for eternal life in the Way of Christ, must act consistently with Divine Truth, Goodness, and Love, or it ceases to witness to its Lord. Secular governments at their best cannot attain to this New Testament ethic, with their practical responsibilities of requiring legal righteousness and of defense against enemies. They must be instructed to obey the Old Testament Law of Justice, then to be as humane as possible. The Church may give ethical guidance to the State, but it cannot accept responsibility for its decisions, as they often involve worldly compromises ruinous to the Church's ability to speak for God. Columba as a presbyter and monk and abbot of Derry, Kells, and Durrow could no longer act as a mere Irish clansman, no matter how hot his blood was running. The Church must be the Church. Helping to cause those three thousand deaths through giving rein to his temper was no churchly act. So Columba repented.

Yet he embraced the penitence of exile as a Divine opportunity. It was not quite the Way of the Cross, for the sorrow he felt in leaving his beloved homeland and his three monasteries was not voluntarily endured for others' sins. The sin was his own. Yet as greatly as was possible, he made of his repentance a glorious service for Christ.

Columba understood the Way of the Cross. He took that way the night he fasted with the couple whose marriage needed healing, praying as he shared their penitent discomfort to bring love back to that household. Christ had gone to the Cross of Calvary to save Columba from the sin of worldliness.

It was not that Columba and other churchmen must have nothing to do with worldly affairs. It is that they cannot use worldly means, such as killing brother men. The means used always shape the ends achieved. The Church's purpose in this world is the Kingdom of Christ's coming on earth as it is in Heaven. Killing doesn't build that Kingdom. The way of the Cross does. Lesser means not inconsistent with Christ's loving will may also help. Columba did not cease to be a statesmanlike churchman. His act of crowning Aidan as king of Dalriada, passing over Conall's descendants and Aidan's elder brother, proved statesmanlike. Aidan was a strong king. Columba is said to have warned him that his descendants would have God's favor in reigning, so long as they did no evil to Columba's successors or to his kindred in Ireland. Cummene the White is quoted by Adomnan as the source of this information, and the fulfillment of the judgment sadly came in Cummene's abbacy.

When Columba took his newly crowned King Aidan to the great convention at Drumceatt in 575, he was not at all bashful in using his Christian and royal influence for statesmanly purposes: first to help his kinsmen in Irish Dalriada to become free of double taxation, to Aidan and to Aed mac Ainmere, high king of Tara; secondly, to both protect and discipline the bards. Yet, all of this was for purposes of peace and helpfulness in matters of which he had full practical understanding, and could in no manner be accused of conduct unbecoming to a man of God.

There is some evidence that Columba visited King Brude's court at Inverness twice, on the latter occasion to improve peaceful relations between King Aidan of Dalriada and King Brude, and that at the same time, he secured the good offices of King Brude to protect missions to the Orkneys and Outer Hebrides. Others believe that Columba's only mission to Inverness came later, in the time of Aidan, and had this purpose of creating peaceful relations. Whatever were the facts, under either assumption, Columba was not averse to using his Christian statesmanship in social action to achieve peaceful relations between kings.

We also have Adomnan's account of Columba's threatening Broichan the Druid with death because he would not release an Irish slave-woman "as an act of human kindness." The woman, set free, was handed over to Columba's envoys and presumably sent back to Ireland. If we can believe anything about this double-miracle tale, it shows Columba opposed to slavery as an inhumane practice, and active at least once in forcing an unwilling slaveholder to release his human property. The tactic reported was questionable. The slave was an Irish woman. There is no evidence that Columba led a general crusade against slavery in Ireland or Dalriada, though he is said to have attempted to secure at the convention of Drumceatt, unsuccessfully, ordinances for the protection of women, of men under holy orders, or in religious communities, and of children against acts of violence in war and peace. These were similar to Adomnan's Law accepted by the Council at Birr in 697. There is a strong tradition of constructive, peaceful, social action in the Celtic Church of Ireland and Scotland from the time of Patrick through the time of Adomnan, limited practically by the hardness of heart of the populace and by what peaceful persuasion could accomplish.

Still, the Celtic Church kept its independence from control by kings. The location óf Columba's monasteries on islands away from the courts of Dunadd and Inverness was for more than eremetic solitude. It guaranteed distinctive freedom from secular domination. Kings came to Iona as suppliants for anointing, shriving, inspiration, wisdom, and burial. Columba would be no pawn of State. He served the King of Kings.

9. With regard to the ninth essential of The Way: humble non-hierarchical church polity, Columba's refusal after his ordination as a presbyter ever to consider becoming a bishop is clear evidence. He followed the Irish custom of having a bishop among his monks in the monastery from time to time to perform ordinations, but subject to his orders as abbot.

Adomnan tells one story of a humble stranger who hid his bishop's orders when he came to visit Iona. He was asked to assist Columba with the Eucharist on the Lord's Day. Suddenly, it was revealed to Columba as he watched him that the stranger was a bishop, so he said, "Christ bless you brother; break this bread alone according to the episcopal rite. Now we know you are a bishop: why until now have you tried to conceal yourself, so that the reverence due to you was not paid by us?" The Andersons think this story was either made up or embellished by Adomnan after his visits to Northumbria and his conversion to the elevation of the episcopacy, and does not in this form represent Columba's emphasis.[41] Adomnan was the first to set up a bishop's chair at Iona. Columba, as an abbot, respected bishops according to their functions in the Irish Church. All unconsciously, his own leadership capability, in organizing at least six monasteries, three in Ireland, and in building up the Columban Paruchiae, set the stage for the later competition of the Armagh bishopric to become an archepiscopal see. When this sort of worldly glory dominated the church, the humility to receive the Holy Spirit soon flew away and the true glory had departed.

10. Columba was also totally unaware of any departure from the life of the one ecumenical Catholic Church. Monasticism had been accepted as one of the ordered ways one could exercise a Christian ministry throughout the Church. The rituals, tonsure, and dating of Easter practiced in the Irish churches from the time of Patrick had come from the East and Rome, originally, and until Columbanus went back to the Continent and Augustine came to Canterbury, the Celtic churches knew nothing different but tolerance of variety in things non-essential. They followed the Scripture teaching as best they

could, welcomed brother-Christians from many lands as students with warm hospitality, and never doubted that there was one Church universal. The doctrinal disputes of the East never reached their insular isolation, and they had a broad toleration from their Druid heritage that did not stickle about fine points of doctrine. Monasteries varied in strictness of discipline according to the leadership of their founding abbots, and there were penitentials of varying severity. The Columban church, like its Irish mother-church, practiced the complete independence and self-sufficiency of inspiration by the Holy Spirit which Patrick had given them.

Adomnan represents Columba as prophesying the Easter dispute which later wracked the Celtic churches. He tacks onto the end of the most appealing story about the encouragement of Ernene at the monastery of Clonmacnois a statement that, while Columba was a guest there,

he prophesied also many other things by revelation of the Holy Spirit: that is to say, concerning the great dispute that after many days arose among the churches of Ireland over the diversity in time of the Easter festival.

Adomnan didn't dare make Columba take sides in the dispute, but he had to bring it in, possibly with the hope that if the saint were thought to have anticipated it, the new proposed uniformity could not be so strongly opposed by his followers.

It was a sad development that the calculation of the date of Easter became the symbol and point of argument in the power struggle projected to squelch the liberty of Celtic Christianity. Yet, when Columba died, this was still a century in the future. George MacLeod has reminded us that later papal claims were nowhere being made in Columba's day. Rigorous uniformity had not yet emerged to bedevil love, and unity was still conceived as enriched and not endangered by variations on a common theme. In such an atmosphere, Columba sent his best poem, on the Glories of Creation, to the pope, who acknowledged its genius but would not put it in the Vatican Library, since it made reference to the salvation wrought on Calvary in only one verse. Columba, nettled but challenged, wrote his great Redemption Hymn.[42] Diversity enriched still in those days. And still, there was so much mission work for the world-wide Kingdom of Christ to be done by those who loved the fulness of His Way. Eastern Britain and much of the Continent of Europe lay in shambles after the barbarian invasions. It was not the Benedictines, but the Celtic monks, with their free and independent spirit, their evangelistic missionary zeal, and pastoral concern for people everywhere who must undertake that task.

Chapter VI

THE WAY COMES TO THE ANGLO-SAXONS

Hickety, pickety, my black hen:
She lays eggs for gentle-men.
Gentle-men come every day
To see what my black hen doth lay.

Take my yoke upon you, and learn from me;
for I am gentle and lowly in heart.
—Matt. 5:5

How often would I have gathered your children
as a hen gathers her brood under her wings.
—Matt. 23-37

Christ's Church is fruitful of new life under those who are gentle in His Way, meek and lowly in heart. She cannot produce much for those who adopt the proud, authoritative, coercive ways of the world. Nowhere is this better illustrated than in the experiences of the two types of saints who, in their contrasting ways, brought Christianity to the heathen Saxons, Angles, and Jutes who were to become the English people. It is the difference in fruitfulness between Augustine of Canterbury and Aidan of Lindisfarne; between Wilfrid and Cuthbert.

After the Battle of Badon Hill and the illusory time of prosperity and decay that followed, there was no unifying power in Britain to check the onslaught of the Anglo-Saxons. Breaking out of their coastal reserve and joined by swarms of kinsmen from overseas, they overran England. Weakened by the plague, lacking in morale and leadership, their faith decadent, the Roman-Christian Celtic population fell back into Wales and Cornwall, or sailed for Brittany, leaving their cities and villas and churches destroyed. So bitter were their feelings against the ruthless heathen invaders that they made no attempt to win them to Christ. The Anglo-Saxons who settled down to farm the greater part of the island were completely pagan.

The first mission to convert them came from Rome. Long before he became Pope, Gregory the Great saw some fair-haired, blue-eyed boys being sold in the Roman slave-market. Asking of what people these handsome lads might be, he was told, "They are Angles from Britain." "Not Angles but Angels!" he replied, and conceived the plan of a mission to their land. Unable to undertake it himself at the time, he remembered when he attained to papal power. In 596, he commissioned his friend Augustine, prior of Saint Andrew's monastery on the Coelian Hill in Rome with a company of forty monks to convert the English.

They were all accustomed to receiving orders, and there was not one courageous man of independent faith and initiative among them. They had traveled only so far as southern Gaul when, overcome with fear, they sent Augustine back to Rome to beg Gregory to recall so dangerous a mission. Gregory was of no such mind. With one letter, he shamed and encouraged his timid missioners, and with another, he instructed Archbishop Etherius of Arles to welcome and provision them.

Reaching Kent in 597, they found their fears completely unfounded, for King Ethelbert had already married a Frankish princess, Bertha, on condition that she be allowed to practice her Christian faith. Her chaplain, a Bishop Liudhard, was already there, conducting worship in a partly refurbished old Celtic church building. Augustine and his monks landed on the Isle of Thanet, and when King Ethelbert came to investigate, so impressed him with their symbols, prayers, singing of the litany, and preaching that he readily granted them freedom to preach in his realm, and quarters in the town of Canterbury. There, by their exemplary piety and preaching, they soon converted the king, and Augustine set up his episcopal see. Having so proved his success, he traveled back to Arles, and was there consecrated archbishop of the English. When he wrote to Rome to inform Gregory of these glad tidings, he asked the pope a number of questions about how to proceed. Fortunately, the Venerable Bede has included them in his *History*, with full text of the pontiff's answers.

Augustine's seventh question was, "What are to be our relations with the bishops of Gaul and Britain?" Pope Gregory replied that he gave him no authority over the bishops of Gaul, and he was to take no official action there without the authority of the bishop of Arles; but that all the bishops of Britain were committed to his charge, to use his authority "to instruct the unlearned, to strengthen the weak, and correct the misguided."[1] The pope sent Augustine more colleagues, and the pallium to wear as archbishop when solemnizing mass. Among the new recruits were Mellitus, Justus, Paulinus, and Rufianus. With them, they brought many sacred vessels, vestments, altar coverings, relics, and many books, also a letter instructing Augustine to consecrate twelve bishops to sees under his jurisdiction, including one at London and one at York. This was more than Augustine was ready to do.

When he had repaired the church at Canterbury, built a monastery, and converted many in Kent, Augustine, with the aid of King Ethelbert, summoned the Welsh bishops in the year 603 to meet him in conference on the bank of the River Severn. He urged them in Christian unity to join him in preaching the Gospel to the heathen Anglo-Saxons. Bede tells us they had two conferences. At the first, they could not agree to Augustine's authority in setting the date of Easter, and in changing some other customs. They agreed to another conference, only after Augustine had demonstrated his miraculous power by healing a blind man whom they failed to help. At the second conference, seven British bishops attended, first visiting a wise and prudent hermit to ask him whether they should abandon their own traditions at Augustine's demand. The hermit advised them to test whether Augustine were a man of God by observing his meekness and humility in rising to greet them. Bede says, " . . . it happened that Augustine remained seated in his chair. Seeing this, they became angry, accusing him of pride, and taking pains to contradict all that he said."

It all depends upon who tells the story, on the main facts of which both sides agree, except that probably there was only one meeting. The questioning of the hermit and the test of Augustine's humility agreed upon make little sense if the Welsh bishops had already had one long conference with Augustine, had observed him, and had witnessed such an impressive healing miracle. The miracle story sounds like standard hagiography.

We heard the account as told in the Welsh tradition from Canon Harold Rue, the retired librarian of Llandaff Cathedral. When the Welsh bishops received the summons from Augustine and King Ethelbert of the Saxons to meet the archbishop at the fords of the Severn, they were troubled. This was a prelate from Rome, of a tradition foreign to their heritage. They had never had a prelate. Their own tradition was from Gaul, was more Eastern in nature and in ritual, through Irenaeus of Lyons, a disciple of Polycarp, who was a disciple of John, the Beloved Apostle of Ephesus. Their tonsure, shaving the fore part of the head, their mode of baptism, once only, not three times, and their worship ritual had been hallowed by nearly three hundred years of faithful observance from ancient Apostolic authority. Why should they take orders from this foreigner from Rome, who had joined himself to the hated and untrustworthy Saxon king? Maybe this was just a cover for further Saxon aggression!

While traveling toward the Severn River to meet Augustine, the Welsh bishops remembered there was a famous hermit known for his wisdom living in a cave in the wilds hard by, and decided to call upon him and ask his sage advice. When they explained their dilemma he replied,

If this man Augustine is truly a man of God he will be a humble man, and will receive you humbly, proving it by standing to greet you as an equal humble fellow-servant of Christ. If he does, listen to him. But if he receives you sitting, reject him.

Augustine arrived at the place on the English side of the Severn which is still called "Aust" first, and had set up his archbishop's throne. When the Welsh bishops came up from the ferry, they found him sitting in vestments and pallium to receive them, expecting them to honor his authority and do him obeisance. They were not impressed by his pomp. He brought up in their conversation the need for changing the date of their observance of Easter, and the "rude tonsure of the rough men of Wales." It was the ancient slave-tonsure from the East, shaving all hair forward from a line across the head above the ears, denoting humble slavery to Christ. The Celtic bishops argued that they had received their traditions from their fathers, saying, "Who are you from Peter, when we are from the great St. John?" The ritual differences were picayune; the real issue was authority, power!

The Venerable Bede says that Augustine narrowed his requirements to three: conformity with Rome on the date of Easter, the form of Baptism, and joining the mission to the Anglo-Saxons. When they refused, Augustine lost patience. He threatened them with a judgment which was also a dire prophecy.

If they refused to accept peace with fellow-Christians, they would be forced to accept war at the hands of enemies; and if they refused to preach to the English the way of life, they would eventually suffer at their hands the penalty of death.[2]

It was the wrong thing to have said: it confirmed the Welsh bishops' suspicions of Saxon perfidy. They replied that they had had war with the Saxons for over a hundred years, so this was nothing new, and nothing different from what they had expected of Augustine, allied with Ethelbert. They refused to accept his authority and withdrew. So the Welsh did not submit to the sovereignty of Canterbury, and kept their freedom until the twelfth century.

The Celtic bishops had read Augustine accurately. He was a small-spirited man, of no real personal courage, or inner empowerment of the Holy Spirit. This had been proved early in the mission by his cowardly running back to Gregory in Rome. He was an organization man, dependent upon the artificial authority of office and hierarchical backing. He had to set up that throne and assert his formal sovereignty from the start, or he never could have ruled those strong-minded, independent Welsh bishops. He represented the very type of Church leadership always produced by the humanly subservient hierarchical system: office-proud, vain, efficient when following orders but lacking in spiritual depth or freedom to respond to the inner Voice of God. He lacked the inner power of the meek, who can dare to be humble because of their direct trust in and submission to God. His type has difficulty reaching people's hearts. It is usually preferred by kings.

Even with Ethelbert's sponsorship, Augustine's mission had limited results. When he died in 604, he had consecrated only two bishops, Mellitus to London and Justus to Rochester, only twenty-four miles west of Canterbury. Save for the temporary success of Paulinus in Northumbria, the evangelizing work of his mission for Rome was barely extended north of the Thames.[3] So Augustine's achievement was limited to the south-east corner of England. Even when Pope Honorius I in 635 sent another mission under Birinius, instructed to take the faith farther inland, it landed among the West Saxons and was confined to establishing the See of Dorchester.[4]

Yet if Augustine was wrong in losing his temper at Aust, the Welsh bishops were also wrong in refusing to join in the mission to convert the Anglo-Saxons. In time, they suffered the dire judgment Augustine foretold. Bede recounts how, some while later, Ethelfrid, the Saxon king of Mercia, led an army against the Welsh south of Chester. Nearby was the huge monastery of Bangor Iscoed on Dee, with over 2100 monks. Twelve hundred and fifty of these monks had come out to pray for the battle, guarded while they prayed apart from the battlefield. The heathen King Ethelfrid counted their praying a form of fighting. Attacking them first, he routed their guard and slaughtered 1200 of the monks before he destroyed the Welsh army.[5]

The opportunity for Paulinus's mission to Northumbria came in 625, when King Edwin of that realm, having extended his domains over most of England, Wales, and the Isles of Anglesey and Man, sought the hand of Princess Ethelberga of Kent in marriage. Her brother, King Eadbald, said she could not marry a heathen. Thereupon, Edwin promised freedom of worship for her and her attendants, and even said he would accept Christ's religion if he and his advisers decided it appeared more holy and acceptable than their own. So Paulinus was consecrated bishop, and sent to York with the betrothed princess. Immediately, he began to toil unceasingly, not only to guard the queen's faith, but to convert Edwin and his people.

There had been other influences upon Edwin before Paulinus came. Bede tells a long tale of Edwin's experience when a young fugitive at the court of Redwald, king of the Angles, when his life was endangered. A strange visitor came and prophesied his future kingship, and a better and wiser guidance for his life and salvation than anything known to his parents or kinfolk. It would be known by the sign he gave by laying his right hand on Edwin's head. Welsh sources earlier than

Bede contain a strong tradition that Edwin was baptized by the Briton Rhun, son of Urien, a former warrior who became a priest. John T. McNeill reports some modern scholars favoring this account, recalling Bede's bias against the Britons as predisposing him not to recognize any such activity of a British priest.[6] So Urien or Rhun may have helped predispose Edwin to listen to Paulinus.

Edwin's protection from the assault of an assassin, and the easy birth of an infant daughter, both on the same Easter eve, Paulinus claiming that his prayers had assured the safe and painless delivery of the child, made the king more open to conviction. Paulinus also showed knowledge of Edwin's earlier Christian encounter by giving him the sign, laying his right hand on his head in blessing. Pope Boniface, at Paulinus' prompting, sent impressive letters to both the king and queen. Finally, the king called a council of his principal advisers. Coifi, his chief priest in the worship of Wotan and the other Germanic gods, expressed himself as favorably disposed to the change. Another influential counsellor said we may compare man's life on earth to the swift flight of a sparrow through a banqueting-hall, in one door and out another. Inside, he is safe from the winter's storms, but after a few moments of comfort, he vanishes into the wintry world without. If this new teaching brings any more certain knowledge of man's life than this, it should be followed. Other elders agreed. Coifi wanted to hear more teaching from Paulinus about God, and hearing it, publicly acknowledged it to be superior. Thereupon, the king professed faith in Christ, his counselors followed suit, and Coifi himself volunteered to signalize the change by profaning the altars and shrines of the idols at which he had performed. Mounting a horse, he rode to the pagan temple, speared the image of Wotan, and told his companions to set fire to the temple, full of joy in his worship of the true God! On Easter day, 627, the king, his two sons by a former marriage, the infant daughter, and many of his subjects were baptized. For six more years, Paulinus carried on a prosperous mission in Northumbria, reaching out with Edwin's help to the provinces of East Anglia and Lindsey.

Then tragedy struck. In the Battle of Heathfield, Edwin was slain. There came a pagan reaction, and Paulinus fled with the widowed queen and her children back to Kent. Only one cleric, James the Deacon, remained at York, living out his days in a village nearby, and after peace was restored, teaching the church music of Rome and Canterbury.

Somehow the Christian faith as taught by Paulinus failed to strike deep roots. Osric, a cousin of Edwin who had received baptism from Paulinus, became king of Deira between the Humber and the Tyne; while Eanfrid, son of Ethelfrid, became king of Bernicia from the Tyne northward to the Forth. Eanfrid had been baptized at Iona. Both reverted to idolatry in the pagan reaction after Edwin's death, but both were also soon slain by Cadwallon, the British warrior chieftain who had won the battle of Heathfield from Edwin. Eanfrid's brother, Oswald, who likewise had grown up in exile at Iona, was a deeply sincere Christian. Inheriting the crown, he mustered a small but dedicated Christian army. He erected a Cross, and before dawn on the day of the battle, had his soldiers kneel about it in prayer to the "true and living God Almighty," asking His mercy and protection. Advancing upon Cadwallon's huge army at the first light of dawn, they won the Battle of Heavenfield in 633 near Hexham, and Cadwallon was slain. Adomnan tells of Oswald having a vision of Columba on the night before the battle, promising him the victory.

So, having secured his kingdom, this devout Christian king, instead of reviving the Canterbury mission, sent to the Scottish elders at Iona where he had received his own Christian faith, asking them to send a bishop to teach and win his people in Northumbria to the religion of Christ. This was not to be the earliest nor the only mission by Irishmen in England during this period. King Sigebert of the East Angles, while in exile in Gaul, was influenced by the Irish missionary Columban, who sent one of his Frankish disciples, Felix, back with Sigebert in 630, where, with the oversight of Archbishop Honorius of Canterbury, Felix conducted a successful mission for seventeen years. Part of that time, he was aided by a celebrated Irish preacher, Fursey (Saint Fursa).[7]

In response to King Oswald's appeal, Abbot Sigene and his council of monks at Iona first sent a bishop-monk named Corman, a man of austere disposition and severe bearing, and the English refused to listen to him. He soon returned to Iona, reporting to his brethren that he had been unable to achieve anything because the English were "an ungovernable people, of an obstinate and barbarous temperament." Corman was not a humble, gentle man.

In a protracted meeting of the Iona Council to decide how better to meet the Northumbrian request, another brother, Aidan, said to Corman,

Brother, it seems to me that you were too severe on your ignorant hearers. You should have followed the practice of the Apostles, and begun by giving them the milk of simpler teaching, and gradually nourished them with the word of God until they were capable of greater perfection and able to follow the loftier precepts of Christ.

Here was a humble, discreet man. So they consecrated Aidan bishop, and sent him as their missionary to the English, to King Oswald's court.

True to the heritage of the Celtic saints, Aidan wanted an island like Iona, expressive of the Church's independence of the secular life of this world, a safe and untroubled haven for seclusion and worship and the cultivation of the spirit, and a base for sailing out on missionary errands to any part of the coast. He found what he wanted: the Isle of Lindisfarne, just off the coast south of the mouth of the Tweed, with a causeway of sand linking it to the mainland twice daily at low tide. It was not too far from Oswald's capital at Bamburgh. Oswald readily appointed it to be Aidan's see, and here the abbot-bishop and his monks built their cells and simple abbey church.

Since Aidan was not fluent in the English tongue at first, Oswald the king volunteered to be his interpreter. Soon they were traveling together the length and breadth of the kingdom, Aidan preaching in his Celtic tongue, and Oswald, who knew it well from his years as a royal refugee at Iona, translating the word of God to his ealdormen and thanes. Soon many more Scots arrived, says Bede and "proclaimed the word of God with great devotion in all the provinces under Oswald's rule." Churches were built. People flocked to them gladly to hear the Word preached. Those in priest's orders baptized those who believed (bishops not being required). The king, of his bounty, gave lands and endowments to establish monasteries. So, led by two humble, sincere loving Christians, their king and their bishop, the people of Northumbria rapidly became Christian according to the evangelical Columban tradition from Iona.

Bede, whose grandparents were probably converted under Aidan, says that time showed he was "remarkable not only for discretion, but for the other virtues as well . . . a man of outstanding gentleness, holiness and moderation." Only one fact marred his ministry in Bede's otherwise enthusiastic acclaim: "He had a zeal in God, but not according to knowledge, in that he kept Easter in accordance with the customs of his own nation."[8] Yet Bede is ungrudging in his praise of the beloved bishop's love of the poor, his honest straightforwardness, the simple austerity of his life, and his gift for reaching men's hearts. In tribute to Aidan, he wrote:

Among other evidences of his holy life, he gave his clergy an inspiring example of self-discipline and continence, and the highest recommendation of his teaching to all was that he and his followers lived as they taught. He never sought or cared for any worldly possessions, and loved to give away to the poor who chanced to meet him whatever he received from kings or wealthy folk. Whether in town or country he always travelled on foot unless compelled by necessity to ride; and whatever people he met on his walks, whether high or low, he stopped and spoke to them. If they were heathen, he urged them to be baptized; and if they were Christians, he strengthened their faith, and inspired them by word and deed to live a good life and to be generous to others. His life is in marked contrast to the apathy of our times, for all who walked with him, whether monks or layfolk, were required to meditate, that is, either to read the Scriptures or to learn the Psalter . . . [9]

Another use to which he frequently put gifts from the wealthy was to ransom any who had been sold unjustly as slaves. Many of those whom he ransomed in this way became his disciples, and after training them, he ordained them to the priesthood.

Oswald reigned only eight years, falling in battle at the age of thirty-eight when the King of Mercia surprised his forces at Maserfield in 641. Yet the Christian order he and Aidan had established was not shattered. Aidan was able to renew his work, though at first, he had little encouragement from Oswald's brother Oswy, who became king of Bernicia. He had full support from Oswy's second cousin, Oswin, son of Osric, king of Deira. Bede tells a tale illustrative of their friendship, of Oswin's generosity, and of Aidan's unworldliness. Though the bishop usually traveled on foot, the better to converse with people, Oswin gave him a very fine horse to ride on rough journeys or when crossing rivers. One day, while mounted on the horse, Aidan met a poor man who asked for alms, and impulsively dismounted and gave him the horse with all its rich trappings. Oswin heard of this and chided the bishop for so undervaluing his gift. "What are you saying, Your Majesty?" replied Aidan. "Is this child of a mare more valuable to you than this child of God?" Whereupon the king knelt at the bishop's feet and promised never to enquire how much of his bounty Aidan gave away to God's children.

In 651, Oswin was captured and treacherously put to death by Oswy, and eleven days later, after sixteen fruitful years as bishop of Northumbria, Aidan died of age and grief. Bede says in requiem:

> He cultivated peace and love, purity and humility; he was above anger and greed, and despised pride and conceit; he set himself to keep as well as to teach the laws of God, and was diligent in study and prayer. He used his priestly authority to check the proud and powerful; he tenderly comforted the sick; he relieved and protected the poor. To sum up in brief what I have learned from those who knew him, he took pains never to neglect anything that he had learned from the writings of the evangelists, apostles and prophets, and set himself to carry them out with all his powers.
>
> I greatly admire and love all these things about Aidan, because I have no doubt that they are pleasing to God; but I cannot approve or commend his failure to observe Easter at the proper time, whether he did it through ignorance of the canonical times, or in deference to the customs of his own nation. But this in him I do approve, that in keeping his Easter he believed, worshipped and taught exactly what we do, namely the redemption of the human race through the Passion, Resurrection and Ascension into heaven of the man Jesus Christ, the Mediator between God and man.[10]

After Aidan's death, the tide so turned against paganism that even Oswy, having taken over Deira, found himself under compulsion, either of popular will or of conscience, to return to the policy of his brother Oswald. He dedicated his daughter Elfled to become a nun, endowing the child with lands for a future nunnery. In 654, he defeated Penda of Mercia in a decisive battle in which the old pagan was slain, so that his committed Christian son, Peada, came to that throne. Now Oswy promoted the Christian cause in neighboring kingdoms, sending Cedd, a Northumbrian trained under Aidan who had been serving in Mercia, into Essex. After Cedd's death in 664, his former work in Mercia was carried on by his brother Chad, another Lindisfarne-trained pupil of Aidan. Peada of Mercia was baptized by Finan, successor to Aidan at Lindisfarne, in 653, and having gained authority in part of his father's kingdom, before the old man's death, had invited and supported the Irish and English monks there. Under Oswy's kingship, Diuma, another Irishman also ordained by Finan, became the first bishop of Mercia. His successors, Ceollach and Trumhere, were also Scots-trained.[11] So before the Synod of Whitby, mainly as the result of the sustained effort, dauntless zeal and singular persuasiveness of the Lindisfarne men and their Scots-Irish Celtic mentors, England was predominantly and permanently Christian. From the Firth of Forth to the south shores of Essex on the Thames, there was a fraternity of churches and monasteries owing their faith and practices to Lindisfarne and the Celtic Church from which it sprang. In thirty years, without knowing it, the tiny island south of Berwick-on-Tweed had become the spiritual capital of Christian England. As Bishop J.B. Lightfoot wrote in 1890, "Augustine was the Apostle of Kent, but Aidan was the Apostle of England."[12] God makes humble, gentle men of independent faith his fruitful missioners.

THE SYNOD OF WHITBY

That England, though so predominantly evangelized by the Celtic Church from Iona and Lindisfarne, should soon be under the Rome-Canterbury hierarchy was the result of a queer combination of causes, religious, domestic and political. At the time, the issue was not seen as we here describe it. There was no acknowledged open division between Iona and Rome. Centuries of isolation since times when the bishop of Rome held no more authority than other bishops in the scattered, growing Christian Church had resulted in no deviations in doctrine: only in minor practices, particularly the way of calculating the date of Easter. No disunity was intended. The Celtic practice for dating Easter had come to Britain from Rome through attendance of British bishops at the Council of Arles in 314. When Felix, of Celtic training, was sent by Columban from Gaul to serve in East Anglia, he received approval from Canterbury. During the period of evangelization, there was so much pioneering work to do that no one was jealous about who did it. Oswald, king of Northumbria, was visiting King Cynigils of the West Saxons at the time that king was baptized by

Birinius, the missionary from Rome. Oswald greeted him as a Christian brother as he came up from the baptismal font, offered him an alliance, took him as his godson, married his daughter, and the two kings jointly gave Birinius the city of Dorchester for his episcopal see.[13] They were all one in the Spirit, one in the Lord.

Yet as new generations of young leaders came on, the minor differences were magnified. Some of the young men traveled for schooling to Gaul where changed customs had come, and came home filled with superior learning and disdain for the old-fashioned, insular Celtic ways. One Scot named Ronan disputed with Bishop Finan, the successor of Aidan, about the date of Easter, only making the unconvinced bishop the more stubborn. His successor, Colman, was a no-less-determined Irishman. Meanwhile, a brilliant young English lad, Wilfrid, who had been brought up in the evangelical tradition of Iona in Northumbria, and had spent two years at Lindisfarne, was sent with royal patronage to study in Rome. He also studied with Archbishop Dalfin at Lyons in Gaul, who ordained him deacon with the Roman tonsure. Returning to Northumbria, Wilfrid became the teacher of the king's son, Alchfrid, who thus became an enthusiast of the new movement for change. A Bishop Agilbert from Wessex came to visit Northumbria, eager to cooperate with Wilfrid and Alchfrid, and at the prince's bidding, ordained Wilfrid a Presbyter. Alchfrid gave Wilfrid the monastery of Ripon. He had recently given the same land to some Scottish monks, but required of them that they change to Roman traditions. They had left rather than alter their Celtic customs.[14]

The issue became critical because of a domestic problem in King Oswy's royal household. Oswy's second wife was the princess Eanfled, daughter of Edwin of Northumbria and his Queen Ethelberga from Kent. Eanfled had been brought up in Kent after her father's death. Since she had been born on Easter, and was baptized by Paulinus in Northumbria on the day of the Roman celebration of Easter in 627, she loved this Easter date, and brought a Kentish priest, Romanus, as her chaplain to continue to adhere to that custom. So there was confusion in the king's household, for when the king had finished his Lenten fast and was celebrating Easter, the queen and her attendants were still fasting and keeping Palm Sunday. Oswy, having been instructed and baptized by the Scots, was not inclined to break from the Celtic custom, but the domestic situation was a nuisance, and Prince Alchfrid pressured him to do something about it. So, while Bishop Agilbert of Wessex was on hand, it was decided to hold a synod to put an end to this dispute and other matters of church difference, such as the tonsure of the monks, etc.

The place chosen for the meeting was the double monastery at Whitby then called Streanaeshalch (meaning "Bay of the Beacon") and presided over by the Abbess Hilda. Hilda had been related to King Edwin. As abbess of Hartlepool and later of Whitby, she helped to train many future leaders of the Church. The Synod was held in 664, or 663 by a newer reckoning, and many interested laymen and clergy attended.

Leading the debate for the Columban side was Colman, bishop of Lindisfarne, who was accompanied by his Celtic monks. He had the support of the Abbess Hilda and the venerable Bishop Cedd, who served as interpreter. For the Roman side, there were Bishop Agilbert of Dorchester with his priests Wilfrid and Agatho, the queen's chaplain Romanus, the elderly James the Deacon, whom Paulinus had left behind, and Prince Alchfrid. King Oswy presided. He opened the proceedings by observing that all who serve one God should observe one rule of life, and all who hope for one kingdom in heaven should not differ in celebrating the sacraments of heaven. So the synod's determination of the truer tradition should be accepted by all. Then he called upon Colman to explain his rite and its origin.

Colman said he followed the Easter customs of his forefathers, men beloved by God who received them from the blessed evangelist Saint John. The king then called upon Agilbert, who asked that Wilfrid might substitute for him, as they agreed on the whole matter and Wilfrid could speak in English. Wilfrid began by telling how he had found the same Easter customs observed not only in Italy and Gaul where he had traveled, but throughout the whole world wherever the Church of Christ has spread, yet "the only people who stupidly contend against the whole world are these Scots and their partners in obstinacy the Picts and Britons, who inhabit only a portion of these, the two uttermost islands of the ocean." Colman asked if then the Apostle John was stupid, and Wilfrid knew enough church history to explain that John, in the early Jewish period of the Church, following the customs of the Jewish law, used to begin the Feast of Easter on the fourteenth day of the first lunar month, whether it fell on a Sabbath or not. But Peter had begun the practice of celebrating Easter on the morrow of the Sabbath, the Lord's Day falling on the fifteenth to the twenty-first day of that moon. The Council of Nicea had confirmed this Roman practice. So Colman was following neither John nor Peter. Columba, and they who loved him, undeniably true servants of God, served Him in primitive simplicity only because no one had come to show them a more perfect way. Yet can Columba take precedence over Peter, the Prince of the Apostles to whom the Lord said, "Thou art Peter, and upon this rock I will build my Church, and the gates of hell shall not prevail against it; and I[3]will give unto thee the keys of the kingdom of heaven."?

"Is it true, Colman," asked the king, "that these words were spoken to that Peter by our Lord?" Colman had to admit it, and could produce no similar authority given to Columba. "Then," said the king, "I tell you Peter is the guardian of the gates of heaven, and I shall not contradict him. I shall obey his commands in everything to the best of my knowledge and ability; otherwise, when I come to the gates of heaven, there may be no one to open them, because he who holds the key has turned away."

The king had spoken, and none could then voice a disagreement. The debate was closed and the great missionary work of the Celts in England had ended. Colman and all the other Columban monks who would not give up their tonsure and date of Easter returned to the land of the Scots to confer with their associates on further courses of action, while Cedd and others who were willing to abandon the Scots customs for the Roman and now English rites, returned to their positions. Tuda, a South of Ireland bishop who had there already accepted the Roman Easter and tonsure, became bishop of Northumbria.[15]

They must have sensed something they did not argue at Whitby, that the issue went far deeper than the trifles dealt with in the discussion. These included other issues not recorded by Bede. Dating of Easter, tonsure of monks, differences in the rite of baptism, and about how you consecrate a bishop were insignificant matters beside the ultimate issue: that of Celtic independence versus integration into the Roman ecclesiastical system. Iona stood for freedom and autonomy; Rome had developed into an authoritarian hierarchy. What was even more to the point, the hierarchical system is more useful to kings.

As told in the *Life of Wilfrid* by Eddius Stephanus, Oswy had more to do with bringing the argument to a close than Bede's account discloses. After Wilfrid's learned discussion of the lunar cycles, "Oswiu asked them with a smile on his face, 'Tell me, which is greater in the Kingdom of Heaven, Columba or Peter?' " And when they all with one accord cited the passage of the keys of the Kingdom, Oswiu gave his decision.[16] The smile was a giveaway. Oswiu knew what question to ask as he had predetermined the issue.

History may not exactly repeat itself, but the Council of Nicea was more germane to the Synod of Whitby than anything Wilfrid could cite about Easter cycles. Both were called by civil rulers, dominated by their personalities, and brought to quick decisions defined by them. There is much reason to doubt that the Emperor Constantine was ever a deeply sincere Christian, as he grew more vindictive and dictatorial with power, and postponed his baptism until his deathbed. The growing strength of the Church in the Roman Empire had caused him to see that he must ride it cannily to power, and then bend it to his policy. Nicea was called to make the Church more useful to serve his power needs. Oswy too, was no fool. Nor is there evidence, really, that his penitence after the foul murder of his good Christian cousin, King Oswin, was genuine. He too became a promoter of the Church for political reasons. He promoted Columban missions, just so long as they were useful to him. Now there was presented to him the alternative not only of unity with the rest of the Christian world, and of the resolution of the disunity of his domestic household, but of an orderly ecclesiastical system run by authority as he understood it. Here were diocesan bishops to be organized under a future archbishop who could work hand and glove with a king, a system honed to usefulness to civil rulers by three hundred fifty years of accommodation since Constantine. The Roman clerics were smart to raise and keep the argument on Easter dating. The Columban monks were too naive to realize the hoax. King Oswy could help the Romanists to resolve the argument their way, on very pious Scriptural grounds, and, at the same time, gain a much more tractable and promising ecclesiastical establishment. As a king, he understood power, where it may reside in the Church, and prove more wieldy and usable for royal purposes. So, though the ostensible religious questions at Nicea and

Whitby were largely diverse, the basic outcome was the same. At each, the civil ruler got a more usable tool. In each instance, the Church bargained to lose its soul.

Of course, these were long-range results. The contribution of the Celtic Church to England did not immediately or ever completely die, for most of the converts trained by the evangelical monks from Iona, Lindisfarne, and the North of Ireland remained. Only thirty Englishmen left with Colman and his Irish monks when they went to found a new monastery on the Island of Innisbofin. A Celtic party remained strong in Northumbria well into the eighth century, and there were Celtic survivals in Mercia and Wessex until much later. Colman's last request of King Oswy was that Eata, abbot of Melrose, be made abbot also of the remaining English monks left behind at Lindisfarne. Eata was a staunch supporter of the customs of the Columban church who had resigned the abbacy of Ripon and led his monks away when Prince Alchfrid had demanded they conform to Roman customs. Eata brought with him from Melrose his prior, Cuthbert, whose character, evangelical zeal and devotion were in the high tradition of Aidan. The willingness of such men to bend to the new regime did not mean the surrender of their basic emphases. Young Englishmen continued to swarm to Irish monasteries for learning and Christian training. The abbot Eadfrid, scribe of the beautiful Lindisfarne Gospels, was one of them. As we shall see in the next chapter, many English missionaries trained in Ireland joined with the Irish who thronged to convert the Continental German tribes, chief among them Willibrord who went to Frisia with eleven companions in 690. Even Boniface, who labored to Romanize the work of the Irish missionaries on the Continent, may have received his evangelical passion and zeal indirectly from Celtic sources.

CUTHBERT OR WILFRID

The lives of two outstanding seventh-century saints, who both received their early training in the Columban church and became bishops under the new order, illustrate best the spiritual contrast between the two traditions. Fortunately, for those who wish to get the full impact of the contrast, Bede's *Life of Cuthbert* and Eddius' *Life of Wilfrid* are to be read in one volume, along with *The Voyage of St. Brendan,* beautifully translated by J.F. Webb in a convenient Penguin Classic, *Lives of the Saints.*

Cuthbert was born near Melrose in what is called the Border Country of Scotland.[17] A robust lad, he joined in games and carefree play with other children, and being agile and quick-witted, was usually a winner. One day, when the children were romping and contorting in a field, a little three-year-old ran up to Cuthbert and told him that a boy who was to become a bishop should be more solemn. Cuthbert remembered this. Stricken later with a lame knee, he was given helpful advice for its cure by a horseman dressed in white. He concluded this must have been an angel.

Serving as a shepherd boy on the Lammermoors, spending the watches of the night like Patrick in prayer, one night he saw a light streaming from the skies, and heard as it were heavenly choirs welcoming the soul of some holy man to heaven. Next day, he learned that at the time of his vision, Aidan, the holy Bishop of Lindisfarne, had passed to heaven. That was the year 651. Delivering the sheep back to their owners, he resolved to enter a monastery. He rode to Melrose where the Prior Boisil was widely known for his sublime virtue. Boisil perceived the earnest sincerity of the lad, and welcomed him to the tonsured brotherhood.

As a young monk, Cuthbert excelled in zeal for strict discipline, watching, praying, working, and reading harder than anyone else. He abstained from all alcoholic drink, but ate enough to keep strong and robust, lest his work should suffer.

Cuthbert was one of the monks sent by Abbot Eata to Ripon when Prince Alchfrid gave them the ground, but who left rather than change to Roman practices. Boisil was aging, and took Cuthbert into his confidence, giving him special Scripture training in the Gospel of John, and hinting that one day Cuthbert would become a bishop. On Boisil's death, Cuthbert succeeded him as prior of Melrose Abbey.

Cuthbert served as prior with holy zeal for the remainder of his thirteen years at Melrose. Inside the monastery, he counseled the monks on the religious life, and set a high example of it himself. Outside in the world, he strove to convert people for miles around from their foolish ways to a delight in the promised joys of heaven. During the plague, some who had professed Christ had reverted to idolatry. To bring back both kinds of sinners, he often did the rounds of the villages, on horseback or more often on foot, preaching the way of truth. Everyone gathered round at his call on the village green, and people listened eagerly to his preaching, and acted upon it.

Such was the skill of his teaching, such his power of driving his lessons home, and so gloriously did his angelic countenance shine forth that none dared keep back from him even the closest secrets of their hearts. They confessed their sins openly . . . and made amends by "fruits worthy of repentance" as he commanded.

He searched out the rugged places of the hills which other preachers dreaded to visit because of their poverty and squalor. He was so keen to preach, he would stay away weeks or a month with the rough hill folk. So largely due to Cuthbert's efforts, the last heathen race of North Britain, the Angles, were converted to Christ.[18]

After the Synod of Whitby, when Colman departed and Abbot Eata was given the added abbacy of Lindisfarne, Eata transferred Cuthbert there as prior. By teaching and example, he took charge of the remaining monks, some of whom preferred the old way of life and resisted. Eventually, he won them by kindly patience and forbearance, with firmness bringing them around little by little to a better frame of mind, keeping calm and unruffled by their insults. He also kept up his custom of frequent visits to the common people of the neighborhood, and became famous for his prayers restoring the sick and suffering. In his zeal for prayer, he would keep vigil three or four nights at a stretch without even taking to his bed at night, still doing manual work or making the rounds of the island by day to drive away the heaviness of sleep. He upbraided the monks for their softness in being annoyed if anyone awakened them at the wrong moment, as he himself welcomed being wakened any time to turn his mind to something useful. His sorrow for sin, thirst for righteousness, and sympathy for others were legend.

After many years, he retired to a life of contemplation on little Farne Island, nine miles southeast of Lindisfarne. There, as a soldier of Christ, he battled with the Devil. With the help of the monks, he built an enclosure with a hut, an oratory, and a guest shelter, and there lived completely alone for nine years, so avid in prayer that he took little care of his physical needs. He never removed his boots for months on end. The Celtic monks, in their eagerness to subjugate the flesh, never learned that "cleanliness is next to Godliness!"

Still, many people came to visit him from remote parts of Britain, confiding their temptations and troubles. They were never disappointed. No one left unconsoled or untreated:

Those beset with worry he brought back to the joy of Heaven. He showed them that both good fortune and bad were transitory in this world. To men beset with temptation he would skilfully disclose all the wiles of the Devil, explaining that a soul lacking in the love of God or man is easily caught in the Devil's nets, while one that is strong in the faith can with God's grace brush them aside like so many spiders' webs.

When brethren marveled at his way of life, he modestly pointed to abbots and priors like Boisil, whom he called superior. He performed many healing miracles, and often foretold events. In one prophecy, he confided to his closest friends the fear that he would be elected bishop, saying he was not worthy and would serve only two years.

A great Synod at Twyford presided over by Archbishop Theodore and attended by King Egfrid unanimously elected Cuthbert bishop for Northumbria. He would not answer the summons of messengers to abandon his hermitage until the king in person, Bishop Trumwine, and other distinguished men took boat to the island, knelt, and implored him with tears to consent. Remembering the words of Boisil, and recognizing the unanimous decision of the assembly, he reluctantly consented. He was consecrated at York on Easter Day of 685. He was intended for the vacant see of Hexham, but at his request, Eata was sent there and he was installed at Lindisfarne. There he followed the Apostolic example, adorning his office with good works, by prayer, teaching, and example leading his flock, making his Bishop's rounds for ordaining and confirmation. Bede says:

Above all else he was afire with heavenly love, unassumingly patient, devoted to unceasing prayer, and kindly to all who came to him for comfort.

After two years in his bishopric, he felt death drawing near and returned to his island hermitage. Leaving instructions for a humble burial in a stone coffin he had prepared, Saint Cuthbert passed to his heavenly reward on March 20, 687. Lightfoot has said, "He left a fame behind him which no churchman north of the Humber has ever surpassed or even rivalled." Cuthbert truly tried to follow the way of his Lord. He was a humble, gentle man.

Wilfrid, the Grand Abbot of Ripon

According to his newer Roman lights, Wilfrid was faithful too. Eddius Stephanus, who wrote Wilfrid's life,[19] is his great admirer, calls him "a Bishop worthy before God," was eager to preserve his memory accurately, and says, "simply to know what kind of a man he was is in itself a sure way to virtue." When he embarks on "the holy life and merits of the blessed Bishop Wilfrid," what he tells is substantially confirmed by the Venerable Bede's *History*.

Wilfrid, born in 633, was an obedient boy to his parents, beloved of all, handsome, well-proportioned, gentle, modest, and controlled—"swift to hear and slow to speak." A cruel stepmother's presence helped to decide him to leave his well-to-do home at fourteen. His father sent him richly caparisoned with servants to the court of King Oswy to find favor with Queen Eanfled. She sponsored his desire to seek Divine service in the Church, and assigned him as a servant to a paralyzed nobleman who had decided to become a monk at Lindisfarne. There Wilfrid served for two years, zealously learning the whole Psalter and other books by heart, and won the love of all by his devotion.

Yet he yearned to visit Rome, and his master consented. The queen sent him to the Kentish royal court, where, handsomely outfitted and in the company of a Bishop Baducing, another nobleman going to Rome, he was sent on his way. There arose some difference, compared by his biographer to that between Paul and Barnabas over John Mark, between the high-spirited young enthusiast and the austere bishop, for they parted company at Lyons. The bishop proceeded at once to Rome, while young Wilfrid remained in Lyons, making a great friend of Archbishop Dalfinus there. The archbishop wanted to adopt him as a son, marry him to his niece, and promote him in the civil government of Gaul. His judgment may not have been far wrong.

Yet Wilfrid professed his religious purpose to continue in his divine vocation and to proceed to Rome, and was sent off well provided with guides and supplies. In Rome, he visited many saints' shrines, and found in Boniface the Archdeacon an able teacher of the New Testament, of the Canon Law, and of the calculation of Easter. Boniface presented him to the pope, who gave him his blessing. With many holy relics, he returned to Dalfinus at Lyons, where he studied for three years, and received ordination as a deacon and the Roman tonsure from Dalfinus's hand.

Returning to Northumbria, proud of his adoption of the Roman way, he found a pupil, friend, and ally in Prince Alchfrid, who gave him the monastery of Ripon with forty hides of land. There he soon won approval by his organizing ability, charity, and generosity. Soon came Bishop Agilbert from Gaul, who had been serving at Dorchester, to aid their cause. Agilbert ordained Wilfrid a presbyter, and let him take the lead for the Roman cause in debate with Colman of Lindisfarne at the Synod of Whitby. After Wilfrid won the debate, it was natural for the king's counselors to elect him to fill Colman's vacant see at the young age of thirty. After an exemplary declination, he thought it better not to flee from God's blessing, but requested that he might travel to Gaul to receive ordination to the episcopate from unquestionably orthodox sources. The Romanist party were now questioning whether British ordinations were fully valid in the new sacramentarian definition of the Apostolic Succession.

The kings sent Wilfrid in great state at vast expense to be ordained by at least fourteen Catholic bishops, Agilbert, now bishop of Paris, among them. Wilfrid was borne into the oratory aloft on a golden throne by nine bishops to the accompaniment of chanting choirs. Heady honors for a lad of thirty years! Yet while all this was taking so much time, Oswy allowed the Celtic party to have Chad ordained and installed in the waiting vacant see. They sent Chad to Canterbury for ordination, but it was the year 665 when that archbishopric was vacant, and the bishops who officiated were Wini of Wessex and "two bishops of the British nation."[20] When Wilfrid returned, he could only withdraw to his abbacy at Ripon, and could use his new episcopate only when the kings of Mercia and Kent summoned him for ordinations. Wilfrid introduced the Benedictine rule in his monastery, and in others he founded in Mercia for King Wulfhere.

When Archbishop Theodore, newly installed in Canterbury, came from Kent to Northumbria, he deposed Chad, who humbly consented to Wilfrid's installation in York. Theodore would not recognize the validity of Chad's ordination, so he allowed himself to be reordained with Roman rites and was installed as bishop of Litchfield in Mercia. In York, Wilfrid rebuilt the old church built by Paulinus, then built a glorious new stone church at Ripon. At the impressive dedication service, standing at the altar before assembled kings and company, Wilfrid read off a list of the Church properties in their realms which had been deserted by earlier British clergy when fleeing from the Saxons, suggesting God would be pleased if the kings would give these lands to him. The kings complied handsomely, and Wilfrid feasted them for three days.

Later Wilfrid backed King Egfrid, son of Oswy of Northumbria, in a successful war with King Wulfhere of Mercia, the victory extending Wilfrid's jurisdiction. He was pious and self-disciplined, ruling well, and received many handsome bequests. At Hexham, he built another glorious stone church, and when one of the young masons fell from a high pinnacle, he was healed with the help of Wilfrid's prayers.

It was too much too fast. King Egfrid's Queen Iurminburgh became envious of Wilfrid's temporal glories, and she turned the king against him. They convinced Archbishop Theodore of Canterbury that Wilfrid was getting the big head, and though they could point to no chargeable reprehensible conduct, while Wilfrid was away, they divided his see and consecrated three bishops over parts of his territory. When Wilfrid challenged their action, the king and archbishop acknowledged there were no charges against him. After all, pride in office and in earthly glory were no longer faults in the Church that ordained him bishop. It was a purely jurisdictional decision. Wilfrid decided to take his case to the Holy See at Rome.

Apparently, there were plots to intercept him on the direct route through Gaul, but Wilfrid landed in Friesland. There he preached to vast crowds with the evangelical zeal he had learned at Lindisfarne, and baptized many chiefs and thousands of converts, beginning the work later carried forward by his friend and pupil, Willibrord. He remained at this work all winter. Then, contacting friends on the way, he was saved from the false attempts of his English enemies to thwart his journey, and safely reached Rome.

Pope Agatho had already received Archbishop Theodore's

reports. When they read Wilfrid's well-written petition, the Roman Synod decided in his favor, and agreed to his suggestion that he, Wilfrid, should summon a council in Northumbria to help him choose coadjutors to be consecrated by the Archbishop of Canterbury to replace the usurpers who had been installed. They even let him represent the northern part of Britain and Ireland in signing the statement of a council of many bishops on Orthodoxy currently being held in Rome.

Wilfrid returned with these Orders of the Holy See to show to Archbishop Theodore and King Egfrid. When he read them before the king and clergy, he was accused of bribing the pope, and cast into prison for nine months, the king in a rage defying the pope's judgment and despoiling Wilfrid of all but his clothing. He was hidden away in a dungeon. Wilfrid submitted without rancor, and the king later tried to bribe him by offering him part of his diocese if he would say the orders sent by the Pope were not genuine. Wilfrid humbly refused.

When the queen fell deathly ill at the nunnery at Coldingham, the abbess, King Oswy's sister, called it judgment for their treatment of Wilfrid. Thereupon, the king released him to go into exile with his friends. In Mercia, he was welcomed by Sheriff Berhtwald, a nephew of Mercia's king. The Sheriff gave him a plot of land where he founded a little monastery, but threats from King Egfrid through the king of Mercia drove Wilfrid on to Wessex. There, the queen's influence forced him to move on again. Finally in Sussex, he found a territory, remote enough and still heathen, where he was needed and welcome. The people were suffering from famine, and did not know how to fish. Wilfrid taught them to fish and saved them from famine, so that they were more than glad to listen to his message of salvation from spiritual starvation. With Gospel preaching, he converted the king and queen and their people, and was given a handsome estate for his episcopal see by King Aethelwalh. If only all of his energies might have been given to missionary evangelism! Founding a monastery on the estate given him, he discovered 250 male and female slaves there, and freed them.

Finding Cadwalla, a royal exile from Wessex in Sussex, Wilfrid befriended him and helped him, so that when Cadwalla recovered the throne of West Saxony, Wilfrid became his bishop as well.

By this time, the Archbishop Theodore, aging and

conscience-stricken, hearing of Wilfrid's success in the neighboring kingdoms, decided to call Wilfrid to him and honor the injunctions of the Roman see. Inviting Wilfrid and Bishop Erconwald to London, he confessed his wrong and expressed his wish that Wilfrid should succeed him as archbishop. Wilfrid forgave him, and asked him to write to his friends about the reconciliation, asking that at least part of his confiscated properties be restored. The archbishop matter might be left to a future council. Theodore wrote to the kings. Egfrid had been killed in battle, and the new king, his half-brother Aldfrid, called Wilfrid back from exile, and restored to him the abbacy of Hexham, the see of York, and the abbacy of Ripon with their revenues, driving out the usurping bishops. Wilfrid possessed the lands and titles for five years.

Then Wilfrid and Aldfrid quarreled over lands and properties, and Aldfrid banished him from Northumbria. Wilfrid was just too big a person for a mere king to have around! Again Wilfrid went into exile in Mercia. Archbishop Theodore had been succeeded by Archbishop Berhtwald at Canterbury. They now held a synod in Northumbria at Austerfield. They invited Wilfrid to attend, promising to honor the pope's decrees, but when Wilfrid attended, an altercation broke out. He confronted an endeavor to trick him into signing in advance a promise to obey whatever that synod might decree. So they might strip him of all his offices and properties with his advance acquiescence! Again, he appealed to Rome.

It required another long journey afoot to the Eternal City. Again the pope, now John, called a synod of bishops and clergy to hear Wilfrid's petition. He asked the Holy See's judgment since his assailants, in contravention of Pope Agatho's decrees, had robbed him of his bishopric, monasteries, and possessions. The representatives of Archbishop Berhtwald of Canterbury charged Wilfrid with rejecting the authority of his archbishop. Wilfrid replied that the archbishop had refused to tell him what he would decree, and had demanded that he sign a written promise in advance to submit to his every judgment whatever, no matter how impossible they might prove to be. He had promised to obey so long as the archbishop's decisions tallied with Canon Law and the decrees of the former pope's synods. After seventy sessions lasting four months, taking up every charge the archbishop had sent against Wilfrid, he was completely exonerated. Bishop Berhtwald was ordered to convene a synod where the usurping bishops would be required to give evidence of their charges, to solve the issue amicably in England if possible, and, if not, to bring their charges again to Rome, facing possibility of excommunication.

Wilfrid had to make the laborious journey back to England. He was over seventy, and had a stroke in Gaul on the way. Yet he recovered after a vision that promised him several more years of life, and returned to confront Archbishop Berhtwald, who submitted with fear and alacrity to the papal bull. King Aethilred of Mercia received Wilfrid with joyous tears. Only Aldfrid of Northumbria refused to change his mind, until, stricken with a serious illness and fearful it was a judgment, he vowed, if he were spared to carry out the pope's commands, and that his son would do so if he could not be healed. The king died. His immediate successor, Eadwulf was also stubborn, and was driven from office after two months. Aldfrid's son, Osred now came to the throne as a ward of Wilfrid. A synod was held, which, after hearing of Alfrid's deathbed vow, yielded at last. Wilfrid received all his titles, monasteries, and properties, and there was peace.

Yet soon thereafter, on his way to Hexham, Wilfrid suffered another stroke. Again he recovered, with the help of many prayers, and had eighteen months more to settle his affairs. He decided how to divide his properties and treasures, made the round of his monasteries giving them his legacies and guarantees of future support, and finally at Oundle, after two more strokes, gave his friends his blessing and died. He was seventy-six years of age. They took his body back to Ripon for burial in the great Church of Saint Peter he had built, and sufficient miraculous portents after his death guaranteed his elevation to sainthood.

Wilfrid's life was a tragedy. By all the rules of the Roman tradition, he was completely innocent and in the right, yet he had abandoned the early training in humble poverty and gentle meekness he had learned at Lindisfarne. The very system he had espoused, with the collaboration of archbishops and kings in this world's strategies, had proved his undoing. Let any churchmen have too much glory, and the envy of this world's rulers and of lesser brethren in the cloth will collaborate to bring him down. Princes of the Church are too wont to listen to princes of this world. Even when the papacy was right, the system did not work for peace and justice until too late. A life by which much greater good might have been done was largely wasted. By the coveting love of properties and offices, The Way, with its humility and. gentleness and self-sacrificing service, is forsaken and the Holy Spirit finds His avenues of inspiration blocked.

Still, kings were not ready to learn. Under King Aldfrid, the Abbot Coelfrid of Jarrow and Wearmouth introduced the Benedictine rule. He was the strong advocate of the Romanizing changes who convinced Adomnan of Iona to adopt the new ways. Nechtan IV, the Pictish King of Inverness, seeking to improve relations with Northumbria and hearing of the advantages of the Roman system for civil rulers, sent a delegation to Northumbria, around 710 or thereafter, asking advice. Coelfrid's reply, probably written by Bede, convinced that king, and Nechtan ordered the new Easter tables and coronal tonsure for all monks throughout his kingdom. Again the Columban monks were resistant. At about this time, Egbert, the Englishman who had long been a student in Ireland, went to live at Iona. Helped by the pressure of King Nechtan, he was able to convince the Iona monks to adopt the Roman Easter in 716. Then, in 718, King Nechtan decreed the expulsion from his realm of all remaining nonconformists, and the Columban monks who would not yield left for Wales, the last bastion of Celtic independence. The Benedictines took over and the Church was in the possession of the kings—and soon lost its soul.

Such a statement is always relative, however. In Scotland and England, there were many faithful Christians to carry on the Gospel tradition. It was a long time in Scotland before the Church of Rome gained full dominion there. Only through the influence of the saintly Queen Margaret of the latter part of the eleventh ccentury was Scotland brought under full papal control, and Andrew was substituted for John as the Patron Saint of Scotland. The Irish monks who came in to replace the Columbans, the Keledie or Culdees of Loch Leven and at Kilrymont by Saint Andrews, though suppressed by Margaret's son, King David, in the twelfth century, still had remnants in the fourteenth. Unorganized spiritual influences remained in unrecorded places. So it is possible to maintain that seeds of independence, evangelical faith, and freedom which is of the Spirit, sown by the Celtic Church, finally sprouted in the Reformation.

Map: Celtic-Inspired Missions: Irish and English, 6th through 9th Centuries

Chapter VII

THE WAY TAKEN TO RENEW AND WIN THE CONTINENT

The joy of new life in Christ must be shared with those who know Him not! While Columba was evangelizing the Picts in the northwestern end of the earth, and before Aidan was sent from Iona to Northumbria, the great Celtic mission movement to reconvert the former Roman Continent and evangelize the Germanic tribes had begun. There was often a joyous abandon in the spirit with which those Celtic monks embraced voluntary exile, their *"peregrinatio."*

The Latin *Voyage of St. Brendan* is a ninth-century, tongue-in-cheek spoof, yet it reflects the rollicking humor with which many sailed away they knew not where! A monk called Barinthus visited Brendan, began to weep, and threw himself full-length in sadness upon the ground. Brendan kissed him and said, "Father, your visit ought to fill us with joy, not sadness. Surely you came with the intention of cheering us up, so preach the word of God to us and then regale our spirits with an account of the wonders you have seen on your voyage over the sea." So Barinthus told them about his visit to the Island of Delights, and a farther visit to an isle called "the Land of Promise of the Saints," where it was daylight all the time, and without eating a bite or drinking a mouthful, they felt so replete that anyone might have thought they were full of new wine. Thereupon, Brendan chose fourteen monks, and they all sailed away westward to find the entrancing isle. One island they landed upon and built a fire upon to cook their fish surprisingly turned out to be a whale. We need not here recount all of the wonders of that voyage. Yet there was a real Brendan who in 558 founded the monastery of Clonfert, and who went away on a famous voyage from 565 to 573 with the unwieldy number of thirty-three companions. Maps made before the voyage of Columbus located Brendan's Isle near the mythical island of Antilla. Sometimes it was confused with the Canary Islands or Madiera. Four expeditions to find it set out from the Canaries between 1526 and 1721, and hope of finding it persisted until 1759 when it was realized that the belief was due to mirages.

Under the year 891, the *Anglo-Saxon Chronicle* tells of three men with just such carefree wanderlust:

> And three Scots came to King Alfred from Ireland in a boat without oars. They had left home bent on serving God in a state of pilgrimage, they cared not where. Their boat was made of two-and-a-half hides and contained enough provisions to last them seven days, and within a week they landed in Cornwall and shortly afterwards came to King Alfred. They were called Dubslane, Macbeth and Maelinmun.

There is evidence of Irish monastic settlement in Iceland (Thule) before the arrival of the Norsemen.

Our point is that the freedom and individuality and variety of the Celtic tradition allowed for vast differences in the motivations of the pilgrims who swarmed overseas from Ireland during those blessed centuries. Undoubtedly, love of adventure, wanderlust, was one of the motives. Even of such an ascetic, disciplined, religiously devoted missionary as Columban, his biographer Jonas writes,

> After he had been many years in the cloister he longed to see strange lands, in obedience to the command the Lord gave to Abraham, "Get thee out of thy country and from thy kindred and from thy father's house to a land which I will show thee."

Most people act from mixed motives, and even when religious motives were dominant, they were not always missionary. Among the Psalms they memorized regularly was the fifty-fifth, with its sixth and seventh verses:

> O that I had wings like a dove,
>   I would fly away and be at rest;
> Yea I would wander far,
>   I would lodge in the wilderness, Selah.

"Dove" was the monastic name given Columba and Columban. The ascetic ideal appealed to many: to be an anchorite was to make the supreme self-sacrifice, the fittest crown of the renunciation in which they had engaged. They went into exile from their beloved country "for the love of God," "for the name of the Lord," "for the love of the Name of Christ," "for the healing of the soul," "in order to win a heavenly fatherland."

When we hear that they called themselves "peregrini," we must not translate that simply "pilgrims," Pilgrims take a pious journey to some shrine for some special devotion, then return home to resume their normal life. Later, from the eighth century on, there were many such pilgrims who swarmed from Ireland and England over the highways of Europe to visit Rome or even the Holy Land. Not so these earlier peregrini. They were rather voluntary exiles, who had pledged not to return to their native land, usually for the remainder of their lives, whether or not they undertook any missionary duties. They were soldiers of Christ, enlisted in a battle with the Devil, and the spiritual hosts of wickedness within their own souls, with the beatific vision and heaven as their rewards.[1]

Yet among the heirs of the tradition of Patrick and Columba, the missionary motive was also strong. They thrilled to the same Bible texts in which their Lord commanded his disciples to take the Gospel to the whole world. As Dom Gougaud says:

> For close upon 400 years Irish saints, filled with burning missionary zeal, labored incessantly to spread the Christian faith and monastic discipline in Gaul, Belgium, Alsace, in Alemannia, in Franconia, in Italy, along the course of the Danube and down the valley of the Rhine.[2]

They were joined in this by their English converts. In the seventh century, they went to ravaged Gaul, Italy, and Switzerland. In the eighth century, it was extended to the low countries and Germany. In the ninth century, the thrust was to further Teutonic peoples, a mission questionably completed by the forcible conversion of the Saxons. In the tenth, eleventh, and twelfth centuries, the Scandinavians were brought into the fold. All of these missions, except the incorporation of the Saxons, were manned chiefly by missionaries from the British Isles.[3]

They were a picturesque crew, the Irish *peregrini,* with their queer tonsure and homespun woolen cowls, their zeal sometimes inspiring but often annoying to the less ascetic and less evangelically inclined churchmen of the Continent. Nor did they tamely conform to the ecclesiastical organization of the lands to which they went. Their wandering bishops had little experience and less patience with the Roman-inherited territorial diocesan rule of the local bishops into whose poorly evangelized territories they sometimes moved. In their Irish monasteries, bishops had been subordinate to abbots in rule and discipline, so in their monasteries on the Continent, they largely ignored the local territorial bishops and resisted submission to their rule. Nor did they submit to kings or popes!

The first and greatest of them was Columban. Some twenty years younger than Columba, he left Ireland for Gaul seven years before that year in which Columba died and Pope Gregory sent Augustine to Kent. Though some German scholars have called him Columba the Younger, there is no evidence of personal connection between the two great missionary leaders, and in Latin texts, he is known as "Columbanus." Tall, vigorous, commanding like Columba, and also an eloquent preacher and gifted poet, he surpassed Columba in the austerity of his discipline and the range of his learning, but lacked the diplomatic discretion, tact, and gentleness the missionary to the Picts learned so grievously before leaving Ireland.

Scholarship has two advantages in knowing Columban. His biographer, Jonas, wrote within a few years after Columban's death, having traveled where he had worked and inteviewed persons who had known him intimately, and, unlike Adomnan, had more interest in telling biographical facts than miracle stories. Furthermore, many of Columban's writings have been preserved: a monastic rule and penitential, letters, sermons, and both light and serious Latin poetry.

Columban was born sometime around 541 in Leinster. As a boy, his parents encouraged him to begin the study of grammar, rhetoric, geometry, and the Holy Scriptures. When, in time, his good looks attracted the forward attentions of "lascivious maidens," he asked counsel of a godly woman, who reminded him of the ills associated with Eve, Delilah, and Bathsheba, and advised him to leave his home territory. Jonas, reporting the firmness of his resolution to flee these dangers, uses the figurative language of Jerome, that he stepped over the prostrate body of his pleading mother. From southeast Ireland, he sought the northwest, enrolling in the monastery at

Gleenish on Lough Erne. There he was schooled under Abbot Sinell, a strict disciplinarian who had studied under Finian of Clonard and Comgall of Bangor. Having studied the Bible with Sinell long enough to write a commentary on the Psalter and some hymns, he went to Bangor under Comgall. There he stayed for twenty-some-odd years of study and teaching until, as a ripened monk in his mid-forties, he applied to the abbot for permission to go on pilgrimage. Recruiting a band of twelve monks to be his companions in exile, he sailed from Ulster in about the year 590, landed in Brittany, whence they passed through into the heart of Frankish Gaul.

In Gaul, there was dire need of Christian renewal. The early days of evangelization under the Roman Empire, of Irenaeus in the late second century and Martin of Tours in the late third, and of the strong influence upon the British Church in the days of Germanus of Auxerre were now centuries past. Wave after wave of barbarian invasion had flowed in from the East as the Roman Empire collapsed, each new inroad leaving the survivors of the former civilization fewer, more isolated, and less influential. As the social order disintegrated, the towns of Roman days had steadily fallen into decay, and the Church, striving to maintain some order amid the chaos, had grown weaker and decadent as well.

Writing his *Historia Franconum* at the very time Columban arrived, Gregory of Tours chronicles an endless succession of acts of brutality and ferocity in the Merovingian realm, accepting them with melancholy pessimism, and no vision of anything better, or of hope born of spiritual judgment. The degradation of standards among the ruling Franks and the coarsening of life was universal. The ruling barbarians, while they covertly admired and in some ways aped the people they had conquered, dragged even the surviving leaders of the Church down toward their own level. Guilty of simony themselves, these clerics had little moral and spiritual influence. Surviving pagan cults had taken on new life. Superstition masqueraded as faith.

Into this society, notorious for cruelties, murders, gluttony, drunkenness, and flagrant sexual irregularities, came Columban and his little band of twelve Irish monks, preaching the victory of Christ on the Cross over the power of the Devil, presenting the rebuke of an austere life and stringent practice of pure virtues to raw consciences and fearful souls eager for the medicine of confession and penance. Columban and his brothers engaged in some itinerant preaching even before they sought a place to settle.

Gregory of Tours says there was one good king, among the royal ruffians of the time, Guntram of Burgandy, who did many favors for churches. Columba approached him, or his successor Childebert II (593), asking permission to establish a monastery. The place the missionary chose was the old abandoned fort of Anagrates in the western foothills of the Vosges Mountains, far from the royal court, among a fragment of the Germanic Suevi tribe left behind during westward migration. Though accustomed to eating only one coarse meal a day, they nearly starved while getting settled, until a farmer seeking prayers for his sick wife brought horse-loads of food, and a not-too-distant abbot with a Briton name, Caramtog, came to their aid. Soon crowds were thronging the old fort, bringing their sick to be healed through Columban's prayers. The need for quiet to cultivate his soul led Columban to spend some holy days in a secret retreat. There, by gentle persuasion, he expelled a bear from the hollow of a rock he wanted for a devotional site, and subsisted on wild apples, herbs, and water.

The rigor of Columban's discipline was no deterrent to recruits. Holiness in that degraded time proved popular. Men thronged to join the devoted band, repenting of their sins, willing to labor hard in penance, their sheer numbers and the need for more arable land forcing Columban to begin another center at Luxeuil, eight miles to the south. There were the ruins of an old Roman town with only a few pagan inhabitants, with wild beasts from the hills often coming down to the outskirts. This became the main community, and recruits continued to pour in, some of them scions of prominent families, until it numbered in the thousands. A third foundation became necessary three miles away at Fontaines. Columban kept command of all three foundations, moving freely between them, leaving provosts to govern in his absence. All lived under the rule Columban framed, much more strict than the Benedictine, with absolute obedience to the abbot, as much silence as possible, a minimum of coarse food, deprivation from sufficient sleep, and a long enumeration of sins with severer penalties than the Benedictine Penitential prescribed.

For about ten years, the mission had peace, with growing numbers of converts and widening influence in the area, until its very success caused trouble. These converts were celebrating the Celtic Easter. Columban had neglected to secure the approval of the nominal bishops of the area who had hitherto neglected these people, and he had failed to keep on good terms with the succeeding kings of Burgundy. Worldly bishops and a depraved court found his presence intolerable.

From the bishops' point of view, the followers of Columban were schismatic. There was no charge of doctrinal heresy, for Columban's teachings were thoroughly orthodox in theology. Still, in Gaul all Christians were subject to bishops, including all abbots and monks, and all observed the Roman Easter. Now here were numerous adherents of the new monasteries in no way recognizing episcopal authority and observing the Irish Easter date. Columban, anticipating part of this difficulty, wrote a letter to Pope Gregory the Great around the year 600 contending with forthright good humor for the Irish Easter, hoping perhaps for some word of tolerance for the diversity. His clever playfulness in alluding to an earlier pope, Leo the Great, with the wry use of a Scripture quotation, "a living dog is better than a dead Leo," might have opened him to the charge of impertinence. He warmly praised Gregory as an author, but this was hardly enough to accredit him to the pope, and there is no record that Gregory replied.

In 603, Columban was summoned by the bishops to answer for his irregularities before their synod meeting at Chalons sur Saône. He replied by letter, in conciliatory good temper, but with no sign of yielding. He argued on the Easter question, claiming support of Eusebius and Jerome, but pleading for love and reciprocal tolerance, quoting 1 Thessalonians: "Prove all things, hold what is good." He rather chided the bishops on two scores of their neglect, quoting "he who shuns the toil of opposing sinful men is a hireling," and suggesting that if all would choose to cast off pride and "be humble and poor for Christ's sake," all God's people might "enjoy a true peace." Obviously, Columban felt under no obligation to obey the bishops, and they took no further action to oust him.

Far more serious was his altercation with the royal household. Since 597, the nominal ruler of Burgundy was Theuderic II, a profligate young prince, but the real master of the realm was his dominating grandmother, Brunhilda. She was capable, but utterly unscrupulous and brutal. A contemporary historian charges her with instigating the murder of the bishop of Vienne. The biographer of Columban says she encouraged her grandson in debauchery in order to retain power in her own hands. Columban aroused her ire by his open disapproval of the concubines. She thereupon called upon him to come and bless Theuderic's illegitimate sons. Columban came before the court in high anger, cursed the boys as the offspring of harlotry, and foretold that they would never come to royal power. Theuderic as a boy had visited Luxeuil and had some admiration for Columban, so he sent a peace offering of some food and wine from the royal kitchen. Columban threw it on the ground saying, "The gifts of the wicked are an abomination to the Most High, for it is not fitting that the mouths of the servants of God should be polluted by his food." Theuderic ordered him seized and taken to Besançon prison where he took opportunity to preach to a large band of condemned prisoners. It is a wonder his throat was not slit. Theuderic instead, still in awe of his character and knowing how the people revered him, ordered his deportation back to Ireland. Having vowed to be a pilgrim in exile for life, Columban could not welcome this. The Irish among his monks were to be expelled with him. One of them, Deicola, unable to keep up with the band, bade Columba farewell and dropped by the wayside. Able to build himself a hut in the wilds, he soon overcame the hostility of a local priest, and founded the well-known monastery of Lure.

Led across France by way of Auxerre and down the Loire, Columban cured a blind man at Orleans, prayed all night at the tomb of Saint Martin at Tours, and was placed, with his companions, on shipboard at Nantes. Hostile winds blew the ship back into the harbor time and again, and finally beached it. This sufficient omen convinced the superstitious guards to look the other way when Columban, his companions, and their possessions had been taken off to lighten the ship and refloat it. They picked up their belongings and walked away.

To return to Luxeuil would have been futile. Columban decided to make for Lombardy in the north of Italy, by way of more favorable Frankish realms. Clothaire II of Neustria welcomed him at Soissons, but he went on to Metz where King Theudebert II of Austrasia consented to a new missionary enterprise in the northern lake region of Switzerland. They sailed up the Rhine and its tributary to Tuggen on the Timmat, where they stirred pagan animosity against them by destroying idols and spilling out wine consecrated to Woden. Yet they made some converts, one of the monks, Gall, having learned to converse in German. Being unwelcome to local authorities, they went on to the eastern end of Lake Constance at Bregenz where they spent some months setting up another monastery.

Yet Columban had his heart set on going farther into Lombardy. According to another writer than Jonas, a Walahfrid Strabo of the ninth century, there was some altercation between Columban and Gall. The superior insisted that Gall's plea of illness was a cover for his desire to stay in Switzerland where he could speak the language. Some of the monks stayed with Gaul, to found what became the famous monastery of Saint Gall. Columban, with a diminished band, took an Alpine pass into the plain of Lombardy, traveling via Milan to Pavia. Here the king, Agilulf, an Arian who had married a Bavarian Orthodox Catholic wife, gave them hospitality, and assigned them a monastery site at Bobbio on a tributary of the Po thirty miles from Genoa. On the property was an ancient decayed church, traditionally founded by Peter the Apostle. This they rebuilt, and surrounded it with other needed buildings. Columban, already in his seventies, shouldered lumber in the construction along with the rest.[4]

Back in Burgundy, the long-discontented nobles, with the willing help of Clothaire II of Neustria, overthrew the cruel dowager Brunhilda, executing her most brutally. Clothaire, now leading the Franks, sent a donation to Bobbio and invited Columban back to Luxeuil. Columban declined with thanks, preferring to foster Church renewal in Italy.

He had already written a treatise against Arianism, since coming into the domain of the Arian Lombards, counting on the popularity of Queen Theudelinda, the orthodox Catholic from Bavaria, to help him win over the king and his subjects. This purpose was obstructed by an old controversy among the Catholics of the area known as the issue of the "Three Chapters," which, so long as it continued, made Catholic orthodoxy unattractive to the Arian Lombards.

The Three Chapters issue stemmed from the activities of the great Emperor Justinian (527-565), who had made himself master of the Church more than any other Eastern Emperor. He had injected himself into the Monophysite controversy over the theological definition of the relation between the divine and human natures in the person of Christ. Eastern theologians had not been satisfied with the Creed of Chalcedon (451), the Alexandrians claiming it was too Nestorian, and calling themselves Monophysites, believers in one nature. This Monophysite protest was used by nationalists in Egypt and Syria, who wanted to throw off the political domination of Constantinople. So threatened with disruption, much imperial policy for two centuries was aimed at the adjustment of this theological controversy. Justinian convened and dominated the Fifth Ecumenical Council in Constantinople in 553. It adopted Justinian's definition of the issue, condemning the "Three Chapters." These were: (1) the person and writings of Theodore of Mopsuestia, revered leader of the school of Antioch more than a century previous; (2) the writings of Theodoret of Cyrrhus in criticism of Cyril; and (3) a letter of Ibas of Edessa to Maris the Persian. Theodoret and Ibas had been approved by the Council of Chalcedon, so that this action diluted the Council of Chalcedon, making Cyril's interpretation of it mandatory. Pope Vigilius, though in Constantinople at the time, refused to share in these proceedings, but within a year, under mistreatment and pressure from the emperor, yielded.

The action of Constantinople was resisted for some time in North Africa, and the yielding attitude of the pope led to a schismatic separation of North Italy from Rome which lasted until the time of Gregory the Great, and in the neighborhing Illyricum and Istria even longer. The purpose of the condemnation of the Thee Chapters had failed; the Monophysites of Egypt and Syria were not reconciled, resulting in the Coptic Churches of Egypt and Abyssinia and the Jacobite Church of the East to this day. It is this council's aftermath which was disturbing the Church in Lombardy in 614, and caused Columban to address a long letter to Pope Boniface IV from Bobbio.

As an Irish Celtic Christian who believed the Church should settle her own affairs, and who opposed all domination of Christ's Body by secular rulers, Columban was basically rebellious against all such high-handed interference as that of Emperor Justinian, and contemptuous of the pusillanimity of Pope Vigilius. In his letter to Pope Boniface, he held Vigilius at fault for submitting to the emperor, and so responsible for the perpetuation of the controversy. He asked the pope to convoke a conference or a council to settle the issue, indicating that King Agilulf and Queen Theudelinda had asked him to make the request, as they were deeply concerned by the continuing harsh conflict between Catholics in their realm, but wanted the Church to settle its own affairs. His words reveal his convictions about the relationship of Church and State, reflecting Peter's words before the Sanhedrin, "We must obey God rather than men." King, queen, and all others, he says, are asking action from the pope to make peace: "Let the king follow the King, do you follow Peter, and let the whole Church follow you."[5]

When Columban wrote to Boniface, he was unaware of any issue of papal authority in the Celtic churches. It was half a century before Whitby, and he had left Ireland thirteen years before Augustine's attempt to assert papal authority over the Welsh bishops at the River Severn. There is no hint of obsequious submission to an infallible authority in his tone. Among the complimentary phrases scattered through the letter are "fairest head of all the churches of Europe" and "head of the churches of the world saving the singular prerogative of the place of our Lord's resurrection,"—both setting some limits. Columban laments the ill repute (infamia) of the Chair of Peter, being shocked by the widespread suspicion he has found that heresy is condoned. "One must grieve and mourn if in the Apostolic See the Catholic faith is not maintained." Northern Italy, where Columban was laboring, was within the territory of the Roman See, as metropolitan. Jealousy for Boniface's honor, as he expects much of him as the successor of Peter, makes Columban duty-bound to protest what seems to be negligence on the part of the pope. The fear that Boniface is repeating the irresponsibility of Vigilius makes a barbed pun irresistible: *Vigila, atque quaeso, papa, vigila, et iterum dico, vigila; quia forte non bene vigilavit Vigilius.* (Be watchful, then, I beseech you, pope, and again I say, be watchful; since perchance he who was called the Watchman did not watch well). It is the province of the pope to lead: "I strive to stir thee up as the Prince of Leaders." He should "defend the faith of a synod." Though assuming the right of the pope to lead, Columban was assuming his own right to monitor the policy of the pope when he was remiss in the discharge of his ecclesiastical duty. He asks for a conference or a council, not for a papal bull! Some have accused him of insolence, others have commended his independence as shown in the free manner he used in addressing Boniface. Others have linked him with the later medieval Conciliarists who preceded the great Reformers. Columban only reflected the attitude carried over among the isolated Irish from earlier centuries before the papacy ever claimed or was accorded such great prerogatives. He contrasts how "we Irish" have always been constant in the faith, and reminds Boniface of "the freedom of discussion characteristic of my native land."[6] He was not discussing the powers of the Roman See to act in the practical situation he faced, which was stalling his missionary work. He was claiming them, prodding their due exercise at the same time that he assumed an antiquated perspective, or should we say a Christian perspective, on their limits!

The evangelistic preaching of Columban was tireless. Jonas reminded his readers repeatedly, "Wherever he went he proclaimed the Gospel word." Thirteen sermons, probably preached in Milan in 612, have been preserved. They are hortatory sermons, aimed at winning a decision for Christ. They are full of exclamatory apostrophes and rhetorical questions, the work of a scholarly homilete. Like American frontier preachers of the early 1800s, Columban did not shrink from warning of hell-fire and commending the blissful concerns of heaven. He waxes eloquent about the greatness of God as Creator and Redeemer, and contrasts the unworthiness of this fleeting and insecure earthly existence with the eternal glory of the life to come. All is vanity in this life, except as a pilgrimage toward the heavenly regions.[7]

Around 616, that pilgrimage came to an end on this earth for Columban. As he lay dying at Bobbio, he remembered Gall, whom he had left behind ill at Lake Constance, and sent him his abbatial staff. By this time, Saint Gall was well on the way toward the conversion of the Alamanni to Christ, and to becoming the greatest figure in the founding of the Swiss Church.

OTHER IRISH MISSIONS

Columban was not the first or only Irish missionary to Italy. In the sixth century, Ursus, leaving Ireland, spent some years in southern France, then crossed the Alps to Aosto.An Irish monk of the same period, Fridian, became bishop of Lucca and labored successfully for the conversion of the Lombards.

In 640, Kilian, bishop of Wurzburg, and his priest Coloman and deacon Totnam were martyred.

In 678, we saw Wilfrid, the Northumbrian Englishman trained by the Celts, preaching with marked success in Frisia of the Lowlands on one of his trips to Rome. Irish monks had been there before him. Another Northumbrian lad, Willibrord, had spent his boyhood in Wilfrid's monastery at Ripon, and had left for Ireland during Wilfrid's trouble with the king of Northumbria and the archbishop of Canterbury. In Ireland, he was inspired by another Englishman, Egbert, to follow up Wilfrid's preaching mission in Frisia. In 690, he went with eleven companions from Ireland as an Apostle to the Netherlands, working first at Utrecht. After the favorable Carolingian expansion under Pepin of Heristal, Utrecht became his archepiscopal see with authority from the pope. He labored for forty-four years in southern Frisia, leaving Christianity firmly rooted when he died at age eighty-one.

Suidbert, an Englishman, went to the Boructuari east of Frisia, and won many converts. Two Irishmen, Caidoc and Fricor, evangelized the valley of the Somme. Valery, Omer, and Bertin left an Irish imprint upon northern France. Fursey, whom we mentioned as serving in East Anglia, later joined this mission. Fridolin, who may have been Irish, worked among the Alamanni in the Black Forest near Basel, and founded a monastery on the Rhine. Pirmin, either Irish or Anglo-Saxon, evangelized in Alamannia, from Lake Constance to Alsace.

Following up this early evangelization with authority from the pope came the great missionary statesman, Winfrith Boniface, an English monk from Sussex who combined the evangelizing zeal Wilfrid had brought to his part of England with a passion to bring all of the missions pioneered by the Celts on the Continent under Roman regulation. He worked for a time with Willibrord in Frisia, then was commissioned by the pope to serve in Germany. In 723, he greatly impressed the pagans of Hesse by chopping down the sacred oak of Woden at Geismar. When it was half cut, a gust of wind toppled and split the great oak, impressing all with his miraculous powers. Soon all of Hesse was turning to the faith. He went on to Thuringia, Bavaria, then back among the Franks and into Frisia, where he was martyred in 754. In most places, he brought under hierarchical control Germans whom the Celts had already won to Christ. McNeill commends the truth of Philip Schaff's remark, "He reaped the fruit of their labors, and destroyed their further usefulness, which he might have secured by a liberal Christian policy."[8]

Still, the Irish kept on evangelizing. They went into Moravia in the eighth century. At Modra has been found the foundation of an Irish-type stone church, built around 800, evidence of conversions flourishing before that date. In the eleventh century, there were a group of monasteries known in Germany as the Schottenklöster. First the Monastery of Saint Peter at Ratisbon grew so large, it spawned a daughter-house, Saint James at Ratisbon, which in turn planted foundations at Wurzburg, Erfurt, Nurnberg, Constance, Vienna, Menninger, Eichstadt, and Kelheim. In 1089, some monks from Saint James at Ratisbon found their way into Russia. With the help of Vratislav II, Christian ruler of Bohemia, they reached Kiev in 1089, leaving there a lasting impression.[9]

Our chief interest, however, is in the spiritual renewal which came to those areas where the Church had become corrupt and decadent as a result of the merging of Christianity with the state policy of the late Roman Empire, and the fall of the empire to the barbarians. Nowhere is this better seen than in the multiplication of Columban's monasteries in the Frankish kingdoms after he was expelled from Luxeuil. Later historians are wont to criticize him as an overzealous Puritan, uncompromising and tactless, for raging against the immorality of the young king, as though a more tolerant approach would have served Christ's purpose better. But when were God's prophets ever compromising? The very fact that he fearlessly risked his life confronting the sinfulness of the king aroused a tremendous moral revulsion against the court and against corruption, on the part of the nobles and the people alike. A soft approach does not bring reformation. Holy zeal is needed to bring moral decency out of chaos. Reform came mightily. Meanwhile, his three monasteries multiplied to unbelievable numbers, not despite but because of the moral strictness of their discipline. Latourette reports Wilhelm Levison as the authority for more than fifty foundations.[10] McNeill estimates sixty by the end of the seventh century,[11] and in a note, after quoting Walker as conservatively numbering the abbeys, nunneries, and hermitages stemming from Columban's work during the seventh century as "no less than fifty three," cites the work of Margaret Stokes, in *Three Months in the Forests of France in Search of Vestiges of Irish Saints,* listing sixty-three founders who were Columban's disciples and holds the total of daughter institutions to have been 105.[12] Columban's spiritual influence can further be measured by the list of twenty-one saints drawn from among his monastic followers during twenty years. Oscar D. Watkins, who lists them from Montalembert, repeats the tribute of Adso of Montier-en-Der, ca 968:

And now what place, what city, does not rejoice in having for its ruler a bishop or an abbot trained in the discipline of that holy man (Columban)? For it is certain that by virtue of his authority almost the whole land of the Franks has been for the first time properly furnished with regular institutions.[13]

For most historians, the seventh century and the first half of the eighth mark the lowest ebb of European civilization in the Dark Ages. Yet this was the period of the greatest wave and flowering of art and learning in Christian Ireland. Then into the schools and settlements, the monasteries and nunneries founded by the abbots, bishop-abbots, bishops without sees and abbesses from Ireland on the Continent, and into the courts of kings who learned to appreciate their scholarship, there flowed a steady stream of scholars, heirs of the combined Christian, Classical, and Druidic traditions of learning taught in the Irish monastic universities. Alcuin, an Englishman who had been taught by Scots at York was head of Charlemagne's palace school. The most illustrious of the Irish scholars on the Continent was John Scotus Eriugena, (810-77) whom Charles the Bald commissioned to translate from the Greek the famous treatise known as the *Pseudo-Dionysius.* His greatest original work, *On The Division of Nature,* is a treatise in philosophical theology. Among his many minor works was a commentary on the Prologue to John's Gospel.

Charlemagne sent an Irish monk named Dumgal over the Alps into newly conquered Lombardy, where at Pavia, not far from Bobbio, he organized a school. When Lothair visited it in 825, he found it so promising that he decided to develop it into the chief center of liberal studies in Lombardy. So the University of Pavia, founded by an Irishman, flourishes to this day. Among its pupils was one Christopher Columbus, who, in the fifteenth century, found a new world soon to receive the seeds of Celtic liberty.

At the court of Charles the Bald at Liege in the mid-ninth century, the leading scholar and literary celebrity was Sedilius Scottus, who gathered a number of other Irish scholars about him. To him, as a well-known poet, has sometimes been ascribed a delightful poem which captures some of the spirit of the lonely Celtic peregrini. Diana Leatham, in her *Celtric Sunrise* informs us it was written by a lonely Irish monk in the far-off monastery of Saint Paul in Austria. She furnishes this delightful translation from the Latin by Robin Flower:

The Scholar and His Cat

I and Pangur Ban, my cat,
'Tis a like task we are at:
Hunting mice is his delight,
Hunting words I sit all night.

Better far than praise of men,
'Tis to sit with book and pen;
Pangur bears me no ill will,
He too plies his simple skill.

'Tis a merry thing to see,
At our tasks how glad are we,
When at home we sit and find
Entertainment to our mind.

Oftentimes a mouse will stray
In the hero Pangur's way;
Oftentimes my keen thought set
Takes a meaning in its net.

'Gainst the wall he sets his eye,
Full and fierce and sharp and sly;
'Gainst the wall of knowledge I
All my little wisdom try.

When a mouse darts from its den,
O how glad is Pangur then!
O what gladness do I prove
When I solve the doubts I love.

So in peace our tasks we ply,
Pangur Ben, my cat, and I;
In our arts we find our bliss,
I have mine and he has his.

Practice every day has made
Pangur perfect at his trade;
I get wisdom day and night
Turning darkness into light.[14]

With rare good humor, with real Christian humility, with dedication to truth and right and love from Christ, "turning darkness into light," His light was brought to the Dark Ages.

To most historians, the fact that the Celtic Churches could not defend themselves, and were swallowed up by the organizing genius of the Roman hierarchy is sufficient proof that they were faulty and impractical. Such a short-sighted pragmatic appraisal would also disapprove of Jesus' humble way of the Cross. Yet the Celtic heritage did not die. Christian believers won to The Way remained in every evangelized land. Wherever the Scriptures were cherished, the charismatic evangelical faith was perennially renewed. In Scotland, there were the Culdees, the remnants of the reformed Celi-Dei, the "Servants of God," active until shortly before the Reformation, non-celibate, many traditions removed from the original order, but preserving the humble service of the Celtic tradition:

> Peace to their shades. The pure Culdees
> Were Albyn's earliest priests of God,
> Ere yet an island of her seas
> By foot of Saxon monk was trod.
> —(Thomas Campbell, *Reullura*)

The Reformation sprang from lands where this heritage remained underground, in England, Bohemia, Germany, and Scotland. John A. Duke, in his *History of the Church of Scotland to the Reformation* (1937), says:

> It was the legacy which the Church of St. Columba bequeathed to the Church which was afterwards to arise in Scotland, which was to be build at the Reformation upon the ruins of the Church of Rome.[15]

We shall leave this grand chapter in our heritage of humble liberty to others.

Chapter VIII

RESURGENCE OF "THE WAY'S"
INDEPENDENCE: 1637-1776

Our American forefathers had an understandable horror of English bishops and archbishops. No Anglican bishop was allowed in the American Colonies until after the Revolution of 1776. To involve American churches in the Bicentennial celebration of our Independence, the National Council of Churches formed and staffed an Ecumenical Task Force. In 1973, its editorial committee issued a publication entitled *The Light In The Steeple–Religion and the American Revolution*. Its third full-page article, after *The Boston Tea Party* and *The Great Awakening* is entitled, *No Lords: Temporal Or Spiritual*. This significant historical piece explains why, with reason, the persistent efforts of Anglicans to have a bishop of the Church of England appointed to the Colonies were always successfully resisted, both in the Colonies and in the Mother Country.

In the colonies north of Maryland, where most of the colonists were Dissenters who had emigrated to escape Erastian bishop rule, in order to embrace religious independence, the colonial charters guaranteed religious freedom. Yet there was justifiable fear of Anglican connivance to maneuver the revoking of those charters. A Dr. Samuel Johnson, a former Congregational clergyman who had defected to the Anglican Church, was made rector of King's College in New York, now Columbia University. He attempted to bring that institution under complete Anglican control. This plan was thwarted by the writings of a Presbyterian lawyer named William Livingston, who publicized the pretensions of the Anglicans in *The New York Mercury*. Dr. Johnson drafted a proposal for the appointment of an Anglican bishop, and sent a covering letter with the copy for the Archbishop of Canterbury. It read:

> It is of the utmost importance for the best good of the colony that the Church (of England) be propagated and if possible be supported (by taxation); and if at the same time their charters (from the King) were demolished and they could be reduced under the management of a wise and good governor and council appointed by the King, I believe they would in a little time grow to a good sort of people and it would be one of the best of all the provinces.[1]

Little wonder that when Anglicans explained that the bishop they wanted would have no secular powers, they were not always believed!

In the southern colonies, where the Anglican Church was established until Thomas Jefferson separated Church and State in Virginia, the Anglican laity opposed having a colonial bishop because they preferred no interference with their control of local vestries over the rectors they employed. In Great Britain itself, a Committee of Dissenting Deputies of Parliament had great influence with the Whig Government and with the House of Hanover in blocking the plans of the Established Church. John Adams later wrote:

> ... the apprehension of Episcopacy contributed ... as much as any other cause to arouse the attention not only of the inquiring mind but of the common people, and urge them to close thinking on the constitutional authority of Parliament over the colonies.

After the Revolutionary War, there was no opposition when the organization of the Episcopal church in the new country involved the electing of two of its rectors as bishops. They were now not "monarchical" bishops under establishment by the government with secular powers, such as the colonists had feared. Erastianism was made unconstitutional by the "no establishment of religion" clause in the new Bill of Rights.

Erastianism is the doctrine that favors state supremacy in ecclesiastical affairs. Thomas Erastus (1524-1583), a German-Swiss churchman whose name became associated with the theory, did not so directly express it in the broad general sense.

Erastianism was one of the worst unsolved problems left by the Protestant Reformation, both on the Continent and in England and Scotland. The principle of "Cujus regio, ejus religio" (As the ruler, so the religion) whereby the established religion in each German principality was determined by the personal religious convictions of the ruling prince, meant coercion to uniformity of religion for any subjects who disagreed. A similar attempt was made to coerce religious conformity in the British realms.

We have seen how the ancient Christian Church allowed itself to be used by the Roman Emperors following Constantine the Great, and how Augustine of Hippo tried to extricate the Church after the fall of the empire in his book, *Of The City of God*. The Eastern Orthodox Church remained under the power of emperors from Constantinople, while the West identified the Roman Catholic Church with the City of God, and the Roman popes attained the power to crown and dethrone kings. Any lower clergy than popes were still largely subject to kings, so archbishops and diocesan bishops were very useful to the state. While they kept their original independence, only the Celtic churches were free from this Erastian corruption, and could be the Church of Christ, subject only to her Lord.

The Reformation was not a purely religious reform. The reformers made common cause with civil rulers who wanted independence to form nation states in the modern pattern, so the resulting Protestant churches, while free from Rome, were variously subject to national powers to which they were beholden for such liberty as they attained. Free in doctrine and in worship and church government from the dictates of the Roman hierarchy, and tasting the wonderful experience of a personal faith in Christ through the teachings of great spiritual leaders and fellowship in the study of the newly opened Bible, they were yet hindered from the full expression of their ancient original Christian heritage by acts of kings and parliaments.

We shall now survey enough seventeenth century religious history to be reminded how reformed Christians in Britain, recalled by study of the Scriptures to the principles of their own ancient Celtic Christian heritage, suffered and sacrificed for religious liberty and toleration. Here three of the so-called Nursery Rhymes become more than suggestive, for they had their origin in and illustrate this very history.

Sing a song of sixpence, a pocket full of rye,
   Four and twenty black-birds baked in a pie;
When the pie was opened the birds began to sing:
   Wasn't that a dainty dish to set before the King?

The King was in his counting house, counting out his money,
   The Queen was in the parlour, eating bread and honey,
The maid was in the garden, hanging out the clothes:
   Along came a black-bird and snipped off her nose.

According to our Historian of Mother Goose, this cleverly written satire lampoons Henry the Eighth's real motives in breaking with Rome and making England Protestant: his greed to loot the Church by seizing the lush abbey revenues; and his desire for Anne Boleyn. The "song of sixpence" is the Church dole. The "pocket full of rye" is the fat fields of grain all over England owned by the friars. The blackbirds are the Augustinian black canons. In even more literal detail, a huge pie so constructed is said to have been borne to the king by Jack Horner, stuffed to his delight with four and twenty deeds of abbey lands dispatched to Henry by the abbot of Newstead. Established by Henry II as a priory for the Black Canons of the Order of Saint Augustine, rich Newstead Abbey shared the general fate precipitated by the King's sweeping order. But before those blackbirds made their pie of the deeds, melodiously to sing when opened by the rapacious kingly precentor, they weighted large chests with choicest treasures and sank them in a nearby lake. Henry is seen counting his money, the queen stuffing herself in consequence of lonely neglect. In the garden, he spies the buxom maid, and some say the snipping of her nose was accomplished by the king's high clerical blackbird, obeying Henry's secret command to break her engagement to young Lord Percy, a noble pupil in the Cardinal's own household.[2] Others hint that more than a nose was eventually snipped.

It would be sufficient for us if the rhyme only generally described the sad Erastian plight of the clergy, having to sing for the ruler who makes it hot for them, and unable to get back at him except for an occasional snip at one of his servants. At any rate, England never had a proper Reformation. Nothing much was changed except that the liturgy now was in English instead of Latin, and Henry himself acted as pope, defining his own divine rights as king, with Erastianism in its worst form fastened upon Church and people.

This bore its wicked fruit two generations later, during the reign of James I of England and VI of Scotland. James was the son of Mary Queen of Scots. His reign was supposed to bring peace by uniting the two realms. Believing in his divine right to rule the Church as he pleased, James determined to conform the Scottish Kirk to Anglicanism.

Scotland had enjoyed a much more thorough reformation than had England. John Knox had led her into a quite thorough Protestant reform, with the assistance and approval of the Scottish Parliament. First he had written for them a Calvinistic Confession of Faith. In 1560, he led the First General Assembly of the Scottish Kirk in presenting to the Scottish Parliament the first *Book of Discipline,* providing that in each parish the minister and elders elected by the congregation would form a disciplinary board later called the Session; that in each town there would be meetings of ministers and elders for discussion which developed into presbyteries, and that there should be a synod for each larger district, and a general assembly for the whole Kirk. In 1564, the general assembly adopted John Knox's liturgy, a *Book of Common Order* allowing for free prayer.

During James's childhood, in 1572, the Regent Morton had secured nominal recognition of the older medieval episcopate in Scotland, largely as a means of gaining possession of church lands. Yet in 1581, the Kirk General Assembly gave full authority to the presbyteries, and in 1592, in spite of James's opposition, the king and Scottish Parliament were compelled to recognize the Presbyterian system. Determined to substitute a royally controlled episcopacy, James was strong enough by 1597 to insist that he alone had the right to call general assemblies. By exiling Presbyterian leaders, he was able in 1610 to establish two High Commission Courts for ecclesiastical cases, each presided over by an archbishop; to procure for the formerly nominal Scottish bishops their new episcopal consecration in the Apostolic Succession from English bishops, and in 1612 could so pack the Scottish Parliament that it gave back diocesan jurisdiction to these bishops. Those who speak airily about how the Scottish Kirk once had bishops should be made to recite this history of when and how!

In 1625, James was succeeded by his son Charles I, an even greater believer in the divine right of kings. Charles made William Laud, a vigorous anti-Calvinist and the actual founder of the Anglo-Catholic position, bishop of London in 1628, and Archbishop of Canterbury in 1633. With the support of the king, Laud forced conformity on England with a heavy hand. By this time the Puritan movement had grown strong in England, and Laud's oppression drove over 20,000 Puritans to emigrate to America between 1628 and 1640.

Then the king and his archbishop turned their attention to Scotland. In June 1636, new *Canons and Constitutions Ecclesiasticall Gathered and Put in Force for the Government of the Church of Scotland* were published with the king's warrant at Aberdeen. Laud had learned in Scotland that the actions of 1610 and 1612, reinstating the episcopate and making all prior Presbyterian books of discipline obsolete, had never been implemented with new canons. He simply took the canons of the Church of England of 1604, amended them here and there with his own notions, and imposed what had been written against the English Puritans upon the Scottish Kirk. Here were no Presbyterian courts, no provision for Ruling Elders, but "Church Wardens," and deacons were made over into the Anglican model. Hugh Watt, my former professor of Church History at New College, Edinburgh says, "The Church of Scotland was no longer to be an episcopacy superimposed on Presbyterianism: it was to be episcopacy pure and simple."[3] Ordinations were made nearly sacramental, and the directions for the Eucharist all but implied transubstantiation. Extemporary prayer and the discretionary ritual of John Knox's liturgy were prohibited. All were required to use a proposed *Book of Common Prayer* no one had ever seen. The king's supremacy in all Church matters was uncompromisingly laid down, with the claim that King Charles had inherited the power "that the godly kings had among the Jews." Chapter VIII said that no synod could alter "any Rubric, Article, Canon, Doctrinal or Disciplinary Whatsoever." Royal absolutism had thrown down the gauntlet to a Scottish Kirk and people reared in the tradition of independence. Then in 1637, Laud brought out the new liturgy. It was an amended Church of England Liturgy he was scheming to impose soon upon the English Church to make it more Catholic, with a plea for uniformity after he had imposed it upon the Church in Scotland.

> Two legs sat upon three legs,
> Up jumps two legs,
> Picks up three legs,
> And throws it after four legs.

This conundrum circulated popularly to express assent to one result! On July 23, 1637, in Saint Giles's Cathedral in Edinburgh, when Dean Hannay began to read the Liturgy from Archbishop Laud's new Church Service Book, an irate Scottish woman named Jenny Geddes, who had been sitting on the three-legged stool she had brought dutifully to Church, rose up in her Presbyterian wrath and hurled it at the offending dean. Some say her aim was good; others that she missed. Some say she fittingly expressed her indignation in "guid braw Scot." Hugh Watt, the historian, says, "Whether the words were ever spoken or not, the traditional 'Fause loon, dost thou daur say Mass at ma lug?' fitly sums up the Scottish feeling."[4] The result was a riot, and tradition has it: "Soon thereafter in Greyfriars Kirkyard an excited multitude signed 'A National Covenant to Defend the True Religion,' drawing blood from their own arms in lieu of ink!"

But that is not quite how it was. Scottish people do not do their great deeds so rashly and without proper thought. They do them "decently and in order!" So Hugh Watt insists rightly that sufficient attention be given to the way the National Covenant was drawn up and presented. And does not the riddle end: "And throws it after four legs"? Jenny Geddes was really aiming after proper action by the Four Tables, of the separate committees of the Nobles, Gentry, Burghers, and Clergymen which were quickly formed.[5]

Actually, the final crisis which produced the Covenant was on February 19, 1638 at Stirling. There, in a proclamation, Charles assumed full responsibility for the obnoxious canons and the Liturgy. Then a general rally in Edinburgh decided upon the Covenant, and Alexander Henderson of Leuchars was chosen to draw it up. On February 27th, it was read to the nobles in John Galloway's house and some phrases adjusted. In the afternoon, it was submitted to the commissioners of the presbyteries in the summer house in the yard, and with slight amendments approved. The amended draft was approved by the whole ministry, except one. On Wednesday, February 28, the Parchment Copy was read in the forenoon, and the great meeting was called for Greyfriars Church at 2 P.M. There, after devotional exercises and a speech, the covenant was produced and read, and the signing began at 4 P.M., first the noblemen, then the barons. It lasted until 8 P.M. with the signing of the ministers next day in Tailors' Hall, and a General Signing in

Edinburgh beginning April 1—all decently and in order!

The leaders of Scotland would not be coerced nor divided. They determined to uphold the former purity of religion, and resist the recent innovations to the uttermost. They chose the Reverend Henderson of Leuchars to draft the covenant, as his protest was already published:

The Kirk of Scotland is an independent Kirk, and her own pastors should be most able to discern and direct what do best seem our measure of reformation; and what may serve most for the good of the people.

The Covenant was a most solemn engagement before God:

" . . . to recover the purity and liberty of the Gospel as it was established and professed" before the late innovations. We promise and swear by the Great Name of the Lord our God . . . that we shall defend the aforesaid religion to the uttermost of the powers that God hath put in our hands all the days of our life, . . . also to the mutual defense and assistance every one of us of another in the same cause of maintaining the true religion and His Majesty's authority with our best counsel, our bodies, means, and whole power against all sorts of persons whatsoever.

This was not a general rebellion. It was not just a question between two liturgies or two forms of Church government. It was a matter of spiritual autonomy. It was the issue of religious freedom, of the right to worship God according to the dictates of their own consciences. Erastianism is a denial of Christianity itself. As John T. McNeill has said:

. . . a church that is reduced to impotence by the state is more pitiable than a church that is persecuted. The church is naturally a free communion; it is still this if it suffers in exercising its freedom, but not if it ceases to exercise it. Communion dies under compulsion, and union itself becomes meaningless.[6]

In December, a Scottish general assembly deposed the bishops and repealed the whole structure of innovations James and Charles had erected since 1597.

Charles had gone too far to retreat, and began to raise forces to suppress what he considered to be rebellion. Yet the Scots were too formidable and he patched up a truce in 1639. In 1640, he had to call an English Parliament to get funds for more troops, the "Short Parliament," which he soon dissolved because they brought up difficult matters. Observing his purpose, the Scots invaded England in such numbers that he was forced to treat and to guarantee the expenses of a Scottish army of occupation. To pay for this, he had to summon another Parliament. When it gathered in November of 1640, the Presbyterian-Puritans had an evident majority and the "Long Parliament" was in session.

This Parliament began by casting Archbishop Laud into prison and abolishing the English episcopacy. In July 1643, it set up the Westminster Assembly of Divines to formulate a fully reformed church for England. When a Militia Bill was introduced to transfer the command of the military from king to Parliament, Charles tried to arrest John Pym and other Commons leaders, and it was civil war.

At first, the king with his amateur cavalry of hunting squires, the Cavaliers, had the advantage, and Parliament needed Scottish military help. To secure it, the English and Scottish Parliaments entered into the Solemn League and Covenant in 1643, pledging the largest possible uniformity in religion in England, Scotland, and Ireland, and opposing "prelacy."

The Westminister Assembly of 121 clergymen and 30 laymen named by Parliament were now joined by Scottish commissioners, Presbyterian theologians, without vote but exercising great influence. The assembly had only advisory status: Parliament kept the power of enactment in its own hands. In 1644, it presented to Parliament a *Directory of Worship* and a completely Presbyterian system of *Church Government*. In 1646, it laid before them the famous *Westminster Confession of Faith,* and in 1647, the *Larger Catechism* for pulpit exposition, and a *Shorter Catechism* meant for the training of children. These were strongly Calvinistic documents, emphasizing the "covenant doctrine" which contrasts the "covenant of works" through the Law with the "covenant of grace" through Christ. Approved by both Parliament and the Scottish General Assembly, these documents were never put in operation in England, but became the constitution of the Church of Scotland and of her daughter churches in America and elsewhere.

Meanwhile, the civil war proceeded fitfully:

> The lion and the unicorn
> Were fighting for the crown;
> The lion beat the unicorn
> All around the town.

Some gave them white bread,
Some gave them brown,
Some gave them plum cake
And sent them out of town.

Written by a Cavalier partisan, the rhyme also reflects the determination of the wealthy city of London to keep it "out of town," Charles I as "The Lion," having appealed for help from Ireland from the Catholic army the Earl of Strafford had organized there, and the indignant Scots as "the unicorn" joining Cromwell under the Solemn League and Covenant, had not met in deciding battle during the winter of 1643-44 when the lion seemed to be beating the unicorn "all around the town."[7] On July 2, the Roundheads, Scots, and Oliver Cromwell's new cavalry of picked "religious men" defeated the royal army on Marston Moor near York, though the Parliamentary forces were defeated in the west at Lostwithiel. In June 1645, Cromwell and Sir Thomas Fairfax with a New Model Army, composed largely of Independents, decisively defeated the Royalists at Naseby and Langport. Charles surrendered to the Scots who handed him over to Parliament.

Cromwell and his Congregational, Baptist, and Puritan Independents were almost as much opposed to a Presbyterian establishment as they were to the Anglican. King Charles now used this division to intrigue with the Scots, promising to honor the "Solemn League and Covenant," if they would invade England again, this time against Cromwell. Cromwell scattered the Scottish army near Preston, making his army supreme in England. In December, he purged Parliament of all the Presbyterians, leaving only a rump of sixty Independents. He abolished the House of Lords, and had King Charles tried for treason. The king was executed January 30, 1649. After subjugating Ireland and Scotland, defeating the forces of Charles's son, and dismissing the rump Parliament, Cromwell ruled as military dictator, calling himself the "Protector" until his death in 1658. His religious policy was a practice of toleration, except for Roman Catholics and High Anglicans.

When his weak son Richard succeeded as "Protector," Royalists and Presbyterians combined to restore the monarchy. Charles II enlisted the Presbyterians by raising their hope of equal treatment with a declaration "of liberty to tender consciences," but he was thoroughly immoral, weak, and indifferent to religion, with promises not to be trusted. It would have taken a stronger determined king to stem the tide of reaction running against Puritanism. The first Parliament chosen after the Restoration was fiercely Royalist and Anglican. In May 1662, a new Act of Uniformity received royal assent, requiring universal use of a new Prayer Book with 600 alterations in the Anglican direction, and an oath of "unfeigned assent" by all clergy, and proscribing taking arms against the king "on any pretense whatever." So Puritans were effectively barred from the Church. From 1,500 to 2,000 ministers refused to take the oaths and gave up their places. By the Conventicle Acts of 1664 and 1670, any persons attending worship gatherings not in accord with the Prayer Book became subject to fines, imprisonment, and ultimate transportation, and deprived ministers were forbidden to teach school or to dwell within five miles of their former charges. The Test Act of 1673 required all military and civil officers to take Communion by Anglican rites or forfeit their posts.

When James II succeeded his brother in 1685, he defied both the Tory Parliament and the Tory Church by introducing Roman Catholics into high military, educational, and civil offices, and in 1688 issued a Declaration of Indulgence giving toleration to Catholics as well as Dissenters. Seven bishops were tried in London for refusing to read this Declaration in Church, and acquitted. Whigs and Tories now combined to enthrone William and Mary of Orange in a bloodless revolution. A Toleration Act in 1689 gave freedom to all Protestant forms of worship.

THE RESTORATION IN SCOTLAND

For Scotland, the Restoration of the Crown had brought great turmoil and suffering. Parliament in 1661 annulled all acts affecting religion passed after 1633, restoring episcopacy as in the time of Charles I. Four bishops consecrated in England were appointed to Scotland, chief of them James Sharp, a renegade Presbyterian, as archbishop of Saint Andrews. All office-holders were required to renounce the covenants of 1638 and 1643. Heavy fines were enacted by Parliament for absence from worship in episcopally governed churches. Many Presbyterian ministers were deprived, and when their parishioners absented themselves from worship under the new subservient minister, they were fined, and soldiers were quartered on any refusing to pay. Covenanters rose in the Pentland Rising and were ruthlessly crushed. In 1679, Archbishop Sharp was murdered. An armed rising of Covenanters was crushed at Bothwell Bridge and the insurgents were treated with extreme cruelty. The king's brother James was put in charge of Scottish affairs. Now the extreme Presbyterians, called Cameronians for their leader Richard Cameron, became a hunted folk.

When James was crowned James II and VII in 1685, Parliament made death the penalty for attending a "conventicle" and it was the "Killing time." The Martyr's Monument in Greyfriars Churchyard, blackened by time, reads:

> Halt passenger, take heed what you do see,
> This tomb doth shew, for what some men did die.
> Here lies interr'd the dust of those who stood
> 'Gainst perjury, resisting unto blood;
> Adhering to the Covenants, and laws
> Establishing the same, which was the cause
> Of Prelatists abjur'd. Though here their dust
> Lies mixt with murderers, and other crew,
> Whom justice justly did to death pursue;
> But as for them, no cause was to be found
> Worthy of death but only they were sound,
> Constant and steadfast, zealous witnessing
> For the Prerogatives of CHRIST their KING.
> Which truths were sealed by famous Guthrie's head,
> And all along to Mr. Rennick's blood.
> They did endure the wrath of enemies
> Reproaches, torments, deaths and injuries,
> But yet they're those who from such troubles came,
> And now triumph in glory with the LAMB.

From May 27th 1661 that the most noble Marquis of Argyle was beheaded, to the 17th of Febry. 1688 that Mr. James Rennick suffered, were one way or other Murdered and Destroyed for the same cause, about eighteen thousand of whom were execute at Edinburgh about an hundred of Noblemen, Gentlemen, Ministers and others; noble Martyrs for JESUS CHRIST. The most of them lie there.

In the far corner of the same churchyard, within its high wall in 1679, 1200 Covenanters were imprisoned for five months, unhoused and almost unfed. Our religious liberty was bought with a dear price! From this oppression, our forefathers sought freedom for their faith in America—and there, strangely enough, the Puritans of New England (not the Pilgrims) were such children of their age that they organized their Colony in Massachusetts with their own brand of religious intolerance. Only when Roger Williams was hounded out of the strict Massachusetts Bay Colony for his Baptist views, and wandering through winter snows found friends among the Indians, and founded the new town of Providence, Rhode Island, on the expressed principle of complete religious liberty and toleration in 1636, was the inherent genius of Christ's Way again properly recognized. In Geneva, Switzerland, in the impressive Reformation Monument stretching along the park hillside, standing with the great reformers is one American, Roger Williams. Because of the insistence of his Rhode Island, the First Amendment, forbidding any establishment of religion or prohibiting the free exercise thereof in the United States of America, is in the Bill of Rights in our Constitution.

During the seventeenth century's persecution and intolerance, many Scots and Scots-Irish of ancient Celtic heritage came to America, settling chiefly in the middle colonies. They formed their Presbyterian churches into presbyteries, and in 1716, the General Presbytery of Philadelphia became so unwieldy they divided it into four, and of them formed the Synod of Philadelphia. By the Adopting Act of 1729, they adopted the *Westminster Confession of Faith* and the *Longer and Shorter Catechisms* as being "in all the essential and necessary articles" good forms and sound words and systems of Christian doctrine; but agreed to peaceful disagreement in extra-essentials with friendship, kindness, and brotherly love. They made one change in the original *Westminster Confession of Faith*. They expressly denied to civil magistrates "the power to persecute any for their religion." This power the original Confession had granted. It was the first official declaration by an organized church on American soil of the principle of the Separation of Church and State and the absolute freedom of conscience.[8]

THE GREAT AWAKENING

While it is generally understood that opposition to Erastianism and prelacy featured in the Revolution of 1776, this fails to plumb the depths of the religious background. A deeper source must be sought in the widespread resurgance of experiential Christianity in the Colonies known as The Great Awakening, for this movement of spiritual renewal unifed the colonies with a new independent religious consciousness. The Great Awakening swept over all of the Colonies, with two special centers, one in New England Puritanism under the leadership of the Colonies' greatest theologian, Jonathan Edwards; the second and most culturally significant in the Middle Colonies, under the leadership of the Log College Presbyterians sparked by William Tennent, Sr. All had their faith kindled and inflamed by the preaching of George Whitefield. This resurgence of evangelical Puritanism, with its Christian theological foundation for liberty and its ecclesiastical representative democracy, furnished a broader religious basis for the new commonwealth than the Deism of intellectual founding fathers like Thomas Jefferson and Benjamin Franklin, whose common core beliefs in the rights of man under God were written into the founding documents. Evangelical Christians and Deists collaborated in the cause of liberty and independence.

To understand the Great Awakening, one must delve into a little-known controversy among Presbyterians in the middle colonies between formalist ministers and those who had an experiential knowledge of The Way in Christ. It was nearly a hundred years since the first great migration of Puritans to New England. Freed from persecution, colonial Christians had lost some of their original zeal. Harvard College, founded to furnish a Puritan ministry, had become aridly intellectual. Yale, founded later by those more evangelical, was drifting in the same direction. As life on the seaboard became more prosperous and secure, the temptations to worldliness increased, while out on the western frontier, hard conditions in sparse settlements under threats of marauding Indians and characterized by rough and lawless elements eroded Christian moral standards.

In Pennsylvania, Maryland, and Delaware, the Scots and Scotch-Irish had formed Presbyterian churches while New Englanders of Presbyterian sentiments had churches in New York, Connecticut, and on Long Island. Some of the ministers from Ireland were renegades who had forged their credentials.[9] They came from Ulster, where Presbyterianism, while intensely and polemically orthodox in doctrine, was peculiarly devoid of deep and fervent piety at this time.[10] Difficult frontier conditions called for a zeal, piety, and personal religious initiative which few of these ministers possessed, especially in Donegal

Presbytery, westernmost in Pennsylvania. In the absence of a sufficient number of talented and spiritually minded clergymen, local church sessions had accepted any trained minister they could find, often someone who had left Scotland or Ireland for reasons other than deep missionary convictions. It was a time of spiritual aridity in Scotland and the North of Ireland. A controversy over strict subscription to the Westminster Confession of Faith and other constitutional standards was splitting the church, the strict subscriptionists tending to be not the more devoted ministers, but often those who would substitute doctrinal orthodoxy for real piety and moral surrender to Christ. This controversy was transported to the colonies as formal subscriptionists who had other difficulties in the home countries sought a new opportunity in the new world. They looked to their professional, educated status and protection by the courts of the Church to guarantee them a living. Soon they became involved in disputes with their frontier congregations where they failed to win financial support and were frequently chargeable with drunkenness and worse immoralities. They sought greater power in presbyteries and synods to protect them from ouster and to compel the laity to pay their salaries.

When the first Synod was formed with four presbyteries, Philadelphia, New Castle, Long Island, and Donegal, factions began to appear. Some protested the synod's laxity in disciplining unworthy and scandalous ministers. There was tension over the matter of strictness of subscription to the doctrines of the *Westminster Confession of Faith,* and difference of opinion regarding the rights of presbytery over against the rights and power of the synod. In general, the morally lax were strict doctrinal subscriptionists who favored synod control, while the evangelicals, who were more biblically than creedally oriented, preferred independent sovereignty of presbyteries, and were determined to awaken the Church from a state of great decline in vital piety.[11]

The evangelicals were called "Log College men" from their identification with a school built of logs in 1735 at Neshaminy Pennsylvania by William Tennent, Sr. for the training of young ministers. During its first five years, seven very capable young ministers received training in this school, and in subsequent years, their number was increased to twenty-one. No opposition was raised against the ordination of the first four prepared, incuding Tennent's three sons. The examiners were well pleased with the quality of their scholarship. As theological education was in the doldrums in Scotland at this time, and many Presbyterian ministers in Ireland and Puritans in England had received similar training in private academies, there was Old-World precedent.

Yet, as factionalism grew in the synod, opposition appeared. From Tennent's warmly evangelical piety, the graduates were strongly revivalist in spirit and "different." They were enthusiastic for a revival that had begun to spread abroad influenced by a Dutch Reformed Dominie, Theodorus Jacobus Frelinghuysen in New Jersey. One of Tennent's sons, Gilbert Tennent became a successful revivalist preacher, preaching in New York and Perth Amboy. William Tennent, Jr. led a revival in Freehold and Gilbert Tennent at New Brunswick at the same time that Jonathan Edwards's revival was becoming known in Massachusetts. The Tennent "Log College" men joined with a group of Puritan ministers of New England background in the synod to sponsor an overture requiring all candidates for the ministry to be examined as to their piety. The main body of Scotch-Irish clergy, strongly subscriptionist and antirevival in sentiment, began to oppose the ordination of Log College trained men, refusing to consider any minister adequately educated who was not from a Scottish or New England university, and "Log College" became a term of scorn.[12]

The synod at this time was about equally divided between the Scotch-Irish formalists on one hand and the Tennent "Log College" group, with the Puritans of New England background, on the other. In 1736, when eleven New Englanders and two leading Tennent men were absent, and of twenty present, sixteen were of the Scotch-Irish subscriptionist party, the synod passed a new Adopting Act requiring strict subscription to the Westminster Confession and other standards, setting aside the former more liberal adopting act of 1729. They also took action usurping former rights of presbyteries in seating ministers.[13] In 1738, with only twenty-eight of forty-seven members present, the synod again dominated by the Scotch-Irish majority forbade the "intrusion" of preachers in wide territories claimed by existing congregations, to stop revivalists from going into communities without regular preaching. They were bent on eliminating the revival. The Tennent group secured the erecting of a large new presbytery, New Brunswick, so they could license and ordain a group of godly, well-qualified young men for the ministry.[14] Thereupon, the opposition passed an overture requiring any applicant for ordination without a New England or European college degree to be examined by a committee of synod and all candidates for licensure to be examined by synod. Gilbert Tennent charged this was intended to wreck his father's attempts to train a godly ministry.

The revivals brought about by the Log College men were not fly-by-night stirrings of emotional enthusiasm. They carried on for several months, or as long as two consecutive years, with deep soul concern and counsel with the minister, resulting in many new births, forsaking self-righteousness for the righteousness of Christ alone for salvation. People were no longer content with the mere form, without the life and power of Godliness.

In 1739, with the New England group absent, the committee examining the records of New Brunswick Presbytery found it had examined and licensed one John Rowland, violating synod's act requiring prior synod examination. New Brunswick Presbytery claimed this had always been a presbytery prerogative and synod's act was in error. The question raised was whether, in Presbyterianism, the real seat of authority lies in presbytery or in higher judicatories. The Tennents claimed power for the presbytery. The anti-revival formalists had control of the synod. No form of government had as yet been adopted by the synod. Everything depended upon arguments from English and Scottish precedents, or upon majority vote at a given synod session. Gilbert Tennent argued that giving synod such power was like adopting the legislative powers of the hierarchy of the Church of England.[15] A synod able to legislate as it pleased would soon equal the Church of England in bigotry and intolerance. Synod found Rowland's licensure illegal and New Brunswick Presbytery guilty of violating the laws of the church. They took preliminary steps to erect a seminary with no recognition of the "Log College." They claimed the revival movement was fanatical, striking at all but its own adherents blindly, indiscriminately, and perversely. Tennent's small minority group faced control by a determined synod majority opposition.

That fall of 1739, George Whitefield, a young Anglican of Methodist leanings, stopped off unannounced in Philadelphia en route to Georgia where he had founded an orphanage. When the engaging young preacher of twenty-four preached in an Anglican Church in Philadelphia and then from the Court House steps, great crowds were electrified. On November 10, William Tennent, Sr., hitherto unknown to Whitefield, called upon him and invited him to assist the revival begun by the Log College men. Soon he was making an evangelistic tour of the churches of the Log College men and the New England group. In one month, he had preached to many thousands, morals were reformed, and the spiritual life of many churches was greatly revived.[16] It was not all his doing. When he left the borders of the synod where groundwork had been laid by evangelical pastors, he preached to only tiny congregations, as in a spiritual desert, but where they had been tilling the spiritual soil, the Great Awakening blossomed. This was true also among the New England background group of churches in the New York Presbytery, where preaching had been influenced by Jonathan Edwards's great revival in New England. Now there was intense widespread interest in this form of faith that meant something to ordinary folk among the laity of the entire synod. Lay enthusiasm altered the balance of power in the synod, in favor of the Tennants. Newspapers took up the news of the awakening and gave it tremendous publicity. Jonathan Edwards and Gilbert Tennent published books, articles and sermons.

In 1740, flushed with enthusiasm, Gilbert Tennent overreached to preach in Nottingham Church of Donegal Presbytery a sermon on "The Danger of an Unconverted Ministry," charging the opponents of the revival with being themselves unregenerate, and urging his hearers to pray for those under the ministry of unconverted ministers. This precipitated a controversy over the nature of the "call" to the ministry. The New Englanders and Log College men agreed that

A minister of Jesus that has never experienced a regenerating change; that has not received Christ the Lord, that does not walk in the steps of His humble and self-denying Life is one of the greatest Solecisms in Nature, a personal contradiction of his character and often proves an extensive mischief to the Church of Christ.

But a minister's labor depends not upon his personal holiness, but upon his "calling." Yet there is a difference between God's call and the presbytery's ordination. This the anti-revival party denied. They insisted that every man duly set apart by the church is truly "called of God." From what had been transpiring, it was evident that when acts of a judicatory are deemed acts of God, ugly clericalism may become rampant, immoral ministers be readily exonerated, and other ministers and laity forced to accept dubious products of presbyterial and synodical trickery without protest.[17] For the revival party, the rights of the church were greater than the rights of the clergy.[18] Defeated by the controlled synod, the Log College men appealed to the laity. The issue was for or against any real revival of spiritual and ethical life in the church. After the Nottingham sermon, the spiritual strife was out in the open.

At this juncture, Whitefield came again, on April 13, 1740, as popular as before and more so. He joined with the Tennents in a triumphant revival campaign through the middle Colonies, and made many friends among the New York Presbytery group, led by Jonathan Dickinson. When synod met in May, this New England background group tried to mediate peace. Neither side was ready. Answering Gilbert Tennent's Nottingham sermon, anti-revivalists in New Castle Presbytery attacked Whitefield's theology in a pamphlet claiming he was a Papist in disguise, and the whole revival a fake.[19] The ensuing pamphlet battle was printed by Benjamin Franklin.

After protracted preaching tours in the New York and Philadelphia areas, Whitefield persuaded Gilbert Tennent to undertake an evangelistic tour of the New England churches. He campaigned from December to March 1741 with great success, attracting phenomenal crowds in Boston. At New Haven, over half of the Yale College students were converted under Tennent's preaching, furnishing a promising pool for future recruits for the ministry.[20]

When the synod met in Philadelphia in May 1741, barely half of the members were present. The entire group of New England Puritan background were absent. The anti-revival formalists had sixteen present, the Log College men seven, and three non-aligned men answered the roll call. The anti-revivalists introduced a written "Protestation," levying accusations against the revivalists, demanding ironclad subscription to the Confession, complete submission to the orders of the synod, that no one accused of violating such orders be allowed to sit in synod, that synod recognize the New Brunswick Presbytery men to have forfeited their right to sit in synod by rejecting synod's rule on the examination of ministerial candidates, and that unless the Log College men gave complete satisfaction, signers of the Protestation would not be bound by any action in which they continued to sit, but would declare themselves to be the true synod, and the others to be schismatics. There was a confused rush of the bare majority to sign this "Protestation," and thus, illegally and without a trial, the Log College men were ousted. There was no vote taken and none recorded. Though synod membership at the time was forty-seven, the vote would probably have been twelve to ten.[21] The rejected revivalists tried to protest the illegal action, then organized themselves as the Conjunct Presbyteries of New Brunswick and Londonderry.

When the synod next met in Philadelphia in 1742, seven members of the New England group from New York Presbytery were present, and called for a committee to heal the breach. Tennent and his group were willing. The anti-revivalists would not withdraw their signed "Protestation," and declared the case closed. Thereupon, the New England group laid a protest before the synod alleging its procedure had been illegal. Their leader, Jonathan Dickenson, issued a carefully prepared pamphlet in defense of the revival entitled *A Display of God's Special Grace*. In 1745, the ousted Conjunct Presbyteries and the New York Presbytery joined to form the Synod of New York, known as "New Side," whereas the remaining Synod of Philadelphia was called "Old Side." The "New Side" synod was based on the less strict Adopting Act of 1729, provided for strict discipline but a looser adherence to the doctrinal standards, stressing ministerial life and conduct equally with orthodoxy in doctrine, the revival as "a work of God's glorious grace," and a striving for irenic relations with Philadelphia and New England.[22]

The revival had released a tremendous new spiritual life, surging spontaneously and largely unguided all through the Colonies, needing church order to save it from subjectivity and rampant individualism. The Tennent group and other "New Side" men accepted the responsibility, conducting an amazing missionary, evangelistic, and church-organizing program as far as the western part of Pennsylvania, in the "spiritual desert" of southern New Jersey, to the "Great Valley" of Virginia and the Carolinas.[23] Thus, they became the genius and future of American Presbyterianism.[24]

The Log College having ceased to function in 1744, two years before William Tennent, Sr.'s death, the new synod needed a school to train their ministry. Many converted Yale students were recruited, but not enough to meet the crying need. Jonathan Dickenson and others in New York Presbytery secured a New Jersey Charter on October 22, 1746, and were joined by the Log College alumni so that the College of New Jersey inherited its traditions. Jonathan Dickenson became the first president, the school beginning in his home in Elizabethtown later becoming Princeton University and Seminary.[25] Funds were raised in the British Isles, despite a vicious letter-writing campaign of the "Old Side" partisans to frustrate the mission.[26]

The "New Side" also sent forth a mission to evangelize the Indians with three missionaries: John Sargent, Azariah Horton, and David Brainerd.[27] They were also broadly ecumenical in spirit, having fellowship with other denominations. Gilbert Tennent defined their position:

All Societies who profess Christianity, and retain the Foundation Principles thereof, notwithstanding their different Denominations and Diversities of Sentiments in smaller things are in Reality but One Church of Christ, but several Branches, (more or less pure in minute Points) of one visible kingdom of the Messiah, whose Honour and Interest, rightly understood, is one and the same.[28]

So they recognized a true church in each of the many evangelical Protestant denominations about them.[29]

Thus, there was no question where the strength and future of the church lay. Floundering at first to organize and bring order out of the tremendous numbers of new converts, the New Side grew by leaps and bounds. Meanwhile, the Old Side, its ministers traditional, formalist, and often charged with moral failures, disowning the revival and lacking in evangelistic and missionary zeal, withered and shrank. In the seventeen years between the schism and the reuniting overtured by the New York Synod "New Side" in 1758, the Old Side ministry had dwindled from twenty-seven to twenty-three, while the New Side had grown from twenty-two to seventy-three ministers, serving a growing church and itinerating the far frontiers. The "New Side," with a surrendered, experiential faith in Christ had all the characteristics for church renewal. They were evangelistic, biblically grounded, and educational, devoted in piety, charismatic in the Holy Spirit, sound but not picayune in doctrine, strongly missionary, strongly Puritan in personal ethics, constructive in social ethics as we shall see, humbly ordered in polity, and broadly ecumenical. New Side renewal in Christ determined the fruitful future of the church.

SPIRITUAL UNDERGIRDING OF AMERICAN INDEPENDENCE

A people newly aroused to the importance of religious liberty of conscience by the Great Awakening were eager to support the move for American independence. So long as the Colonies were under English rule, there was great danger to religious freedom. The united Synod of New York and Philadelphia of the Presbyterian Church in the Middle Colonies approached the General Association of Connecticut, the agency of the Congregational churches of New England, and together they formed an association. Yearly, from 1766 to 1775, the two churches conferred, and resisted the schemes of the governors of some of the Colonies to make the Anglican church official.

When the struggle for independence loomed, the churches took no official action. Yet nearly two-thirds of the population of the colonies had a Calvinist background, and nearly 900,000 of the 3,000,000 population had Scottish or Scotch-Irish ancestry. There was no question on which side they were active as citizens. Ranke, the German historian said, "John Calvin is the practical founder of America." English leaders of the day spoke of the revolution as a "Presbyterian rebellion." Horace Walpole facetiously remarked in the English Parliament, "Cousin America has run off with a Presbyterian parson."

If any individual parson were to be named, it would be John Witherspoon, a clergyman who signed the Declaration of Independence and was a member of the Continental Congress. He was not exactly a parson, being the President of the College of New Jersey, started by the New Side men and later moved to Princeton. Witherspoon was from Scotland, an adherent of the realist Scottish "common sense" theology opposed to rigid, idealistic predestinarianism. When he arrived, he found two faculty members, Jonathan Edwards, Jr. and Joseph Periam, promoting the "New Divinity" of the Edwards-Bellamy-Hopkins school of thought, with its stress on complete predestination and Divine Sovereignty among the students. He was wise enough not to start an open theological conflict, but young Edwards and Periam left the college after Witherspoon's first year. In his philosophical lectures, Witherspoon consistently opposed all forms of idealism.[30] As a strong believer in religious and civil liberty, he was soon active in the movement for independence. Though absent from most Presbytery meetings from 1776 until the end of the Revolution because of his civic activities, he was appointed to preside at the opening session of the first Presbyterian General Assembly of 1789.

Many Anglicans in the colonies were Royalist in sympathy, and a large contingent emigrated to Canada. Others supported the Revolution. George Washington was a Vestryman of the Anglican Church, but he was also a Freemason. His beliefs and sentiments were more in line with his Masonry than with his church. The Masonic Lodges were hotbeds for freedom. The Boston Tea Party has been called an adjourned meeting of the Boston Lodge. The Deism which predominated in the religious beliefs of many of the American Founding Fathers may have been derived in large measure from the Masonic philosophy with its belief in God, Freedom under Law, and Immortality. Similar beliefs are found in the writings of the seventeenth-century philosophers of democracy, such as John Locke and John Milton. Milton had published a series of pamphlets against episcopacy in 1641, and defended the execution of Charles I. Thomas Jefferson derived his principles of democracy for the American republic from these writers. Calvinist theology, which centers in the sovereignty of God, enabled Congregationalists, Baptists, and Presbyterians to make common cause with Deists for liberty. Deism in Freemasonry may be of ancient origin. Freemasonry traces itself back through the medieval craft guilds. Its interest in Pythagorean geometry, immortality, and its practice of memorization raises the interesting question whether its traditions might go back to the times of the Celtic Church, when Columba protected the Guild of the Bards at Drumceatt. We leave this question for research by some interested Freemason.

When the American Revolution was won, the Presbyterians had been so prominent among its proponents that some other religionists expressed concern, lest that denomination might be rewarded with some special preferment or privilege in the new nation. Some even suspected them of coveting the position of a national church. The Synod of New York and Philadelphia, acting before there was a general assembly, gave assurance that on principle they could not allow any privilege from government not equally shared by all other religious bodies. The declaration reads:

It having been represented to Synod that the Presbyterian Church suffers in the opinion of other denominations from an apprehension that they hold intolerant principles, the synod do solemnly and publicly declare that they ever have, and still do renounce and abhor the principles of intolerance; and we do believe that all peaceable members of civil society ought to be protected in the full and free exercise of their religion.[31]

When the United States of America was formed, both the representative democracy of its structure and the protection of the liberty of its citizens, including their religious liberty, were profoundly influenced by the model so many of its citizens had in their Calvinistic churches. Also, the realistic concern for the abuse of power, which determined the elaborate and careful provision for checks and balances between the executive, legislative, and judicial branches of government, reflected the Church's doctrine of human sin whereby power so readily corrupts.

With such a close collaboration and influence in the formation of this Republic, there has been a danger that Protestant churchmen should identify Christianity with the American Dream, so losing their Christian spiritual independence, by succumbing to an idealistic nationalism. This is safeguarded against by the realization that America has never been a Christian nation. The amount of religion in the founding documents has always been limited to an Old Testament or Deistic belief in the Creator and His Law, not faith in the saving grace of Jesus Christ. So long as the Church remains evangelical, a wholesome tension remains, while Christians may sing with heartfelt enthusiasm:

America! America!
God mend thine every flaw;
Confirm thy soul in self-control
Thy liberty in law!

Chapter IX

"THE WAY" IN CHRIST LARGELY FORSAKEN

We should now be prepared to ask with greater balance and depth of comprehension why we have been suffering such sad decline and spiritual barrenness in the old-line denominations of the Protestant church in America and elsewhere for nearly two decades. The loss began in church school membership and attendance, was clearly visible in church membership when declining growth became a net loss in my denomination in 1966, and at the same time congregational giving to General Missions began to shrink. Being a United Presbyterian, the writer has close knowledge only within his own communion, but recognizes the failure to be common in varying degrees in sister denominations.

Many external circumstances may be blamed for this condition: the secularization of the general culture; the effects of television; prolonged prosperity; increased dependence upon the welfare state; dismay and pessimism from the Vietnam War, etc. Yet not all religious groups have been similarly affected. Dean Kelley, formerly of the National Council of Churches has written a revealing book entitled *Why Conservative Churches Are Growing,* comparing the similar decline in the mainline Protestant denominations with a concurrent tremendous growth in conservative denominations like the Southern Baptists, and a vast expansion in conservative and faith missions abroad in the same period. Kelley's explanation is that Christianity has kept its meaning in the conservative churches, but this meaning has

United Presbyterian Church Trends

	Church Membership	Church School Membership	Total Receipts Reported by Congregations	Congregation Giving to General Assembly General Mission
1965	+ 5,783	− 64,423	+$ 11,950,816	+$ 438,159
1966	− 10,039	− 51,564	+ 7,951,142	− 53,064
1967	− 29,822	− 70,905	+· 28,274,969	+ 299,419
1968	− 39,037	− 99,451	− 3,553,648	− 1,300,425
1969	− 56,964	− 118,114	+ 3,329,417	− 867,090
1970	− 76,969	− 86,661	+ 4,664,848	− 1,828,078
1971	− 74,422	− 99,898	+ 11,013,724	− 2,625,890
1972	−104,612	− 94,435	+ 4,389,864	− 2,027,101
1973	− 99,705	− 20,117	+ 37,614,993	− 2,246,080
1974	− 85,514	− 49,888	+ 32,320,212	+ 974,983*
Total Change	−571,301	− 755,456	+$137,956,337	−$9,235,167

*Includes $1.4 million from the Emergency Appeal

Derived from:
(1) Minutes of General Assembly, Part II 1974 Statistics
(2) Comparative Statistics, 1974, Research Division, Support Agency
(3) Letter, Research Division, Support Agency
(4) Minutes, General Assembly Mission Council 3-17-75.
Published in *The Presbyterian Layman,* Feb. 1976.

been largely lost in the old mainline churches, whose leaders have tried to define a new meaning. This new meaning is the role the leadership thinks the faithful ought to see in the social situation. So they lift up a lofty social standard in the hope that the members will rally around it, recognize their newly defined duty, and do it. It has not worked. The flag-waving leaders have found themselves at greater and greater distance from their ostensible followers, waving the flag more frantically as the gap has widened.[1] Kelley is not clear as to how the attenuated religious meaning may be recovered, but suggests the mainline churches should furnish the religion the people want, or do better in inspiring their members to the "meaning system" of social action, or "throw in the sponge and settle for being a promiscuous social club."[2]

Recently, a more trenchant attempt to analyze the decline of the writer's denomination has been published by John R. Fry entitled *The Trivialization of the United Presbyterian Church.*[3] It is a bitterly angry book, the dedication page reading, "To Religion's Cultured Despisers: You are right." Fry blames the bureaucracy of the denomination for policies he considers picayune: the emphasis upon reconciliation in a world of rank injustice; the preoccupation with the redefinition of the word "mission," the embracing of reorganization as a means of retreat from social conflict. This is a case of the pot calling the kettle black; the excoriation of a left-of-center establishment by a more extreme leftist for whom the only definition of the church's call from God is simply "to undertake the works of love and justice as an institution among other institutions in a modern world."[4] For him, the social issues of the twentieth century, as he sees them, are determinative for the church, rather than the teaching and Spirit of Jesus Christ, and his only optimism is "that the plain ugly problems of a late twentieth-century world will prevail over every obscurantism and force the church to face them."[5]

Neither of these writers plumb the depths of the problem, of how the ever-available, all-sufficient meaning of "faith in Christ" became miscontrued, attenuated, and largely lost in the theological jargon and promotional verbosity of the bureaucracies of the mainline denominations, so that loyalty to Christ who makes all things new but who is "the same yesterday, today, yea and forever" has become less and less operative, or not seen in terms of what the denominational leaders have been promoting. As the pastor of a leading progressive "late-suburban becoming inner city" church in a middle-sized midwestern city, whose intelligent members, leaders in their community, had thrilled in 1957 to be hosts of the General Assembly, and who kept informed as to what was going on, I was plunged deeper and deeper into the sad dilemma of how to keep them loyal and enthusiastic toward the local church and denominational benevolences when the policies of the denomination grew more and more demon-ridden to alienate them. From this vantage viewpoint, caught sadly in the midst of the growing disaffection, sent every year I wished to the General Assembly as an observer by my concerned congregation, the mounting disaster was becoming threatening as early as 1961. The dominant off-center establishment, a coalition of neo-orthodox and liberals with similar social outlook, virtually unopposed, were becoming more and more self-assured, manipulative, and less able to listen as the church was blown into the troubled waters of the '60s. First our Sunday school teachers complained of articles in the official Christian education magazines containing propaganda favoring life in Red China. It was not that our people opposed all Christian social teaching and social action. They were aware of the Calvinist tradition of social reform. When word came down requesting that all sessions adopt a policy of accepting members without regard to race, our session said, "Why not? We have always assumed this if the opportunity came." One elder led in organizing Presbytery's Commission on Religion and Race. Yet it was the uncritical idealistic leftist naiveté in general assembly statements and the editorial policy of the denominational magazine *Presbyterian Life* that created opposition. So many members were angered and upset by the magazine, that though I had been on its founding committee, and had done some of the first promotional speaking in synods for *Presbyterian Life,* it was impossible to prevent our session from discontinuing the "Every Home Plan" which circulated it to our entire membership.

Why, when the Civil Rights movement had gotten out of hand and the Blacks were rioting and burning cities and looting, did the General Assembly leadership encourage their threatening demands in Minneapolis? Why did the General Council give its docketed time to allow James Forman to make his ridiculous demand for $50,000,000 from the General Assembly at San Antonio? Why the repeated gifts of benevolent funds to a radical socialist organization in Colombia over the protests of the Colombian Presbyterian Church? Over two years before the Angela Davis fiasco, our members' refusal to give to general benevolences had brought about the policy of allowing them the discretion of designating their benevolence portion to session-designated specific objects, for which we secured Projects Outside the Budget from the mission boards. The gift of $10,000 from the Legal Defense Fund toward the defense of an avowed Communist, Angela Davis, could have been explained as a Black Commission's "goof" which was censured by the General Assembly, and the furor modified some, if the Stated Clerk and other leaders had not shown their opposition to the mild Assembly rebuke by writing in impassioned support of the grant.

Sometimes it seemed as though the leadership, in their stubbornness, had an unconscious death wish for the church if it refused to take their determined path. Many mature ministers of larger churches, beloved by their congregations, said they were so tired of the struggle, they could hardly wait to retire. Meanwhile, the official promotional propaganda from headquarters in all of the controlled publications rang the changes on the same cliché "in words" which the perceptive lay people either suspicioned for their double entendre or laughed at as so much bureaucratic gobblede-gook. One of our youth teachers wrote a knowing spoof:

> I'd never need a "shrink," I think
> If I could just "relate";
> Or better yet if I could learn
> How to "communicate."
> If "reconciliation" could
> Unite me with my brother,
> And "sensitivity training" would
> Improve me as a mother;
> If I could hold a "dialogue"—
> Prove my "identity";
> Or better yet participate
> In some "group therapy";
> And "find myself"—become "involved"
> In something "meaningful";
> And "do my thing" and learn to "love"
> Then they'd say, "Beautiful!"
> Do all these things, then I'll be "free"—
> But I think I'm that already:
> What I really believe I need, my friend,
> Is a new dictionary!!
>
> —*Dorie Volk*

Reconciliation sociology and humanistic psychology together aren't the Gospel.

Of course, it was more than verbal juggling. Even the *Yearbook of Prayer for Missions,* which we had used for years with our daily devotions to supply the benevolence objects for our intercession, was reedited as a propaganda piece for the new theology of the "Church in Mission," as long beloved hospitals and schools were given to secular health-service charities and independent boards of trustees, and National Missions funds funneled into new projects of strategic social change. The new theology went deeper. If God has already reconciled the world to himself, and "God is where the action is," then God must be seen at work in the secular world wherever reconciliation, and the feeding of the hungry, and the giving of justice in terms of greater equality is going on. With monistic predestined and deterministic views of history, God must be active in the spread of Communism and Third World Socialism in this century, and Christians had better join God's reconciling work there and get with it! Christians who still believe God wants us to be free to obey Him and worship Him, and who think the Free Enterprise System by which they support our superior economy is the lesser of evils in a universally compromised with evil world, decided they would stop giving their hard-earned benevolence dollars into the hands of a church establishment bent on dismantling that system. The manipulators of the church establishments, World Council, National Council, and the leaders of the mainline denominations were either stupid, naive, idealistic dupes of the Marxist subverters, or, if smart, committed to the intrigue. So the intelligent, socially conservative great majority of the laymen, who still loved their church and its formerly trustworthy worldwide benevolence program, faced a crucial dilemma. That they still wanted to give to benevolences was proved by the oversubscription of the popular Fifty Million Fund, when each congregation was allowed to select its own specific objects overseas and at home with the promise that every cent would be spent where designated. Yet the cuts in giving to general benevolences jeopardized the annual support of those same objects, and the salaries of the evangelistically minded missionaries whose work the new-theology minded officials might cut out first! Worse, the feelings of suspicion and antagonism pervading the whole church made local evangelism and every other call to loving Christian service doubly difficult.

To see how far our leadership has been taking us from the Eternal Way In Christ, we must now examine what has been happening to the ten characteristics we have found essential to New Testament Christianity, strongly evident in the life of the Celtic churches as they brought the light of the Gospel for renewal after the Dark Ages, and in the Gospel movement of the Great Awakening that laid the foundations of evangelical Protestantism for a free America. Perhaps a renewal of a broad, fruitful, balanced, non-polarized, experiential faith in Christ involves a renewed acceptance of and devotion to these ten characteristics of that faith which it has always used and favored where the genuine Christian action is!

I. Evangelical Faith

Patrick gave "the eternal grace of the laver of salvation" to heathen tribes, proclaiming boldly the Name of the Lord. Patrick's *Confession* told of his sharing "such great grace that many people through me should be regenerated to God and afterwards confirmed." An evangelical faith expresses itself in fruitful evangelism. Evangelism is the propagating, recruiting activity of the church, whereby the redeemed in Christ share the life-transforming grace of God they have received with others who need both the abundant life in this world and the eternal salvation it offers. All through the '60s, vital evangelistic leadership had been missing in the United Presbyterian Church. The former "pre-Assembly Conference on Evangelism" became a sounding board for the fads in social radicalism favored to condition the commissioners' minds. Then in 1969, word came back to the hustings that the assembly had heard some good speakers on evangelism. Hopeful that the National Division of Evangelism had finally reawakened, the Committee in Nebraska scheduled a Pre-Synod Evangelism Dialogue, inviting the leaders of the division.

It was a revealing exhibition. First the Associate For Theological Studies of the Division of Evangelism tried to redefine evangelism for our time in terms of the "community-creating power of the gospel." "Evangelism must become involvement in reconciliation," he said. "The day of the theology of the Word is over. The day of the theology of Communion is in." Claiming that "Calvin saw evangelism as engagement in the reconciling activity of the common life," he affirmed, "We must listen to the world and its cry—the alienation of life, the existential disruption of human society, man's cry for reconciliation and communion."

He was not concerned about reconciliation to God, but our reconciliation with men in the world community. Since God is acting in the world today, evangelism is to reconcile the common life of mankind without concern for gaining members for our churches. He did speak about introduction into the life of love, and quoted Luther as saying "My neighbor is Christ to me." But he said the concern is not now guilt, but alienation. "The act of love needs to precede the words or our talk is empty."

The next speaker, our Nebraska pastor who has been moderator of the General Assembly, began by remarking, "My understanding of evangelism has changed across the years but I am not yet up to what we have just heard." He warned against making evangelism so broad, it loses its meaning, saying, "The evangelism I'm interested in is that which perpetuates the historical dialogue between God and man. It must be confrontation, an encounter with Jesus, or it isn't evangelism." That was more like it!

Then the associate chairman of the Division of Evangelism spoke on "New Styles and Strategies for Renewal in Mission." He said we are confronted by deep-rooted revolutionary forces, and the gospel of reconciliation can be brought to bear only if the churches will cooperate in planned ventures. The local church is too limited an instrument for mission. Presbytery as a flexible instrument must so serve. Social action strategies formulated at synod and presbytery levels must be implemented at the congregational level. If ministers prove uncooperative, presbytery should develop means to remove ineffective and emotionally disturbed ministers; and where ministers become involved in controversial issues with their churches, presbytery support and commendation should be given.

Significant growth should come through open dialogue in Presbytery on moot issues . . . Though power and politics have been seen as less than Christian, power is an instrument for change and therefore for mission.

In this, it was evident that the mission of the church was considered synonymous with social change, and that ministers who differed from this position, if he had his way, would be considered ineffective, and if they protested, considered emotionally disturbed, and removed from leadership in their churches. It sounded like the Russian way of dealing with dissidents! So the socialistic mind cannot abide or tolerate independence and freedom!

Finally, the chairman of the Division of Evangelism spoke on "The Crisis In The Nation." He said the nation and we are under judgment of God. The mercy of God is needed for our attitudes in three areas: race relations, war and peace, and poverty. First, the church must be more involved in the race problem. Second, the Vietnamese War was not only the nation's problem, but the problem of the church. The cross superimposed upon the flag has alienated more people from the cross than from the flag. Thirdly, there is poverty in the most affluent nation upon earth, and thank God we have learned that Thanksgiving baskets won't cure it. Solutions must be sought in structural change in the economy. Judgment may well be upon us because churches are so timid. Sessions should support cadres of members as they involve themselves in community problems, using general assembly actions on social issues as guidelines. Clusters of churches may join in such joint ministry in mission, with sessions giving leadership. This is the meaning and task of evangelism in a changing world.

In the discussion which followed, a pastor from a small town arose and said he had brought an elder along in hopes they would receive some help toward improving the evangelistic outreach of their church. Now he was nonplussed. There was no race problem in his town: every citizen was a Caucasian. He could not imagine how speaking about the Vietnam War would bring people to Christ. There was no poverty in his town. What should they do for evangelism?

Attempting to answer, the chairman of the Division of Evangelism lamely allowed such a small Nebraska town was different from the urbanized industrial East most characteristic of present-day America. He fumbled about and was visibly at a loss for an adequate answer.

Finally, a preacher with a droll sense of humor stretched his legs on the front row and drawled, "Well, I guess ministers in small Nebraska towns are just going to have to preach the Gospel!" The conference dissolved in wry laughter at the expense of the Division of Evangelism.

Later, in hopes of sharing some understanding of why people in the churches were losing confidence in our denominational leaders, I told this story to a moderator of the General Assembly who was obviously "in" with the liberal establishment. The only answer was, "You boys in Nebraska shouldn't have treated him that way. It has made him so defensive!"

There has been no sufficient willingness to admit that such a one-sided emphasis has contributed to the polarization wracking the church. For years, there has been no balancing emphasis upon winning people to a life-changing personal relationship with Jesus Christ. Year after year social action was redefined and pushed as evangelism to expose commissioners to the radical side of social issues known to be coming before the General Assembly. Those responsible probably were sincere in the belief that a more liberal social thrust on the part of the church would be the only means of convincing modern non-Christians of the church's relevance in our changing world. They scheduled speakers who would repeat their own convictions. The church's tragedy has followed the capture of her bureaucracy, almost completely, by people of a point of view far to the left of the center of her lay constituency. These leaders felt they had a mandate to rule or ruin, as modern prophets of God's righteousness. His righteousness was defined by them, talking among themselves.

When a "Celebration of Evangelism" was organized by ministers cognizant of the true need, and held in Cincinnati, it drew tremendous interest and enthusiasm. The Division of Evangelism was not the initiator, could hardly oppose, but barely cooperated. Still, they did not get the message. At the "Urbana '76" Intervarsity Christian Fellowship missionary convention, the eleventh triennial North American student gathering, of the 17,112 in attendance, the largest denominational representation, 1,046 were United Presbyterians! They must seek evangelical inspiration somewhere!

There are people of genuine evangelical faith in our churches. Most of them are not lacking in some social vision as well, but they doubt that a mere social stance will convert anybody. They believe that sinners must be led to a saving, personal relationship with Jesus Christ before they have the inner motivation to love as Christ loved, and to bear the Cross rather than the Hammer and Sickle in complex social situations, and that there is a fundamental difference. Usually, they are of independent disposition, often considered intractable by the church's organization-minded bureaucrats. The church must first return to genuinely representative democracy, and take people of varying viewpoints into its councils. It must really believe that to "maintain the unity of the Spirit in the bonds of peace" under one Lord we must rejoice that "His gifts were that some should be apostles, some prophets, some evangelists, some pastors and teachers for the equipment of the saints for the work of ministry" (Eph. 4:4-13), and let each exercise his different gift that the whole body may upbuild itself in love! It remains to be seen whether this one denomination's new leadership under drastic reorganization will have that breadth of vision. A new "Risk Evangelism" program is projected. Certainly, a stance in evangelism true to the full broad truth of the New Testament Gospel, more like that of the Celtic churches and the Great Awakening, is needed if any branch of the church is to be capable of furthering Christian renewal in our time.

II. Biblically Enlightened

Of Patrick, it was said, "In the Sacred Volume sacred treasure he findeth." He built his church upon Scripture truth, searching it broadly and responding to its inspiration as the Holy Spirit inspired him to understand it. Each little new congregation became a Bible school.

It is not easy to answer the question whether our churches have been mining the treasures of the Bible helpfully for this age. Certainly, there has been more knowledge about the Bible available, historical, archaeological, and geographical, and a spate of new translations making the Scriptures more understandable to the average reader. Yet I wonder if the average church member seeks and finds the Word of God to meet his needs as well as our fathers did.

Forty years ago, it was thought that the neo-Orthodox movement, led by the Swiss theologian Karl Barth, would return the learned leaders of the churches back to the Word of God in the Bible. "The Word of God" was said to be Barth's central concept. When neo-orthodoxy became strong in our denomination's leadership, seeming to offer a strongly Bible-centered middle ground between former liberal and fundamentalist extremes, many hoped its influence in the new *Faith and Life* curriculum for our church schools would be helpful. The old *Group-Graded Uniform Lessons* needed improving. At first, the new lesson books and teachers' helps, strong on Bible history, looked promising, even if they did offer so much academic detail. Church school teaching took on new life. Strangely, however, after some years, the attractive textbooks on Old and New Testament History, on different department levels for the church schools, were shelved, the curricular helps became more child-experience centered and/or more concerned with modern social problems. Then, after a quarter century, a new completely different curriculum was introduced, featuring the teaching methodology of the public schools. Somehow through all of this, the simple, personal, moral, and spiritual teachings of the Bible received less emphasis. Church-school-trained adolescents in pastors' communicant classes could not tell the Ten Commandments or their meaning. There was no time for the memorizing of great Scripture passages and key memory verses. The Bible became less and less a book of life demanding obedience and supplying saving faith, and church school attendance dwindled. Strangely, it has continued high in more conservative denominations stressing simple Bible teaching.

One cause may have been the way Barthian theology deceived our biblical expectations. As Gustaf Wingren, professor of Systematic Theology at the University of Lund, Sweden, says, "That which disappears from our attention through the theological work of Barth in this generation is the living and active God of the Bible, this God who continually creates and gives."[6] Promising to return from liberal philosophical theology to the word of God in the Bible Barth actually remained a philosophical idealist of the school of Schelling. His theology is all in the realm of ideas, not of moral reality. The main question with Barth is not that we become right with God, but that we have knowledge of God. Barth claims that the only knowledge we have of God comes from the one revelation of God in the incarnation of Jesus Christ. He, therefore, denies all of the natural theology taught in the Bible, and the revelation of the moral law in the Old Testament, and in the conscience of man through God's general creation. Law he would derive only from the love learned from the Gospel. So the biblical order of the revelation of the moral law prior to and in preparation for the Gospel is abandoned. As he is an idealist, evil for Barth has no real objective existence. There is no Devil, no evil power,[7] no kingdom of evil which must be destroyed, nothing actively evil in man which must die in order that the new man may be born.[8] Therefore, the problem of man's sin and guilt and need for forgiveness and salvation fades away just as it does in modern society with its relativistic ethics. For Barth, God has already reconciled the world to Himself through the one revelation in Christ, and all men need only to be informed about this. Repentance and guilt are unnecessary. Barth is essentially a Universalist. In one of his *Prison Sermons,* he claims that the unrepentant thief was surely saved by his having been crucified along with Jesus.[9] Little wonder that preaching and church

304

school teaching derived from Barthianism have muted moral teaching, conversion, the inner struggle with the Tempter, and the real meaning of the Cross and Resurrection. The Barthian system selects from and distorts the Word of God as it is revealed so variedly, realistically, and progressively throughout the Old and New Testaments.

That today's church people are hungry for the truth in the Bible is evident from the phenomenal success in churches of many denominations of the Bethel Bible Study Course of the Rev. Harley A. Swiggum. It requires pupils training to be its teachers to pledge weekly attendance for two years, and the memorizing of where hundreds of "concepts" are to be found throughout the Bible. These "concepts" are simple denotations of important Bible events and teachings helpful toward knowledge of Bible content. The course obviously fills a gap left in the churches' programs of education.

III. Humble Piety

Have our churches been training people in the practice of humble prayer and devoted service? Or has activism for what are considered larger social causes been so avidly stressed that humility has been forgotten, prayer neglected, and "piety" confused with "pietism" has become a term of opprobrium? Has promotion of the "big, major issues" obscured the importance of personal sacrificial service and charitable giving?

I first became aware of the trend in 1957 when we were hosting the general assembly in Omaha. A local women's committee met with a woman sent from headquarters to plan for the women's meetings. Our women reported with concern that when they suggested that the planning session open with prayer, the headquarters leader said, "We don't take time for that anymore."

Years ago, the election of moderators of general assemblies used to show careful regard for the humility of the candidates put forward by their presbyteries or friends. If any candidate was seen to be too eager for the honor, this worked against his election. Election was supposed to be public recognition for many years of humble, significant service and genuine spiritual leadership in the Lord's vineyard. In recent years, because some youth advisory delegates requested it, the candidates are required to campaign for the office by exposing themselves to public questioning on controversial issues of the day, and by answering a series of questions before the whole assembly in lieu of seconding speeches by their friends. Humility is sacrificed to competitive platform suavity and political charisma. The competition for the honor is crass, and few seem to mind it.

Our local church supported a National Missionary to the Indians in Sills, Arizona. She loved her people, serving them with sacrificial devotion. Her simple letters telling of her work with her people were an inspiration. Then we learned she had been dismissed because new National Missions philosophy called for a man to work at social strategy in the area, and there were not funds for both. After a time of unemployment, the board rehired her to work among Spanish-speaking people in a slum parish in El Paso, Texas. Again, her letters were of human, personal experiences, warm and loving. Then, after a few years, she was again unemployed because the church had brought in a new man to direct strategic social mission for the Chicanos in that presbytery. She wanted to work more with Spanish-speaking Americans, so she spent her own money to attend a language school for Latin-American missionaries in Central America to improve her Spanish. Then she offered herself to the board, again without response. Finally, she found a presbytery-approved mission in Tracy, California, and was engaged to serve there in a work raising its own funds. Soon, she was the head of this mission. Our session elected to send some discretionary benevolence funds to her mission. In the value judgment of many rank-and-file-Christians, social strategy does not take precedence over humble, loving service.

Our people needed to learn to pray together. Old-fashioned prayer meetings went out long ago. Our denomination offered no helps. We heard of small groups for prayer and sharing of faith and spiritual growth basic in the *Faith At Work* movement. After taking some couples for experiential participation and training at the spiritual renewal meeting of a Baptist Church in Sioux Fall, S.D., we were helped by *Faith At Work* volunteers from far and near with a very inspirational weekend at our church. Soon we had ten small volunteer prayer groups meeting weekly in homes of our members and their friends. Therefrom, we had people able to witness to life-changing experiences in Christ through the power of the Holy Spirit from the pulpit of our church. Yes, these people learned they must not act "holier than thou," and small prayer groups were not everyone's cup of tea, but piety is not a "dirty word," and for some, prayer leads to rededicated service. Jesus took his disciples apart to pray, then back to serve!

IV. Charismatic Ministry

Patrick, Columba, and Columban were guided and illumined in their ministry by the Holy Spirit. Therefore, they were independent of human direction, possessed "second sight," and were contagious with spiritual inspiration. There is no evidence that glossolalia (speaking with tongues) had any part in their ministry. Silence was more often cherished in their rule. Yet the manifold fruits of the Spirit were there in abundant measure: "love, joy, peace, patience, kindness, goodness, faithfulness, gentleness, self-control." (Gal. 5:22) Healing by faith was frequent.

Henry Pitney Van Dusen predicted a return to personal knowledge of the Holy Spirit in our time. It has come, albeit slowly. The Pentecostal churches which overemphasize glossolalia, if we follow 1 Cor. 14, are among the fastest-growing communions. Of late, we have seen the growth of charismatic movements in many denominations, including our Roman brethren. Dr. George F. MacLeod of the Iona Community has shown a special interest in the charismatic ministry in late years, searching more deeply into the Iona heritage.

Yet recently, our denomination has been redefining the ministry in terms that describe the "call" in purely ecclesiastical terms, rather than by the inner summons of the Holy Spirit. A general assembly study of the Holy Spirit was informative, but not too inspirational. How can anyone meet the spiritual demands, trials, disappointments, temptations, challenges, defeats, and opportunities of today's Christian ministry without the inner guidance and power of the Holy Spirit Jesus promised us? For church renewal, share Him we must!

V. A Realistic, Trinitarian, Personal, Bi-Worldly Theology

Ethical and theological realism were assumed in the New Testament and dominated the thinking of the Celtic churches. The preference for abstract philosophical ideas in Greek thought was early resisted. God and Satan, good and evil are real. This world, with its created natural order in which Christ participated by His incarnation is real, over against its unreality in Platonism. Heaven and hell are real prospects. Human sin, death, and the struggle with the Tempter are real, and required a drastic remedy in the victory of Christ on the Cross and by the Resurrection. The defilement of human personality by what comes out of sin-corrupted human hearts is still alienating people from God, regardless of modern social permissiveness. These are not just ideas to be played with, juggled with, believed, or disbelieved without serious consequences. What we do in response to these realities determines whether we really live, eternally, here and hereafter.

Many who call themselves Christians in the twentieth century think differently. I recall the controversy stirred thirty-five years ago, when, after losing the battle with leukemia in our only boy, I wrote an article for *The Presbyterian Tribune* entitled "Give The Devil His Due." "Such archaic superstition," they said, and "Such an attempt to escape responsibility for our wrong choices by blaming it on the Devil!" As though yielding to the Tempter were not always our own responsible choice! Since that time, the writings of Clive Staples Lewis such as *The Great Divorce* and *The Screwtape Letters,* and the rediscovery of the realistic atonement doctrine of the Early Church, of Irenaeus, and of Luther, by Gustav Aulen of Lund, Sweden, in his *Christus Victor,* have made realistic biblical theology more intellectually respectable. Meanwhile, pragmatically, to win the battle with cancer, drug abuse, prejudice, or any other evil, we had better believe they are real. Christianity, if it is to merit enthusiastic acceptance, must free itself of idealistic distortions that hamper needed morale for life's real battles!

Characteristically, the two theologians who have had the greatest influence upon the old-line Protestant leadership in America this century have both been idealists; both have denied the personal activity of God the Father in relationship with people in this world; both have muted evangelical conversion; and both entered theology carrying a prior devotion to socialism. Paul Tillich and Karl Barth have appealed to the liberal left and the neo-orthodox middle ground of churchmen in our time with quite different systems of thought, yet have been more alike than has been commonly realized. Their practical effect has been nearly identical: both deriving their ethics from the ideal principle of agape love; both denigrating moral law in relativistic situational terms; and both emphasizing idealistic social solutions.

Paul Tillich and his wife belonged to an avant-garde set in Berlin after World War I, when his thinking was strongly influenced by Karl Marx and he became deeply involved in the movement called religious socialism. Hoping to help Germany lead the way toward a radical reconstruction of society, based on the view of man in the Old Testament prophets, whose ideas he found echoed in Marx, he entered an academic career in philosophical theology. The Nazis smashed his immediate hopes and he had to leave Germany. Reinhold Niebuhr made a place for him at Union Theological Seminary, New York.

Tillich's denial of God's personal activity in human lives is clearly told in the appraisal of his theologian friend and interpreter Nels F.S. Ferré in the lead article *Tillich and the Nature of Transcendence* in the reprint symposium from *Religion in Life*, Winter 1966, entitled *Paul Tillich, Retrospect and Future.* When Tillich uses the term "the unconditioned" *(das Unbedingte)*, for God, a neutral noun, he means it. "He actually did not believe in the Christian God who raises the dead and who works personally in human history."[10] "In the deepest sense, he, more than anyone else, is the father of our American death-of-God theologians." Two of them dedicated a collaborative book to him.[11] He once said that his intellectual father was Schelling, the idealist precursor of Hegel.[12]

God for him is no seer who created the world, who foresaw the needs of the world, and who works purposefully with each person and event. There is . . . no purposing providence and no companion who understands . . . no concrete help for human history . . . no total goal toward which history moves. Tillich simply cannot be put within the framework of Christian theology . . . His position cannot be held or confined within the Christian faith without fundamentally altering and destroying it.[13]

Tillich wrote with two faces: theologically from within the circle of Christian faith, and then philosophically what he actually believed. So he could state in his *Systematic Theology* that incarnation (of Jesus) is indispensable to the Christian faith; and also that incarnation, historically and factually speaking, is blasphemy or nonsense.[14]

That Tillich was never converted to evangelical, life-changing faith in Christ is obvious from the publication of two recent books revealing his personal life, one by his widow, the other by his student, longtime friend and colleague at Union, the New York psychoanalyst, Rollo May. In a chapter on Tillich's love for women, May says he "seems to have been psychologically incapable of investing his love openly and completely in the one woman whom he married."

Though Tillich in a measure opposed the God-is-dead theologians, he claimed God does not exist, meaning God is not a part of the space-time order, but rather is the "Ground of Being." Tillich also used the term "the Ultimate," sometimes "the Divine," always distant intellectual terms, never personal. Nels Ferré hoped he could persuade him to accept the term "Spirit." In *Morality and Beyond,* Tillich derives his ethics from a double dependence: upon agape love and *kairos,* which is the manner of love's embodiment in concrete contents to fit new situations in ever changing times. Writing of the need to accept the loss of liberty under socialism, he says, "One must not condemn the collectivist and authoritarian forms of equality just because they negate equality's liberal and democratic forms." Love may demand a transformation in this *kairos.*[15]

Tillich became known as the "Theologian of Culture" with brilliant insight into the religious dimensions of art and literature. In 1951, he delivered a series of lectures in Berlin on the subject of Utopia, the concluding lecture, "Critique and Justification of Utopia," contending for the validity and efficacy of the utopian ideal. Tillich is buried in New Harmony, Indiana where Robert Owen led a secular utopian community in the 1820s. The wife of a descendent of Owen, having contributed to the historic restoration of the town, became an admirer of Tillich at Union, and added a park named for the theologian by the shrine for the Harmonists. He attended the dedication and consented to be buried there as appropriate to his ideals.[16]

The importance of Karl Barth's similar social orientation may be more difficult for many to believe. An early liberal socialist, Barth reacted violently to the support given by German liberals, including his theological teachers, to the Kaiser's war policy in World War I. He led a neo-orthodox, theological reaction against liberalism. His idea of God was so transcendent that he could believe God touched human history only once after the Creation: in his great act of reconciliation with mankind in the Incarnation. In the Cross and Resurrection, God's reconciling work was accomplished for everyone. So Christ is the only revelation of God. This Barth stressed when he wrote the *Declaration of Barmen*, resisting Hitler's messianic claims for the German Pastors' Emergency League. Christ's love is the only revelation for ethics, which must be derived situationally from agape. Therefore, the chief ethical task is social reconciliation. Friedrich-Wilhelm Marquardt of the Free University of Berlin has published in 1972 a 358-page volume in German, well received by German scholarship, entitled *Theologie und Sozialismus—Das Beispiel Karl Barths* (Theology and Socialism—the Example of Karl Barth) stating the following thesis in the Introduction, page 15:

> In this book the assertion will be maintained that there is not only a vague trace, but a distinctly recognizable and demonstrable influence of Socialism upon the theological thinking of Karl Barth.

By teaching a unitarianism of the Second Person of the Trinity, and neglecting natural theology, moral law, and the Holy Spirit's inspiration of liberty, Barth could erect a great theological system which conditions his followers' politics to advanced social idealism without their realizing it. The authors and proponents of the Presbyterian *Confession of '67* were largely Barthian. The chief purpose was to gain constitutional ground in the United Presbyterian Church for defining the church's mission in terms of universal social reconciliation. In their Barthian interpretation, the main thrust of the "ministry of reconciliation" enjoined in 2 Corinthians 5 is not "be ye reconciled to God," for God has done all of that already. It is rather "be reconciled with all social dissidents and alienated groups." Our reconciliation with the Marxists is more important than their conversion!

Like Barth, the authors and proponents of the new United Presbyterian *Confession of '67* were using neo-orthodox theology to rationalize their social idealism. Early Barthianism, with its universal reconciliationism chosen as the one all-comprehensive motif of the Gospel, seemed to justify their desire. Actually, it places reconciliation in the place of God as an idol. As though He is reconciled to Communistic atheism and oppression! Universal reconciliationism becomes the deification of compromise with evil aggressors so long as they are social idealists! One possible explanation of this monstrous error is that its perpetrators were so frightened by John Foster Dulles' "brinkmanship" as secretary of state, and the rattling of nuclear bombs, and the prospect that the world might end a la Nevil Shute's *On The Beach,* "not with a bang but a whimper," since they trusted no historic Christian eschatology, that they wanted to rationalize compromise with every aggressive evil power and threatening minority in the effort to guarantee peace. They will not admit that this offers a perfect "patsy" set-up for the Leninist, sophisticated strategy of implacable aggression: "Two steps forward and one step back." Still we have those who would heal the wound of God's people lightly saying "Peace, peace," when there is no peace![17]

The current theological bright light from German scholarship is the theology of hope. The guiding light of the revolutionary wing of this new movement is Jürgen Moltmann. In his thinking, Christ becomes a typical Marxist-humanist, championing the cause of the downtrodden masses against existing power-structures. In *Religion, Revolution and the Future* Moltmann says, "We no longer view the structures of society as given by nature or by God, but know that because they are made by man they can also be changed by man."[18] The hope of utopia is in the collaboration of humanistic Marxism and humanistic: chiliastic Christianity.

The predominance of such thinking in liberal seminaries in recent decades, among the more outspoken professors and the loudest students, will help to explain the polarization of our churches. Too much theological thinking has been the attempt to say "me too" to the Marxists, and to go them one better in the espousal of social idealism. When they accuse us of preaching "pie in the sky bye and bye when you die," we have too often scrambled to prove ourselves more this-worldly and secular, quite neglecting the two-worldly, eternal dimension of our historic faith, with its real but quite different concern for this world. The Way in Christ for church renewal must stress the ethical imperative of eternal life here and hereafter.

Lest the reader despair of theologians, and fear that the church is lost to the Marxists, may I assure you that this is a passing phase. There are at least two major theologians writing and speaking in terms that bid to outshine the pro-Marxists. The first is Wolfhart Pannenberg of Munich, the original proponent of the Theology of Hope, whose independent thinking Jürgen Moltmann has endeavored to twist out of context. Pannenberg is a historical realist who breaks out of the context of idealistic dialectical theology, and affirms the centrality of the Christ event, with the historicity of His Ressurection in a new style of natural theology. The reality of history attains completion only in its end, so history receives its unity from God's end purpose for it. In the destiny of Jesus, this end has come and been seen in advance. Sharing it, each individual gains freedom over against the power of Satan. No human government can successfully attain peace and justice, but the Community of the Faithful, sharing God's love for the world must serve society amid history's tensions.

Another theological movement derives from the newer Einsteinian cosmology, with its thorough rejection of the dualism we inherited from the Greek idealists. Einsteinian physics replaces the simple causal connections and natural laws of Newtonian physics, which have informed the philosophy of atheistic scientific positivism and older liberal theology, with concepts of field structure and field laws and the infinite dimensions of quantum mechanics outdating prior thought. In 1972, Professor Thomas F. Torrance of New College (School of Theology) in Edinburgh, Scotland, lectured a Church Leaders' Conference in Birmingham, England, on *The Church in the New Era of Scientific and Cosmological Change.* He said:

Unfortunately . . . the Ptolemaic cosmology, together with the philosophical and cultural dualism between the intelligible and sensible realms, was introduced into Christianity through St. Augustine, and has affected the whole of western Christianity ever since. . . . For the first time then, in the history of thought, Christian theology finds itself in the throes of a new scientific culture which is not antithetical to it, but which operates with a non-dualistic outlook upon the universe, which is not inconsistent with the Christian faith, even at the crucial points of creation and incarnation. This also means that the theology most relevant to the post-Einsteinian world is that of classical Patristic theology. . . . . Perhaps the worst thing Churchmen could do would be to lose their nerve at the wide gap opening up between historic Christianity and modern patterns of human behavior, and allow themselves to be panicked by the avant-gardes into translating the Christian message into current social manifestations which are themselves part of the sickness of humanity. That is, alas, the line so often pursued by reactionary liberals in the name of "involvement," as though the Church were a sort of religious discotheque, whereas I want to challenge them to follow the example of the Greek Fathers in undertaking the courageous revolutionary task of the Christian reconstruction of the foundations of culture: nothing less is worthy of the Christian Gospel.[19]

Let us pray for more such theologians to lead us in the needed renewal!

VI. Missionary Dedication

One of the tragedies of recent church history has been the shrinking of the overseas missions programs of the major old-line American Protestant denominations. At the same time, conservative and faith-mission denominations have greatly increased their foreign mission enterprises. It is a complex situation, with many factors.

Some countries in which we had huge mission investment have been closed to our missions: especially China, when the Communists took over in 1948, and all of our hospitals, universities, middle schools, and social settlements were confiscated and our missionaries sent home.

Part of the decrease in the number of foreign missionaries is due to the success of our missions, in training nationals to leadership in now self-governing churches, turning the work of administration, pastoral service, and even missionary expansion within their countries over to them, decreasing the number of Americans needed in many fields.

Yet much of the decrease has been forced by insufficient benevolence funds, as sending denominations have received smaller mission contributions from their members at the very time when inflation and increasing costs around the world have made it far more expensive to keep a missionary in the field. The reason for shrinking gifts to official denominational benevolences when local church support giving has increased and there has been increased support of projects closer to home, such as Presbytery enterprises, is variously explained. A large factor has been growing disaffection and mistrust of denominational leadership because of the change in the philosophy of mission, and strongly emotional opposition to certain widely publicized controversial projects. The tragic result has been that since the decision about which mission works to close has been in the hands of executives being criticized for their sponsorship

314

of new policies, there has been some cause for evangelistic missionaries to fear they were the first ones being recalled. So the withholding of funds has backfired, to the detriment of the very missionaries the withholders would favor.

It is too soon to gauge what to expect from the leaders and from the churches under the new reorganization of the United Presbyterian Church. It stands to reason that the merging of the board responsible for foreign missions into a united program agency, responsible also for national missions and Christian education, and the scattering of mission responsibility in regional synods may further weaken the world mission emphasis. Something deeply real and convincing must be done to restore trust and enthusiasm for a renewed world mission program in the denominations, or more and more consecrated funds will go to independent missionaries and mission projects. Christ's great commission still commands!

VII. Steadfast Personal Morality

With church membership in the United States at a higher percentage of the population than at any other time in the nation's history, the past twenty years have witnessed a rapid decline in personal moral conduct. Crime has multiplied. Murder, rape, burglary, and theft all have increased in alarming proportion. Corrupt practices in business and graft and corruption in politics threaten the stability of our free society. Sexual immorality has increased to the degree that many think we are undergoing a sexual revolution, permanently departing from Christian standards of chastity and purity as the honored ideal. Increasing divorce threatens the stability of the family, and one of the causes is the increasing acceptance of hedonism rather than self-disciplined keeping of covenants, in obedience to God as the basis of personal conduct.

Where has the church stood in the midst of this debacle? Has the Christian fellowship been a tower of strength to all who have needed help in resisting the temptations of the world in our time, an effective rescue agency capable of snatching victims from Satan's slavery and restoring them to lives of victorious goodness in Christ, and a clear definer of The Way of Christ on all the dangerous moral issues which have arisen? Have we been the salt of the earth, a purifying, seasoning, moral preservative? Have we been the light of the world, illuminating the moral darkness with the clear rays of Christ's truth? The church cannot accept full responsibility for all that goes on in the world, for its effective, committed membership is not a controlling majority in society. Still, it is the duty of Christ's people to give clear moral leadership for all who will follow, and to offer effective redemption from evil to all who will respond. In this important part of her ministry, while many local congregations have remained true to the New Testament Gospel, and some ministers have preached and served with steadfast moral consistency and faithfulness, others have faltered and weakly compromised, while the denominational leadership, the church's official periodicals, and supposed Christian education materials have exhibited policies adding to the moral uncertainty.

Several causes of this faltering moral leadership are obvious:

1. Concentration upon vast, seemingly more important social issues to the neglect and disparagement of problems of personal morality. In our presbytery, if issues of personal conduct were raised, it was called "nit-picking." A minister considered a hero because he had marched for racial justice at Hattiesburg, Mississippi thought the payment of his personal bills unimportant and had to be bailed out of threatened bankruptcy. His theology was strongly Barthian! Some socially idealistic young ministers were not faithful to their wives.

2. The fear of alienating rebellious youth, leading to excessive coddling and moral leniency. Parents have widely made this mistake, failing to take firm moral stands, for fear of losing their youngsters, when what the protesting young often really wanted was a strong definition of right and a sure curb on their folly, to give them assurance of the moral order and proof they were loved. Church leaders likewise proved fallacious in muting clear Christian standards, hoping thereby to remain popular with rebelling youth.

One widespread instance was church acceptance of the heretical rock opera *Jesus Christ Superstar*. Written by two young atheists, its portrayal of Jesus as a weak seeker of popular adulation, emotionally dependent upon Mary Magdalene, and inferior in judgment to the socialist-minded Judas, was obviously sacrilegious by clear Christian standards. Yet many churches scheduled its use to please rock-music entranced young people.

At the General Assembly of the United Presbyterian Church in Chicago in 1969, a band of "hippies" were condoned as they made nuisances of themselves, interrupting the communion service with calculated misconduct, lying in the aisles in amorous poses during business sessions, releasing balloons, and were given time on the platform to defame the church using inexcusable four-letter words.

The church's response to the youth rebellion in granting undue prerogatives to callow youth in its business procedures is widely regarded an advance with changing times, with few courageous enough to question its wisdom. Of course, the idealistic leftists welcome it, for young people, inexperienced with living in the real world, can be counted upon to give enthusiastic support to idealistic proposals, while it is harder for the realistic opponents of such schemes to voice their critical objections in the presence of innocent adolescents. The young "Advisory Commissioners" at Chicago, well primed by the liberal young adult leaders with whom they met for group caucus, crowded the microphones to speak on all controversial issues, and were given such undue deference, it worked to the detriment of wise, serious debate. It must be recognized that some Youth Advisory Commissioners spoke well in criticism of the Sex Report, where their idealism needed to be heard on a subject where they had primary responsibility. Yet, the net effect of this coddling upon the moral authority and social responsibility of the church may well be questioned.

3. The uncritical assumption that every change is necessary in changing times. Because things generally are said to be bad, any proposed change, even in moral standards, is liable to be welcomed as good, or at least with the willingness to experiment. So the Chicago General Assembly, confronted with a 20,000 word report entitled *Sexuality and the Human Community*, favoring opinions that premarital and extramarital sexual relations are not necessarily sinful nor to be condemned, and belittling injunctions against such conduct as mere "conventions . . . the culture-bound wisdom of a part of the community: to wit, the white, Protestant and middle-class part," did not adopt it, but did send it down to the churches to be studied!

4. The substitution, in ethical theory, of ideal abstractions for the living God. So "agape and kairos" for the disciples of Tillich, and "reconciliation" for the Barthians become effectual idols, usurping the place of the personal Heavenly Father and

the indwelling Christ and His teachings in the New Testament as the ultimate norms and guides to all human conduct. More popularly, many think "Love is God" is no different from the Scripture truth "God is love."

At the Chicago Assembly, I asked one of the obstreperous "hippie" appearing group where he was from. He said from San Francisco Seminary which had helped him to attend the assembly. Asked what he believed, he replied, "I believe in 'Thou shalt not kill,' and in love." "What kind of love do you mean?" I inquired. "Do you mean 'eros,' or 'filia,' or 'agape,' the morally responsible mature love that really cares?" "Anything that turns me on!" he replied. "These couples who are lying around on the floor together, are they married?" I asked. "Some of us are married," he replied, "but we don't ask that question!"

So the "love" ethic becomes what people want to make of it, often mere humanistic sentimentality, a form of hedonism mistaken for Christianity. A similar, sentimental misunderstanding of Christian love accounts for the defense of homosexuality as "neither sin nor sickness" in a recent church publication.

5. Widespread teaching and adoption among churchmen of "Situation Ethics" as defined by Joseph Fletcher in his popular book by that title. Fletcher, an Episcopal clergyman and professor, had his book published by the Presbyterian Westminster Press. When he was dean of the traveling Cathedral of the Diocese of Southern Ohio in 1940, I sat in a course he opened to Cincinnati clergymen. Sensing the trend of his economic argument, I challenged his social belief. He admitted to being a theoretical communist. In his *Situation Ethics, A New Morality,* he approvingly quotes Nikolai Lenin when Lenin once asked Tolstoyan idealists, "If the end does not justify the means, then in the name of sanity and justice what does?"[20] In the casuistry of Fletcher's book, by the multiplying of exceptional cases in which two or more ethical considerations conflict, he seeks to degrade the authority of moral law. Situational ethics teaches the subordination of all other laws, rules, principles, or axioms to agape love in each special situation. It assumes the average person to have the ability to see the full implications of agape love in complex situations, so as to justify their departure from common moral rules. The inability of even very intelligent people to do this adequately is illustrated by the participants in the Watergate break-in. One of them said he was confused by a leading churchman's teaching of situational ethics, thinking the

importance of the election for the good of humanity justified such a minor infraction of law, especially with the approval of the White House.

6. The confusion of Christian ethics with secular academic thinking through soliciting the opinions of "experts." The policy of church bodies in appointing special committees to bring in reports on ethical matters results in so-called experts in sociology, psychiatry, psychology, academic ethics, etc., being placed on the committee, or being consulted with too great deference to their opinions. Their thinking is often derived from secular academic sources and current social statistics. This may explain the Sex Report to the General Assembly of 1969. The assumption is that the changing social environment brought about by scientific discoveries and popular changes in attitude makes the ethical teachings of the New Testament obsolete.

The church must make up its mind whether Jesus Christ who said, "my words will not pass away" is truly her Lord. If He is, we cannot just call Him "Lord! Lord!" and not do what He says. For what He says in the realm of personal ethics, about honesty, about hating, about being pure in heart and thinking as well as in conduct, about how any kind of evil including fornication defiles personality (Mark 7:21-23) is in the area of Jesus' own Divinely true expertise. In this, He is not superseded by any later ethical authority whatsoever, if He is Lord! Church renewal awaits the recovery of true moral authority under Christ.

This ethic will put spiritual well-being above material comfort in the scale of values. No hedonistic humanism can satisfy anyone who, in Christ, is assured of eternal life. This world is important, but life at home with the Lord is more important, and this life must be disciplined for the soul growth that prepares for that glorious eventuality. Here we have a motivation which will make virtue of the necessity now to eat less, use up less energy, and conserve the world's dwindling resources. Either Christian spiritual purposes must inspire a free, voluntary simpler way of life, or it will be forced upon us by social controls destructive of liberty. Where the Spirit of the Lord is, there is freedom through voluntary self-discipline. It is time that Christians should outgrow the fear of being taunted with the accusation of being "other-worldly" as if that were a term of opprobrium. We must be proud that our faith in abundant spiritual living in this world and in the next makes us more eager to serve the real well-being of potentially eternal sons and daughters of God in both worlds. The love of Christ in our hearts requires such an eternal-life ethic.

Certainly we must meet the perennial danger in stressing personal morality, that Christians may become self-righteous pharisaic legalists, and think they may gain heaven by earning "Brownie-points." Such a pietism was no doubt the aim of the derision of the Barthian reformists who sought in the '60s to reeducate the Presbyterian ministry. Seminars for ministers were held across the church on "The Nature of the Ministry," with a textbook advising ministers to study, not to set a moral example to their congregations. I asked whether I should take up chewing tobacco or going out with my neighbors' wives! It was a complete repudiation of Paul's advice to Timothy.[21] If it was an attempt to counterbalance Victorianism in American Christianity, it was a bit late. Some said it was because Barth liked his beer. So the students at one seminary forsook the coffee shop on campus where they had formerly held their discussions for the tavern across the street, and when as graduates these emancipated theologs took our midwestern churches, flaunting their new-found Christian liberty, the silly furors they caused divided churches and made no end of trouble for the synod executive. All temperance lessons were discontinued in the Christian Education curricula, so that a truly important social issue became totally neglected. The abhorrence for personal morals has sounded like the teaching of Marcion, who would have tossed the Old Testament and other moral books out of the Scriptures, and was condemned as a heretic by the Church of the second century.

All followers of Tillich and Barth and other idealists who would overintellectualize the faith should heed Immanuel Kant's *Critique of Practical Reason,* in which he proved that ethical understanding provides a more trustworthy path to final truth than "pure reason," using the intellect. Better they need to hear Jesus for whom obedience was always more important than doctrine.[22] Our Lord said that the moral surrender that cleanses and integrates the inner life must be the prerequisite of knowledge of God in Him:

Blessed are the pure in heart, for they shall see God.

The priority of moral obediences was clarified for me in an

experience of Scriptural illumination in 1948 in Shanghai. Completing a lecture tour for the Board of Foreign Missions, sharing "New Life Movement" methods of evangelism with Chinese Christians, I was invited to a Chinese Christian Business Men's Luncheon Club. Following my remarks, an honored guest, Mr. Doho Yen, was asked to comment. I was told that Mr. Yen was the managing editor of *Sin Wan Pao,* the largest circulating daily newspaper in the Orient, and was not a Christian, but a prospect for evangelism. He began to speak in rapid Chinese, a Chinese pastor seated by me whispering a digest translation in my ear. "He says that he is convinced that Christ has the only answer to the world's problem, as he has read the New Testament carefully. Yet he is not ready to profess faith in Him until he knows Him better. He asks you how he may get to know Him better."

As I was called upon by the chairman of the meeting to respond, I prayed earnestly for guidance. Even as I was rising to my feet, two relevant truths from John's Gospel flashed into my needy foreconsciousness, and I was given to say, "Mr. Yen, I am glad that you have studied the New Testament and are already acquainted with the life of Jesus and his teachings, and are convinced that He has the answer to the world-wide problems of humanity. Yet now I must point out that you are asking for the wrong sequence: more knowledge before you will obey and follow Him. Christ asks us to follow Him in faith and obedience in order that we may know. He said, 'If any man's will is to do His will he shall know,'[23] and again, 'If you continue in my word, you are truly my disciples, and you will know the truth, and the truth will make you free.'[24] The time comes when we must surrender our wills and become obedient disciples, as we already know enough to judge and choose the best. Then as we grow in the Christian way of life we are given personal experiences of His forgiving love and helpful Presence and power whereby we know Him more and more."

I wish I might report Mr. Yen's decision. It was a trying time, for the Communists were advancing southward from Peking toward Shanghai, making it doubly difficult for so prominent a citizen to declare for Christ. Before we were ordered out of China the next day, I was told that Mr. Yen was seriously considering the reply the Holy Spirit had given me. Personal surrender to moral obedience is the main pre-requisite to spiritual renewal.

VIII. Socially Constructive

Jesus' realistic social ethic of the Kingdom of God on earth was relative to people's "hardness of heart," and required demonstration in the special fellowship of His Church dedicated to agape love. The Celtic Church largely preserved this social ethic, though its later ascetic monasticism makes this witness bizarre to us. Yet this is a marginal consideration. Does our almost exclusive preoccupation with idealistic social change accurately express the Gospel?

When we say it does not, we are not denying the social responsibility of Christians, nor of the Church. We cannot say that the personal Gospel of individual conversion and nurture is the whole and only work of the Church. Too often, personally enthusiastic Christians have been satisfied to coddle their own pious feelings and "pass by on the other side," ignoring brethren in need. Yet too often, the advocates of particular programs of social change have kept the argument on the general issue of whether the church has any social responsibility, and may involve itself in any social action, as though opposition to their specific programs amounted to a general denial. This has prevented adequate critical scrutiny of their particular social theorizing, their specific projects, their means of getting seeming churchwide approval through social action resolutions in church courts, and the scheme by which they have wangled support from church funds. So the bureaucracy has aligned itself in secular partisan politics at the opposite pole from most of its constituency. It is no new danger in Calvinist churches. Writing the biography of Sir Walter Scott who lived a century and a half ago, Hesketh Pearson says:

> In Scotland religion was a firm ground of friction, and he (Scott) hated the enthusiasm which made it "a motive and a pretext for particular lines of thinking in politics and in temporal affairs." This was a spirit which did nothing but evil, "disuniting families, setting children in opposition to parents, and teaching as I think a new way of going to the Devil for God's sake."[25]

Of course, Jesus himself said His faith would divide families. The question in each particular event is whether it is His faith, or some proud human assumption which is made the issue. Unfortunately, social action gives such marvelous scope for what the Greeks called "hubris" and the Hebrew-Christian tradition calls "original sin." When Dietrich Bonhöffer said that humanity has "now come of age," and we must therefore accept complete responsibility for the world's future, he was rather ruling out the prerogatives of Divine Providence and urging us to bite off more than we can chew. Being fellow workmen with God is heady business if we are not humbly aware that His is the larger role. We must make sure it is really His plan we are so eager to promote, and that we go about doing it in His way, with the real backing and approval of His people. Otherwise, we may become laughingstocks like the man Jesus told about who began to build a tower and was not able to finish it. We have responsibility in social action, but it is a far more modest and humble one than scheming to control the whole secular world. Our churches have been straining to do so much more than they have lay backing for, so much more than they know how to do, or ever can do well, at the same time that they have been neglecting more fruitful aspects of their work for humanity which they are equipped to do well, and which might in the long run make them socially more effectual.

To have credible opinions in this controversial field, one must have had some experience in social action through the years. Through most of my ministry, I was so active promoting and participating in this applied Christianity that I have had queer feelings of guilt in recent years when it has been so overdone. Stanley Jones was right when he said that if Christianity doesn't begin with evangelism, it never begins: if it ends with evangelism, it ends! So community activity and the perennial battle with civic corruption consumed much of my energy through the years. In Galesburg, Illinois, I battled quite immaturely with the Custer Machine. In Sioux City, Iowa, it was with the criminal control of the Department of Public Safety, and with a communist-directed jurisdictional strike at the Swift Packing Plant. In Cincinnati, there was work helping the interracial integration of an inner-city church, and for Protestants and Other Americans United for the Separation of Church and State in ending Roman Catholic control of public school boards and milking of school taxes in North College Hill and Saint Bernard. Experience taught more and more realism. In Omaha, there was more than one reason for marching in protest marches with our Black brethren when the children were killed in the bombing of the Black church in Birmingham, and in honor of Dr. Martin Luther King at the time of his assassination. Solid citizen support of the Christian Black community was needed to prevent seizure of social leadership by radical subversives.

In Dundee Church, Omaha, the outstanding spiritual leader was a solidly converted, twice-born elder, an attorney named Joseph M. Emmert. He was chairman for Evangelism of the Council of Churches and led a city-wide personal evangelism crusade with the help of the old Federal Council of Churches Department of Evangelism, which won more decisions and new church members than the Billy Sunday Campaign years before. Becoming president of the Omaha Council of Churches, he asked me to serve the Community Relations Committee. Later, when a particularly scandalous condition developed in the local judiciary, it was his knowledge of legal conditions and planning which enabled us to secure the cooperation of leading Jewish, Roman Catholic, and Protestant attorneys to analyze and pinpoint the evils, and to mobilize the public conscience of all three religious communities to enter the judgeship election, and put in a reform slate of municipal and district judges of all three faiths who transformed the law enforcement in Omaha. This activity led to a term on the board of the Omaha Community Chest, and later six years by mayor's appointment on the Omaha Human Relations Board. When I was chairman, we persuaded the City Council to enact the area's first Fair Employment Practice law. More realistic insight came conducting preliminary adjudication of cases from charges of unfair employment practice.

My most informative stint was a six-year term on the Advisory Committee for Social Action of our General Assembly from 1948 to 1954. The appointment came after writing letters to a magazine in support of a brother minister's right to pulpit freedom as a pacifist in World War II. Not sharing his opinion, I contended for his right to freedom to dissent on grounds of conscience. On the Advisory Committee, my mediating position, sometimes encouraging the right-wing businessmen to speak up, may have surprised some staff persons. One of the laymen, Mr. Lem Jones, president of Stoever Candy Company of Kansas City, had been president of the National Council of Presbyterian Men in the days before that organization was taken over and controlled by the headquarters bureaucracy, when they used to be called "the Republican Party at its prayers." I found the businessmen on our Committee frustrated and threatening to walk out, as they were no match in theory and loquaciousness for the leftists, including a certain liberal professor of sociology who talked very freely. The businessmen needed to be encouraged to say what they thought, as they represented a far larger constituency in the church. They needed to recognize that the committee could not recommend actions to the general assembly unless it had a true consensus, including their participating agreement and support. During those years, the General Assemblies received no very wild, leftist recommendations from its Advisory Committee on Social Action.

In the General Assembly of 1961, serving on the Standing Committee on Social Action revealed how the department, along with the boards, was moving farther left. Also how the method of forming the standing committees in the Election Sections all but guarantees a leftist Committee on Social Action. Eager beavers usually got their committee choice! Then the division of labor into subcommittees to formulate the separate positions being considered on the basis of committee members' interest helped to favor passage of any resolution strongly supported by the department. The rush of business and avalanche of reports during the last days of the Assembly protected most Standing Committee recommendations from effective floor opposition. So the actual process was far from fair representative democracy.

It was no great surprise, therefore, to learn from Paul Ramsey's book, *Who Speaks For The Church?* how the 1966 Geneva Conference of Church and Society of the World Council of Churches arrived in so brief a time at its pronouncements on so many deeply controversial world issues. Being a professor of Religion at Princeton University, Dr. Ramsey was an advisory resource person at this Conference with opportunity to view the process firsthand. There the delegates had opportunity to choose the issue of their greatest interest for drafting and discussion in a subcommittee, and then the subcommittee leaders presented their findings before the crowded final meetings of the Conference as a whole, rendering effective opposition to subcommittee proposals very difficult. The subcommittee which drafted and put through the strong statement against American military policy in Vietnam, seeming to speak as the Christian conscience of the world's Protestant and Orthodox Churches, consisted of four persons: leftist Professor John C. Bennett, president of Union Theological Seminary in New York; Metropolitan Nicodim of the Russian Orthodox Church, Moscow; Albert Laham, a lawyer from Lebanon; and an observer from India, A.K. Thampy, businessman.[26]

In 1970, Dundee Church, Omaha, acted socially by sending one of our able young elders, after years of church and community leadership, to the United States House of Representatives. As a freshman Congressman, John Y. McCollister went with other presbyterian legislators to a meeting called by the Moderator and Stated Clerk of his General Assembly. There he was appalled when presented the bulky stack of resolutions on so many crucial controversial secular issues before the United States and the world, passed by one week's meeting of the General Assembly: issues on which Congress committees struggle for months to get competent knowledge. Led by Congressman Clarence J. Brown of the Seventh Ohio District, these conscientious Presbyterian churchmen in Congress addressed and signed a letter of concerned protest to the Stated Clerk saying in part:

As public servants who are also Presbyterians, we belong to different political parties and hold divergent philosophies on questions of public policy relating to the political, economic, social and international issues of the day which the temporary occupants of the hierarchy of our church feel constrained to address. We acknowledge that our divergent views on temporal matters often spring from common spiritual and religious convictions and question that our political differences make us any less Christian and Presbyterian.
. . . we feel obliged to petition the current leaders of our church to concentrate more on the issues which unite us as men of goodwill seeking personal salvation and less on those conceits which divide us as partisans on transitory issues.

Was this protest signed by nineteen Presbyterian Congressmen critical of current church practice ever publicized or heeded?

Our social-activist churchmen, in their eagerness to be "involved" in current social change, and to prove their religion "relevant" to every issue dominating the public mind, have often failed to study what Jesus meant when He said His Church would be "in the world" yet not "of the world." They have little heeded the strategy of our Celtic Church fathers in planting their headquarters for mission in independent islands off the coast, as Iona and Lindisfarne. To be the Church, the

Church must be separate not only from the State, but also from each current phase of civilization, what in German is called the "Zeitgeist." The advocates of a completely secular Christianity are seeking the impossible. Involved in the common life as we must be to earn a living and to be good citizens, and influential as the Church should be for the common good, we must also maintain a certain detachment in our special fellowship as Christians. From this, we may view the limitations of any viable culture-complex, containing as it must the world's unregenerate multitudes. The Church cannot act redemptively upon the world's life if she fails to maintain a better life within her own household of faith. So there must be a certain independence of the Church from human culture, and from the current sociology, economics, and politics of secular civilization, even as there must be legal separation of Church and State. H. Richard Niebuhr in his searching analysis, *Christ and Culture* says:

The relation of the authority of Jesus Christ to the authority of culture is such that every Christian must often feel himself claimed by the Lord to reject the world and its kingdoms with their pluralism and temporalism, their makeshift compromises of many interests, their hypnotic obsession by the love of life and the fear of death. The movement of withdrawal and renunciation is a necessary element in every Christian life, even though it be followed by an equally necessary movement of responsible engagement in cultural tasks. Where this is lacking Christian faith quickly degenerates into a utilitarian device for the attainment of personal prosperity or public peace; and some imagined idol called by His Name takes the place of Jesus Christ the Lord. What is necessary in the individual life is also required in the existence of the Church. If Romans 13 is not balanced by I John the Church becomes the instrument of the State, unable to point men to their transpolitical destiny and their suprapolitical loyalty; unable also to engage in political tasks save as one more group of power-hungry or security-seeking men.[27]

Niebuhr clearly points out how often we see the mote in our brother's eye in this regard, and miss the log in our own. So, conservatives who attack the cultural-protestantism of liberals often do not realize that their own stance assumes a loyalty to an earlier American social organization and cultural pattern of laissez-faire frontier days, whereas when Marxist Christians criticize the "bourgeois Christianity" of democratic and individualistic liberalism, they do so from their own stance which identifies Christ with socialism. The terms differ, but the logic remains the same: Christ is identified with what men conceive to be their finest ideals, their noblest institutions, their best dreams.[28]

Our churches have undoubtedly been too greatly involved in and compromised with the materialism and injustices of our free-enterprise culture. Ever since being called to the ministry from a university course in Business Administration, the writer has been keenly aware of the greed assumed and aggravated in a profit economy, and of the injustices and sufferings of the incompetent inherent in a competitive society. My feeble attempts in preaching and teaching and ameliorative social action have no doubt been grossly inadequate. Yet I believe that the idealists who embrace the envisioned alternative of International or Third World Socialism as their goal are fleeing from evils they know and hate to greater evils they will not contemplate: evils of unhampered political tyranny of rulers and of moral stagnation of the masses kept in security. With these evils also, Christ cannot be identified.

Further, I believe that joining in "united fronts" making common cause with politico-economic organizations for idealistic reasons when these bodies are committed to worldly, un-Christian means of achieving their goals is a false activity on the part of the Church and a betrayal of the Way of Christ. We have been told that we must embrace the "Revolution." Sometimes the word is meant very figuratively, with moral and spiritual content, as when Jesus may rightly be called a "revolutionist." Yet often what is intended is something else, an identification of Christianity with revolutionary socialism, or a teaming up with it in the achievement of common humanistic aims which involves compromise with its violent and dishonest subversive means. The giving of benevolence funds by the World Council of Churches to violent revolutionary organizations in South Africa is a case in point. This makes the Church "of the world," participant in their terrorist acts even though it is done because the Church agrees with their opposition to racism, and the money is specified to be spent for food and medicinal supplies. Jesus would not join the Zealots in his day against the slavery and oppression of the Roman Empire. For all their members' participation, the churches did not endorse the American Revolution nor support it with their church funds. As a clergyman, Columba had no business stirring up a just war. The Church has its own means of example, persuasion, and conversion, and must work for peace and justice within all societies by its own methods. When it joins the world, it loses its right to represent Christ, the world's Redeemer.

One cause of confusion in Church social action has been failure to recognize the two types of ethics in which Christians are inescapably involved, unless they become like Trappist monks: in the Church and in secular society. Here we need to recall the old Covenant Theology, with its differentiation between the Covenant of Law and the Covenant of Grace. Sometimes we have assumed this difference applied only to separate periods of history divided by Calvary: "dispensations" they were called. The Old Testament dispensation was when God dealt with humanity according to the Law; the New Testament dispensation since He revealed His Grace in Christ. Yet when we think in terms of social ethics, the Covenant of Law still holds for nations and cultures. "Blessed is the nation whose God is the Lord" is as true today as it was in the tenth century B.C., and the "Lord" here is still the God of righteousness and judgment. Nations are not judged by Christian standards. No nation is really Christian. Even in America only about 40 percent are even formal Church members. The other 60 percent cannot be assumed to be responsive to Christian motivation, or to understand anything about the grace of agape-love. Therefore, the attempt simplistically to apply the highest Christian principles and ideals in social legislation has been largely irrelevant and doomed to practical failure. The Tillichian and Barthian attempt to derive all ethics, personal and social, from Christian agape-love is an idealistic exercise in futility. It is impossible to enforce love and mercy by law. Legal restraint is ineffectual when applied to people on matters they are incapable of understanding. Inner motives cannot be compelled. Even the Tenth Commandment never could be enforced. Therefore, in social action, the primary principle is that of justice. Granted that Shakespeare's Merchant of Venice taught a great moderating truth. Mercy must sometimes temper justice when legal penalties are being imposed upon human beings. Certainly also, we must seek to apply unselfish caring love in human relations wherever we can in this world, and we dare not excuse ourselves as Christians in being callously less than humane in our conduct in the world of business and politics. Yet unredeemed human nature still needs the constraint of strict legal justice if society is to continue to exist. Christian idealists, who assume there are no culpable sinners in the world, and can be expected to show up as "bleeding hearts" to obstruct imposition of every real penalty for crime, only tend to make Christ's way seem ridiculous. Likewise, those who always support idealistic social legislation because it satisfies their sentimentality with no compunction to discover the probable realistic results, when selfish people begin to take unfair advantage of it and bureaucrats make a boondoggle of it, are similarly engaging in futility. Because the world remains so imperfect, its laws and our best social action must be accommodated to its evils. So social action is the proper primary area for situational ethics.

Meanwhile in the Church, the colony of heaven on earth, where all should be assumed to have received the grace of God's forgiving love and to be motivated by agape, our Covenant of Grace rules. Here we should be able to work out its higher implications in a fostering fellowship. Here the way of the Cross is appreciated rather than being resented as a "stumbling block" or "foolishness." Here the world should be able to view the demonstration of the best Way in its true glory. To be sure, the Church also is not perfect, being composed of only partly transformed sinners. Yet it is a fellowship of the redeemed with Christ's help, therefore with higher standards of social ethics than the world can know.

The inability or unwillingness of Tillichians and Barthians to see this difference, with the continuing value of both ethical systems, has led to a strange anomaly in American history: leading churchmen joining with militant atheists in forbidding the teaching of the religion of the Old Covenant of Law and engaging in prayer in our public schools. They have been certain there should be no religion expressed, except that controlled by the churches or other religious bodies, and have denigrated the religion that inspired the foundation of this Democracy, when only 10 percent of the colonists at most belonged to any church. They have deprived the vast majority of schoolchildren who go to no church schools of any moral training, and of the amount of Divine truth which was in the common-core faith. When the Denver General Assembly of the United Presbyterian Church lined us up against allowing the common knowledge of the Old Covenant that might help keep the nation decent, and forbade the common teaching of that belief in God, liberty under law, and immortality, on which this democracy was founded, fearing this might detract from the higher revelation in Christ, where were the Freemasons and other believers in liberty with knowledge of Old Testament and American history? Barthian socialistic idealism was scoring another point in its contest with old-fashioned liberalism and its institutions.

Confronted with the record of the churches in idealistic social action in recent decades, one might be tempted to yield to the conspiratorial theory, accusing people broadsidedly of conscious complicity in subversion. For the vast majority, this is not true. Most believers in Barthian theology and some who follow Tillich refuse to believe this book's claim of social motivation in their theology. Most social activist churchmen are not given to analyzing their sentiments. They are left-of-center by disposition, and have gone along emotionally and uncritically with the major trend of the Church's leadership in our time. There may be a core of consciously socialistic conspirators. The English Fabian Society, started by George Bernard Shaw, Beatrice and Sydney Webb, et al, with its plan to change the meaning of the West's ideal words like "democracy" and "liberty," to gradually penetrate all of the professions that shape public opinion to change the mind-set of the Western nations toward socialism, capturing the schools, the churches, the news media, etc., has been so successful, it must have continuing organized existence. Yet mostly, the process has not needed to be clandestine. The natural man wants to believe its doctrine of human nature, of the natural goodness of mankind when uncorrupted by evil environmental influences, taught two centuries ago by the French Romanticist Jean Jacques Rousseau and popularized in American education by John Dewey. This has helped the common mind to favor idealism, even as Rousseau helped to prepare France for her ghastly idealistic Revolution.

The doctrine that man's life is primarily controlled by social conditioning and environmental influences, denying any importance to heredity, has been helped by major emphases in the budding science of sociology. If inborn individual differences may be ignored, it greatly helps sociology's statistical methods. If social services are expanded, more social workers are needed. If social determinism is allowed, sociology becomes that much more important. If social legislation can cure society, sociological idealism is vindicated. Most college students who enter law, teaching, the ministry, writing, etc. seldom take more dismal, difficult courses in economics or political science, but take a popular course in sociology to learn all they want to know about society, and they seldom criticize the dogmas fed them in many such college courses. So they are conditioned favorably to social idealism.

Further, people readily sentimentalize about what they dislike around them, and can criticize with lofty feelings of broad moral superiority. Socialistic idealism plays upon this penchant. Its ideal vision of the future utopia and its sentimental idealism appeal to the youthful and the theoretical mind. To have theoretical competency to prescribe for all mankind's problems, with no need of the drudgery of real objective experience and observation, gives wings to upstart adolescent rebellion.

Given all of these factors in an affluent culture, where many older Church bureaucrats formed a deep dislike for the "capitalistic system" during the doldrums of the Great Depression, and where others feel guilty about the wealth they have inherited in a world with so many "have-not" peoples, and with the widespread desire to feel we might really "take this sorry scheme of things entire and mold it nearer to our hearts' desire," and the conspiracy becomes only a small part of the cause.

The sad wonder is how so many could forsake the One who is the real continuing source of our hopes, both personal and social. The following lines were an attempt to express that deeper, more lasting hope, written for the "Dundee Newscaster" in 1972. They may be sung to the old campfire song tune, "If There Were Witchcraft."

Christ of God's Kingdom

When we are younger we are so eager
 To see the world made perfect in our time,
That we would go for each promise speaker
 Of ideals quickly won by human climb;
But in this real world no men are perfect,
 And new world orders do not grow on trees;
In fondest daydreams there is no magic
 To conquer sin or build good by degrees.
Chorus:
 Christ of God's Kingdom, constant and true;
 Savior, Perfecter, we still need you!

When men are saying, how with new science
    Mankind has now finally "come of age,"
And Christ betraying give their obeisance
    To human programs currently the rage;
When superficial "relevant" churchmen
    Would reconcile us all to worldly aims,
We need the Gospel of His true Church, when
    He calls to change and guide us with His claims.
Chorus:

God has not left us alone to fashion
    His Kingdom fair in one convulsive jump,
Nor e'er bereft us of His compassion
    While we were coaxing many a foolish bump!
He sent His Son to begin His Kingdom
    Here on this earth, immersed in human sin;
When we are won to His highest wisdom
    By faith in Him we build and others win.
Chorus:

This world will never achieve perfection
    Until all men in Him have been reborn,
Whose Cross forever, Whose Resurrection
    Must reconcile to God all from Him torn.
The way of love is no simple feeling,
    Nor sentimental choice of some ideal,
His Way above is our cross revealing—
    Says we must suffer here to make it real!
Chorus:
    Christ of God's Kingdom, constant and true,
    Savior, Perfecter, we still need you!

IX. Humble Non-Authoritarian Church Polity

Jesus washed his disciples' feet, shaming them for wanting chief seats at the table in His Kingdom. He told them they must not adopt the proud ways of Gentile rulers in the conduct of His Church's affairs, lording it over people and glorying to wield authority. In the Celtic churches, there were never any higher spiritual leaders than bishops, and they were willing to submit to abbots in temporal rule. Humility was practiced as the first essential of holiness. The ideal of the first Beatitude, it was necessary if a churchman were to win the voluntary following that meant real leadership in things of the Spirit. What has been the trend in Church polity and administration in recent decades?

It cannot be said that polity is the major determining factor in the growth and decline of denominations. While some of the fastest growing bodies have independent congregational polities, such as the Southern Baptists and Pentecostals, the Northern Baptists, the Congregationalists, and the Disciples of Christ having similar church government have shared in the general decline.

When mergers have been consummated, the merged denomination has tended to adopt more of the polity of the member having more organization. The United Church of Christ has a polity more like the former Evangelical and Reformed Church than the Congregational Christian.

Regardless of polity, denominational policies have tended to adopt secular patterns of government and business, increasing the size of bureaucratic establishments, multiplying executives and staffs for the new services offered the churches, whether used or not. Church offices, like government bureaus, once opened are hard to close. Yet shrinking benevolences helped to cause a tremendous reorganization of United Presbyterian staffs recently, merging boards and agencies, and terminating the services of many executives. This was done after engaging the advice of business consultants. It is too early to assess the results.

Concurrently, United Presbyterians have undergone another major dislocation in the forming of a smaller number of large regional synods, usually combining several state-sized synods. Ostensibly to distribute power and responsibility for National Missions from the National General Assembly level one step toward the grass roots, it has actually removed synods one step away from the grass roots. Other intervening agencies comparable to former synods in area and administration are being formed to take their place. Since pastors went to synod every year in most states, and now become delegate to regional synods every five years, these new bodies are less responsive to their constituencies and will be more controlled by the officialdom. More significantly, the staff executives on every level will be more beholden to and supervised by the powers above. Presbyterian polity in traditional theory gave preference to supervision from the grass-roots up, making the Presbytery,

334

composed of ministers and elders in equal numbers in a local area, the prime judicatory with indeterminate powers. Any powers of higher judicatories, such as synods and the General Assembly, had to be specifically delegated and granted by the Presbyteries. Synod executives grew out of National Missions, and were supervised by a Committee on Field Personnel of that board for that part of their work, the other part being beholden to the local synod. In the new order, all executives are recommended and their work reviewed yearly by a personnel-supervising body in the next higher level of administration, tending to concentrate personnel power at the top and approaching the old straight line of responsibility and hierarchical pattern of polity. Such authority from the top down was what the ancient Church took over from the Roman Empire.

In the new *Confession of '67*, without much debate, there was introduced a constitutional statement which says that the mission of the Church has been conducted historically under various polities, and that any and all are acceptable. This looks like preparation for future mergers in which Presbyterian polity and liberty might be sacrificed for the sake of unity with acceptance of episcopal or even arch-episcopal authority. The formation of larger regional synods would facilitate such a process. They are not advantageous to the conduct and support of the former synod-level projects, such as homes for senior citizens, youth camps, and campus ministries at state universities. In every body, there are those so organizationally minded that seemingly efficient lines of administrative supervision take precedence over liberty and spiritual inspiration. This increases as staffs grow. Eternal vigilance must aye be the price of freedom. The monetary cost of executives grows higher and higher, despite recent protests of salaries given the newly reorganized officialdom. Where are the humble servants of Christ like the former leaders of the Foreign Mission Board (COEMAR), whose example helped to hold United Presbyterian executive remuneration more comparable to that of humble ministers and missionaries?

X. Ecumenical Unity of Spirit with Rich Variety

Jesus prayed that his followers might all be one in Spirit, even as He was spiritually one with the Father, even though separately conditioned by the Incarnation. He wanted visible evidence of that oneness so that all men might have opportunity to see it and believe. The Celtic churches, enjoying a rich variety in churches and monasteries, knew nothing but that oneness until the Rome-Canterbury authorities breached it with strange new demands of conformity and power, refusing to recognize Celtic Church ordinations, and insisting upon reordinations under a new superstitious, sacramentarian doctrine of Apostolic Succession. Must the oneness be through one hierarchical ecclesiastical power structure? Or could it be visible in mutual recognition, frequent intercommunion, and the sharing of service projects in Christian love, without the necessity of a controlled uniformity? This issue has divided and weakened the churches afflicted with it in recent years again, turning the promising ecumenical movement into a nightmare of power politics.

Before the end of the nineteenth century, there had come a decline of denominational rivalries in the United States and Canada. Voluntary associations to cooperate for Christian purposes such as the YMCA, the YWCA, Christian Endeavor and The Student Volunteer Movement, showed the unifying trend. The world missionary endeavors of the churches made plain the impropriety of transferring denominational differences to foreign mission fields. A Home Missions Council in 1908 was followed by the World Missionary Conference in Edinburgh in 1910, resulting in the Foreign Missions Conference of North American and the Federation of Women's Boards for Foreign Missions. More representative of the denominations than these voluntary bodies was the Federal Council of the Churches of Christ in America, composed of official delegates from cooperating churches in 1908, and the later organization of the World Council of Churches, both councils for consultation and cooperative action, not organic unions of churches. A movement for the organic union of several different denominations began in Canada.

An even more ambitious movement began in England at Lambeth in 1888. The Anglican Church has long looked upon itself as a possible bridge for reuniting the whole of Christendom, possibly joining with the very similar Eastern Orthodox communions to reunite scattered Protestants with the Roman Catholics. They consider their highly sacramental ordination in the Apostolic Succession of the Historic Episcopate to offer such an advantage. So they determined to foster unions with

Protestant bodies, being willing to make other concessions but always insisting upon the reordination of the other denominations' clergy, thereby subjecting them to the power of Anglican Episcopal authority. They adopted a declaration called *The Lambeth Quadrilateral*, calling for unions on four principles: the Scriptures, the Nicene Creed, the Two Sacraments, and the Historic Episcopate.

Anglicans themselves have never been of one mind in this. Evangelically minded, low and broad churchmen protested from the start. In 1902, the Rev. H. Hensley Henson, canon of Westminster and later bishop of Durham, told their church congress, "To invite non-episcopal Churches to treat with you, and at the same time to propound as a preliminary assumption the invalidity of their ministry and the doubtfulness of their Eucharist is to perpetuate an absurdity as well as to offer an insult." The General Convention of the Protestant Episcopal Church in the United States inaugurated a plan for a World Conference on Faith and Order aimed at the examination of all issues of theology and polity which might effect the reunion of Christendom.

In the 1940s, there was a serious attempt to unite the Episcopal Church in the United States and the Presbyterian Church, U.S.A. Having collaborated in Cincinnati with a very broad churchman, Bishop Henry Hobson, in the Black-White integration of a Presbyterian-Episcopal union congregation, I was hopeful when the preliminary plans to unite the two denominations did not require reordination of Presbyterian ministers. We had elected my ministerial father, Dr. William B. Lampe of St. Louis to be Moderator of the General Assembly at Minneapolis in 1945. He told me what happened just prior to the General Assembly at Atlantic City in 1946. The leader of the Episcopal negotiating committee for the proposed union approached him with considerable embarrassment to inform him that at that late hour, the Plan of Union would have to be amended. The High Episcopalians had balked, with an ultimatum that if the Lambeth conditions preserving Apostolic Succession were not kept, they would secede and maintain the pure Episcopal Church tradition.

Dr. Lampe said, "Then you mean it is all off unless the Presbyterian Church agrees to have your bishops reordain our ministers?"

The Episcopal brother believed it could be softened a bit

with some sort of a mutual laying on of hands, thus sharing our two rich heritages.

"Whom would that fool?" asked Dr. Lampe. "If I laid my hands upon an Episcopal clergyman no one would think that changed his ministry, but if one of your bishops laid his hands on me you would think that something was added to my ordination. Then by accepting that ceremony I would be agreeing that all of the baptisms and Lord's Suppers I had performed in my ministry before that date were lacking in something with which my ministry would be more valid from then on! How would I explain that to parents of babies I have baptized? I can tell you right now that neither I nor most Presbyterian ministers would agree to collaborate in such a superstition."

"Then I suppose this terminates our Plan of Union," said the Episcopal representative. It did. When Dr. Lampe recounted this conversation, I determined that the next time there was a proposed union including the Anglicans, I would make sure this issue was not concealed until almost too late. In 1958, the Lambeth Conference of Anglican bishops from all over the world strongly proposed promotion of unions with other churches, always maintaining the "historic episcopate." Obviously, Lambeth proposed to take advantage of the popular ecumenical movement to foster other Whitbys and to extend its own power.

In December 1960, the issue arose again. The Stated Clerk of the United Presbyterian Church, Dr. Eugene Carson Blake, upstaged the meeting of the National Council of Churches by reading, from the nearby pulpit of Bishop James Pike's Cathedral, a plan of merger with the Episcopalians and other agreeing denominations. When it was examined carefully, there indeed was the provision for the camouflaged reordination of all other clergy by the Episcopal bishops in a ceremony of mutual laying-on-of-hands! I began to write articles clarifying the issue historically in our national magazine, *Presbyterian Life,* and prepared to go as a commissioner to our General Assembly at Buffalo to help lead the opposition. One of my associate ministers opined, "If any bishop ever tries to lay his hand on Ed's head he'd better wear asbestos gloves!"

In an article entitled "Lambeth or Geneva," in our *Dundee Newscaster* for May 5, 1961, I pointed out that many Episcopalians, including my friend Mr. Charles P. Taft of Cincinnati, former president of the National Council of Churches, opposed the proposal. Mr. Taft said that the plan did not seem to leave room for pluralism of Protestant churches in a community. "Many laymen do not like this. Pluralism permits diversity, but Dr. Blake's plan seems to contemplate organic union." Mr. Taft said he preferred the approach of the Faith and Order Commission of the World Council of Churches, encouraging cooperation and union but preserving local option and diversity. Dr. John Heuss, rector of Trinity Protestant Episcopal Church, New York, strongly opposed the plan, and pointed out that the American Episcopal Church, being part of the worldwide Anglican Communion, "could not morally act on any plan of union with non-Episcopal Churches until such proposals have received the approval of the Lambeth Conference which will not meet until 1968." By their still Erastian polity, the British bishops and the archbishop who lead the Lambeth Conference are appointed by the British government. Where would that place the merged denomination in prospect? I concluded my little article with the following verses:

Lambeth Ballad

The Bishops met in Lambeth,
 In London of the Queen,
Where trappings of great Empire
 Are still much to be seen;
Three-hundred-ten church Noblemen
 From over all the world,
The hope of spiritual sovereignty
 Where Britain's flag has furled.

They did not need to say it—
 Words would be indiscreet:
Dominion and authority
 With Bishops aye must meet;
Political dominion
 For England now was o'er,
But spirits brave could glory save
 For England as of yore.

Let history's clear pattern
 Instruct the timid soul:
When Roman Empire sagged and fell
 What Bishop kept her whole?

Where Emperor tiara wore
    And "Pontifex" was named,
Yon Pope in Rome made spiritual home
    For all that Empire tamed.

"We must not speak of Empire,
    This word is now passé,
And any hint colonial
    Must sure be hid away;
But there's another gambit
    For those who'd save the Queen:
The word is 'Ecumenical,'
    The fairest to be seen!

"We fended off Geneva
    When Henry wanted wives,
And Scotia's theologians
    When Cromwell saved our lives;
Now should we be unmindful
    Of this, our heritage,
And let Geneva lead the new
    Bright Ecumenic Age?

"There is a Newbigin-ning
    On India's southern strand,
It's ordination isn't quite
    Our Apostolic stand;
But we can still recover
    Our highest claim this late:
Be sure to make each union take
    Our high Episcopate!

"We have not been forehanded
    In Canada or Japan:
We should have seen our destiny
    When unions first began;
But now we'll lead the vanguard
    In other likely lands,
Persuading all to mutual
    Sweet laying-on-of-hands!"

Forth went the noble Bishops,
    Of one the name was Pike,
He had a Presbyterian friend
    With whom he saw alike:

A leader ecumenical
    And Stated Clerk to boot,
Who wanted much to mentor such
    A union plan afoot.

The pace of National Council
    For Blake was now too slow;
They spoke in San Francisco
    And Blake-Pike stole the show.
Their scheme has some momentum
    And if we do not balk
We all may soon be Pikers
    And do the Lambeth Walk!

One reference may need comment. Bishop Lesslie Newbigin led in forming a Union Church of South India in which the reordination of non-Episcopal clergy was not immediately required, knowing that in thirty years, all the clergy of the merged body would have received the proper Apostolic Succession through placing all new ordinations in bishops' hands. The Anglicans accepted this compromise with great difficulty, and in the later North India Union were able to achieve the reordination requirement from the start. I confess to having some difficulty with my intercessory prayers when using the new Yearbook of Prayer for Missions when we must pray for "Rt. Rev." So-and-So serving in the Union Church of North India!

The issue was clearly drawn for us at the Eucharistic Service of the Anglican Pilgrimage to Glastonbury in 1971. On the previous Sunday in Liverpool, we had experienced a deeply moving communion in the great Liverpool Cathedral, partaking of the elements at the express invitation of a warden of the Cathedral, and "discerning the Body of Christ" in the Christian fellowship of that place with our good friends, Mr. and Mrs. John Turner of the British Bible Society there. On Wednesday, we had our interview with Canon Harold Rue of Llandaff Cathedral, who gave us the Welsh version of the meeting of the British bishops with Augustine of Canterbury at the River Severn in A.D. 603 when Augustine pompously remained seated. Then on Saturday, we joined in the Forty-third Year of the Anglican Pilgrimage to Glastonbury Abbey.

Only six persons were present for Mattins at Saint Benedict Church early in the morning, but a great throng came to participate in and behold the Parade of Banners from Saint John's Church to the abbey grounds where Holy Eucharist was to be celebrated at eleven. One glance at the Order of Service told us it would be "High." It was entitled *"The Order of the Holy Eucharist of the Blessed Virgin Mary,"* and began with an Introit, "Hail O Mother Most Holy." Then we read the statement on the Order of Service meant especially for us:

An invitation to make the pilgrimage is addressed to all members of the Church of England, and those in Communion with her; also to all "separated brethren" who, though unable to join with us in Communion, wish to share in our penitence and devotion.

We decided to remain until after the sermon by the Right Reverend the Lord Bishop of Saint Albans. When the sermon began, we were nonplussed. The voice was coming over the loudspeaking system, but there was no preacher at either the pulpit of the lectern. Then we discovered why. The Right Reverend Lord Bishop was seated, preaching from an improvised bishop's throne set up among the ruins of the abbey for the occasion, as the occasional nodding of his head in emphasis gave evidence! Just like Augustine at the River Severn! They have not learned in nearly 1400 years.

For me to bow down and receive an Anglican bishop's "laying-on-of-hands" so that I would then belong to the exclusive orders of the "Apostolic Succession of the Historic Episcopate," and thereby be associated in spirit only with those who so draw their robes about them in superior isolation from humbler Christian "separated brethren" would be a grievous sacrilege. Division is most grievous at the Table of the Lord. The Body of Christ is the Church composed of all believers at any place. The Apostle Paul made it clear in his letter to the erring Corinthians:

For any one who eats and drinks without discerning the body eats and drinks judgment upon himself, (1 Cor. 11:29).

At the Buffalo General Assembly of 1961, we did not vote to promote the proposed union. It was clearly stated in the compromise we passed that this was only to be a "Consultation."[29] Yet each plan put forth by the "Consultation On Church Union" has had strong promotion by our denomination, through its papers and leaders ever since. When one Assembly unexpectedly voted to leave COCU, the present Stated Clerk was quite irate. The evidence of his non-compliance assured me I need have no fear in voicing my dissent against General Assembly actions. We are back in COCU now again, and the promotion of schemes to deprive us of our liberty, representative democracy, independence, and diversity keeps on, to date each one worse than its predecessor. The last scheme would have abolished the office of Ruling Elder, taken the calling of pastors out of local church hands, and combined all local churches in various clusters in each town. Since the promoters of COCU are the same radical social actionists, by and large, who want to use the churches for radical change in society, how they must itch for the power it would give them to rule those millions of the merged Church and the Church coffers of all those fat, conservative denominations under picked dedicated radicals as archbishops. Perhaps they'll be as devoted to social utopia as the former Red Dean of Canterbury! But what if reaction should come in politics, and fascist-minded archbishops gained that power?

In all of our ten basic criteria of essential, original Christianity, our major old-line Protestant denominations are measureably found wanting. In Europe, the condition has been aggravated by formal relationships with national governments, and the identification of Christianity with sentimental social humanism has sometimes been more advanced. We have not been far behind. Is this why the churches in Europe and in America have been in the doldrums?

Some readers may consider my criticisms too subjective, too selective, too negative, too confined to one denomination, and therefore unfair as a basis for generalization. I could only be honest and tell it as I have seen it. People in other denominations must judge their own. Curiously, I have observed how the social action fads seem to hit many of the denominations at the same time. There were unnecessarily radical sex reports in several national assemblies the same year. The same world seems to be calling the tune for all of us. Granted that I have not spoken of the good programs of the ecumenical movement, like the worldwide disaster relief of Church World Service, and the cooperation of churches from many denominations in Billy Graham Crusades, in which I have rejoiced to participate. It was heartening recently when the governing board of Church

World Service resisted the move to include participation in strategic social change in their program.

Happily, not all denominations fit the pattern I have described. By the same ten essential characteristics positively lived, some modern-day churches still change lives, grow, and flourish. Samuel H. Moffett, associate president of the Presbyterian Theological Seminary in Seoul, Korea, told in the November 23, 1973 *Christianity Today*, "What Makes The Korean Church Grow?" Korea has one of the fastest growing churches in the world. The reasons given: "Personal evangelistic witness," "Bible-centered instruction," "the cleansing exhilaration of the Holy Spirit," "prayer," "independent self-government with trained lay-elders," "faithfulness in adversity," "intellectual integrity," "a strong faith," "the Providence of God."

History does not exactly repeat itself, but The Way In Christ in all its basic essentials remains relevant and necessary to the church's mission confronting the massive changes in twentieth century social culture. God's people need the eternal Gospel, and Jesus' teaching still makes all things new. Meanwhile, the special emphases we saw nurtured to prominence by the peculiar history of the Celtic Church in Britain, Ireland, and Scotland, included in these essentials, still bear special stressing. Tolerance without compromise in a religiously pluralistic America and world is an obvious necessity. Spirituality, piety that is not pietism but can resist the blandishments of secularism and the compromises of complete social involvement must be recovered. Moral steadfastness must be recovered to confront increasing rottenness in a hedonistic, materialistic culture. Christian independence from all Erastian controls of governments and of economic-political ideologies must be maintained. Humble churchmen of genuine spirituality must lead. The Celtic heritage, as it stressed the New Testament Way, Truth, and Life in Christ, and inspired the Great Awakening, may reawaken us!

Chapter X

"THE WAY": UNITING AND RENEWING ALL CHURCHES

Jack Spratt could eat no fat,
His wife could eat no lean,
And so betwixt them both you see
They licked the platter clean!

Thanks be to God for human difference, variety, diversity. In family life, problems are solved better and life is incomparably richer just because husband and wife complement each other, have different perspectives, varied dispositions, talents, mental approaches, aesthetic tastes, and physical capacities. Just so long as they are faithful to each other in love, treat one another with consideration and respect, and share the same basic faith and moral standards, other differences need not detract from the union, but only make life more meaningful and interesting. The same is true in the Family of God which is the Church of Jesus Christ.

The true Church, Catholic and Ecumenical, is composed of all people and their children throughout the world who by faith accept Jesus Christ as Son of God and Lord, and are striving, with the help of His indwelling Spirit to live His way. All else is optional. Detailed theologies, liturgies, forms of church government, social groupings in fellowship, priorities in pro- gramming service for a better world, all depend upon combina- tions of historical and personal factors which are open to free choice according to relative likes, dispositions, and judgments. They should not disrupt Christian unity, so long as they do not breach faith in Jesus Christ or defeat His way. His way is humble, loving, kind, just, holy, pure, honest, faithful in keeping covenants. God is good. In philosophical language, ethical categories are primary, and take precedence over intellectual and aesthetic categories in Christian thinking, as well as over physical and material considerations. For Jesus, calling him "Lord, Lord" was less important than doing what He said. If we abide in His word, and are truly His obedient disciples, we shall know the truth that makes us free.

Since God has made people so varied and able thereby to take their places and fulfill their callings in the complex economic, political, intellectual, cultural, and recreational life of society, they cannot help having different interests, tastes, dispositions, and inclinations. Some are more theoretical, others more practical. Some are more progressive, others more conservative. Some are more artistic while others couldn't care less. Some are more active, others more quiescent. Some are more matter-of-fact, others more mystical. Some are more extrovertive and sociable, others want fewer, closer friends to share their deeper, more introvertive lives. Some have rich heritages from former fatherlands they want to pass on to their children. The one God who sent His only Son to save all must want room for all within His Church. Yet, because a deeply satisfying religious allegiance must minister to the whole of one's life, these Christians often prefer to express their faith in worship and fellowship differently with others who share their preferences. Therefore, Christian life proliferates into groupings wherein people with similar tastes feel more at home. They express the infinitely rich variety possible in Christ in those ways most congenial, helpful, and inspirational to them. The God of Creation and Providence made us that way. As the natural theology implied in the First Person of the Trinity informs our thinking, we welcome this diversity.

In Japan, I observed how the Buddhist faith, in an entirely different culture with different religious background, had developed denominations so similar to our Christian branches that I could identify them. There was Zen, with its cultivation of the mystical and its high intellectual simplicity, reminding one in some ways of the Society of Friends. There was Nichiren, with its love of ritual, preferred by the military, having some human kinship with our Episcopalians. Medieval Buddhism had been monastic and ascetic, like monastic Catholicism. The reformation which produced the popular Pure Land Buddhism, Jodo Shinshu, was led by one Shinran who came down from the Holy Mountain to proclaim such works of self-torture unnecessary, saying all one needed to be saved was to express sincere faith in the loving Buddha. So I saw worshipers run into the Jodo Shinshu Temple in Kyoto, bow to the image, pray "Namu Amida Butsu" (Name of the Loving Buddha), or even the shortened form "Nembutsu!" and depart, their faith renewed. It reminded me of the Protestant doctrine of salvation by faith alone, and the practice in revivals of going forward to be saved or revived in faith, with no necessary Church follow-up, and sometimes little change of life. How human we all are!

Therefore, any attempt to dragoon all Christians into uniformity under one authoritative power structure is certain, in the long run, to fail. So failed the medieval Roman attempt, which never did control the East, and eventually broke down in the Protestant Reformation. Actually, Rome herself has long since accepted variety in her monastic movements. How different is a Franciscan from a Dominican or a Jesuit! Similarly, the Consultation on Church Union will fail, so long as it attempts to merge and make uniform under a monarchical hierarchy of episcopal power varied denominations with rich traditions in freedom which should not be lost. Many say COCU is already a lost cause, and no longer merits the amount of attention we are giving it. Rather, it is still a focus of much sincere hope and endeavor for a more real and fruitful Christian unity. It needs guiding toward a more practical and historically possible ecumenicity. The attempt to force a low common-denominator uniformity under monarchical power is attractive to theoretical idealists, given to abstract visions of social perfection, and to devotees of officialdom who rejoice in the wielding of power. COCU was formulated and promoted from among bureaucratic leaders of the denominations, and has never won much grassroots enthusiasm or support, much optimistic propaganda to the contrary notwithstanding. There was a better plan with more acceptance among ministers and laity not long ago. It was not agreeable to the Lambeth Quadrilateral, nor to those who prefer clear lines of authority for administrative efficiency. This plan might be revived and refined.

Before we propose it again, there is need to assess two concepts which have contested for supremacy in the Church since the second century: the Apostolic Succession of the Historic

Episcopate and the earlier Conciliar ideal of Church government. We saw how Ignatius of Antioch began to exalt the authority of bishops, and how Irenaeus, toward the end of the second century, seeking defense against heresies, looked to main city churches where there was a succession of clear tradition from founding Apostles. The two ideas were combined in the Apostolic Succession of the monarchical episcopate, and the rite of ordination formerly shared by presbyters concentrated in episcopal hands. Later, empire control of the Church for state purposes called for a substitution of sacramentarianism with automatic (*ex opere operato*) grace for spiritual change and the work of the Holy Spirit. By the doctrine of Apostolic Succession in ordination as a sacrament in episcopal hands, the bishops gained an instrument of power they are ever loath to give up. For theoretical and ritualistic minds, it is possible to believe that something magical passes through those successively special hands.

It is a symbol of an important spiritual reality. The real Apostolic Succession is a spiritual heritage in Christian leadership. As Christian faith and inspiration for Christian leadership must be caught more than taught, it passes from a John to a Polycarp to an Irenaeus and on through the spiritual succession of Celtic churchmen to a Patrick, then later to a Columba, and eventually to present-day leaders of the Church in Scotland and throughout the world. It passes not so much by the physical laying-on-of-hands, which is only the symbol, but by the contagion of spiritual fatherhood and sonship. As I contemplate my own Apostolic Succession, the sources of many traditions have enriched my ministry through many communions. Primarily, there was William B. Lampe, whose preaching inspired my boyhood and young manhood, who confirmed me, encouraged my ministerial vocation, and led in my ordination by Saint Louis Presbytery. There was an Episcopal clergyman, Prof. Donald McFayden, who opened the progressive Old Testament revelation to me as my teacher of Hebrew History at Washington University. My professors at McCormick Seminary, Andrew C. Zenos, R. Worth Frank, Arthur Hays, George L. Robinson, Ovid R. Sellers, and Floyd V. Filson, contributed richly. Later there were professors in Edinburgh: Kemp-Smith at the "Varsity" and Hugh Watt at New College. A Quaker, Rufus Jones of Haverford; a Baptist, Harry Emerson Fosdick; a Methodist, E. Stanley Jones; an Evangelical and Reformed,

Reinhold Niebuhr and many more, too numerous to mention, have shared in the vital inspiration of my ministry. Spiritual things are spiritually received as well as spiritually discerned. The precious "deposit" which Paul cautioned Timothy to guard must still be passed on.

Yet the constitutional principle whereby the purity of teaching, the needed order, the liberty, communion, and spiritual reality of the Church must be maintained is conciliar as opposed to monarchical. This was so in the early church, beginning with the Council of Jerusalem in A.D. 50, presided over by James, the brother of our Lord. James was not an Apostle! All through the first six centuries, councils were recognized to have final human authority in the Church. The assumption of papal authority was later development. Even in the Middle Ages, not long after Aquinas had affirmed that "submission to the Roman Pontiff is necessary to salvation," and Boniface VIII in *Unum Sanctum* (1302) had made his opinion an authoritative declaration, pronouncing "that submission on the part of every human creature to the Bishop of Rome is altogether necessary for salvation," conciliarism was reaffirmed. There were those who did not see the mediation of the Divine coming down through the pope, but who affirmed that authority in the Church flowed from the Divine Spirit diffused through the Body of the Christian people. Accordingly, the fundamental organ of authority in the Church was a council of the Christian people through their delegated representatives. Marsilius of Padua, in *Defensor Pacis* in 1324, charged the pope with "defacing the beauty of the church, which is her unity" by his upstart absolutist claims. After the Great Western Schism of 1378 when there had been two contending popes, the reuniting Council of Constance claimed in 1415 to "represent the catholic church militant," and to "hold authority directly from Christ" asserting its superiority to all, explicitly including the pope.[1]

All of the great reformers believed in the unity of the Church according to the conciliar principle, and worked for a General Council of all Christians which the pope could not control. Sadly, in England under Henry VIII and his successors, the monarchical principle in Church as well as in State was maintained. The similar conflict in secular politics is between constitutionalism and absolutism. In the latter, the power and authority descend from the ruler, who is not responsible to the ruled. In the former, it rests with the ruled, as the ruled also rule, though usually through delegated and responsible representative bodies. So in Church government, the Divine authority flows not through a papal and episcopal hierarchy, but from the Divine Spirit diffused through the whole body of Christ's people, expressed through their Council of delegated representatives.[2]

What we need is a real return of the Conciliar Principle, in a Federal Union of all the Churches of Christ. Such a plan was proposed by that great saint and prophet in Christ, E. Stanley Jones. Humble servant of the Lord, he turned down the office of bishop in the Methodist Church. I can see him still, during the general manual work period of his Ashram at Saugutuck, going about stooping to pick up stray trash paper and other litter. Stanley, as he always wanted to be called, went up and down the land for years explaining his Federal Union proposal, always getting a good response among the rank and file of Christians. In Federal Union, the denominations of like tradition would be encouraged to merge, but those with rich separated histories and real differing heritages would keep their identities and separate varying witnesses, while joining in one representative democracy of the churches. The continuing Congregationalists would preserve and represent their rich Pilgrim heritage, the Methodists the Wesleyan tradition of the "heart strangely warmed," the Episcopalians the stately beauty of their worship, the liturgical wealth of their Prayer Book, and their Historic Episcopate, the Presbyterians their lay Elders and theological emphasis upon the Sovereignty of God, and the Lutherans their living heritage from the great German Reformer, while Baptists and Disciples of Christ could continue to insist upon immersion, and Pentecostals stress their speaking with tongues.[3]

Wherein would this differ from the present National and World Councils of Churches? It would be the next and proper step forward from these present councils by giving the Federal Union Churches, both National and World, their rightful limited authority and responsibility, requiring them to be more responsive to the will of their constituent branches. Today, the National Council of the Churches of Christ in America and the World Council of Churches are representative consultative bodies, but once they meet, they can only speak for themselves and to the denominations represented, but with no decision-making power, and no means of checking their deliverances, except by expostulation, the cutting of contributions or denominational withdrawal. There is no provision for sending their decisions down for referendum in constituent bodies. They have been speaking too much without sufficient responsibility and authority, and without sufficient safeguards to ensure that their declarations reflect the real concensus of the churches they claim to represent. If the Church needs unified structures to be seen "that the world may believe," Federal Union has more possibility than the directions of consolidation and hierarchical control envisaged by the Consultation on Church Union. Federal Union could attract a truly broad spectrum of denominations, whereas those few who would merge under the Historic Episcopate with "Apostolic Succession" would still compose only a denomination making peculiar claims to a dubious superiority. So it would have great difficulty attracting more of such diverse communions as the Lutherans, Baptists, Friends, and Pentecostals.

Yet all of this is subordinate and secondary to the true unity we profess when we say, "I believe in the Holy Catholic Church." It is the spiritual oneness of all who are in Christ by faith, and are trusting in Him for grace to live His Way. We readily become aware of this unity when "discerning the body" of Christ, we commune with fellow disciples of rich variety the world over, as we did with Anglicans in Liverpool Cathedral, with Russians of the Union Church of Baptists, Mennonites, and Pentecostals in Moscow, and as in 1948 I shared in serving communion on World-Wide Communion Sunday in Hanyang, Central China with a Chinese Anglican priest and a Methodist missionary, using as elements rice cakes and tea. With broad toleration and mutual admiration of our differences in all elective part of our heritages, we can love each other, celebrate the Lord's Supper together, and serve unitedly for those objectives on which we all can agree, or on which some of us may agree as we choose. We can each in our own free way and all together concentrate upon the evangelism, nurture of Christian piety, response to biblical and charismatic inspiration, steadfast moral obedience, non-partisan social reform, and worldwide witness to the Gospel, which is our commission in our common heritage.

This calls for a greater activity in world mission than the churches have ever been willing to furnish with personnel and support. Of late, the world population explosion has been leaving the churches behind. Today's challenge requires a more astute and sacrificial confronting of the secular religions now commanding the total allegiance of hundreds of millions. Most basically, it calls now for a renewed united loyalty to the whole Way In Christ as taught in the New Testament and demonstrated as essential to renewal in the fruitful times of the Celtic churches and in the Great Awakening.

So our vision of Christ's Church winning victory over the "powers of death" may be renewed. The myopic, earthbound vision of the Church as a glorified hierarchical bureaucratic "henchperson" of the secular, boondoggling "Great Society" Welfare State stirs little Divine enthusiasm in spiritually hungry hearts. This has divided, polarized, and defeated us. The Church must be relevant, yes, but to the whole of life, truly glorious in Christ, with both earthly and eternal Divine perspective, thereby keeping its balance. As always, His way calls for free, simple, humble, Spirit-guided service from all of us. "Jesus, knowing that the Father had given all things into his hands, and that he had come from God and was going to God . . . girded himself with a towel . . . " He still challenges us saying, "If anyone would come after me, let him deny himself, and take up his cross daily, and follow me. For whoever would save his life will lose it; and whoever loses his life for my sake will save it."[4]

> Thou hast called us to bear a cross,
> Not Thy Cross that absolves our sins;
> But some cross as it others wins
> By a love that will not count loss.
>
> For our crosses are daily deeds,
> And Thy sacrifice once for all:
> Thy one death all from sin to call,
> Our cross serves lesser human needs.
>
> We would love as Thou hast loved us,
> Thy commandment is strong and clear:
> To abide in Thy love so dear
> By the love which for others does.
>
> Lord, we hear Thy voice calling still,
> "Whosoever would follow me,
> And find life, and a true self be,
> Must lose self in the Father's will."

Lord, we answer Thy loving call,
And with joy would our crosses bear,
Willing others' distress to share
In the love which must care for all.

Only with such free, humble, united service in Christ can
His Church renew its witness in a darkening secular world, with
burgeoning population and shrinking material resources drifting
toward disaster. We want to take up our crosses when we see
His in the light of His Resurrection. Like the ancient Celts, we
see a circle of glory on each cross, the symbol of eternal life in
Him who as Lord already reigns on High, and also in His present earthly Body, the Colony of Heaven.

Providentially, the liberty-loving Celts were used of Christ
for His mission in the ancient Church. Paul's first Gentile
churches were among the Galatae in Asia Minor. Born near
them, he knew their Celtic spirit. He wrote to them: "For freedom Christ as set us free . . . for you are called to freedom,
brethren." Asia Minor became the first area of the Roman Empire thoroughly evangelized. Irenaeus, Celtic-speaking missionary from Asia Minor, became the theologian of Christian
freedom in Celtic Gaul. The British Church was the daughter
of the Church of Gaul. Patrick, a British Celt, took "The Way"
to Ireland unspoiled in its ten original characteristics. Columba
led its spread to Scotland from Iona. Celtic missionaries
evangelized most of Anglo-Saxon England and brought renewal
in Christ to the darkened Continent.

Never efficient organizers, the freedom-loving Celts succumbed to Roman arms, and to the Roman Church which had
adopted Roman ways. Yet the spark of Christian freedom
among them never died. It ignited Wycliff, the Morning Star of
the Reformation, the Puritans and seventeenth-century Scottish
martyrs, and the evangelicals of the Great Awakening. We need
it again!

"Now the Lord is the Spirit, and where the Spirit of the
Lord is, there is freedom!" (2 Cor. 3:17)

NOTES AND REFERENCES

Chapter I: How "The Way" Came to Britain

1. George MacLeod, Founder of the Iona Community, in his Introduction to Diana Leatham's *Celtic Sunrise, An Outline of Celtic Christianity* pp. 8, 9 says, "It is no accident that the last remaining relic of the Celtic Church on Iona is St. John's Cross, standing just outside the Roman Period Abbey at the laying of whose earliest foundation stone that Cross, by then already old, stood sentinel. Nor is it accident that St. John was the Patron Saint of Scotland for centuries before the Roman dominance placed in his head St. Andrew. Least of all, perhaps, was it accident that this same Cross was smashed to smithereens. The Keys demolished it."

2. John 8:31-32
3. John 16:14, 15
4. Matt. 18:20
5. Nora Chadwick, *The Celts*, p. 39
6. Op. Cit. p. 38
7. Bede, *A History of the English Church and People*, I-3, says, "Before Claudius no Roman either before or since Julius Caesar had dared to land on the Island, yet, within a few days, without battle or bloodshed, he received the surrender of the greater part of the Island." Yet the Silures resisted for nine years!
8. Winston Churchill, *A History of the English-speaking Peoples*
9. Gildas the Wise, *Of The Overthrow of Britain*, Sec. 5.
10. Bede, *A History of the English Church and People*, I-2.
11. Katherine Elwes Thomas, in *The Real Parsonages of Mother Goose*, says this rhyme is to be regarded as the start of jingles in England. p. 35.
12. Modern historians specializing in the Middle Ages have preferred to doubt Geoffrey's veracity and to exaggerate his originality. His claim to have translated "a very old book in the British tongue" brought from Brittany by his friend Walter the Archdeacon was believed by his patron, Robert, Earl of Gloucester, and by the contemporary bishops who rewarded his labors with the See of Asaph. Walter the Archdeacon was there, and would needs have been a party to such a deception, had the claim been untrue. In 1917, Sir William Flinders Petrie presented a paper, *Neglected British History*, before the British Academy, reopening the question of the native British or Amorican

source for the early history of Britain. An earlier attempt to identify the Old Welsh Chronicle, *The Brut Tysilio* with Geoffrey's source for the early history had been disdained by scholars, who concluded the Welsh manuscript was only a poor abbreviation of Geoffrey's Latin *Historia*. In 1929, Acton Griscom published the Latin *Historia Regum Britanniae*, together with a literal translation of a similar Welsh manuscript, No. LXI of Jesus College. He claimed there are over fifty such manuscripts awaiting scholarly study. This present writer compared this manuscript in English with an English translation of Geoffrey's *Historia*. There is evident dependence of the *Historia* on something like the Welsh manuscript, with stylistic and imaginative emendations and historical corrections, quite similar to the dependence of the Gospels of Matthew and Luke upon Mark in New Testament studies. When the American Medievalist J.S.P. Tatlock in his magnum opus, *The Legendary History of Britain* (U. of Cal. Press 1950), discounts Griscom and disdains all of the Welsh manuscripts to support the older theory that all are summaries of Geoffrey's *Historia,* impressive as are his details of Medieval history, one surmises that he is unwilling to contemplate an earlier Amorican source because that would take it out of his period of specialization. He seems safe in his special scholarly fief with few to contest his detailed erudition. Yet Flinders Petrie and Acton Griscom are more convincing. The Amorican bias in the manuscripts and in the *Historia* are clear.

13. Dom Luis Gougaud, the French Benedictine Monk, in *Christianity in Celtic Lands* p. 217, says Celtic Britain had no diocesan bishops. When the Welsh clergy joined the fleeing emigrants from the Saxon invasion of Britain toward Brittany, they had abbots, some of them being bishops without diocese. In 845, when Duke Nominoe of Brittany won independence from Charles the Bald and assumed the title, "King of Brittany," he tried to reorganize the Church by the Continental pattern, making the Celtic monastery bishoprics into dioceses with geographical boundaries, and claimed Metropolitan status for the See of Dol. In 862, Pope Nicholas I wrote to King Salomon, Nominoe's successor, declaring all Breton bishops to be suffragens of the Metropolitan See of Tours. Bishop Festiman of Dol had asked the pope for a pallium. In 865, the pope demanded evidence of pontifical documents substantiating claims of Festiman that his predecessors had been metropolitans, claiming no papal ecclesiastical tradition authorized a Breton archbishop. The conflict lasted over 300 years. In 1199, Innocent the Third issued a Bull requiring the bishop of Dol to renounce his canonical rights and submit to the jurisdiction of the See of Tours. So for ten generations, the bards of Brittany's court had incentive to embellish the tales of Arthur, and to grace his coronation in Britain, with the attendance of archbishops to prove the precedent. Gougaud, Op. Cit. 123f.

14. Bede, *A History of the English Church and People,* I-4

15. *English Historical Review,* XXII 767-770.

16. Bede, *A History of the English Church and People,* Author's Preface, page 34 in Penguin Classics Edition, 1955.

17. Caesar Baronius, *Annales Ecclesiastici a Christo Nato ad Annum 1198.*

18. H. F. Scott Stokes, *Glastonbury Abbey Before the Conquest,* a translation of *On The Antiquity of the Church of Glastonbury A.D. 1130* by William of Malmesbury, Note 2, page 50.

19. Gildas the Wise, *The Overthrow of Britain,* par. 8. Haddam and Stubbs,

Councils and Ecclesiastical Documents Vol. 1 p. 24 traces this source for Gildas's statement. Eusebius, under the glow of Constantine's friendship, was all too ready to believe Tertullian's exaggeration. The claim is impossible from what we know of Tiberius, from Lactantius and other more contemporary historians.

20. Kenneth Scott Latourette, *History of the Expansion of Christianity,* Volume I, p. 208.
21. Gildas the Wise, *Of The Conquest of Britain,* par. 9.
22. Bede, Op. Cit., I-8; J.H. Smith, *Constantine the Great,* quotes *Optatus de Schism Donat* 1:22, see quotation and further treatment p. 99 of this book.
23. Bede, Op. Cit. I-8.
24. Bede, Op. Cit. I-13.
25. Bede, Op. Cit. I-26.
26. Bede, Op. Cit. II-2.
27. Eddius Stephanus, *Life of Wilfrid,* Chapter 17 in the Penguin Classic *Lives of the Saints,* 1965.

Chapter II: Christ's Way in Celtic Britain Assessed

1. For the continuing work of God, see Genesis 1:1 in Hebrew, the gerundive form *"bara"* meaning literally "creating." See also John 1:1 and 5:17 where Jesus says he is working with God in his present continuing creation.
2. Matt. 18:20.
3. John 17:21.
4. 2 Cor. 5:17.
5. Irenaeus, *Proof of the Apostolic Preaching,* Sec. 40, 41.
6. Tacitus, *Annals,* XIV 29, 30.
7. Hippolytus, *The Refutation of All Heresies,* Bk. I, Chapter xxii.
8. Hippolytus, *The Refutation of All Heresies,* Bk. I, Chap. ii.
9. Weber and Perry, *History of Philosophy,* pp. 25, 26.
10. Diana Leatham, *Celtic Sunrise,* p. 29.
11. John T. McNeill, *The Celtic Churches,* p. 9.
12. *Westminster Confession of Faith* Chapter XXII Section 2.
13. John 8:31, 32.
14. James Smart, *Quiet Revolution.*
15. Matt. 5:21-24.
16. Matt. 4:4, 7, 10; 15:34; Ps. 22:1; Luke 23:46; Ps. 31:5.
17. Luke 4:16-21; Isa. 61:1, 2,.
18. Mark 2:23-28.
19. John 4:20-24.
20. 2 Cor. 3:6.
21. Irenaeus, *Proof of the Apostolic Preaching,* Sections 86, 87, 89, 90, the latter quotation being from Rom. 7:6.
22. Luke 4:16.
23. Mgr. L. Duchesne, *Christian Worship, Its Origin and Evolution,* Ch. 7.
24. E. Glenn Hinson, "Church History" Course 76A at Louisville Baptist Theological Seminary. I am greatly indebted to Professor Hinson for the research that has brought Early Christian Practices to life.
25. Duchesne, Op. Cit. pp. 192f.

26. Tertullian, *On Penitence,* p. 9.
27. Ibid.
28. John 5:8.
29. Acts 19:1-7. See above, p. 53.
30. Acts 2:1-13.
31. Acts 1:6-8.
32. Gal. 5:5, 1 Cor. 12:3, Eph. 2:8.
33. Gal. 5:22-25.
34. 1 Cor. 12:8-11, 28-31.
35. 1 Cor. 14:1-32.
36. John 20:22, 23.
37. John 16:12, 13.
38. John 16:7-12, 14, 15.
39. 1 John 5:7, 8.
40. 1 John 3:18, 24.
41. 1 Cor. 12:31-13:13.
42. Irenaeus, *Proof of the Apostolic Preaching,* Sec. 7.
43. Irenaeus, Op. Cit. Sec. 9.
44. 2 Cor. 3:17.
45. Irenaeus, Op. Cit. Sec. 3.
46. Ibid., Sec. 6.
47. Ibid., Sec. 11.
48. Irenaeus, *Against Heresies,* Bk. IV, Chap. XXXVII, Sec. 1, 2, 4, 5.
49. Robert F. Evans, *Pelagius, Inquiries and Reappraisals.*
50. Phil. 2:12, 13.
51. Bede, *History of the English Church and People,* I 17-21.
52. Epistle to Diognetus, Chapter 5.
53. Justin Martyr, *Apology,* 14.
54. Irenaeus, *Against Heresies,* Book 4 Ch. 9-1.
55. Ibid. Book 4, Ch. 16.
56. Gildas, *Of the Overthrow and Conquest of Britain,* Part II, Sec. 24.
57. Ibid., Part I, Sec. 26.
58. Ibid., Part III, Sec. 66.
59. Ibid., Part III, Sec. 67.
60. Ibid., Part III, Sec. 110.
61. Matt. 11:2-6.
62. Isa. 9:6.
63. Matt. 5:3, 41; Mark 10:43-45; John 13:12-17; Philem., 1 Timothy 6:1-3.
64. Matt. 24:6, 10:34.
65. Reinhold Niebuhr, *Moral Man and Immoral Society.*
66. Matt. 13:31-33.
67. Matt. 13:24-30.
68. Luke 14:31, 32; Luke 14:28-30.
69. John 17:13-17.
70. Matt. 4:1-11.
71. Matt. 13:47-50.
72. Phil. 3:20.
73. Matt. 5:13-16.
74. Matt. 10:38, 39; 16:24-27.
75. Rom. 13:1-7, 1 Pet. 2:13-17.
76. Rev. 14:8.

77. Bede, *History of the English Church and People,* I-8.
78. W.H.C. Frend, *The Early Church,* pp. 133-136.
79. Ibid., p. 135.
80. 1 Cor. 3:12-15.
81. John 8:32.
82. Optatus, *De Schism Donat,* I-22 quoted in J.H. Smith, *Constantine the Great,* p. 143.
83. Victor, *Epitome de Caesaribus,* quoted in Smith, Op. Cit. p. 60.
84. Eusebius, *Life of Constantine* Ch. 28.
85. Matt. 11:12.
86. Phil. 2:5-8.
87. Mark 10:42-45.
88. John 13:2-15.
89. 1 Tim. 3:1-13; Titus 1:5-9.
90. Matt. 16:18.
91. Phil. 1:1.
92. Acts 6:1-6.
93. Hippolytus, *Apostolic Tradition,* Prayer for the Ordination of a Bishop, III, 3, 4, 5.
94. 1st Council of Carthage on Bishops: *Liberty of Administrative Decision,* Cyprian, ANF V, 379.
95. 2nd Council of Carthage on Bishops; *Equal Powers,* Cyprian, ANF V, 565.
97. Gougaud, *Christianity in Celtic Lands,* pp. 122, 217.
98. Eph. 4:4-6.
99. Eph. 4:2, 3.
100. John 17:20-23.
101. Gal. 2:11-21.
102. 2 Pet. 3:15, 16.

Chapter III: False Ways the British Church Escaped

1. Scottish version of *Humpty Dumpty,* from James Black, *The Unlocked Door,* p. 142.
2. Prov. 16:18.
3. 1 John 1:5.
4. Augustine, *Confessions,* Trans. by E.B. Pusey, Everyman's Ed., Bk. V X-18, p. 86.
5. Ibid., Bk. IV, xv-24, p. 67.
6. Ibid., Bk. III, vii-12, p. 40.
7. Ibid., Bk. VII, xii-18 p. 135.
8. Ibid., Bk. VII, xiii-19 p. 136.
9. Augustine's *Confessions,* Trans. Pusey, Everyman's Ed., Bk. VII, xv-21, p. 137.
10. Ibid., Bk. XII xv-18, pp. 287, 288.
11. Ibid., Bk. XI xxxi-41, p. 277 footnote.
12. Ibid., Bk. X xlii-67, p. 247.
13. Ibid., Bk. XII xxv-34, p. 299.
14. Ibid., Bk. XII xxiv-xxxi, pp. 298-306.
15. Eusebius, *Ecclesiastical History* X-7.

16. Ibid., IV, 35 and 36.
17. Augustine, *The City of God,* Bk. XIX, 5-8.
18. Ibid., Bk. XV.
19. Ibid., Bk. XVII—1.
20. Ibid., Bk. XVIII, 46, 49, 50.
21. Ibid., Bk. XIX, 1-3.
22. Ibid., Bk. XIV, 23-26.
23. Ibid., Bk. XVIII, 46.
24. Ibid., Bk. XVII, 4.
25. Ibid., Bk. XX, 9.
26. Ignatius, *To The Smyrneans,* 9.
27. Acts 5:38, 39.
28. Council of Nicea, Canon 6. See Frend, *The Early Church,* pp. 123, 124.
29. Karl Joseph von Hefele, *Conciliengeschichte,* II, 69.
30. Ibid., II, 116.
31. Ibid., II, 307.
32. Ibid., II, 357.

Chapter IV: The Way in Ireland

1. Don Luis Gougaud, *Christianity in Celtic Lands,* p. 20.
R.P.C. Hanson, *St. Patrick, His Origin and Career,* p. 170.
3. John T. McNeill, *The Celtic Churches,* p. 63.
4. Patrick, *Letter to Coroticus,* 10.
5. Patrick, *Confession,* 1.
6. Patrick, *Letter,* 10.
7. Hanson, Op. Cit., p. 176.
8. Patrick, *Confession,* 1.
9. Ibid., 27.
10. Ibid., 16.
11. Patrick, *Confession,* 2.
12. Ibid., 3.
13. Patrick, *Letter,* 6.
14. Patrick, *Confession,* 34.
15. Ibid., 17.
16. Ibid., 18.
17. Ibid., 19.
18. Ibid., 20-22.
19. Hanson, Op. Cit., 121, 122. McNeill, Op. Cit., p. 61.
20. Hanson, Op. Cit., p. 73.
21. Ibid., p. 140.
22. Patrick, *Letter,* 14.
23. Patrick, *Confession,* 43.
24. Ibid., 23.
25. Ibid., 24.
26. Ibid., 13.
27. Ibid., 27.
28. Ibid., 32.
29. Bede, *Hist. of Eng. Church,* I.17.

30. Patrick, *Confession*, 46.
31. Hughes, *Church in Early Irish Society*, pp. 4-9.
32. Patrick, *Confession*, 35.
33. Ibid., 38.
34. Ibid., 41.
35. Ibid., 14.
36. Patrick, *Letter*, 1.
37. Hughes, Op. Cit., p. 34.
38. Patrick, *Confession*, 21.
39. Ibid., 51, 52.
40. Ibid., 26, 27.
41. Ibid., 32.
42. Ibid., 29, 30.
43. Ibid., 27.
44. Ibid., 26.
45. Ibid., 1.
46. Ibid., 9.
47. Ibid., 10.
48. Ibid., 11.
49. Ibid., 34.
50. Ibid., 46.
51. Ibid., 62.
52. Ibid., 48.
53. Ibid., 49-54.
54. Ibid., 26.
55. Patrick, *Letter*, 10.
56. Ibid., 3.
57. Patrick, *Confession*, 43.
58. Hanson, Op. Cit., pp. 137, 138.
59. Patrick, *Confession*, 38.
60. Hanson, Op. Cit. , p. 77.
61. Patrick, *Confession*, 12.
62. Ibid., 38.
63. Ibid., 39, 40.
64. Ibid., 40, 41
65. Ibid., 55.
66. Ibid., 56.
67. Ibid., 28.
68. Ibid., 58.
69. Ibid., 61.
70. Patrick, *Letter*, 8.
71. Ibid., 10.
72. Ibid., 11.
73. Ibid., 19, 20.
74. Sechnall, *Hymn*, i and xv.
75. Patrick, *Confession*, 14.
76. Ibid., 11.
77. Ibid., 21.
78. Ibid., 26, 29.
79. Ibid., 57, 58.

80. Ibid., 9.
81. Ibid., 13.
82. Ibid., 62.
83. Patrick, *Letter,* 10.
84. Patrick, *Confession,* 24.
85. Ibid., 25.
86. Ibid., 33.
87. Ibid., 34.
88. Ibid., 38.
89. Ibid., 4.
90. Ibid., 60.
91. Ibid., 34.
92. Ibid., 25.
93. Ibid., 34.
94. Ibid., 43.
95. Ibid., 44.
96. Ibid., 7.
97. Ibid., 59.
98. Patrick, *Letter,* 4.
99. Ibid., 18.
100. Ibid., 17.
101. Patrick, *Confession,* 11.
102. Ibid., 37.
103. Ibid., 38-41.
104. Ibid., 19.
105. Ibid., 49.
106. Ibid., 48.
107. Ibid., 41.
108. Ibid., 42.
109. Patrick, *Letter,* 2.
110. Ibid., 8, 9.
111. Ibid., 9.
112. Ibid., 9-14.
113. Hughes, *Church in Early Irish Society,* pp. 44-46.
114. Ibid., pp. 111-120.
115. Patrick, *Confession,* 3.
116. Ibid., 34.
117. Patrick, *Letter,* 5.
118. Ibid., 6.
119. Ibid., 11.
120. Patrick, *Confession,* 26.
121. Hughes, Op. Cit., p. 65.
122. C.J. Godfrey, *The Church in Anglo-Saxon England,* p. 47.
123. Bede, *History of the English Church and People,* III, 27.
124. Hughes, Op. Cit., 76-78, 161.
125. Jane Oliver, *Isle of Glory,* (New York: G.P. Putnam Sons, 1964.)
126. John Ryan, *Irish Monasticism, Origins and Early Development,* p. 106.
127. Ibid., p. 116.
128. Hughes, Op. Cit., p. 114 quoting *Book of Armagh,* 21, b, 2.
129. *Old Ireland,* pp. 44, 45.

Chapter V. The Way in Scotland: Iona

1. Duke, *History of the Church of Scotland to the Reformation*, p. 13.
2. Adomnan, *Life of Columba*, Preface, 3b-4a.
3. Bede, *History of the English Church and People*, III, 4.
4. A. O. and M. O. Anderson, *Adomnan, Life of Columba*, Introduction, p. 23.
5. Ibid., p. 20.
6. Adomnan, Op. Cit., I, 43.
7. Ibid., I, 1.
8. A. O. and M. O. Anderson, Op. Cit., p. 20.
9. Bede, Op. Cit., Introduction, Penguin Classic Ed., p. 15.
10. A. O. and M. O. Anderson, Op. Cit., Introduction, p. 94.
11. Ibid., p. 95.
12. Bede, Op. Cit., V 15; Andersons, Op. Cit., pp. 94-96.
13. Duke, *History of Church of Scotland Before the Reformation*, p. 23.
14. Adomnan, *Life of Columba*, Preface, 5a.
15. John T. McNeill, *The Celtic Churches*, p. 88.
16. James Bulloch, *The Life of the Celtic Church*, p. 13.
17. Adomnan, Op. Cit., III, 2 & 3.
18. A. O. and M. O. Anderson, Op. Cit., Introduction, pp. 72, 73.
19. John T. McNeill, Op. Cit., pp. 89, 124.
20. C. J. Godfrey, *The Church in Anglo-Saxon England*, p. 49.
21. Bede, Op. Cit., III 4; Andersons, Op. Cit., p. 74.
22. Adomnan, *Life of Columba*, Preface 5a.
23. Ibid., III, 23.
24. Ibid., II, 35.
25. Ibid., II, 11.
26. Ibid., III, 32.
27. Ibid., II, 33.
28. Ibid., II, 34.
29. Ibid., I, 37.
30. Ibid., I, 33.
31. Ibid., II, 26.
32. Duke, Op. Cit., p. 33.
33. McNeill, Op. Cit., 96, 97.
34. Adomnan, Op. Cit., III, 5.
35. Ibid., I, 3.
36. Ibid., I, 3.
37. Ibid., I, 1.
38. Ibid., III, 23—186b.
39. Ibid., I, 50.
40. Ibid., I, 1 p. 106.
41. A. O. and M. O. Anderson, Introd. to *Adomnan's Vita Columba*, pp. 25, 102.
42. George MacLeod, Introduction to Diana Leatham's *Celtic Sunrise*, p. 7.

Chapter VI: The Way Comes to the Anglo-Saxons

1. Bede, *History of the English Church and People*, I, 27.
2. Ibid., II, 2.
3. Bulloch, *Life of the Celtic Church*, p. 64.
4. Bede, Op. Cit., III, 7.
5. Ibid., II, 2.
6. J.T. McNeill, *The Celtic Churches*, p. 103.
7. Bede, Op. Cit., III, 19.
8. Ibid., III, 3.
9. Ibid., III, 5.
10. Ibid., III, 17.
11. Ibid., III, 24.
12. Simpson, *The Historical St. Columba*, p. 79.
13. Bede, Op. Cit., III, 7.
14. Ibid., III, 25.
15. Ibid., III, 25, 26.
16. Stephanus Eddius, *Life of Wilfrid*, in Penguin Classic *Lives of Saints*, pp. 142, 143.
17. Bede, *Life of Cuthbert*, in Penguin *Lives of Saints*, translated by J.F. Webb is the source of the subsequent summary.
18. John A. Duke, *Hist. Church of Scotland to the Reformation*, p. 41.
19. Stephanus Eddius, *Life of Wilfrid*, Op. Cit., is the source of most of this summary following.
20. McNeill, Op. Cit., p. 194.

Chapter VII: The Way Taken to Renew and Win the Continent

1. Dom Louis Gougaud, *Gaelic Pioneers of Christianity*, pp. 5, 6. Gougaud, *Christianity in Celtic Lands*, pp. 129f.
2. L. Gougaud, *Gaelic Pioneers of Christianity*, p. 98
3. Kenneth Scott Latourette, *History of the Expansion of Christianity*, Vol. II, p. 78.
4. McNeill, Op. Cit., pp. 158-163.
5. Ibid., p. 164.
6. Ibid., pp. 164, 165.
7. Ibid., p. 167.
8. Ibid., p. 173.
9. Ibid., p. 190.
10. K.S. Latourette, *History of the Expansion of Christianity*, Vol. II. page 43, note 124.
11. McNeill, Op. Cit., p. 166.
12. Ibid., p. 259.
13. Watkins, *History of Penance*, 2 Vols., London 1920, II 626, cited by McNeill.
14. Diana Leatham, *Celtic Sunrise*, pp. 190, 191.
15. John A. Duke, *History of the Church of Scotland to the Reformation*, p. 62.

Chapter VIII: Resurgence of "The Way's" Independence: 1637-1776.

1. Bridenbaugh, *Mitre and Sceptre*, p. 216.
2. K.E. Thomas, *The Real Personages of Mother Goose*, pp. 68-72.
3. Hugh Watt, *Recalling The Scottish Covenants*, p. 4.
4. Watt, Ibid., pp. 59, 60.
5. Thomas, Op. Cit., p. 264.
6. John T. McNeill, *Unitive Protestantism*, p. 263.
7. K.E. Thomas, Op. Cit., 269, 270.
8. William Thomson Hanzsche, *The Presbyterians*, p. 74. A.C. Zenos, *Presbyterianism in America*, p. 56.
9. L.J. Trinterud, *The Forming of an American Tradition*, p. 36.
10. Ibid., p. 36.
11. Ibid., p. 108.
12. Ibid., p. 64.
13. Ibid., p. 68.
14. Ibid., p. 73.
15. Ibid., p. 82.
16. Ibid., p. 86.
17. Ibid., p. 92.
18. Ibid., p. 93.
19. Ibid., p. 100.
20. Ibid., p. 101.
21. Ibid., p. 105.
22. Ibid., p. 121.
23. Ibid., p. 118.
24. Ibid., p. 122.
25. Ibid., pp. 123-125.
26. Ibid., 126.
27. Ibid., 130.
28. Ibid., 132. Gilbert Tennant, *Divine Government–Necessity of Gratitude*, pp. 45f.
29. Ibid., p. 133.
30. Ibid., p. 224.
31. A.C. ZENOS, *Presbyterianism in America*, pp. 66, 67.

Chapter IX: "The Way" in Christ Largely Forsaken

1. Dean Kelley, *Why Conservative Churches Are Growing*, pp. 17, 145.
2. Ibid., p. 146.
3. John R. Fry, *The Trivialization of the United Presbyterian Church*.
4. Fry, Ibid., Preface, viii.
5. Fry, Ibid., p. 73.
6. Gustaf Wingren, *Theology in Conflict, Nygren, Barth, Bultmann*, p. 43.
7. Ibid., 112, 113.
8. Ibid., p. 109.
9. Karl Barth, *The Criminals With Him*, a Prison Sermon reprinted in *A.D.*

Magazine (May 1973)

10. Nels F. S. Ferré *Tillich and the Nature of Transcendence,* in the Symposium, *Paul Tillich Retrospect and Future,* p. 8.

11. Ibid., p. 10.

12. Ibid., p. 11.

13. Ibid., pp. 15, 16.

14. Ibid., p. 7.

15. Paul Tillich, *Morality and Beyond,* p. 92.

16. Robert H. King, *Tillich at New Harmony,* article in *Christian Century* Magazine, Mar. 1, 1972.

17. Jer. 6:14, 8:11.

18. Jürgen Moltmann, *Religion, Revolution and the Future,* p. 135.

19. Thomas F. Torrance, in *New College Bulletin,* Edinburgh, Feb. 1973, pp. 19-23.

20. Joseph Fletcher, *Situation Ethics, A New Morality,* p. 121.

21. 1 Tim. 4:12, 3:2-13.

22. Luke 6:46. Matt. 7:21.

23. John 7:17.

24. John 8:31, 32.

25. Hesketh Pearson, *Sir Walter Scott, His Life and Personality,* p. 115.

26. Paul Ramsey, *Who Speaks For The Church?* p. 83.

27. H. Richard Niebuhr, *Christ and Culture,* p. 68.

28. Ibid., p. 103.

29. See this author's chapter in *The Challenge to Reunion,* compiled by Brown and Scott, McGraw Hill publishers, 1963 p. 198, also John T. McNeill's chapter in the same symposium p. 86.

Chapter X: "The Way," Uniting and Renewing All Churches

1. John T. McNeill, *Unitive Protestanism,* p. 95.

2. Ibid., pp. 89-94.

3. For further development see the author's chapter, *Toward Federal Union for All,* in *The Challenge to Reunion,* Brown & Scott, pp. 198f.

4. Luke 9:23, 24.

BIBLIOGRAPHY

Anderson, A. O. and M. O. *Adomnan's "Life of Columba"*. Edited with translation and notes and with extended historical introduction, London: Thomas Nelson and Sons, 1961.

Augustine. *Confessions*. Translated by E. B. Pusey, Everyman's Edition London: J. M. Dent, 1907; New York: E.P. Dutton, 1926.

————*The City of God*. Lat. *De Civitates Die* in *Basic Writings of St. Augustine*. New York: Random House, 1948.

Baker, George Philip. *Constantine the Great and the Christian Revolution*. New York: Dodd Mead and Co., 1930.

Barclay, William. *The Mind of Paul*. New York: Harper and Bros., 1958.

Baronius, Caesar. *Annales Ecclesiastici a Christo Nato ad Annum 1198*. 37 Vols. 1588-1607 Rome: Friburg, 1887.

Barth, Karl. *Church Dogmatics*. A Selection by Helmut Gollwitzer. Translated and Edited by G.W. Bromiley. New York and Evanston: Harper and Row, 1961.

———— *The Word of God and the Word of Man*. Translated by Douglas Horton. Boston, Mass.: The Pilgrim Press, 1928.

———— "The Criminals With Him". A Prison Sermon Reprinted in *A.D. Magazine*, May 1973.

Bede (Baeda Venerabilis). *A History of the English Church and People (Historia ecclesiastica gentis Anglorum)*. Translated by Leo Shirley-Price. Harmondsworth, England: Penguin Books, Ltd. 1955.

———— *Life of Cuthbert* in *Lives of the Saints*. Translated by J.F. Webb. Harmondsworth, Middlesex, England: Penguin Books, Ltd. 1965.

Bieler, Ludwig. *The Life and Legend of St. Patrick*. Dublin: Clonmore and Reynolds, Ltd., 1949.

———— *St. Patrick and the Coming of Christianity*. Dublin:Gill, 1967.

Black, James. *The Unlocked Door, A Book of Children's Stories*. New York and London: Harpers, 1931.

Bright, John. *The Kingdom of God.* Nashville: Abingdon Press, 1953.

Brown, R. M. and Scott, D. H. *The Challenge to Reunion, the Blake Proposal Under Scrutiny,* a compilation. New York: McGraw Hill, 1963.

Bulloch, James. *The Life of the Celtic Church.* Edinburgh: The St. Andrew Press, 1963.

Butler, Alban. *Lives of the Saints.* Edited by Thurston S.J. and Atwater, Donald. New York: Kenedy, 1956.

Caesar, Julius. *Gallic Wars.* Translated by H.J. Edwards. Loeb Classical Library. Cambridge, Mass.: Harvard University Press, 1963.

Chadwick, Nora K. *The Age of the Saints in the Early Celtic Church.* London: Oxford University Press, 1961.

———— *The Celts.* Harmondsworth, Middlesex, England: Penguin Books, Ltd., 1970.

Chamberlain, Nelson R. *Jurgen Moltmann, Apostle of Hope* Article in *Christianity Today* June 21. 1974.

Churchill, Winston. *A History of the English Speaking Peoples.* London, BPC Publishing, 1971.

Danielou and Marou. *The Christian Centuries.* Vol. 1. New York: McGraw Hill, 1964.

Diognetus, Epistle to. The Ante-Nicene Fathers. Grand Rapids: W.B. Eerdmans, 1951-1957.

Dodd, B. E. and Hermitage, T. C. *The Early Christians in Britain.* London: Longmans Green, 1966.

Duchesne, Mgr. L. *Christian Worship, Its Origin and Evolution.* London: Society for Printing Christian Knowledge, 1940.

Duke, John A. *History of the Church of Scotland to the Reformation.* Edinburgh and London: Oliver and Boyd, 1937. Reprinted 1957.

Eddius, Stephanus. *Life of Wilfrid.* In Penguin Classics. Translated by J.F. Webb. Harmondsworth, Middlesex, England: C. Nicholls & Co. 1965.

Eusebius. *Ecclesiastical History.* Trans. Roy J. Defarrari. *Nicene and Post Nicene Fathers.* Ed Philip Schaff and Henry Wace. Grand Rapids: W.B. Eerdmans Pub. Co. 1952-1957.

———— *Life of Constantine* in same volume.

Evans, Robert F. *Pelagius, Inquiries and Reappraisals.* New York: Seabury Press, 1968.

Ferguson, John. *Pelagius: A Historical and Theological Study.* Cambridge, England: W. Heffer, 1956.

Ferré, Nels F. B. *Tillich and the Nature of Transcendence.* In a Symposium *Paul Tillich, Retrospect and Future.* Nashville and New York: Abingdon, 1966.

Fletcher, Joseph. *Situation Ethics, A New Morality.* Philadelphia: Westminster Press, 1966.

Frend, W. H. C. *The Early Church.* Knowing Christianity Series. Philadelphia and New York: J. Lippincott Co., 1966.

Fry, John R. *The Trivialization of the United Presbyterian Church.* New York: Harper and Row, 1972.

Gallico, Paul. *The Steadfast Man.* A biography of Patrick. Garden City, N.Y.: Doubleday, 1958.

Geoffrey of Monmouth. *Histories of the Kings of Britain (Historia Regum Britonum).* English Translation by Sebastian Evans. New York: E.P. Dutton & Co. 1911.

Gildas the Wise. *The Overthrow of Britain (De Excidio et Conquestu Britanniae).* Translated in *Six Old English Chronicles.* Edited by John Allen Giles. London: H.G. Bohn, 1848.

Godfrey, C. J. *The Church in Anglo-Saxon England.* Cambridge, England: Cambridge University Press, 1962.

Gougaud, Dom Luis. *Christianity in Celtic Lands.* Translated by Maud Joynt. London: Sheed and Ward, 1932.

———— *Gaelic Pioneers of Christianity: The Work and Influences of Irish Monks and Saints in Continental Europe (6th to 12th Centuries).* Dublin: M.H. Gill and Son, 1923.

Green, Michael. *Evangelism in the Early Church.* Grand Rapids: Eerdmans, 1970.

Griscom, Acton. *Geoffrey of Monmouth's Historia Regum Britanniae.* In Latin together with an English Translation of the *Welsh Manuscript No. LXI of the Brut Tysilio* by Robert Ellis Jones. London and New York: Longmans Green, and Co., 1929.

Halliday, F. B. *A Concise History of England From Stonehenge to the Atomic Age.* London: Thames and Hudson, 1966.

Hanna, James A. M. *A History of the Celtic Church.* Ann Arbor, Michigan: Edwards Bros., 1963.

Hanson, R. P. C. *Saint Patrick, His Origin and Career.* New York and Oxford: Oxford University Press, 1968.

Hanzsche, William Thomson. *The Presbyterians.* Philadelphia: Westminster, 1934.

Hefele, Karl Joseph von. *A History of the Councils of the Church.* New York: A.M.S. Press, 1972.

Hinson, E. Glenn. *Early Christian Practices.* Mimeographed Classroom Manual for Church History 76A at Louisville Baptist Seminary.

———— "Baptism in Early Church History." *Review and Expositor* (1968): 23.

Hippolytus of Rome, Saint. *The Refutation of All Heresies.* Ante Nicene Fathers. Grand Rapids: W. B. Eerdmans Pub. Co., 1951-1957.

———— *The Treatise on the Apostolic Tradition.* Edited by Gregory Dix. Reissued, Henry Chadwick. London: Church Historical Society SPCK, 1968.

Home, Gordon F. S. *A. Roman London A.D. 43-457.* London: Eyre & Spottiswoode, 1948.

Hughes, Kathleen. *The Church In Early Irish Society.* Ithaca: Cornell University Press, 1966.

Ignatius. *To the Smyrneans. To the Trallians.* Ante Nicene Fathers.

Grand Rapids: W. B. Eerdman's Pub. Co. 1951-1957.

Irenaeus. *Against Heresies.* The Ante Nicene Fathers. Grand Rapids: W.B. Eerdmans Pub. Co., 1951-1957.

———*Proof of the Apostolic Preaching.* Ancient Christian Writers. Westminster, Md.: Newman, 1952.

Kelley, Dean. *Why Conservative Churches Are Growing.* New York: Harper and Row, 1972.

Kermack, W.R. *The Scottish Highlands, A Short History, c33-1746.* Edinburgh and London: W. and A. K. Johnston & G. W. Bacon Ltd., 1957.

King, Robert H. "Tillich at New Harmony." Article in *Christian Century* (March 1, 1972).

Lactantius. *On the Deaths of the Persecutors.* In McDonald, Sister Mary Francis, O.P. *Lactantius, The Minor Works.* Washington, D.C.: The Catholic University of America Press, 1965.

Latourette, Kenneth Scott. *History of the Expansion of Christianity.* 7 Volumes. New York: Harper and Bros., 1937. Vol.I, 1938; Vol.II.

Leatham, Diana. *Celtic Sunrise, An Outline of Celtic Christianity.* London: Hodder and Stoughton, 1951.

Lewis, Lionell Smithett. *St. Joseph of Arimathea at Glastonbury.* London: Jas. Clark & Co., 1955.

MacNaught, John Campbell. *The Celtic Church and the See of St. Peter.* Oxford: Basil Blackwell, 1927.

McFayden, Donald *Understanding the Apostles' Creed.* New York: The Macmillan Co., 1927.

MacLeod, George.*Introduction* to Leatham, Diana.*Celtic Sunrise.* London: Hodder and Stoughton, 1951.

McNeill, John T.*The Celtic Churches.* Chicago: University of Chicago Press, 1974.

———*Unitive Protestantism.* Richmond: John Knox Press, 1964.

Malmesbury, William of. *Chronicle of the Kings of England to the Reign of Stephen (Gesta Regum).* London: Henry G. Bohn, York St., Covent Garden, 1847.

———*Of the Antiquity of Glastonbury Church (De Antiquitate Glastoniensis Ecclesiae) 63-1126.* Translated by H.F. Scott Stokes in *Glastonbury Abbey Before the Conquest.* Glastonbury: Central Somerset Gazette, 1932.

Manschreck, Clyde L. *A History of Christianity in the World From Persecution to Uncertainty.* Englewood Cliffs, New Jersey: Prentice Hall Inc., 1974.

Marquardt, Freidrich-Wilhelm. *Theologie und Sozialismus, Das Beispiel Karl Barths* (Theology and Socialism, the Example of Karl Barth). Munich, Kaiser Grünewald Publisher, 1972.

Moltmann, Jürgen. *Religion, Revolution and the Future.* New York, Charles Scribners and Sons, 1969.

370

———— *Theology of Hope.* New York and Evanston: Harper and Row, 1967.

Muirchu. *Life of Patrick.* Quoted from: Gallico, Paul. *The Steadfast Man.*

Niebuhr, H. Richard. *Christ and Culture.* New York: Harper and Bros., 1951.

Niebuhr, Reinhold. *Moral Man and Immoral Society.* New York: Charles Scribners, 1932.

Nennius. *Historia Brittonum, Annales Cambriae 956.* Translated in *Six Old English Chronicles.* Edited by John Allen Giles. London: H.G. Bohn, 1848.

Ordinance Survey, Director General of. *Map of Britain in the Dark Ages.* Chessington Surrey: Crown Copyright, 1966.

Pannenberg, Wolfhart. *Jesus, God and Man.* Philadelphia: Westminster, 1968.

Pearson, Hesketh. *Sir Walter Scott, His Life and Personality.* New York: Harper, 1954.

Patrick *(Sucatus Patricius).* Confession and *Letter to Coroticus,* together with the *Hymn in Patrick's Praise,* by St. Sechnall. Translated by Newport J.D. White. London: S P C K, 1961.

Plinius Caecilius Secundus C. *Letters, With an English Translation.* Revised by W. M. L. Hulchman. London: W. Heinemann, 1915.

Pochin-Mould, Daphne D. C. *The Celtic Saints.* New York, Macmillan, 1956.

Ramsey, Paul. *Who Speaks for the Church?* Nashville: Abingdon Press, 1967.

Ryan, John. *Irish Monasticism: Origins and Early Development.* Ithaca: Cornell University Press, 1972.

Simpson, W. Douglas. *The Historical St. Columba.* Edinburgh and London: Oliver Boyd, 1963.

Smart, James. *Quiet Revolution.* Philadelphia: Westminster Press. 1969.

Tacitus, Cornelius. *Annals.* Ed. Hugh Lloyd-Jones. New York: Twayne Publishers, 1964.

———— *Life of Gnaeus Julius Agricola.* Trans. Herbert W. B. Benaric. Indianapolis: Bobbs Merrill, 1967.

Tatlock, J. S. P. *The Legendary History of Britain.* Berkeley: University of California Press, 1959.

Tertullian. *On Penitence* and *To Scapula.* The Ante Nicene Fathers. Grand Rapids: W. B. Eerdman's Pub. Co. 1951-1957.

Thomas, Katherine Elwes. *The Real Personages of Mother Goose.* Boston: Lothrop Lee and Shephard Co., 1930.

Tillich, Paul. *Morality and Beyond.* New York: Harper and Row, 1963.

Torrance, T. F. "The Church in the New Era of Scientific and Cosmological Change." Address in *New College Bulletin,* Vol. VII, No. 1 Edinburgh (Feb. '73).

Torrence, T. F. *Space Time and Incarnation.* London: Oxford University Press, 1969.

————— *God and Rationality.* London: Oxford University Press, 1971.

Trinterud, Leonard J. *The Forming of an American Tradition, a Re-examination of Colonial Presbyterianism.* Philadelphia: The Westminster Press, 1949.

Versfeld, Martinus. *A Guide to the City of God by Augustine of Hippo.* New York: Sheed and Ward, 1958.

Walker, Williston. *A History of the Christian Church.* New York: Charles Scribners and Sons, 1927.

Watkins, Oscar Daniel. *History of Penance.* New York: Burt Franklin, 1961.

Watt, Hugh. *Recalling the Scottish Covenants.* London: T. Nelson and Sons Ltd., 1946.

Weber, Alfred and Perry, Ralph Barton. *History of Philosophy.* New York: Charles Scribners and Sons, 1896 and 1925.

Wingren, Gustaf. *Theology in Conflict: Nygren, Barth, Bultmann.* Translated by Eric H. Walstrom. Philadelphia: Muhlenberg Press, 1958.

Zenos, Andrew C. *Presbyterianism in America.* New York: Thomas Nelson & Sons, 1937.